# OBEDIENCE IN CHURCH & STATE

Cambridge University Press
Fetter Lane, London

*New York*
*Bombay, Calcutta, Madras*
*Toronto*
Macmillan

*Tokyo*
Maruzen Company, Ltd

De vera obedientia.

# An oration ma
de in Latine / by the
right Reuerēde father in God
Stephā bishop of Wiche
stre / now Lorde Chaū
celour of Eng
lande.

With the Preface of Edmonde Bonner than
Archideacon of Leicestre / and the kinges
Maiesties Embassadour in Denmar
ke / and now bishop of London: tou
ching true obedience / Printed
at Hāburgh in Latine / in
officina Frācisci Rhodi
Mense Ianuario /
1536.
And now transla=
ted in to Englishe / and
printed eftsones / in Rome /
before ý castle of .S. Angel / at the signe of .S.
Peter. In nouembre / Anno do. M.D.Liij.

TITLE-PAGE OF *DE VERA OBEDIENTIA*
'Rome' edition

# OBEDIENCE
*IN*
# CHURCH & STATE

THREE POLITICAL TRACTS
by
STEPHEN GARDINER

Edited, with an Introduction, Translation
and Notes

by

PIERRE JANELLE

*Agrégé de l'Université, Professeur*
*au Lycée Kléber Saint Jean*
*Strasbourg*

CAMBRIDGE
AT THE UNIVERSITY PRESS
1930

PRINTED IN GREAT BRITAIN

# PREFACE

I T is scarcely possible to mention all the names of those whose
generous help has made my task easier and enabled me to
find a way out of numerous difficulties. My warmest thanks
are due primarily to the Syndics of the Cambridge University
Press, who allowed photographs of the Corpus Christi manuscript, and of the Berthelet and "Rome" editions of *De vera
obedientia*, to be taken for my use; and to the secretary of the
Press, Mr S. C. Roberts, whose kind assistance has been indeed
invaluable. I must also express my gratefulness to the members
of Corpus Christi College, and especially to the librarian, Sir
Edwyn Hoskyns, Bt., for facilities granted to me for work in
the college library; to Prof. A. F. Pollard, director of the
Institute of Historical Research of the University of London,
for his kind advice and encouragement, and to the members of
the Institute; to Monsignor Martin, and the Abbés Amann and
Mollat, dean and professors of the faculty of Catholic Theology
in Strasbourg; to Prof. Le Bras, of the Strasbourg faculty of
law; to Prof. Marc Bloch, of the Strasbourg faculty of letters;
to Prof. Petit-Dutaillis, director of the Office des Universités in
Paris, for information supplied on many doubtful points; to
Prof. Pitou, of the Lycée Fustel de Coulanges, Strasbourg, for
guidance in regard to difficult parts of the Latin texts; and to
many others who, I am certain, will excuse me for not printing
their names here, and whose kindness will not be forgotten.

PIERRE JANELLE

# CONTENTS

## FRONTISPIECE

Facsimile title-page of *De vera obedientia*, "Rome" edition

# INTRODUCTION

AN exhaustive study of Bishop Stephen Gardiner's political thought does not fall within the scope of the present introduction. The investigation of origins, which it necessarily implies, would take us too far afield, among the theories of the Middle Ages and of the Renaissance; and we must reserve such a discussion for a separate work, in which Gardiner's ideas, both political and religious, will receive full treatment. For the present, we merely wish to account for our reasons, in selecting for publication three of his early writings; to provide the reader with all the information available in regard to them; to point out the internal unity which justifies the title of this book; and to throw some light upon the relations between Gardiner's professed conception of the State, and his moral and religious personality.

Of the three texts which are published in the following pages, one, *De vera obedientia*, was printed immediately after its composition in 1535, and has been reprinted several times since, though never quite satisfactorily, either in the Latin original, or in the English translation ascribed to Bale. The two other texts have never appeared in print, and have seldom been mentioned, still less used, by historians. The earlier one, to which we shall refer, from its first words, as the tract *Si sedes illa*, was written by Gardiner in justification of the execution of Cardinal Fisher, at the same time as *De vera obedientia*. The other one is several years later; it was not penned until 1541, and is part of the controversy between Gardiner and the Strasbourg reformer Martin Bucer, which lasted on till 1548. We need not trouble here to provide the necessary historical background, which may be supplied from many current works of history or reference,[1] and better still from Prof. J. A. Muller's

[1] See in particular the articles in *D.N.B.*, *Encyclopædia Britannica* (by James Gairdner), Cooper's *Athenæ Cantabrigienses* and Gillow's *Dictionary of English Catholics*.

excellent biography, *Stephen Gardiner and the Tudor Reaction*.[1]
Yet a few facts must of necessity be mentioned. Stephen
Gardiner was born about 1497, at Bury St Edmunds. When
about fourteen years of age he was sent to Cambridge to study
law, a subject in which he attained to great proficiency, gradu-
ating after a few years' time as a doctor of civil and canon law.
Meanwhile he had come into touch with, and fallen under the
influence of, the group of humanists who continued the Erasmian tradition at Cambridge; and thus, early in his career, we
find him, in regard to law, a jurist, imbued with Roman or
rather Byzantine notions of the state and the prince; in regard
to letters, a humanist, and a conceited one at that, proud of his
knowledge of Greek, and eager to display his familiarity with
"Tullius" and the Latin comics; in regard to religion, a
humanist of the new school also, well read in Scripture and the
fathers, especially those whom Erasmus and his followers had
lately rediscovered and published; liberal-minded enough to
use his influence in favour of the first Cambridge reformers,
when they had got themselves into trouble; yet himself strictly
conservative in regard to dogma. His personal qualities account
both for his early accession to academic dignities, and for his
rapid rise in court circles. He was certainly kind-hearted, and
full of the spirit of good fellowship, and knew how to make
himself popular; at the same time he was unencumbered with
an excess of scruples, and eager to make his own place in the
world. That such a man should have entered the service of
Cardinal Wolsey, and found quite a congenial atmosphere in the
great man's household, will give rise to no wonder; nor is it
surprising that Henry VIII, who knew how to choose his
servants, should soon have become aware of his exceptional
abilities as a lawyer and linguist, and should have been anxious
to turn them to his own profit.

The divorce question was then coming to the forefront of
English politics. Gardiner was sent on an embassy to Pope
Clement VII in 1528. He was instructed to obtain from him
a decretal commission, enabling the king to have the case tried
in England, and the matter finally settled there, the possibility
of an appeal or of a revocation of the case to Rome being wholly

[1] S.P.C.K. 1926.

precluded. His attitude towards Clement VII has been judged and interpreted in various fashions. Attempts have been made to link it up with his later rejection of papal supremacy in *De vera obedientia*.[1] Yet an ambassador employed on such a delicate mission would scarcely venture upon the expression of personal feelings; he would be sure to adhere strictly to the letter of his instructions. Gardiner, in fact, did "bully" the Pope, but his "bullying", if we judge from his own letters sent home, was no worse than that of Wolsey; and Wolsey himself, to all appearances, sincerely thought that he was acting in the interests of the Church, while urging the Pope to comply with the king's wishes. When the cardinal darkly hinted that Henry VIII might withdraw his support or his allegiance, and that he should not be goaded into open rebellion like the German princes, he certainly did not mean that he wished the king to do so, but that such a calamity should be averted at all costs. There is no reason to think that Gardiner took a different view. Add that no clear distinction was then made between the Pope as the purely spiritual mouthpiece of the Church, as the head of a powerful and self-governing ecclesiastical body, and as one of the petty rulers of Italy. Clement VII was anxious to maintain and if possible to increase his power in the peninsula, and took an active part in the lively game of Italian politics. He thus placed himself on the same level as other temporal princes, and made himself liable to be treated according to the ordinary rules of international politics. Finally Henry VIII's request was that Clement VII should grant a spiritual favour in return for a temporal advantage—the support of a wealthy and influential ally. The Pope was to make an unlawful and immoral use of his authority, but such authority was not denied: it was asserted more emphatically than ever. Gardiner's professional training may have made it natural for him to find a loophole through the letter of a law, while respecting the law in itself. For all those reasons, we may credit his assertion at the beginning of *De vera obedientia* (1535), that up to quite a recent time, he had been in favour of those things which he now impugned—namely papal supremacy.[2] In some respects, however, his journey to Italy

[1] Such is the case in Prof. J. A. Muller's above-mentioned work, p. 27.
[2] *De vera obedientia*, Berthelet ed., fol. 2 b.

may be said to have prepared the ground for his later attack upon the Papacy. Clement VII was then in most distressful circumstances. He had just escaped from Castle S. Angelo, where the Emperor held him a prisoner. Not daring to return to Rome, he had taken up his abode in the small town of Orvieto; and Gardiner himself has left us a somewhat contemptuous account of the meanness of his lodgings and state, and the dwindling numbers of his retinue.[1] Certainly the miserable condition into which the Papacy had fallen could not enhance its prestige in the eyes of Henry VIII's ambassador; and a comparison readily suggested itself with the brilliant court at home, the wealth and power of the English monarch. Then again, during his stay in Italy, Gardiner may have been unfavourably struck with the state of morals among high ecclesiastical circles, and it is possible, though far from certain, that his biting satire of the Roman See in the tract, *Si sedes illa*, may be founded in part upon his memories of 1528.

Though he had but partly succeeded in his mission, Gardiner, on his return home, rose high in the king's favour. He soon occupied a position akin to that of a foreign secretary of nowadays, was promoted to various ecclesiastical preferments, and in 1531, through the agreement of the king and the Pope, was made bishop of Winchester. Meanwhile he had played a not unimportant part in the divorce proceedings of 1529, as a lawyer on the king's side, when the case was tried in England, before the legatine court of Wolsey and Campeggio. Of his doings on that occasion, which have hitherto remained unnoticed, we shall soon have more to say. The bishop of Rochester, John Fisher, had engaged hotly on the side of Queen Katharine. It was Gardiner who bore the brunt of the attack, first writing an answer to Fisher, and then denouncing him in the most violent terms, in an address to the two legates which was read as being the king's own. We publish the opening passage of the latter tract. It is a fitting introduction to *Si sedes illa*. It supplies us with an early expression of the unfriendly attitude which Gardiner was to take up against Fisher in 1535—whether out of sincere dislike of the man, or rather in subservient compliance with the wishes of the king; and the grounds given for

[1] *Letters and Papers,* vol. IV, pt ii, No. 4090, Gardiner and Foxe to Tuke.

that attitude—Fisher's disloyalty towards his sovereign—already foreshadow Gardiner's doctrine of utter, unconditional obedience to the prince.

Up to 1532, it had been possible for a conservative lawyer to view the divorce trial from a merely professional and technical angle; and he might either shut his eyes to the wider issues at stake, or flatter himself with hopes that time would bring a satisfactory solution. But it now became impossible to ignore Henry VIII's attempts to reduce the Church to absolute servitude. The year 1532 witnessed a trial of strength, which eventually ended in the king's victory; but there had been resistance, and it is noteworthy that both in Convocation and in Parliament, Gardiner was among those who opposed the pretensions of the king. The self-same man who but three years later, in *De vera obedientia*, was to deny the existence of any privileges belonging to the spiritual order, and to grant to the English sovereign the powers formerly claimed by Justinian, stood in Parliament by the side of Thomas More in the defence of the rights and liberties of the Church.[1] Between his dignified letter to the king—written to justify his conduct in Convocation,[2] and wrongly called his "submission"—and his two anti-papal tracts, Gardiner's attitude underwent a deep change. Right up to the great crisis, he must have hoped against hope that events would take a more favourable turn. We know that he was one of those who, on August 20, 1533, applied to the Pope for permission to say mass, in case the kingdom were placed under an apostolic interdict. The time was approaching, however, when it would be necessary to take sides for or against the king. He must have been faced with the same alternative, as Fisher, More, and Pole. But when the hour of trial came, he threw in his lot with his royal master. His motives in so doing can only be guessed at. The most important of those may have been purely and simply fear, with an admixture of

[1] *Letters and Papers*, vol. v, No. 1013, Chapuys to Charles V (Vienna Archives) according to which Gardiner seems to have opposed the king's design as a lord spiritual in the Upper House.

[2] MS Cleopatra B, vi, fol. 203 a. Printed by Wilkins in his *Concilia*, vol. III, p. 752, as "Bishop Gardiner's letter of excuse". Amongst other documents referring to the Convocation of April–May, 1532, Wilkins also prints the two answers of the clergy to the king, refusing submission, and drafted by Gardiner (vol. III, pp. 748–53).

ambition, if we are to trust contemporary judgments quoted in a later part of this introduction. The king would hardly be content with a silent submission, and Gardiner, we may suppose, was asked to give a tangible proof that he might be depended upon. Hence his two tracts, *Si sedes illa*, and *De vera obedientia*, which in a way serve the same purpose, that of justifying the rejection of Roman supremacy, and the assumption of quasi-papal powers by the English sovereign. The variations in tone and matter are mostly due to the necessity in which Gardiner was, of adapting his defence of the king's conduct to the requirements of Lutheran Germany, and Catholic, though Gallican, France. *De vera obedientia* is a statement of Gardiner's doctrine in regard to the power of princes; *Si sedes illa* is a particular application of that doctrine to the case of Cardinal Fisher, whose refusal to comply with the will of Henry VIII is represented as a sin against God and man. The king, Gardiner asserts, is the only vicar of God on earth, to whom the sword of power is entrusted; obedience, even to wicked and cruel princes, is an absolute duty on the part of the subject, who has not even the right to question or remonstrate, but must bear ill-treatment modestly, humbly and patiently. The king is accountable to God only. The Pope can pretend to no supremacy of any kind; he is likened to a chaplain, who can be dismissed at will. The Church has no special powers or privileges within the State: its only mission is to teach, but it has no right even to govern itself.

There is good reason to doubt the sincerity of some at least of Gardiner's assertions; but whatever he might think in his heart of hearts as to the respective powers of king and Pope, he was in his temperament the very reverse of an individualist; whether in the State or in the Church, no virtue could in his eyes vie with the essential duty of submission, the foundation of all social and religious order. The theory of the divine power of kings, though in some respects unpalatable, may have seemed to him the only possible one in the circumstances. Since owing to causes which he could not or would not bring himself to judge, the authority of the Pope had passed away, the king's undisputed power was to be the corner-stone of the new social and religious fabric. Let "cæsaro-papism" (a word which he of course never used, but which is more suitable than any), be given a fair and loyal try. And in fact as long as Henry VIII lived, Gardiner never swerved from his unqualified acknowledgment of the king as the all-powerful head of Church and State. To him, the Pope may have seemed incapable of making head against the Lutheran revolt, of preventing the total subversion of the established order of things; the king was the only possible bulwark against the oncoming storm; and not the king only, but other sovereigns as well, first among them the Emperor. Theirs was a religious as well as a political task; they were to preserve the dogmatic unity of the Church grounded upon Christian tradition; hence the obedience due to them as the heads of their respective Churches was conducive to the general weal of Christendom. Such reasoning, if not wholly sincere, may at least have justified Gardiner in his own eyes, and put the best possible construction upon the religious changes which he disliked at heart, though he had not been brave or disinterested enough to withstand them.

This new aspect of Gardiner's theory finds expression in the third tract which we print here, and which we shall refer to as *Contemptum humanæ legis*. Its strange and paradoxical title should lead to no mistake; the question is not really whether the contempt of human law ought to be punished more severely than the transgression of divine law, but whether the unlimited power of the king, now a pope as well, coupled with submission and humbleness on the part of the subject, was to prevail over biblical theocracy, coupled with an acknowledgment of the rights of man. There is, no doubt, real continuity between the doctrine of *De vera obedientia* and that of the *Contemptum humanæ legis*; and yet, a great change seems to have come over Gardiner between 1535 and 1541. No concession is now made to Protestant tastes or phraseology; the very texts of Scripture which, in *De vera obedientia*, were put forward as a lure to the reformers, are now turned into weapons against them. The emphasis is not now laid upon liberation from Rome, but upon the maintenance of beliefs and practices which Protestants considered as essentially Roman. Obviously Gardiner, at heart a conservative, has by now seen the dangers of playing with explosives. He is doing his best to retrieve the situation, by using in favour of the "old religion" that very same supreme headship which, at one time, had been universally considered as tending to its destruction. Thus the three tracts printed in the following pages, not only provide an exposition of the theory of absolute obedience to the prince, as to God's vicar on earth; they also make it clear how such a theory, though it might for a time serve the interests of Protestantism, was in itself wholly contrary to its spirit. The alliance of Protestantism with religious absolutism was unnatural and temporary. Tyndale taught, it is true, the duty of obedience to the sovereign;[1] but he had never dreamt of making the prince a pope.

Gardiner's later career scarcely concerns us here. From the year 1541 to his death in 1555, he only devoted a few brief pages to the question of obedience and the divine power of kings.[2] Throughout the whole of that period his polemical works were concerned with purely religious issues, and devoted to the defence of traditional beliefs and practices. Even his controversy with Bucer, which had begun with a discussion of the disciplinary rights of the sovereign over the Church, was soon to develop on quite different lines, clerical celibacy becoming the main question at issue in the writings which followed the *Contemptum humanæ legis*. We shall therefore leave aside the second part of Gardiner's life, which stands in such marked contrast to the first, and turn to a particular study of his three political tracts.

The first of those is *Si sedes illa*, which we mentioned above as being a justification of the execution of Cardinal Fisher. We know practically nothing of the previous relations between Gardiner and the bishop of Rochester. Fisher had been Chancellor of Cambridge University while Gardiner resided there, first as a student and fellow, then as the master of Trinity Hall. They must have come into touch at that time, and there is no reason to think that they were then on bad terms. It is rather significant that after 1535 the name of Fisher never once occurs in the whole of Gardiner's works and correspondence. The reason for such silence seems fairly obvious. Gardiner, in

---

[1] In his *Obedience of a Christian man.*
[2] In the *Exetasis testimoniorum* (written in 1548), Louvain, 1554, pp. 155–8.

*De vera obedientia*, had treated the bishop of Rochester as an adversary, and without mentioning him, had no doubt glanced at his *Assertionis Lutheranæ confutatio*, and his *Sermon against Luther* of 1521.[1] But within the space of a few years, he had become, if anything, his continuator, in his defence of Catholic dogma and discipline against the Protestants.[2] Now the advocate of Henrician Catholicism would hardly welcome the taunt of popishness, which he could scarcely avoid if he claimed the support of such an ardent champion of the Papacy as Fisher had been. Besides, he knew but too well how basely he had taken advantage of the king's powerful support, and flattered the king's passions, in his vile, hypocritical attack upon his old chancellor; and he certainly disliked to be reminded of it.

As early as 1529—the fact is here noticed for the first time—Gardiner, as the king's supporter in the divorce trial, had engaged hotly against the bishop of Rochester. Fisher, who was the queen's devoted adherent, and had been, with others, appointed her legal adviser, openly declared his opinion on the divorce question in a number of tracts, several of which are still extant. A copy of one of those is preserved among the MSS of Cambridge University Library (MS. 1315 or Ff. v. 25, piece No. 12). It is a demonstration, divided up into six *axiomas*, to the effect that the Pope had full power to grant a dispensation for Henry VIII's first marriage with the wife of his deceased brother, and that consequently the marriage was to be con-

[1] Cf. the whole of the latter part of *De vera obedientia*, which refers to the primacy of Peter. Compare with *Assertionis Lutheranæ confutatio*, 1523, articles xxv and xxvi; *English works of Fisher*, ed. J. E. B. Mayor (Early English Text Society), Sermon against Luther, 1st and 2nd instructions on the gospel, pp. 314–31.

[2] This might be shown by merely comparing the headings of chapters in the controversial works of both writers, what concerns the Papacy being of course left aside. For instance, Fisher asserts, in his *Defensio regiæ assertionis*, the necessity of following the fathers in the interpretation of Scripture; Gardiner takes exactly the same line. Fisher wrote his *De Eucharistia* against Œcolampadius; Gardiner, in his *Annotationes* (Lambeth MS, No. 140) attacked the same man on the same ground; this was, it is true, in 1549 or 1550, in the reign of Edward VI; but for the past ten years he had consistently maintained the same position. It may be noticed also that while Fisher's *De Eucharistia* was translated into German by Luther's great adversary, John Cochlæus, Gardiner seems to have been in friendly touch with the latter by 1546, and certainly was praised by him (cf. P. Janelle, "La Controverse entre Etienne Gardiner et Martin Bucer", in *Revue des sciences religieuses*, Strasbourg, July 1927, pp. 461–2).

sidered as valid. This tract begins with the following words: "Constat inclitissimum Regem Henricum 7$^{\text{mum}}$", etc. Now as it happens, there is in the Public Record Office (State Papers, Henry VIII, vol. 54, fol. 262; *Letters and Papers*, vol. IV, pt iii, No. 5768) a list of *libelli* produced at the divorce trial before the legatine court of Wolsey and Campeggio, in June 1529; Fisher's tract is noticed among those which were brought out "Ex parte regine", under the following title: "Libellus primus Roffen*sis* incipien*s* Constat inuictiss. / *etc*." The answer to this writing is not far to seek. On p. 129 of the same volume (*Letters and Papers*, vol. IV, pt iii, No. 5729) is found a treatise on the divorce beginning with the words "*Quod* ad illud axioma pertinet...". The author then proceeds to confute Fisher's demonstration, beginning with his second *axioma*. This rejoinder was submitted to the bishop of Rochester, who put in marginal notes, in which he expresses his own views in the most lively fashion. The tract is marked with the letter C and entitled "Liber compo*s*itus co*n*tra Roffen*sem*". The calendar of *Letters and Papers* makes no attempt to settle the question of its authorship. Yet the clue is found in the very same volume of State Papers, and it is rather surprising that it should have escaped the notice of the calendarers. In the list of *libelli* which we have just quoted, one of those "exhibited" "ex parte Regis" is referred to in the following words: "Libellus D. Stephani Gardineri incipiens / *quod* ad illud axima [*sic*] *etc*." It is thus made quite certain that the answer to Fisher is Gardiner's own work. If additional confirmation were required, it would be supplied by the handwriting of the MS. This is erroneously stated by *Letters and Papers* (vol. IV, pt iii, No. 5729, p. 2537) to be Wriothesley's, but there can be no reasonable doubt that it is really Gardiner's earlier hand (compare with contemporary letters of his in State Papers, vol. 53, fol. 226 and 275).[1] This has been kindly confirmed for us by no less an expert than Mr R. H. Brodie, Assistant Keeper of the Public Records.

This is not all. Gardiner's refutation of Fisher's *libellus* is of a purely technical nature. When it was penned, the king and

---

[1] It must be noticed that the calendarer consistently mistook Gardiner's hand for Wriothesley's; so that once the necessary substitution is made, his very error lends support to our ascription to Gardiner of C and M, and of *Si sedes illa*.

his adherents no doubt still hoped that the bishop of Rochester might be won over, and accept his adversary's special pleading at least as an excuse to justify an insincere recantation. But Fisher surprised the royal party by the boldness and determination of his attitude. The legatine court had been sitting four times already, when on June 28, 1529, he unexpectedly stepped forward in front of the legates, and freely declared his mind in regard to the king's marriage, the validity of which he strongly asserted. He was ready, he added, like John the Baptist of old, to lay down his life in the defence of holy matrimony. He then handed out to Wolsey and Campeggio a new writing of his on the divorce (cf. Campeggio to Salviati, June 29, 1529, in *Letters and Papers*, vol. IV, pt iii, No. 5732, from Theiner, *Annales*, p. 585; cf. also No. 5734, and bishop of Bayonne to Francis I, *ibid.* No. 5741). The king bitterly resented what he considered as a personal affront, and one which called for immediate retaliation. Fisher's speech may not have been written[1] and has not come down to us; but the king's scathing rejoinder, in the form of a counter-address to the legates, immediately follows Gardiner's writing quoted above, in vol. 54 of the State Papers, Henry VIII. To be more accurate, the volume contains part of the draft, marked M (fol. 218 a to 229 b) and an imperfect copy marked D (fol. 166 a to 217 b). It is quite clear that the draft was divided up into quires, and that those were handed out to several scribes to be copied at the same time. Now the calendar of *Letters and Papers* states "M" to be in Wriothesley's hand, but this is again a mistake. Mr R. H. Brodie concurs in this view, though it must be said that he is less positive as to the hand being Gardiner's, a point on which we feel no serious doubt. It should be added that the paper of D (in particular the watermark) is identical with that of C, which we know to have been used by Gardiner. The very fact that the documents were bound together at an early period, and both submitted to, and annotated by, the bishop of Rochester,

[1] But it is probably the writing handed out to the legates which appears in the above-mentioned list as "Libellus secundus Roffen*sis* incipien*s* / Re-*verendissi*mis in *Christo* pa*t*ribus / etc.", while the king's answer is probably referred to as "Libellus quo delen*tur* deducta per Roffen*sem* incipien*s* / Postqu*am* in hac materia etc.", the first words being slightly misquoted. It may be noted that this writing is not ascribed to the king in this list, though another writing appears in it as "Libellus eiusdem [Regis]".

points to a common origin. Internal evidence brings us to the same conclusion: the rhetorical exordium is quite akin to that of *Si sedes illa* and *De vera obedientia*. For those reasons we have felt no hesitancy in ascribing the king's answer to Gardiner, in printing the opening passage in the following pages, and supplying an English translation.[1] It will make it far less surprising that in *Si sedes illa* Gardiner should have slandered the memory of his old chancellor with such an utter disregard of what he knew to be the truth.

Six years now passed, full of momentous changes. Again and again the two men are found face to face or at any rate in close touch; and yet we can scarcely guess their feelings in regard to each other. In the very same Convocation of April–May 1532, in which Gardiner was foremost in rejecting the king's demands, a committee was appointed to go and consult with Fisher on the questions at issue.[2] Soon after the bishop of Winchester must have finally gone over to the king's side. On April 6, 1533, Fisher was arrested, and placed in Gardiner's custody for the space of more than three months. It was thought best to keep him out of the way while Cranmer was pronouncing the king's divorce from Katharine of Aragon, and while the coronation of Anne Boleyn—at which Gardiner attended—was being celebrated. On April 14, 1534, Fisher refused to take the oath of succession, and was committed to the Tower. According to his Catholic biographer, Dr Richard Hall, several bishops were sent to him to try and gain him over.[3] Among them were Stokesley, Tunstal and Gardiner—three men, be it noted, who up to quite lately had been averse to the religious changes, and whom the king's promises or threats had moved to an unwilling palinode. On November 18, 1534, the refusal to acknowledge the king's supreme headship was made treason by Act of Parliament; and the oath of supremacy was accordingly tendered to Fisher, who persistently refused to take it. On May 20, 1535, Pope Paul III, no doubt hoping that he would thus shield the bishop of Rochester's life, created him a cardinal. This,

---

[1] Our translation is quite independent from that of part of the passage, which was published by J. S. Brewer in his *Reign of Henry VIII* (ed. by James Gairdner, London, 1884), vol. II, pp. 348–51.

[2] Cf. T. E. Bridgett, *Life of blessed John Fisher* (London, 1888), p. 220.

[3] *Ibid.* p. 333, where a passage of Dr Hall's *Life of Fisher*, written during the reign of Philip and Mary, is reproduced.

however, merely incensed the king, and as soon as the news reached England, Fisher was put on his trial. As he still rejected all thought of submission, he was sentenced to death, and sent to the block on June 22, 1535.

The whole of Europe stood aghast at the terrible news, which was received at Rome with grief and horror. Pope Paul III gave vent to his indignation in two letters, one to Ferdinand of Hungary, "King of the Romans", and the other to Francis I, king of France. The Latin text of the latter document, which is dated July 26, 1535, is printed below, from the *Meslanges historiques* of Nicholas Camusat (Troyes, 1619), an English translation being supplied. The Pope's brief to Francis I declared that Henry VIII was deprived of his crown and dominions on account of his crimes; it was thus doubly dangerous, in so far as it might not only justify hostile proceedings on the part of France but also help in raising a rebellion at home. It was necessary to parry the blow, if not to counter-attack, and Gardiner was selected for the purpose. We soon find him at work at the same time upon his answer to the Pope's brief and *De vera obedientia*, which he both mentions in the following undated letter to Thomas Cromwell (State Papers, Henry VIII, vol. 96, fol. 17; *Letters and Papers*, vol. IX, No. 442):[1]

Master secretary after my most harty commendations I sende vnto youe by this berer / myne aunswer to the brief according to your letteres / which aunswer if I might haue had* with me this night / I had entended to haue / polyted and clensed as I haue alredy doon myn oration which / I wyl at London delyuer to bartlet[2] to be prynted / of this aunswer I haue noon other copye but that I nowe sende / which is too rude as in many places ye shal rather perceyve what I meane / thenne pyk out what I saye / —If youe bringe it with youe / I wyl in a daye / and a night put it in mundum[3] / and adde a good portion to thende / that is not yet wryten as I diuised with my lord of cauntorbury / to doo / This vntyl my meating with youe most hartely fare ye wel / From winchestre this sonday

Your loving and<br>assured frende<br>Ste. Winton.

[1] In *Letters and Papers*, vol. IX, p. 143, the letter is conjecturally dated [Sept. 26] but on what grounds is neither stated nor apparent.
[2] To the printer Berthelet, who published *De vera obedientia*.
[3] I.e. bring it to its finished form.

Addressed (on folio 18 b): "To the right honnorable Master Thomas Crumwel principal secretary to the kings highnes".

We have only found in the State Papers one other mention or Gardiner's answer to the brief. In the autumn of 1535, Edward Foxe, bishop of Hereford, was sent to Germany as an ambassador to the Protestant princes, who were then assembled at Smalkalde. Among Cromwell's papers is a "Memorandum for my Lord of Hereford's despatch" (*Letters and Papers*, vol. IX, No. 213, p. 71) which after letters of commendation, a commission, and passports, mentions several books, which Foxe was apparently to take along with him, and among others, "The bishop of Winchester's book, *de Obedientia*, and his answer to the brief...". Now Foxe says, on October 8, that he is to start in a few days (*ibid.* No. 563). The composition of Gardiner's tract would thus fall between some date early in August and the beginning of October. As to the writing itself, it might perhaps now be considered as lost, had not Mr R. H. Brodie, on a question put by Prof. J. A. Muller, once again found the calendar of *Letters and Papers* to be at fault. In vol. 94 of the State Papers, Henry VIII (*Letters and Papers*, vol. VIII, No. 1118, 1-2-3), the following documents are found: from fol. 185 a to 197 b, the first part of the draft of a Latin treatise, headed "answer to the popes bull", and beginning with the words: "Si sedes illa Romana"; from fol. 153 a to 184 a, a fair copy of the same, complete; from fol. 198 a to 213 a, an English translation of the treatise in a contemporary hand. Now the calendar states the draft to be in Wriothesley's hand; but there can be no mistake at all about the hand being Gardiner's. So this writing, which is in fact a methodical refutation of the Pope's brief, is certainly the one mentioned in the letter to Cromwell and in his memorandum. Its authorship is further confirmed by internal evidence; the passages in which Paul III is gibingly compared to St Paul, for instance, are almost exactly parallel in *Si sedes illa* and *De vera obedientia*.[1]

The fair copy was obviously taken from the draft (cf. Latin text, fol. of MS *161 a* : 190 a, *163 b* : 192 b, *171 a* : 196 a), and

[1] Cf. fol. of MS *169 b* : 195 a, and *De vera obedientia*, Latin text, fol. 32 a. There is also a striking likeness between two sentences on fol. 180 b-181 a and *Contemptum humanæ legis*, p. 267 of MS. (In regard to the numbering of pages, cf. note p. lxx.)

the English translation worked out from the fair copy (cf. fol. 211 a of MS). One wonders to what purpose Gardiner's tract was turned into English. *De vera obedientia*, though printed, was apparently never translated until the Protestant exiles on the Continent undertook the task in 1553. The king and court were sufficiently grounded in the Latin tongue, as well as the clerical and intellectual circles whom it might seem useful to persuade. It may have been meant, at one time, to disseminate copies of *Si sedes illa*, in its English garb, among the popular classes, according to Protestant practice; but this does not seem ever to have been done. The translation is clearly not Gardiner's own work; he would not, to be sure, have misunderstood his own reasoning, and made himself guilty of such misconstructions as we repeatedly find in the course of the English version; minor errors it is true most of the time, but occasionally serious. On fol. 201 b of the MS, the ironical *rhetorculus hic* is stupidly rendered by "this yong Rhethoricion"; while on fol. 205 b (*169 a* : 195 a of the Latin text) "in vanitatis crimen facile decidit" is turned into the meaningless clause, "playnely apperith to bee a vayne crime". The translator was obviously no match for Gardiner's classical scholarship. Besides he seems to have been pressed for time, and towards the end of the tract, his style loses all terseness and forcefulness (cf. fol. 209 b). Who it was who thus disfigured Gardiner's able, though displeasing, refutation, cannot easily be ascertained. It seems as if the same man had composed and copied the English version, for a scribe would hardly venture upon such a correction as that on fol. 208 a. Now according to Mr R. H. Brodie, the handwriting may be that of Sir John Tregonwell, a privy councillor, who had been proctor for the king in the divorce case, took part in the proceedings against the Carthusians and Thomas More, and was to be active in the suppression of monasteries; or possibly of Sir William Petre, a friend of the Boleyns, and later a visitor of the lesser monasteries. It seems at any rate that the translator favoured the Reformers, if we are to judge from his use of such an expression as "the disciples of the Lord", which has a strong Protestant flavour (fol. 198 b). The imperfections of his work have seemed no sufficient reason for rejecting his English version and substituting a modern one;

in spite of numerous mistakes, his translation is on the whole accurate; besides it is an interesting specimen of racy, homely, sixteenth-century prose; and much will be found in it that is of value for the history of the English tongue.

Unlike *Si sedes illa*, which we only find mentioned in one or two official papers, *De vera obedientia* was from the first meant for publication. Henry VIII was well aware of the necessity and political efficiency of propaganda, and of the power of the printing-press. As soon as he had resolved to make himself the absolute master of the English Church, he set afoot a great polemical offensive, in the course of which many books were issued in justification of his policy. He was too well acquainted with the real spirit of Protestantism to appeal to the support of Protestant controversialists. Those whom he chose as defenders of his supreme headship, from 1534 to 1539, were conservatives who, like Gardiner, were making the best of an unwelcome situation, and who, after feebly struggling for a time, had let themselves be pressed into his service. Such was the case of Edward Foxe, bishop of Hereford, whose *Opus eximium de vera differentia regiæ potestatis et ecclesiasticæ* was printed in 1534, and reprinted in 1538, by Berthelet; such was also the case of Richard Sampson, dean of the chapel royal, who about the same date, penned his *Oratio, qua docet Anglos, regiæ dignitati cum primis ut obediant...episcopo Romano ne sint audientes...*, which was also published by Berthelet. Tunstal, who in 1533 had made himself obnoxious to Henry VIII by his opposition to the supreme headship in the Northern Convocation,[1] joined with Stokesley in writing a defence of the supremacy for the benefit of Reginald Pole, and in 1539 preached a sermon on the same subject which was again printed by Berthelet (*A sermon of Cuthbert, Bysshop of Duresme upon Palme Sondaye before Kynge Henry the VIII*). As for Bonner, then archdeacon of Leicester, he wrote, as we shall see, the violently anti-papal preface to the Hamburg edition of *De vera obedientia*. It tells a good deal for the strength of Henry VIII's

---

[1] Eustace Chapuys to Charles V, in *Spanish Calendar*, vol. IV, pt ii, No. 1081 (which is more accurate than the condensed version in *Letters and Papers*, vol. IX, No. 653). Tunstal's opposition was to the royal divorce.

character and will, for his inexplicable personal fascination and prestige, and for the awe which the royal dignity and power then inspired, that all those men should have espoused the king's cause, and in appearance at least, espoused it gladly. There must have been, in their renunciation of beliefs which they held dear, something more than physical fear, time-serving and servility.

The only two notices that we have of the composition of *De vera obedientia* are the same which have been mentioned above in connection with *Si sedes illa*. Gardiner's letter to Cromwell proves that his treatise was only placed in the printer's hands some time after the pope's brief had reached England, early in August, 1535; while Cromwell's memorandum makes it clear that by the beginning of October it had come out of the press. It appeared with the following title-page and collation:

(Large engraved border) STEPHA|NI WINTON. | EPISCOPI DE VERA | OBEDIEN-|TIA | ORATIO | Colophon: LONDINI IN AEDIBUS THO. | BERTHELETI REGII IMPRES-|SORIS EX-CVSA. | AN. M.D. XXXV. | CVM PRIVILEGIO.|

1 vol. 4°. Sig. A 1–I 4; folios numbered from 1 to 36, including the title-page.

Immediately after its appearance, *De vera obedientia* embarked upon a curious career, of which the available evidence allows us to get a few glimpses. First, as to its publication in Strasbourg. Edward Foxe, accompanied by another conservative, Nicholas Heath, archdeacon of Stafford—a future archbishop of York under Mary—in due time departed upon his embassy to the German princes, carrying with him, no doubt, a few copies of Gardiner's treatise. On his way to Smalkalde, he called at Strasbourg, where Martin Bucer was then at the head both of the city and of the Reformation movement. Strasbourg was in the sixteenth century a town of considerable importance, less on account of its actual population or power, than because it was one of the main continental centres for the diffusion of ideas. Bucer had been greatly struck with the new turn which things were taking in England; he mentions English affairs in many of his letters throughout the autumn of 1535, the winter and spring of 1536.[1] He was dreaming of a great Protestant alliance, which, according to his temperament, was to be obtained by compromise between opposing parties. Every effort of his diplomatic skill was bent towards the achieving of such a result. England also, he thought, might be induced by gentle means to adhere to the new pact. It is not surprising in the circumstances that he should have hailed with joy the coming of Foxe and Heath. He mentions it in several of his letters as an event of great importance.[2] Unhappily he does not supply us with much information as to Foxe's doings in Strasbourg. We learn from a letter of Zwick to Bullinger that "the English ambassador conferred for three days with learned men of Argentoratum (Strasbourg)....He joined with them in most sharply attacking the pontifical monarchy....He also produced to them some writings of Philippus (Melanchton) and Bucer".[3] Melanchton's book, *De locis communibus* (the *Loci communes rerum theologicarum seu hypotyposes*, published first in 1521), is quoted in Cromwell's above-mentioned memorandum side by side with *De vera obedientia*, and, though nothing is here said of Gardiner's work, we may assume that Foxe left one or several copies in the hands of Bucer and his friends.

After November, 1535, contemporary documents are again dumb, and we have in vain ransacked every available collection for an allusion to the printing of *De vera obedientia* at Strasbourg.[4] Did Foxe suggest it to the Strasbourg reformers, or

[1] Cf. the following collections: *Briefwechsel der Brüder Ambrosius und Thomas Blaurer, 1509–1548*, bearbeitet von Traugott Schiess, Freiburg i. Br. 1908–12; *Centuria Epistolarum Theologicarum ad Ioannem Schwebelium, 1519–1540*, Zweibrücken, 1597; and especially the MS *Thesaurus Epistolicus Reformatorum Alsaticorum*, copied out from various sources by J. W. Baum, and now in the possession of the University Library at Strasbourg. Letters of Bucer to Ambrosius Blaurer, about the middle of November 1535 (*Thesaurus*, vol. VIII, fol. 259 b); to the same, about November 18 (*Briefwechsel*, vol. I, p. 760); to Margareta Blaurer, November 18 (*Briefwechsel*, vol. I, p. 823; *Thesaurus*, vol. VIII, p. 261); to Johann Schwebel, November 18 (*Thesaurus*, vol. VIII, fol. 263; *Centuria*, p. 281); to Ambr. Blaurer, January 8, 1536 (*Thesaurus*, vol. IX, fol. 11); to Bullinger, January 17, 1536 (*Thesaurus*, vol. IX, fol. 15); to Vadianus, January 17, 1536 (*Thesaurus*, vol. IX, fol. 17); and many others.

[2] Cf. in the previous note the letters written during the month of November, 1535.

[3] *Thesaurus Baumianus*, vol. VIII, fol. 261 b, marginal note. The original is in the *Collectio Simleriana* at Zurich. Johann Zwick was, like Ambrosius Blaurer, one of the leaders of the Reformation at Constance.

[4] In addition to the collections quoted in a previous note, we may mention:

did the latter, especially Bucer, eagerly seize the opportunity thus proffered of broadcasting the notable increase in strength that had just accrued to the Protestant party? There was no doubt equal willingness on both sides, but in the present case the Strasbourg reformers assumed the responsibility of the publication, by prefixing to it a preface dedicated "to the pious reader" (*Pio lectori*) which begins with the following words: "The oration on true obedience of the reverend father Stephen, bishop of Winchester, having recently come into our hands, we considered it as impossible, that we should not impart it to thee...".[1] The preface highly commends such "true bishops" as Gardiner, and also praises Cranmer, Foxe, and Heath. It is signed "V. F. Capito, C. Hedio, M. Bucerus et caeteri Ecclesiastae Argentoratenses", but was no doubt really drafted by Bucer, though he modestly placed his name last. More than once, in the following years, he was to make use of dedications to enlist the sympathy and support of the English clergy, if not to compromise them with the Protestant party. He dedicated two of his works to Cranmer and to Foxe respectively, in the course of the year 1536.[2] His purpose in so doing, he writes in his epistle to Foxe, was "to strengthen our people in their hopes of a general agreement of the churches, since they will thus understand that even bishops, and of so great a realm, and principal men with a king in so many ways of surpassing virtue, applied themselves to this matter with such earnestness".[3]

*Briefwechsel Landgraf Philipp's des Grossmüthigen von Hessen mit Bucer*, ed. Max Lenz, Leipzig, 3 vols; *Politische Korrespondenz der Stadt Strassburg im Zeitalter der Reformation*, vol. II, ed. Otto Winckelmann, Strasbourg, 1887; *Corpus Reformatorum*, Correspondence of Melanchton; a number of others, less directly connected with the history of Strasbourg, were also consulted.

[1] *De vera obedientia*, Strasbourg ed. fol. A 2: "Nacti nuper orationem, de uera obedientia R. P. Stephani Episcopi Vuintoniensis, committere non potuimus, quin eam tibi communicaremus...".

[2] The work dedicated to Cranmer was *Metaphrases et enarrationes perpetuæ epistolarum D. Pauli Apostoli....Tomus primus, continens metaphrasim et enarrationem in Epistolam ad Romanos....*Argentorati per Wendelinum Rihelium, mense Martio MDXXXVI; the work dedicated to Foxe was *In sacra quatuor evangelia enarrationes perpetuæ....*Basileæ apud Ioan. Hervagium, anno M.D. XXXVI, mense Septembri. Both dedications were made within a twelvemonth of Foxe's visit to Bucer.

[3] *In sacra quatuor evangelia*, etc. sig. *2: "Postremo ut nostris hominibus animos adderem sperandi amplissimam ecclesiarum consensionem, cum hinc intelligerent etiam Episcopos, et tanti regni, et apud regem tot nominibus excellentem præcipuos, in hanc rem tanto studio incumbere".

On January 17, 1536, Bucer wrote to Vadianus, the St Gall reformer, to try and win him over to his great scheme of a Protestant alliance. He insisted on the fact that England had unanimously rejected the supremacy of Rome, and to lend greater force to his arguments, added, "I send you the oration of the English bishop".[1] This was obviously *De vera obedientia*; but whether in a manuscript copy or in its printed form, and in that case whether in the Berthelet or Strasbourg edition, remains a matter of doubt. In the regular course of things, books were issued for one or the other of the two great Frankfort fairs, in September and March;[2] but it seems likely that owing to the need for speedy action, Gardiner's work had been sent to the press immediately after Foxe's passage, and was ready by January. The Strasbourg edition indeed seems to have been turned out in great haste, and is not nearly so elaborate as contemporary works from the same press; in regard to its type, paper and setting, it is distinctly poor when compared to the editions issued at London and Hamburg. It does not even bear the ornamental mark of the printer to whom the work was entrusted, Wendelin Rihel or Richel (Wendelinus Rihelius), a friend of the Reformers, whose press issued many works of Bucer, Calvin, John Sturm, Sleidan and others.[3] The title-page and collation are as follows:

STEPHANI | VVINTON. EPISCOPI, | Angli, de uera obedientia, oratio. | QVA EX DIVINIS SCRIPTVRIS | hæc mira cum euidentia colliguntur, | tum elegantia exponuntur. |

i. Quàm oporteat humanas traditiones | posthabere præceptis Dei. |

ii. Ro. Pontifici nullum esse in alias Ecclesias | imperium, nullamque iurisdictionem.

iii. Reges, Principes, *et* Magistratus Chri- | stianos, unumquemque suæ Ecclesiæ supre | mum in terris caput esse, *et* religio-|nem cum primis procura-|re debere.

ARGENTINAE, ANNO | M. D. XXXVI. |

[1] *Thesaurus Baumianus*, vol. IX, fol. 17, January 17, 1536, Bucerus Vadiano: "Mitto orationem Anglicani episcopi...".
[2] Cf. E. Doumergue, *Jean Calvin*, Lausanne, 1899, vol. I, p. 593.
[3] Cf. Friedrich Kapp, *Geschichte des deutschen Buchhandels*, Leipzig, 1886, pp. 826 and 848; Heitz und Barack, *Elsässische Büchermarken bis Anfang des 18. Jahrhunderts*, Strassburg, 1892, art. "Wendelin Riehl".

1 vol. 8°. Title-page + sig. A 2 to A 6 + B 2 to E 8 + 2 fol. Folios numbered 1–34 from sig. B 1. Colophon: ARGENTINAE IN AEDIBVS | VVENDELINI RIHELII, | ANNO M. D. XXXVI. |

Having left Strasbourg, Foxe and Heath apparently continued on their journey post-haste, arrived at Erfurt at the beginning of December, then went on to Smalkalde where they opened with the German princes negotiations which dragged on until the beginning of June, and led to no result. Their embassy lies henceforth outside our subject. There were hopes that among the documents which refer to the proceedings at Smalkalde, some allusion to *De vera obedientia* might be found;[1] but none such has been discovered, and we cannot be certain that the book was submitted to the assembled Lutherans, though this is more than likely.

Meanwhile Henry VIII's plan for propaganda on the Continent was developing in other directions as well. On November 3, 1535, Gardiner arrived in Paris on an embassy to Francis I.[2] On November 19, Cromwell sent him twelve copies of his "oration" and as many of that of Sampson, both of which works were no doubt to be placed before the eyes of the French king, in order to induce him to join Henry VIII in his rejection of the Papacy.[3] And yet soon after Gardiner was to declare against a Protestant alliance with the German princes,[4] while at Smalkalde, Foxe and Heath refused to make any concessions to the Lutherans in regard to dogma, insisted on the retention of the "private mass", and declined to go any farther than a

---

[1] Especially in the *Corpus Reformatorum*, Melanchton, vol. II, *passim*.

[2] This date is given by *D.N.B. sub nom.* "Gardiner". On November 18 Gardiner was daily expected at Dijon, where the French court was then in residence (*Letters and Papers*, vol. IX, No. 847, p. 284, Letter of the bishop of Faenza, papal nuncio in France). On December 13 Chapuys wrote to Charles V (*ibid.* No. 964, p. 324) that as far as he could ascertain, Gardiner had gone to France "to persuade the most Christian king to make himself head of the church in his kingdom, on which matter the said bishop has lately made an oration...".

[3] *Letters and Papers*, vol. IX, No. 848.

[4] *The opinion of Gardiner, bishop of Winchester, concerning the articles presented to the King's Highness by the Princes of Germany at the Conference at Smalcald,* etc. Printed in Collier, *Ecclesiastical History*, ed. Barham, 1841, vol. IX, p. 131, record No. 25; from MS Cleopatra E, v, fol. 213.

diplomatic understanding.[1] Gardiner and the other conservatives may have wished, or pretended to wish, other kings to follow Henry VIII's example, and make themselves popes in their respective dominions; but, if they could possibly help, traditional beliefs and forms of worship were thereby to suffer no change.

Reginald Pole had at that time been living in the north of Italy for several years. The king was anxious to enlist his support in favour of his religious policy. More than once he had sent messages to him, requesting his opinion on the divorce and the supreme headship, which opinion he assured him would be heard in a friendly and unprejudiced spirit. Words to the same effect, which in fact were little less than orders, had been used with Fisher and Thomas More, and were no doubt being used with Gardiner and the conservative clergy. To make compliance easier, the king forwarded to Pole works written by the advocates of the royal cause, such as Sampson's *Oration* in 1534. On January 1, 1536, Pole thus informs Contarini that he has received *De vera obedientia*: "Some days ago I had letters from England, and with them a few books, the chief of which is published under the name of the bishop of Winchester....Those were sent to me, to instruct me in that opinion, which the king wishes me to follow, not allowing me to remain silent, whatever I may think. But I willingly bear that they should thus compel me to write, since even if they bade me be silent, I doubt whether I should obey".[2] A few days after, writing to the same friend, Pole reverts to *De vera obedientia*. He agrees with Contarini that the work is "most cunningly written, but made up of the falsest arguments". Those, he says, are poor, and easily refuted; but "however futile the reasoning of those men

[1] Cf. *Corpus Reformatorum*, vol. III, No. 1389, Anton. Musa ad Steph. Rothe and *passim* to No. 1437, especially No. 1407, Responsum legatorum regis Angliæ ad articulos ipsis a Confœderatis d. 25. 1535 Schmalcaldiæ propositos.

[2] *Epistolæ Reginaldi Poli*, ed. Quirini, Brixiæ (Brescia), 1744, vol. II, p. 429: "Ex Anglia accepi superioribus diebus literas, et cum iis libros aliquot, quorum unus est præcipuus, Episcopi Vintoniensis nomine editus... ii ad me transmissi, ut me erudirent in ea sententia, quem Rex me sequi cupit, et utcunque sentiam, me tacere non permittit. Ego vero hanc mihi necessitatem scribendi ab illis imponi libenter fero, qui etiamsi tacere juberent, nescio an obtemperarem".

may be, the theme is a great one, or rather the themes are great, for there are not one but several, and of the greatest weight; which the books of those men have incited me to handle now".[1] Pole then goes on to express his fears, lest his refutation should not be equal to his purpose, then promises to send to Contarini by the next courier the central and most important part of the work he has begun, that in which he "answers those men's reasons" in regard to the primacy of the Pope. What this rejoinder was to be, we know from later correspondence: it developed into his treatise *Pro ecclesiasticæ unitatis defensione*,[2] which was completed at the end of May, 1536, and was soon after presented to Henry VIII.[3] It is not mainly concerned with Gardiner's oration, but with that of Sampson, which Pole had undertaken to confute as soon as it had reached him. Yet *De vera obedientia* certainly strengthened him in his resolve, and thus may be said to have brought about, for its own part, the composition of one of the greatest controversial works in the sixteenth century.

While Foxe and Heath were negotiating with the Lutherans at Smalkalde, Edmund Bonner, then archdeacon of Leicester, had been sent to Denmark on an embassy. On his way to Copenhagen he stopped at Hamburg with his fellow-ambassador Richard Caundish to attend the Protestant diet that was sitting there. On February 14, 1536, they sent letters home from that city. The diet, they say, "began on January 3, with the duke of Lüneburg, the orators of the dukes of Holstein, Saxony, the Elector, the Lansgrave, Lübeck, Lüneburg, Bremen, etc.... They have printed the bishop of Winchester's book, *De vera obedientia*".[4] Bonner must have presented the book to the deputies, and been instrumental in its publication, since he

---

[1] *Epistolæ Reginaldi Poli*, vol. II, pp. 432–3: "Non sine artificio scriptum, sed levissimis argumentis contextum....Sed utcunque illi sunt futiles, argumentum magnum est, vel potius magna sunt, nec unum sed plura, et ea gravissima sunt; ad quæ nunc tractanda me horum libri impulerunt".

[2] This work was not made public until 1555, when it was published, strange to say, in Strasbourg, and by the very same printer who had issued *De vera obedientia*, Wendelin Riehl; the same volume, it is true, includes several anti-papal treatises.

[3] Cf. *Epistolæ Reginaldi Poli*, vol. II, p. 455. On June 8, 1536, Pole writes to Contarini that his book has been placed in the hands of Henry VIII, from whom an answer has already arrived by the same bearer.

[4] *Letters and Papers*, vol. x, No. 303, p. 112.

himself wrote the violently anti-papal preface, which may be in part accounted for by the Protestant atmosphere in which he was placed.[1] The tone is more biting and sarcastic than even that of *Si sedes illa*, the Pope's moral character being reviled in such words as these: "Be thou most firmly persuaded of this, good reader, that if this [royal] marriage had been the only question at issue, the bishop of Rome would have been most easily kept at rest, especially if some morsel or other had been cast before him".[2] Bonner's motives in countenancing the publication of *De vera obedientia* at Hamburg are clear from the opening lines of his preface: "Whereas there be even now undoubtedly some...who think that the quarrel, which is between the most serene majesty of the king of England and France and the bishop of Rome, arose from this, that his royal Majesty joined to himself in marriage the most illustrious and most noble lady Anne, while in fact the matter at stake is far other and contrary...".[3] Gardiner's book will declare the true state of things. Here again, Henry VIII's efforts to "make" opinion are apparent.

Samuel Roffey Maitland, in his eagerness to clear Bonner from all imputations of fickleness or time-serving, has in his *Essays on the Reformation*, attempted to prove that there were no printers at Hamburg in 1536, and that *De vera obedientia* must have been issued by English reformers exiled abroad, the name of Hamburg being a blind. He hints, without positively asserting it, that the preface is a fabrication.[4] One cannot but regret that his habitual sanity should be for once hopelessly at fault, and that he should have launched upon wild and altogether

[1] The translation of this preface ascribed to Bale is reprinted in S. R. Maitland's *Essays on subjects connected with the Reformation in England*, new edition, London, 1899, Essay No. XVIII.

[2] Bonner's preface, Latin text reprinted in *Fasciculus rerum expetendarum et fugiendarum*, ed. Ed. Brown, London, 1690, pp. 800 sqq.: "Illud autem tibi sit persuasissimum, optime lector, Episcopum Romanum, si nihil præter hoc matrimonium esset, facillimè quieturum, præsertim unâ aut alterâ objectâ offâ".

[3] *Ibid.*: "Quandoquidem nonnulli sunt haud dubiè etiam hoc tempore... qui putant controversiam illam, quæ inter Serenissimam Angliæ Franciæque Regis Majestatem et Episcopum Romanum existit, in eo positam esse, quod sua Regia Majestas longe clarissimam ac nobilissimam dominam Annam Matrimonio sibi copularit, quùm reverâ tamen res longe aliter ac diversius sese habeat...".

[4] S. R. Maitland, *op. cit.* Essays XVII, XVIII.

groundless conjectures. The printer Franz Rhodé (Franciscus Rhodus) who published Gardiner's work, is known to have come from Marburg to Hamburg in 1536, and left Hamburg for Danzig in 1539.[1] His text of *De vera obedientia*, was, like that of Strasbourg, taken directly from one of the London copies; this is shown by a number of minor particulars. But his edition, unlike that of Strasbourg, is a credit to his press; its large, fine paper, its clear, elegant type, are almost a match for Berthelet's handiwork, and, by the way, are scarcely the sort of thing that one would expect from destitute exiles printing clandestine broadsheets. The title-page and collation are as follows:

STEPHANI VVINTONIEN-|SIS EPISCOPI DE VERA OBE| dientia, oratio. | VNA CVM PRAEFATIONE EDMVN-|DI BONERI ARCHIDIACONI LEY | cestrensis sereniss. Regiæ ma. | Angliæ in Dania legati, | capita notabili-|ora dictæ | ora-|tionis com-|plectente, | IN QVA ETIAM OSTENDITVR | caussam controuersiæ quæ inter ipsam sereniss. | Regiam Maiestatem & Episcopum Ro-|manum existit, longe aliter ac | diuersius se habere, quam hacte-|nus a vulgo putatum sit. | Hamburgi ex officina Francisci | Rhodi. Mense Ianuario | 1536

1 vol. 4° with broad margins. Sig. 1–iiij + A i–A ij + B i–F iiij. No colophon. The preface takes up sig. ij a–iij b.

Those are all the references that we have been able to gather in regard to the Latin editions of *De vera obedientia*, though others are sure to crop up in contemporary documents, especially the manuscript collections at Strasbourg and Zurich. The number of copies must have been limited from the very first, and although the work was known to the chief English Reformers of the period,[2] there is no reason to think that it was ever widely read. The three editions have by now become rarities, and as early as 1551, at Gardiner's trial under Edward VI, several important witnesses declared that they had never heard of

---

[1] Cf. Friedrich Kapp, *Gesch. des deutschen Buchhandels*, p. 178; J. M. Lappenberg, *Zur Geschichte der Buchdruckerkunst in Hamburg*, Hamburg, 1840, p. xxxvii.

[2] It is mentioned by several of those whose works are reprinted in the Parker Society Publications, such as Pilkington (vol. xxxv, p. 621), Jewel (vol. xxiii, pp. 34, 38; vol. xxvi, p. 1074), Hooper (vol. xxi, pp. 267, 557, 559, 567). No one of those writers, unhappily, brings any new information about Gardiner's treatise.

his treatise against the Pope.[1] Possibly the bishop of Winchester may have preferred, as far as England was concerned, to keep the book under as much as possible.

There could be no difficulty as to the choice of the Latin text to be reprinted here. Berthelet's first edition has been followed, while footnotes point out the variants, mostly unimportant, in the Strasbourg and the Hamburg editions. Some of the marginal notes added by Bucer are also reproduced, as a proof that the Strasbourg reformers naturally placed, or insisted on placing, a Protestant construction upon Gardiner's demonstration. On the contrary, the choice of an English translation gave rise to much perplexity. Was a modern version of sufficient accuracy to be preferred to that which is ascribed to Bale? The latter, which dates back to 1553, is full of gross misconstructions, and requires constant correction. Yet, after due consideration, it has been retained for the following reasons: despite its faults, it conveys the impression which Gardiner's Latin made upon a contemporary reader; it has literary merits of a sort, picturesqueness and liveliness being its most certain qualities. Besides it has never been reprinted face to face with the Latin text, while an opportunity is now given of comparing it with the original, and judging its merits—or shortcomings—accordingly. Footnotes have been appended whenever emendation was necessary.

It is obviously outside our present purpose to go into the extremely knotty question of the authorship and publication of the *Oration of true obedience*—a problem which bears little relation to Gardiner's political ideas. As in the case of most Protestant pamphlets secretly printed at home or abroad, the circumstances in which the *Oration* was issued are altogether mysterious. Yet we have been able to ascertain a few facts. Soon after the accession of Queen Mary in July, 1553, a series

[1] Cf. the official report of Gardiner's trial in Foxe's *Acts and Monuments*, ed. Pratt, pp. 162 sqq. The earl of Wiltshire knew nothing of *De vera obedientia*; nor did the Marquis of Northampton, the Earl of Bedford and Sir William Harbert. It is true that *De vera obedientia* was an argument in favour of Gardiner, against whom they were deposing; yet if the book had been widely known, they could not have affected to be ignorant of it, and the very question put to them would have had no object.

of Protestant pamphlets began to stream out in rapid succession from some clandestine press with clearly defined characteristics, the titles and dates being the following: *An admonishion to the Bishoppes of VVinchester, London and others* (October 1); *VVhether christian faith maye be kepte secret in the heart, without confession therof openly to the worlde* (October 3); *The Communication betwene my Lord Chauncelor and iudge Hales* (October 6); and lastly *De vera obedientia* (October 26). Now it is striking that three out of four of the above should profess to be printed at Roane (Rouen) by one Michael Wood (the *Communication* alone bearing no printer's name), while there can be no possible doubt as to the similarity in paper and type.[1] (The latter is roman, the *w*'s being everywhere of the same face, and slightly larger than the other letters; the peculiar Gothic capitals *A*, *N* and *S*, in the titles, are exactly alike.) Now where this clandestine press was situated we cannot pretend to have discovered. Some would have it that the *Oration* was printed in Germany, presumably because Bale is supposed to have fled there soon after Mary's accession. It may be noted also that the edition used for translation—that of Hamburg— would be more likely to be met with in Germany than elsewhere. It is clear at any rate that the printing of *De vera obedientia* was part of a systematic plan of attack, and that the attack was conducted by an able and resolute adversary. Was that adversary John Bale, bishop of Ossory in Ireland under Edward VI, now, after his adventurous flight, an exile for his faith? Such a view was taken by an eminent scholar, John E. B. Mayor, whose manuscript note to that effect in the first volume of *Athenæ Cantabrigienses* has been reproduced in the additions and corrections of vol. III (p. 69). We may suppose that his opinion rested mainly on internal evidence; at any rate, he suggests no confirmation from what little is known of Bale's movements after his flight from Ireland. The English version published at "Roane" certainly bears the strongest likeness to Bale's controversial style and manner. As the reader will soon find out, unnecessary coarseness has been in more than one place in-

---

[1] The four booklets, be it noted, are bound together in a volume of the Lambeth Library (press-mark A. 4. 13, pieces 3 to 6), and must have been early considered as belonging to the same family.

troduced for its own sake; and the translation, on the whole, is the work of a polemical, irresponsible writer, not that of a scholar or thinker. Perhaps the nearest approach to a proof of Bale's authorship is to be found in the "translatour's conclusion" or·appendix, which we have no reason to reproduce here any more than his preface. It is not to be dismissed as purely "scurrilous", and its literary value is far from negligible. The writer makes use of Gardiner's own comparison of himself, in the face of error and truth, to a man with two wives; who having lived with the one—error—so long as the other—truth— was away and thought to be dead, is now on the latter's reappearance bound to return to her as to his only lawful spouse. Gardiner, we are now told, has again deserted "Goodwife truth" and turned her out of doors, to revert to his first love, "Mistress Rose of Rome". In a few highly picturesque pages, we hear how he took to loathing "olde plaine russet cote Ione of the countrie...alwaies moiling and scraping to get the peny for the world to come", and fondly remembered "what prety knackes... his sweet sugarloafe Mistres Rose...devised to please him, howe softlie she was wont to chirpe him vnder the chin and kisse him...".[1] The delineation of character may appear crude and the expression even more so, yet this broad, homely sketch of a comic play is due to no common pamphleteer; it bears the stamp of true genius—of a sort; it stands out in vivid colours on the dull background of contemporary religious controversy; it is indisputably the work of a master hand. Who apart from Bale, among the English Protestant refugees, was able to write in such a vein? No name suggests itself, tediousness being the main feature in the polemical writings of the Reformers. The "conclusion" to *De vera obedientia* stands at the beginnings of English humour in its most realistic form. Such, no doubt, is the strongest argument in favour of Mayor's contention.

At the same time, if the bishop of Ossory did turn *De vera obedientia* into English, we cannot entertain a high opinion of his literary attainments, and his ignorance of the Latin tongue is indeed surprising in the flowering days of humanism, and on the part of one who had been Gardiner's fellow-student at Cambridge. The English version, it is true, had to be turned

[1] *De vera obedientia*, 1st Roan ed. sig. K i–ii.

out in all haste, hence possibly some of its imperfections. But again, if we are to credit Bale's description of his strange adventures in 1553, it seems quite impossible that he should have been in time to supply the printer with a translation, however hasty, of Gardiner's work, before October 26. On September 8, according to his own statement in *The vocacyon of Johan Bale to the bishoprick of Ossorie in Irelaunde* (1553), he was still at Kilkenny, where his servants were arrested;[1] soon after he fled to Dublin, and a few days later embarked on a small ship, the date of his escape being Michaelmas day, September 29, according to one of his biographers.[2] Then he himself tells us how he was taken prisoner by a Dutch (or rather Flemish) man-of-war, and "tossed to and fro vpon the seas, by the space of xxiiij dayes",[3] before he was set ashore in Catholic Flanders, somewhere in the neighbourhood of Antwerp. There he was kept in a private house,[4] "as a prisoner, by the space of iij wekes" until he was finally allowed to depart. Forty-five days from September 29 bring us to November 13, i.e. eighteen days after the date on which *De vera obedientia* was professedly issued. This seems hard to reconcile with Bale's authorship, unless we are prepared to admit that the translation was written before and somehow or other came into the hands of the printer; or that the date on the title-page is a blind. But this latter assumption would cast suspicion upon the dates of the whole series of pamphlets issued from the same press. Besides we know from the *Chronicle of Queen Jane and two years of Queen Mary* that "about Christmas eve (1553) ther came forth a booke entytled 'De vera obedyentia' imprinted, as yt is saide, at Roane, where it was translated…".[5] The book would of course have left the press some time before; a few weeks would be necessary for smuggling of Protestant literature into England. Perhaps the most reasonable explanation is that the reformer who translated Gardiner's work was not unsuccessfully trying

---

[1] *The Vocacyon of Johan Bale*, etc., in vol. i of the *Harleian Miscellany*, ed. London, 1808, p. 348.

[2] Parker Society, vol. i, p. xi: Biographical notice of Bale by the Rev. Henry Christmas, who unhappily does not quote his source.

[3] *Harleian Miscellany*, 1808, vol. i, p. 357.

[4] *Ibid.* p. 358.

[5] Camden Society, old series, vol. 48, p. 33.

to imitate Bale's manner and emulate his talent. Be this as it may, the question must for the present remain undecided, and the field be left open for future explorers.

Of the *Oration of true obedience*, several editions were issued. The first in date is the one mentioned above, which appeared with the following title-page and collation:

DE VERA OBEDIENTIA | AN O [these three letters in Gothic type] | ration made in Latine by the ry-|ghte Reuerend father in God Ste-|phan B. of VVinchestre, nowe lord | Chau*n*cellour of england, with the | preface of Edmunde Boner, som-|time Archedeaco*n* of Leicestre, and | the kinges maiesties embassa-dour | in Denmarke, *and* sithence B. of Lon-|don, touching true Obedience. | Printed at Hamburgh in La-|tine, In Officina Francisci Rho-|di Mense Ia. M D xxxvi. | And nowe translated into english | and printed by Michael wood:| with the Preface *and* con-|clusion of the traun-|slatour. | ¶ From Roane. xxvi of Octobre M D. l iii | In Readinge marke the Notes | in the margine. | A double mynded man, is inconst*an*t in al his waies. Iac. i.

i vol. 8°. Sigs A i–viii + a i–iiij (title-page and "The translatour to the gentle reader") + sigs b i to i vi, folios numbered i to lx (Bonner's preface and text of *De vera obedientia*) + sigs. I vii–K iv a (The translatovr eftsones to the christen reader). Marginal notes in black letter.

The name of "Roane" as the place of printing may be a blind, though not taken as such in the above-mentioned passage of the *Chronicle of Queen Jane*. What is called the "second Roan edition" is almost similar to the first, and we may suppose that it was rather in the nature of a recasting of the earlier issue, the same fount being used, and advantage being taken of the transformation to introduce some improvements. The title-page and the date are the same, but the pages are slightly higher (thirty lines instead of twenty-eight). The text has now been divided up into paragraphs, the Gothic *r*'s (used on account of a shortage of roman *r*'s) have disappeared, and marginal notes have been added. In the preface and especially in the appendix "to the Christian reader", the style has been touched up in a rather felicitous way. The collation is the following:

1 vol. 8°. Sigs A i–B iiij (the latter folio marked A iiij by mistake) (title-page and translator's preface as above) + Sigs B v to I vi a, folios numbered i to lviii a (Bonner's preface and text) + sigs. I vi b to K iij, folios numbered lviii b to lxiii b (translator's conclusion as above).

Before this edition appeared, the Spanish marriage must have become a common subject for talk, since a marginal note on p. A iiij runs as follows: "Care not for the braue Spaniardes wyll brynge vs a mery world". But as early as November 16 the Commons had petitioned against the queen's matrimonial schemes.

The third edition belongs to a class by itself. It differs from the first two in some important particulars. On its title-page, which we reproduce in facsimile, it professes to be printed "in Rome / before *the* castle of S. Angel / at the signe of S. Peter. In nouembre / Anno do. M.D. L iij". The collation is as follows:

1 vol. 8°, unpag. Sigs A i–B v ("The Preface of the translatour to *the* gentil reader", and Bonner's preface); B vi–H ii (De vera obedientia); H iii–H iiij a (a string of scripture texts headed "Resistaunce of *the* Gospell / is a most manifest sygne of dampnacion.") Black letter throughout. At the bottom of fol. H iiij a is the device of Hugh Singleton, a well-known London printer[1] (a monogram in a shield, surrounded with the inscription "God is my helper"). This of course proves nothing as to the origin of the book.

The most striking discrepancies between the "Rome" and "Roane" editions are in the preface, which has been largely expurgated, amended and polished up, so as to make it less coarse and crude. This may perhaps tend to prove that the "Rome" edition was not issued under the translator's super-

[1] It is rather curious that the same peculiarity should be met with in two other Protestant pamphlets issued two years after, *A confession and declaration of praiers added thervnto by Jhon Knox...vpon the death...of...Edward VI...* (July, 1555) and *An epistle wrytten by John Scory...vnto all the faythful that be in pryson in Englande...*(1555). Both bear Hugh Singleton's mark at the end, while the former, like *De vera obedientia*, professes to be "Imprinted in Rome, before the Castel of S. Aungel / at the signe of Sainct Peter". The two pamphlets are bound together as pieces 6 and 7 of vol. xxxi. 8. 13 in the Library at Lambeth.

vision, but by other reformers who were conscious of the discredit which an utter lack of decency was sure to bring upon them as a body. Bale himself, at any rate, would not be likely to place a curb upon his freedom of speech. All this matters little, however, as far as our immediate purpose is concerned, for the translation itself is identical in the three editions, misprints only being corrected. The "Rome" text being both the latest and cleanest, has been selected for reproduction here. The marginal notes are retained; they again emphasize the use made by Gardiner of Protestant forms of speech, while they make it no less clear that, despite his outward concessions, he fell far short of true Protestant standards. The notes are particularly heavy towards the end, where reference is made to the breaking of unlawful oaths; this is referred by the translator to "vows of chastity unadvisedly made", in other words to the case of religious men and women who have left their orders and married. This might be considered as another presumption in favour of the authorship of Bale, himself an unfrocked Carmelite friar; for he was most sensitive on the question of vows, on which he constantly kept harping. But this of course might to a lesser degree apply to other English reformers.

A word must here be said of the previous reprints of *De vera obedientia*.[1] Before the age of controversies had come to an end, the Latin original was twice republished in the seventeenth century, in both cases quite accurately; first by Melchior Goldast, who used the Strasbourg text, in the successive issues of his *Monarchia Sancti Romani Imperii* (e.g. Hanoviæ 1612, tom. i, p. 716); then from the Hamburg text, together with Bonner's preface, in Edward Brown's appendix to his edition of the *Fasciculus rerum expetendarum et fugiendarum* (London, 1690, vol. II, pp. 800–20). As for the English translation ascribed to Bale, it only reappeared in the nineteenth century. It is found as an appendix to William Stevens's *Memoirs of the life and martyrdom of John Bradford* (London, 1832), but this reprint of the Rome text is, in the judgment of S. R. Maitland,

---

[1] A concise but complete bibliography will be found in J. A. Muller, *Stephen Gardiner and the Tudor reaction.* Cf. also J. Gillow, *Dictionary of English Catholics*, and S. R. Maitland, *Essays on the Reformation*, Essays XVII–XIX.

so careless and full of blunders as to be utterly worthless.[1] The same edition was used in 1870 by B. A. Heywood, whose reproduction of it in *The royal supremacy in matters ecclesiastical in pre-Reformation times*, is faithful and exact, but has become almost as rare as the original. On the whole, *De vera obedientia* is seldom within the reach of the historical student, and it is hoped that the present reprint will supply a deficiency.

If we judge Gardiner's feelings rightly, we may fancy that he was anything but flattered or gratified by Bucer's complimentary preface to his treatise. He had played up to the Protestants for diplomatic motives, but he had no wish to be held up to the whole world as one of their friends and supporters. Bucer himself soon realized his mistake. From the year 1539 onwards, he handles Gardiner roughly in his private correspondence, bewails his influence upon Henry VIII, calls him "the corrupter of the English church", the "devilish bishop".[2] Gardiner, he says in an interesting letter to the Landgrave of Hesse, is responsible for the maintenance of Catholic beliefs in England: "It is to be deplored", he adds, "that this and other raving bishops in England should have, with those of France, devised means to maintain themselves in their pomp, and thereby to turn their kings from us and pure religion; namely by helping them to remove the Pope, but then putting themselves together with their kings in the place of the Pope".[3] Gardiner is here credited with a scheme for the establishment of Cæsaropapism, buttressed by a strong episcopacy, both in England and in France. It is a trick of the devil, Bucer says, to replace an old worn-out Pope by new ones. Henry VIII is seeking the support of the Emperor for his policy, and the marriage of priests has of course no chance either in his dominions or in

[1] S. R. Maitland, *Essays on the Reformation*, Essays XVII–XIX.

[2] "Den verderber der Englischen Kirchen", Bucer to Philip, Landgrave of Hesse, October 16, 1539, in Lenz (Max), *Briefwechsel Landgraf Philipp's von Hessen mit Bucer*, vol. I, p. 110, "den teuflishen bischove von Wincestren", *ibid.* p. 244, November 26, 1540.

[3] "Es ist auch zu besorgen, dasz dieser und andere geschwinde Bischove in Engelland mit denen in Frankreich dies Mittel bedacht haben, sich in ihrem [*sic*] Pracht zu erhalten, wo sich ihre Konige von uns und der reinen religion dadurch abwendeten, dasz sie ihnen hulfen den Papst entsetzen und sich aber sampt ihren Konigen an des Statt einsetzeten", *ibid.* vol. I, p. 100, September 16, 1539.

those of Francis I.[1] Here we already find all the main points of the controversy with Gardiner, which Bucer was to begin in no friendly spirit, though with outward meekness and courtesy; while the bishop of Winchester, on his part, entertained no high opinion of the Strasbourg reformer, "a man", he says, "whom he had never seen before; but who", he adds contemptuously, and perhaps sarcastically, "was not altogether unknown to him, on account of his books and published writings".[2]

The Diet of Ratisbon was to bring the two adversaries face to face. We need not enlarge upon this huge assembly, to which men flocked from all parts of Europe. The Emperor was attempting to re-unite divided Christendom under his own sceptre; an attempt distinct from, and to some extent opposed to, that of the Pope and the majority of the Italian cardinals, which was to mature in the Council of Trent. It need scarcely be pointed out that Charles V had no wish to make himself the head of the Church in the same sense as Henry VIII had done. He wished to retain the authority of the Pope over the whole of Christendom, were it but in hopes that the Papacy would become finally attached to imperial interests; which would of course necessarily ensue, if he succeeded by his own means in bringing back the Protestants to the fold. The Church would remain papal, while the Pope would be little more than a servant or chaplain of the Emperor—a position curiously akin to that which Gardiner, in *De vera obedientia*, had stated to be his by right.[3] In the circumstances, Henry VIII's attitude appears as highly significant. Charles V's scheme of imperial Catholicism seemed to offer to him a chance of reverting to the unity of the Church, of preserving traditional beliefs and forms of worship, of quieting whatever qualms of conscience he may have felt, without sacrificing any of the newly-acquired rights of the crown. Impelled by such motives no doubt, he sent Gardiner, by now the recognized head of the conservatives, to Ratisbon as his representative; not indeed to take part in the official debates or

[1] Lenz (Max), *Briefwechsel Landgraf Philipp's von Hessen mit Bucer*, vol. I, p. 100, September 16, 1539.
[2] "...cum ego tecum homine mihi non antea viso, libris tamen tuis et scriptis in publicum emissis non omnino ignoto...contuli", *Stephani Winton. episcopi angli ad Martinum Bucerum...conquestio*, ed. Cologne, 1545, sig. A ij.
[3] Berthelet edition, fol. 32 a.

negotiations, but to feel the way and see what might be done by purely diplomatic means[1]. The bishop of Winchester was placed in a curious position; officially at least he gave up nothing of Henry VIII's pretensions to a full supremacy over the English Church; while at the same time he was conducting with Italian or imperial diplomats, negotiations which actually paved the way for the return of England to the obedience of the Roman See,[2] and to which he later referred as having had such an object.[3] But in fact England's submission was to be conditional upon the acceptance by Rome of Henry VIII's own terms; and there need be no absolute contradiction between Gardiner's defence of the king's rights over the Church in his controversy with Bucer, and his efforts to effect a reconciliation with the Papacy. How the Ratisbon debates proceeded; how a committee of six was formed—three Catholics and three Protestants, all moderates, with Bucer on the Protestant side—to discuss the matters at issue; how Gardiner attempted to carry out his mission, and to get into touch with Pole; how in fact his purpose was defeated, owing to anti-papal opposition at home, and to the failure of the Diet to achieve its main object; are points which need not detain us here. What really matters is that he appeared at Ratisbon as the defender of that special and long-forgotten form of Catholicism in which the king, even if he granted the Pope a primacy of honour, was to rule the Church by divine right.

On December 12, 1540, a certain Dr Heinrich Kopp wrote from Antwerp to the council of thirteen who ruled Strasbourg, that the bishop of Winchester had passed through the town on December 10 with 140 horses. He carried with him, we hear, a heap of books, and was accompanied by a few young men

[1] Gardiner does not appear in the *Narrationes colloquii Ratisponensis* (*Corpus Reformatorum*, vol. IV) or in the *Acta Colloquii in Comitiis Imperii Ratisponae habiti*, published by Bucer at Strasbourg in 1542.

[2] Cf. on Gardiner's direct or indirect negotiations with the Roman See the very definite evidence supplied by the *Nuntiaturberichte aus Deutschland*, Part I, vol. VII, *Berichte vom Regensburger und Speierer Reichstag 1541, 1542*, ed. by Ludwig Cardauns, pp. 37, 38, 50, 73 (Letters of Morone and Sanzio to Farnese).

[3] In his sermon of the first Sunday in Advent, December 2, 1555 (*Concio reveren. d. Stephani Episcopi vintonien....habita dominica prima adventus...*, Romæ, 1555, sig. d iiij).

of learning.[1] Travelling by easy stages, he eventually reached Nuremberg some time before March 28, and there discussed the theological problem of justification with the reformer Osiander, taking a definitely Catholic line.[2] Soon after he must have arrived at Ratisbon, for the public sittings of the Diet began on April 5. No evidence is extant as to the date of his first meeting with Bucer. What passed between the two men is chiefly known to us through Gardiner, who referred to the controversy again and again in his English and Latin works. Bucer, he tells us, was the first to seek an interview, which was haughtily granted: "I wish to further truth," Gardiner was to say to his adversary on leaving Ratisbon, "and if such was not the case, I should have admitted neither you nor Alesius to conference with me".[3] Bucer, who knew what sudden turns things had been taking in England for the past three or four years, had, we may think, not yet lost his hopes of enlisting for the Protestant party the support of such a valuable ally as the bishop of Winchester. Alesius was the Scottish reformer Alexander Aless, whom he had brought with him to the first meeting, and who took part in the discussion. In addition to him there were numerous witnesses, including, possibly, John Calvin,[4] and also probably some of those "young men of learning" who were in Gardiner's train. "I do not make use against you," the latter was to say in his *Epistola* to Bucer, "of the authority of witnesses, who were present at our debate, and who still remain alive; nor would you accept them unless they were in league with you, for such only you call pious and trustworthy".[5] Of the actual circumstances of the disputation we know little more. One particular detail struck Bucer to such a point, that

[1] *Politische Korrespondenz der Stadt Strassburg*, ed. by O. Winckelmann, vol. III, p. 139.
[2] *Corpus Reformatorum*, vol. IV, No. 2170, letter of Osiander to Justus Jonas, from Nuremberg, March 28, 1541. Cf. No. 2172, letter of Melanchton to Justus Jonas, March 29, 1541.
[3] Cf. *Contemptum humanæ legis*, p. 272.
[4] At any rate Calvin, who was present at Ratisbon, was acquainted with the detail of the controversy. Cf. *Corpus Reformatorum*, vol. LXXI, p. 134, Prælectio in Amos, cap. vii, v. 10–13.
[5] *Stephani Winton....ad Martinum Bucerum Epistola*, Ingolstadii, 1546, sig. A 3 b. "Non utor in te autoritate testium, qui praesentes nostro sermoni interfuerunt, adhuc superstites, neque enim recipis nisi conjuratos, quos solos pios vocas, et dignos fide".

he recalled it as late as 1547, in his *Gratulatio* to the English people upon the accession of Edward VI. "I saw him", he says of Gardiner, "so much inflamed with the dispute, that the veins of his hands—a thing which I have never beheld in any other man—swelled and throbbed, whenever he heard from us a thing which displeased him; especially if any such thing had been uttered by the most learned and truly pious theologian, Alexander Alesius...".[1] This was denied by Gardiner in his rejoinder; if he had been tempted to shake, it would have been, he says, with laughter at the stupidity of Alesius.[2] But the story, whether fanciful or not, took firm root among the English Protestants. It is found anew, in a somewhat improved version, in Nicholas Carr's letter, written on the occasion of Bucer's death in 1551. We are now favoured with further details on the *portentum*, the "monstrous appearance". "In Gardiner's right hand", we hear, "between the thumb and forefinger,...a certain vein first swelling, palpitated with such a rapid and visible motion, that all those who saw him, said he had come readier to fight than to dispute, and better prepared for arms than for counsel".[3]

Gardiner's adversaries may have made more of the tale than it was really worth; but the very heat with which he denied it, and reviled Bucer in his various tracts against him, is rather damaging evidence; and he must certainly plead guilty to the charge of excessive violence. The ambassador and counsellor of the mighty sovereign of England felt neither sympathy nor reverence for the unfrocked monk who had the audacity to oppose him. He considered him as a sectarian rebel to whom

---

[1] *Gratulatio Martini Buceri ad ecclesiam Anglicanam*...1548 (November), p. 53: "Equidem autem ita ardere eum vidi contentione, ut venae ejus in manibus, quod in nullo unquam homine vidi, subsilirent, et tremerent, quoties audiret a nobis, quod offendebat; maxime si quid tale dixisset doctissimus, et vere pius theologus, Alexander Alesius, quem unum mecum adduxeram...".

[2] *Exetasis testimoniorum*..., Lovanii, 1554 (really composed in 1548), pp. 2–3. Aless is here referred to as "ineptus Scotus...quo homine ineptiorem...arbitror me vidisse neminem...qui ex gente fidem habet infamam".

[3] *De obitu doctissimi et sanctissimi...Martini Buceri*... Londini, 1551, sig. e i *b*: "In dextra ejus manu, inter pollicem et indicem,...vena quaedam intumescens, tam celeri et perspicuo motu palpitaret, ut omnes qui illum aspexerant, ad pugnandum quam ad disputandum, ad arma quam ad consilium paratiorem venisse dicerent".

he, as a bishop, without stooping to a discussion on equal terms, might bend down to help him back into the right way. Had not Bucer once before "sung his palinode"?[1] On the other hand the Strasbourg reformer, who was conscious of his inferiority in mere power and driving force, made the best possible use of his coolness and self-restraint, and goaded his adversary into unbridled wrath, while himself preserving the most innocent-looking composure all the while. The actual progress of the discussion must be elicited from conflicting documents. Bucer's account of it is late and as we shall see, is rendered untrustworthy by an obvious misstatement. As to Gardiner's account, we can easily piece it together from several of his works, English and Latin. In the *Examination of the hunter*, written in answer to William Turner's *Huntyng of the Romishe fox*, he "reherses his communication with Bucer...with whome", he says, "vpon the desyre he had to confer with me I told hym i was glad to speak. Who when he cam to me after the maner of Germany made a long oration vnto me conteynyng only the zeale he had to the truthe for trying out where of / he sayd he was desyrous to talk with me / I told hym i was glad to hear hym speak so indifferently. But for as myche / all autorite / wher by to press one another was clerely taken away by dissention / I told hym that Scripture was out of autorite / to any one parte / becaus both partes wolde applye to theyr partye / theyr own interpretation and there in stand obstinately...and therfore i sayde for want of autorite to proue / i wold vse Socrates maner of disputyng with hym / *and* pres hym / which he shuld hymself grant / he sayd he was content / Then i asked him where in / and he sayd he cared not / but he thought / that the mariage of prestes was very cruelly handled / to forbid it *sub pœna mortis*. I told he was a sore aduersari in thys becaus the mater touched hym self how be it the kyngis maiesti myght forbid it / of the payn i wold reson with hym afterwarde / and dowted not but the extremite of payn was in respect of the multitude mercifully to kepe them by feare / from danger / rather then cruel as he

---

[1] Cf. *Contemptum humanæ legis*, p. 272 and note. This no doubt refers to Bucer's change of attitude on the question of the Lord's Supper, when he gave up Zwinglianism to take up the intermediate position which may be considered as specially his own.

calleth it…".[1] Then Bucer asked by what authority the king might forbid marriage; Gardiner replied that the king had the same authority as a father, to whom absolute obedience was due. Besides it was proved by a passage in I Cor. vii, 37, that a father might keep his daughter a virgin out of his own free-will. On being shown the passage, Bucer seemed to be thunderstruck; then handed the book to Aless, who then referred to the beginning of the chapter, no doubt to vv. 2 and 9, in which marriage is recommended for the avoidance of fornication.

We have substantially the same story in the *Conquestio ad Martinum Bucerum*.[2] The discussion on I Cor. vii later developed into a war of pamphlets which lasted on till 1548 and which we have described elsewhere.[3] This, however, was but a side-issue at Ratisbon, and the main debate now followed, its subject being the authority of kings in matters religious. Gardiner granted to the prince disciplinary powers akin to those of the Pope, which Bucer and his friends could in no wise accept. The debate must have occupied several sittings, though we have no direct evidence to that effect. At any rate, after being begun orally, it was continued in writing, while Gardiner was still at Ratisbon: "At that time", he was to write in 1544, addressing Bucer, "we took occasion (of the oral discussion) to send private letters to each other and pursued more at large and more clearly what in our talk had occurred by the way. I myself even then, fearing lest any false charge should be brought forward, while the recent memory of present things was still fresh, declared in letters written to you, what had been done in conference; so that you might, while we were still in each other's presence, reproach me with any misrepresentation, if you thought from my words that I meant to turn any such against you. Now you know what you answered to my letters and what I again wrote to you. Indeed I am still preserving the writings in the original hands,

---

[1] *The examination of a prowd praesumptuous hunter*, etc. This short tract is now lost, but was reproduced by Turner in *The rescuynge of the Romishe fox* (1545), where the above passage is found on sigs. L i b–L ii a.
[2] *Stephani Winton….ad Martinum Bucerum…conquestio*, Coloniæ, 1545, sig. A iij b.
[3] In the article mentioned at the end of note 2, p. xvii.

as certain proofs of most evident truth".[1] Gardiner reverts to
the subject in his *Epistola ad Martinum Bucerum* of 1546,
stating that while at Ratisbon, he composed an *extempore* answer
to Bucer, "let this be said", he adds, "without any bragging".[2]
From the above-quoted passages, we gather that the bishop of
Winchester sent two memoranda in succession to his adversary.
One of those memoranda, or at least a fragment of it, though
little noticed, has been known almost from the very first. In
1546, while the dispute on I Cor. vii was at its fiercest, Gardiner
repeatedly taunted Bucer with misrepresentation of what had
passed in 1541: "Why do you not publish", he said, "my
writing which is in your hands?... You suppress what I wrote".[3]
After ignoring the taunt for two years, Bucer at last grudgingly
reprinted a paragraph of the memorandum.[4] As to the subject
of the latter there can be no doubt. It is only concerned with the
interpretation of Paul's epistle and the power of a father to con-
strain his children to celibacy. It obviously refers to the earlier
part of the discussion and must be considered as first in date.

As for the second memorandum, it is happily extant in a
manuscript copy, the very same one, we may think, which
Gardiner says he had kept for reference. Though well-known
to bibliographers,[5] its connection with the Ratisbon debate has
not yet been pointed out. It is found in the Parker Collection[6]

---

[1] *Ad Martinum Bucerum Conquestio*, Coloniæ, 1545, sig. A ij: "Quo tempore,
arrepta inde occasione, literis privatis ultro citroque missis, quod inter
loquendum obiter inciderat, latius atque apertius sumus prosecuti. Ego
enim jam tum ne quid inde calumniae nasceretur veritus, cum adhuc recens
praesentium memoria vigeret, quod inter conferendum agebatur, datis ad
te literis sum testatus, hoc nimirum consilio, ut praesens praesenti calumniam
objiceres, si quam forte ex verbis putasses intendendam. Tu vero quid meis
literis responderis, et quid item iterum tibi rescripserim, scis. Certe apud
me servantur ipsa autographa, indubiae veritatis clarissima testimonia".

[2] *Ad Martinum Bucerum Epistola*, Ingolstadii, 1546, sig. A 3 b: "...ut qui
extemporali facultate (quod sine jactantia sit dictum) tibi Ratisbonæ scripto
privatim responderim...".

[3] *Ad Martinum Bucerum Epistola*, sig. A 3 b: "Quin scripta quae apud te
sunt mea aedis..."; sig. A 4 a: "Illa quae scripsi supprimis".

[4] *Gratulatio*, p. 55.

[5] It is mentioned in Gillow's *Dictionary of English Catholics* among other
writings dated 1554; in *D.N.B.* without a date, *sub. nom.* Gardiner; and in
James's *Catalogue of the C.C.C. MSS*. Prof. J. A. Muller rightly ascribes it
to the latter part of Henry VIII's reign.

[6] This collection contains many papers which were in Gardiner's hands
at some time or other.

at Corpus Christi College, Cambridge, vol. CXIII, piece No. 34, pp. 255–274—twenty closely written pages in thin, clear italics, obviously not Gardiner's hand, but that of a scribe or secretary. This is the hitherto unpublished writing which we reprint below, as Gardiner's third political tract. Its title runs as follows: *Contemptum humanæ legis iusta authoritate latæ grauius et seuerius vindicandum quam diuinæ legis qualemcunque transgressionem.* The last few pages of this tractate provide us with information which leaves no possible doubt as to the circumstances and time of its composition.[1] We hear of the Scot Aless, whom Gardiner admitted to conference together with Bucer; of Bucer's virtuous indignation at the pomp of the bishop of Winchester's embassy; we find passing references to the earlier part of the debate on I Cor. vii; and finally Gardiner tells us that he is writing on the very eve of his departure: "I am getting ready", he says, "to start on my journey, and am not at leisure to answer" Bucer's admonition on the duties of a true bishop.[2] When Gardiner left Ratisbon is not exactly known. On July 4 he is said to be "negotiating more than usual with his Majesty"[3] (i.e. the Emperor), but on the same day there is a rumour going "that he is recalled, and fears for his life, because he has recommended church reunion to his king".[4] There is reason to think that shortly after that date, having penned his second answer to Bucer, he in fact began his progress back to Flanders and England. It appears from a letter of the Spanish reformer Dryander (Francesco de Enzinas) to Edmund Crispin at Oxford, written on September 22, that before September 10 Gardiner had been halting at Louvain;[5] and we know that

[1] Pp. 272–4 of the MS.
[2] *Ibid.*, p. 273: "Ego ad iter me paro, nec vacat respondere... etc.".
[3] Sanzio to Farnese, Ratisbon, July 4: "Che l' amistà con Inghilterra et il ragionamento del casamento va strecto et il vescovo Trieste [Wincester] negocia più del solito con S. Mtà...". In *Nuntiaturberichte*, vol. VII, ed. by Ludwig Cardauns, p. 73, No. 34.
[4] Morone to Farnese, Ratisbon, July 4: "Man sagt, der Bischof von Winchester sei zurückgerufen, und fürchte für sein Leben, weil er dem Könige zur Union geraten habe...". In *Regesten und Briefe des Cardinals Gasparo Contarini*, ed. by Fr. Dittrich, Braunsberg, 1881, p. 209.
[5] The letter was produced at Gardiner's trial and is found in Foxe's *Acts and Monuments* (ed. Josiah Pratt, vol. VI, p. 139). Dryander says he arrived at Antwerp on September 21 and had spent ten days at Louvain; it seems from the wording of his letter that Gardiner's Louvain adventure had taken place before, and that he heard it related by his host.

his ambassador's train compelled him to travel by slow stages.

Bucer's account of the controversy in the *Gratulatio* agrees with the above in regard to the subjects handled, but reverses the order, and places the discussion on clerical celibacy and the father's power over his daughter after that of the king's authority over the Church.[1] Bucer also denies having complied with Gardiner's request as to the method to be followed in debate, and declares that he proclaimed the infallibility and all-sufficiency of Scripture as a test of truth. But the trustworthiness of his statements may with good reason be questioned. When challenged to justify his charges against Gardiner in regard to I Cor. vii, he is compelled to acknowledge that he cannot substantiate them by means of his adversary's writing.[2] In the same passage, he denounces "Winchester's horrible dogma, that the transgression of human laws is rightly to be punished more heavily than that of divine laws".[3] Now this was written under Edward VI, when Gardiner had no means to make himself publicly heard in his own defence; but if we refer to the Corpus Christi MS, we find that as early as 1541 he had been careful to reject such an interpretation of his thought, and to make it clear that he compared the *contempt* of human law on the one hand, and *some transgression* of divine law on the other.[4] In the *Exetasis* composed in 1548, while he was in disfavour and soon to be imprisoned, he again takes exception to Bucer's "calumny", and devotes a few pages to its refutation.[5] He very exactly confirms his statements of seven years before. "You have", he says to Bucer, "my explanation, set forth in my own hand, which methinks you were greatly afraid of publishing".[6] But now, though the treatment of the subject be substantially the same, the tone is different. Gardiner still very reasonably contends that it is impossible for the prince to chastise every breach of "God's law"—i.e. the moral law—and that he must attend primarily to the preservation of the State by punishing

---

[1] *Gratulatio*, p. 55.  [2] *Ibid.* p. 49.
[3] *Ibid.* p. 55: "Horribile Vintoniensis dogma humanarum legum quam divinarum transgressionem recte puniri gravius".
[4] Cf. *Contemptum humanæ legis*, pp. 260 sqq.
[5] *Exetasis testimoniorum*, Lovanii, 1554, pp. 155–8.
[6] *Ibid.* p. 155.

1

those who infringe "human laws", and thereby "perturb human society".[1] Yet he is less insistent now upon the disciplinary rights of the prince over the Church. His defence of what he himself calls a "paradox" appears as merely theoretical: the heart has gone out of it. Writing more than twelve months after the death of Henry VIII, he had begun to realize that the absolute power of the sovereign in matters religious might easily cut both ways, and in particular might be used against that Catholic tradition which he held dearest; shortly after he was to plead the rights of conscience against the authority of the State. With the passing of Henry VIII, Cæsaro-papism had suffered its deathblow; no other Justinian was thenceforth to sit on the English throne.

Having now ascertained the circumstances in which the three tracts appeared, we are better able to determine their true character, and the relation they bear to Gardiner's own personal views and beliefs. First of all, one point is clear. Whether they reflect his deeper feelings or not, *Si sedes illa* and *De vera obedientia* were not written with the object of expressing and furthering truth as such, but in view of a political result to be achieved, and so as to take political circumstances into account. They are diplomatic documents, drafted in order to strengthen Henry VIII's position after the breach with Rome. Lest a united Europe should turn against him at the Pope's call, he was compelled to find allies on the Continent. Thus in dealing with the various Powers, he had to take up the attitude best calculated to enlist their sympathies, and therefore to adapt himself to their various temperaments. This had to be done skilfully, and Gardiner was entrusted with the work. His position in regard to his royal master was that for which his professional training fitted him best; that of an advocate who deems it no breach of the moral law to strive for his client's victory by all means, fair or foul. His devotion to the interests of Henry VIII, whether spontaneous or compelled, is the only possible explanation for the many instances of deliberate falsehood which the two anti-papal tracts offer. This does not mean, however, that they are grossly and callously insincere. Gardiner

[1] *Exetasis testimoniorum*, Lovanii, 1554, p. 158.

must have at least tried to persuade himself that his client was in the right. Hence, while some passages are no better than pieces of diplomatic make-believe, others contain a measure at least of truthfulness, while on some points, Gardiner was not to recant his early opinions even after his return to the Roman Church under Mary.

These remarks may be easily verified by a careful examination of Gardiner's two anti-papal tracts, allowance being made for their difference in character and tone. The former is adapted, as we said, to the requirements of Gallican France, the latter, to those of Lutheran Germany. Again, while *De vera obedientia* is a regular treatise on royal supremacy, a demonstration conducted according to the rules of logic, *Si sedes illa* has no pretensions to unity or even consistency. It closely follows the Pope's brief which it is meant to confute, taking up each point in its turn, irrespective of the others. Its purpose is not to persuade by clear, cold reasoning, but to carry the reader along and rouse his feelings—whether noble, such as patriotism or loyalty to the sovereign, or ignoble, such as hatred, greed, and envy. In places, it looks as if Gardiner had wished to flatter the lowest instincts of the populace. Though himself a lover of episcopal or ambassadorial pomp, he denounces the Pope for "sitting among the crowd of his cardinals, in flashing gold and dazzling white, glorified by his tiara" (fol. 175 a). On the whole, the style is that of the bar, oratorical and inflated. In its moral aspect, *Si sedes illa* is, in parts at least, a monument of the most repulsive hypocrisy. Gardiner is here found at his lowest. He knew old bishop Fisher for what he really was, a devoted adherent of the Roman See, who considered the cardinal's hat sent to him by the Pope as a supreme honour of which he was unworthy, and heroically laid down his life in the defence of papal supremacy. Now the character which Gardiner gives to his old chancellor is that of an inconsistent poltroon, who viewed death with terror and would have bought life at any price. He makes Fisher address the Pope from his grave and complain to him of his elevation to the cardinalate in such words as the following: "You burdened me with that odious title of a cardinal, when prison and the charge laid against me had robbed me of all honour.... To express what I feel in a word, you attended to your own cause, not mine, since I would rather have lived a private person than died a cardinal" (fol. *171 b*–196 b and *172 a*–197 a of Latin MSS). Gardiner's bad faith here borders on the ludicrous, but it is bad faith all the same. It was no doubt the height of diplomatic skill to turn the Pope's stoutest champion and the victim of Henry VIII's lust for power into a supporter of absolute obedience to the prince; to make him confess that he had tainted the purity of his conscience by his "treason", and charge Paul III with inhuman cruelty. But the attempt is scarcely creditable to Gardiner's moral character, still less to his sense of humour.

The main theme handled in *Si sedes illa* is such as to evoke a ready response from Henry VIII's brother-prince, himself a most touchy person in regard to his independence from the ecclesiastical power. The duty of unconditional submission to the sovereign is clearly asserted. Fisher "resisted his prince and God's commandment (of obedience) against all law as well divine as human" (fol. *170 b*–196 a). Then comes a denial of any papal primacy founded on the law of God, and of any subordination of England to the Holy See. On the other hand, we find little that reminds us of Protestant habits of speech. In his conclusion Gardiner exhorts his readers to "embrace the sincere doctrine of Christ" and to become "not papistical, but evangelical" (fol. 183 b). But in other places the translator alone must be held responsible for the Protestant ring of such phrases as "the father Jesus Christ" (fol. 211 b of the English MS) or "the grace of God in spirite" (fol. 207 b). Gardiner was no doubt careful not to scare Francis I by any religious innovations, while trying to detach from him Rome, and induce him to declare himself the supreme head of the Church in France. Hence the essential element of *Si sedes illa* is not doctrinal novelty, but satire, ruthless and scathing, of Roman abuses and vices. The first few lines give the keynote to the whole. Rome has no regard for real holiness, but only for her own profit; she rejoices in the slaughter of men, women and children, whom she unhesitatingly sacrifices to her own interests; those who stand in her way are cast into dungeons and secretly murdered; cardinals' hats are sold for money, or lavished upon the Pope's nephews or even bastards. Such themes were not infrequently harped upon by French satirists in the late Middle Ages. Rabelais, who had been staying at Rome for some time, was soon to take them up again in the fourth book of his *Pantagruel*.[1] Gardiner's denunciation of Rome was sure to find a hearing in French court circles, although Francis I might, in talk with the papal legate, affect the most uncompromising devotion to the interests of the Holy See.[2]

*De vera obedientia* had quite another purpose. It was meant for a different public, which was to be addressed in a different tone. The clever way in which Gardiner adapted himself to his various audiences, is the best possible proof that his utterances are not to be taken at their face value. There can be no question of sincerity in his over-skilful imitation of Protestant phraseology. The whole of *De vera obedientia* is sprinkled with expressions which are meant to deceive; they grant much in appearance, and in fact grant nothing at all. The king, we are told in one place, "approaches God through faith, which is the only way of access" (fol. 12 a). The words are in one sense perfectly orthodox, yet they suggest justification by faith alone. In another place, Gardiner seems to borrow the words "obedientia vera, quæ est hominis proprie christiani", from the title of Tyndale's work, *The obedience of a Christian man*; the translator was not slow in taking the hint. Again, the return to Gospel truth which Gardiner repeatedly mentions may be understood merely of royal supremacy over the Church, or of Lutheran innovations in belief and worship. We find references to "the freedom, which is now brought to us by the Gospel"—Luther's "Christian liberty" (fol. 8 a); to "the light of the Gospel, which has now succeeded to darkness" (fol. 31 b); to "the voice of truth, which had been long buried" (fol. 36 a). What is more, concessions seem to be made to the Protestants on points on

---

[1] Cf. Chapters XLV to LIV (ed. Louis Moland-Henri Clouzot, pp. 139–166), especially Chapter L, in which the Pope is said to be ordered by his Decretals "à feu incontinent Empereurs, Rois, Ducz, Princes, Republicques, et à sang mettre,...les spolier de leurs biens, les deposseder de leurs Royaulmes, les proscrire, les anathematizer, etc.". Cf. also the end of Chapter LI.

[2] Cf. the letters of the Papal nuncio in Paris, Paolo da Carpi, bishop of Faenza, to Rome in 1535–6. For instance in his letter of July 3, 1535 (Vatican library, Nunziatura Gallica sub Paulo III, vol. ii°, fol. 240 sqq.), we hear that Francis I has promised to him to sacrifice his own life, if need be, for the conservation of the apostolic see ("per conservatione della quale dice Sua Maestà spenderià se sarà bisogno la vita propria").

which Gardiner was soon to prove their irreconcilable adversary. A few lines are devoted to the "adulteries, and worse crimes" perpetrated by the clergy under cover of their religious name and raiment (fol. 14 a). Turner, Bale and Bucer were to speak no worse. Again, Gardiner negligently flings into the discussion a few words from Scripture which Protestants had made their own, when he states that papal jurisdiction is "according to the traditions of men" (fol. 18 a). That in using such words, or exposing the "advowtry" of priests, Gardiner was merely playing a part, and one distasteful to himself, his controversial works were soon to prove, and first in date among them, as we shall see, the *Contemptum humanae legis* itself. We also know that after 1536 he was to take his stand against the indiscriminate diffusion of the Bible, and to assert in the most forcible terms that tradition was of equal value for the settlement of doctrine and discipline. Yet *De vera obedientia* seems to be permeated with Protestant biblicism. The king's supremacy is justified by numerous examples from the Old Testament. Scripture is repeatedly stated to be all-sufficient: "the Scriptures, we hear, dictated by the Holy Ghost himself, offer to us the most certain voice of God" (fol. 7 a–b); there is no exception from obedience to the prince, since "none such is mentioned in that law, which if you add anything to, or take anything from, you are a wicked man" (fol. 13 b); in the matter of the king's divorce, "the judgment of Scripture alone would have been enough" (fol. 8 b). All these concessions to Protestant tastes or tenets are even more obvious in the English version of the treatise, in which they are carefully stressed; yet Gardiner's lip-service was not a sufficient disguise, and at best he only appeared as a half-hearted adherent of the Reformation. This is made clear in various marginal notes of the English edition, such as that in which the translator gives vent to his indignation at finding Dunstan, an archbishop and a monk, referred to as a most holy man (sig. D vii b, "Rome" edition), or scouts the mere thought of a primacy of honour, which Gardiner says was in past times deservedly granted to the Pope (sig. G ij a).

*De vera obedientia oratio*, an oration indeed, and an advocate's work, to be heard recited aloud rather than perused in private;

with advocate's tricks almost too apparent in places: "Why should I recall", Gardiner cries out, "the solicitude of King Jehoshaphat?" and he recalls it (fol. 16 a); "We need not spend any time in searching Old Testament Scriptures", and yet he does (fol. 23 a). He is not, however, necessarily insincere whenever he lapses into false oratory. We shall attempt to discern which of his assertions were in agreement with his inmost beliefs or with his opinions of the moment, and not merely assumed for reasons of interest or fear. Taking things as a whole, to begin with, it is noteworthy that Gardiner himself, at various periods of his life, repeatedly declared that he had written *De vera obedientia* unwillingly, and that his contemporaries generally took the same view. Soon after the treatise was composed he went to France as an ambassador, and there was in touch with the papal nuncio, Paolo da Carpi, bishop of Faenza. The latter wrote to Rome on March 27, 1536: "I find that Winchester has an extreme desire to see his king again in the right way, and that he made that book by force, not having the strength to suffer patiently the death, which was clearly preparing for him".[1] An obscure Protestant courtier, William Palmer, writing a satirical poem on Gardiner in 1547, makes him address the Pope almost in the same words:

> I made a boke namyde true obedience
> where in I provyde the kynge / the supreme hed
> Of ynglonde / and Irelonde next under Christe
> but truly father yt was not in my harte
> For if the kynge the trouthe had ye-wiste
> I had lost my hedde for pleynge that parte.[2]

It is true that in 1551, when Gardiner was tried under the protectorate of Warwick for his adherence to the old religion, he presented articles in his defence, in which he submitted that

---

[1] Vatican Library, Nunziatura Gallica sub Paulo III, vol. ii⁰, fol. 202: "Trovo che Vincestra desidera extremamente vedere il suo Re ritornato a buon camino, et ch' il fece quel libro per forza non havendo forza di patir la morte patientemente, che chiaramente se gli apparecchia". ("Apparecchia" seems to be a mistake for "apparecchiava".)

[2] Trinity College, Cambridge, MS. No. 613, *The disclosinge of the practyse of Stephyn Gardyner...*, fol. 17 a, st. 4–5. On the authorship, date and character of this poem, cf. Pierre Janelle, *An unpublished poem on bishop Stephen Gardiner*, in the Bulletin of the (London) Institute of Historical Research, June and October, 1928, and February, 1929.

in 1535 he had published a book against the pope. But *De vera obedientia* was here used as a weapon in legal warfare, and such a use implies nothing as to Gardiner's own opinions. The witnesses who confirmed his statement on this point were precisely Catholics such as Sir Edward Carne (later an ambassador to Rome under Mary), Bishop Tunstal, Gardiner's chaplain William Medowe, and many other favourers of the old religion.[1] They were fighting, under persecution, with the weapons that were left to them.

In the reign of Queen Mary, when Gardiner, broken down with ill-health, was feeling the approach of death, and reviewing his past life, he made it quite clear that but for his royal master's pressing request, he would never have openly declared against Rome. He was most likely referring to *De vera obedientia* when he said, in his sermon of December 2, 1554, that in the time of Henry VIII, "we spoke and did those things, which only ministered to lust and greed".[2] The very text of the sermon is significant: "Hora est nos jam de somno surgere"—"it is time for us to rise from our sleep".[3] In discussion with "heretics", who taunted him with his anti-papal treatise, he declared that he had sinned through weakness, and exhorted them to follow him in his return to the Roman Church.[4] His unwillingness to declare against the Holy See is confirmed by the very tone and style of his two anti-papal tracts. In *Si sedes illa*, it is true, he does his very best to handle the Pope roughly. In one place, he more than hints that Paul III is inspired by the evil one: "He does not conceal whose spirit inspires him, and whom he acknowledges for his father (fol. 179 b)". Elsewhere, we find an elaborate comparison between the Pope and a courtesan— both earning money in a shameful fashion (fols. 181 b–182 a). But in *De vera obedientia* his newly-assumed hostility towards the Roman See appears to cause him a good deal of uneasiness. In two important passages of the tract he awkwardly excuses

---

[1] Cf. Foxe, *Acts and Monuments*, ed. Pratt, vol. vi, pp. 185, 188, 202, etc.
[2] *Concio reveren. d. Stephani*...Romæ apud Antonium Bladum, 1555, sig. A ij *b*: "Cum ea diceremus et faceremus, quæ libidine et avaritiæ tantum inservirent".
[3] *Ibid.* sig. A ij a.
[4] Cf. for instance, Foxe, *Acts and Monuments*, ed. Pratt, vol. vi, p. 625, first examination of Laurence Saunders.

himself for having so suddenly changed his views. The first few pages are devoted to a far too rhetorical exordium, in which he describes the effect produced upon him by the blinding light of truth, and almost compares his conversion to that of St Paul; he confesses that up to quite recently he held opinions altogether opposed to those he is now proclaiming. In the concluding pages of the book, he is at even greater pains to justify the breaking of his oath to the Pope. Throughout the whole work, he adopts a tone of heavyish banter, perhaps meant as an imitation of Erasmus' irony, which suggests anything but plain candour. On the whole, whereas in *Si sedes illa* he very freely reviles the Pope, in *De vera obedientia* he treats him with far greater moderation; he affects to wish him well, and suggests that he might even now enjoy a primacy of honour, were he but worthy of it. This difference between the two tracts again confirms our surmise as to his real sympathies. *Si sedes illa* was to remain unprinted and unsigned; under the cover of secrecy, a man who had not Fisher's character and fortitude might stoop to the work cut out for him, and allow himself a generous use of insult and calumny. However, Gardiner had not lost all self-respect, and when it came to making a profession of faith in a work that was to appear in print under his own name, he could scarcely nerve himself to swallow the bitter cup which the king had prepared for him. He felt he was going to be publicly branded as a turncoat by his late associates. Hence the obvious embarrassment which he tried to conceal by means of rhetorical artifices. The style of *De vera obedientia*, if compared with that of other works, in which he very directly and unhesitatingly utters his mind, will perhaps supply the best possible proof that he felt no inclination for the part he was requested to play.

Thus, taking things roughly, we may say that in penning *De vera obedientia* Gardiner was not sincere. Nor were his contemporaries the men to indulge in fine distinctions on the point. To them there were no degrees in the rejection of the Papacy. One must be for the Pope or against him. Gardiner had been known as a supporter of the old religion; he had now gone over to the opposite side; he was therefore untrue to himself. In such a simple way was the question settled, in the heat of party strife. Yet, as we said, there are shades in Gardiner's untruthfulness. There are some among his early opinions which he never publicly recanted. For instance, both in *Si sedes illa* and in *De vera obedientia* he very firmly asserts that papal supremacy is not founded on Holy Writ, that the words, "Tu es Petrus", etc. granted Peter no superiority of power over the other apostles, and that anyhow such superiority did not descend to Peter's successors. Now when he returned to the Roman Church under Mary, Gardiner repeatedly accounted for his motives in so doing, either in public sermons or at the trial of heresy cases. He said that he repented *De vera obedientia*. He confessed his sin in having broken from the unity of the Church, and his joy at the occasion now offered of reverting to it. "That sleep which oppressed us long and heavily, and that we must shake away with all our labour and zeal, that sleep was our separation from the unity of the Catholic faith, and of the Apostolic See".[1] The evils of disunion, the need of a supreme authority for the avoidance of dissensions and the declaration of dogma, now again induced the bishop of Winchester to submit to the Holy See. Protestant "variations" had gradually persuaded him that the authority of the Church must not be diffused throughout the whole body, but entrusted to one common head. Weighty reasons no doubt; and yet, reasons of convenience only, reasons purely human. One would expect something more in Gardiner's recantation: some acknowledgment at least of the Pope's claim to be the vicar of God, of the divine origin of the Papacy. But no such acknowledgment appears, and for all we know, we may think that to his dying day he went on looking at the Papacy, as, indeed, a necessary coping-stone to the fabric of the Church, but yet as a purely human institution. His disregard of Roman claims may perhaps be accounted for by his early training, which would no doubt have left in him some of the scepticism of Erasmus. His discussion of Peter's primacy in *De vera obedientia* bears a scholarly appearance; his reference to the spurious

---

[1] *Concio reveren. d. Stephani episcopi vintonien.*, Romæ, 1555 (sermon of December 2, 1554), sig. A ij a: "Somnus, qui graviter et diu nos omnes oppressit, nobis jam omni opera et studio excutiendus, somnum hunc appello nostram ab unitate Catholicæ fidei, et Sedis Apostolicæ discessionem".

donation of Constantine[1] shows that like other humanists, he was not to be taken in by the fabrications of papal lawyers.

To what extent Gardiner, despite the obvious contrasts in his career, may have remained consistent with himself, and accordingly truthful, will appear more clearly, if we attempt to determine what he really meant when rejecting papal supremacy. The latter may be understood in various senses: it may be the purely spiritual authority of the Pope to decide matters of doctrine and direct the religious life of the Catholic body; or it may mean papal jurisdiction over the clergy and even over the laity, in so far as these are Christians; a jurisdiction finally destructive of national sovereignty and independence, and bound to come into conflict with the civil power. In his two anti-Roman tracts, Gardiner neither upholds nor rejects the former kind of supremacy: he never once mentions it. On the other hand, he very distinctly states his objections to anything like a papal overlordship. We know the bishop of Winchester to have been a patriot;[2] no wonder that in *Si sedes illa* he should first of all defend his country's independence against Roman encroachments (fols. *165 b* : 194 a sqq.) and indignantly deny that England should be tributary to the Holy See. In *De vera obedientia*, he supplies us with a very clear definition of what he means by papal supremacy, "that pontifical power which they call ecclesiastical" (fol. 13 b), a power of government, taxation, patronage and jurisdiction, which ought properly to be the king's, but has been robbed from him by the Roman See. To achieve their object, the Popes have taken care to prevent princes from attending to the moral discipline of their peoples, despite the contrary injunction of the Bible (fol. 15 b). Should kings agree to papal pretensions, they would not only neglect all those of their subjects who wear a religious habit, but also refrain from taking heed of most of the crimes committed by

[1] *Si sedes illa*, fol. *166 b* : 194 b of MS.
[2] Cf. for instance *A declaration of svche true articles*, etc. (against George Joye), London, 1546, 8⁰ ed. sig. C vii b–C viii a: "We englyshe men to whome god hath giuen many victories vnder the banner of saynte George..."; *ibid.* CLXXIX a: "To be a good christen man, and an english man"; CLXXIX b: that we may live "lyke christen men, with christen men, and englyshe men, with english men".

laymen (fols. 15 b–16 a). Thereupon follows a whole succession of historical examples from the Old Testament and the early centuries of the Church, to show that many pious rulers have been supreme over the ecclesiastical body as a whole. In other words, we find here no properly religious objection to the exercise of the papal function.[1] Gardiner's attack on the Papacy has little in common with that of Tyndale and other Protestant controversialists, who consider the Roman See as the main source of doctrinal errors, such as justification by works, or idolatrous practices such as indulgences, pilgrimages, and the worship of saints. *De vera obedientia* stands, in that respect, in full contrast to Tyndale's *Obedience of a Christian man*. Its natural associations are rather to be sought among contemporary defenders of the authority of the State, whose opposition to ecclesiastical privileges implied no dislike of the old religion, its beliefs and organization. Such was Henry Standish, the provincial of the English Franciscans, who as early as 1515 had declared against clerical exemptions; such again was the lawyer Christopher St German, who engaged in controversy with Thomas More, and who first supporting the State against the Church, eventually came to support the king against the Pope. For indeed there was but one step from the one to the other. The Papacy was in itself the emblem and safeguard of ecclesiastical independence; and while taking his stand against the Roman See, Gardiner was denying those very liberties of the Church which he had so warmly defended only three years before.

Yet, one should guard against the false impression that must of necessity arise, if the word jurisdiction is here understood in too narrow a sense. The powers of which Gardiner, in *De vera obedientia*, recommends the transfer to the king, go far beyond the ordinary routine of Church tribunals. After rehearsing the names of Hebrew kings who appointed high priests, he comes at last to the most telling example, that of the Byzantine Emperor who attempted to rival the spiritual power of the Popes, and whose behaviour he apparently wishes Henry VIII

---

[1] Cf. in particular fol. 31 a: "I shall not contend thus much about the primacy...but this I deny, that the bishop of Rome should have been made first by God in regard to any absolute worldly power: that is the question at issue, on which the whole cause turns".

to emulate. Justinian, he says, "made laws on the holy trinity, on the Catholic faith, on bishops, clerks, heretics, etc." (fol. 19 a). This indeed goes very near to claiming for the king powers which the Pope himself did not enjoy in an undisputed fashion at the time. If the prince is free to decide what is faith and what is heresy, is he not the supreme authority for the declaration of dogma? And indeed Gardiner seems to have granted as much in practice—at least as long as Henry VIII lived. His letters to Cranmer, written in 1547, a few months after the king's death, are highly significant. When the Henrician formularies of faith were drafted, he says, the question of justification was referred to the king, who decided against the Protestant doctrine: such a decision was final; Cranmer ought to bow down to it and to persist no more in a wholly needless discussion.[1] This, however, should not be mistaken for a full acknowledgment of the king's spiritual power; it may be in part accounted for by Gardiner's personal devotion and loyalty to his royal master, in part by the fact that Henry VIII had decided in a Catholic sense. Under Edward VI, when the English Church was being made Protestant in the king's name, Gardiner evidenced far less respect for the authority of the sovereign. The prince, we may think, was entitled, in his view, to pronounce on matters of belief only in so far as he was in agreement with the orthodox faith. The power to declare dogma finally remained vested in the universal Church. What organ of the Church was to be its mouthpiece, Gardiner never declared, even when most hotly engaging in the defence of religious tradition. But he always believed in one Catholic truth, and plainly declared as much even while exalting the prince's spiritual power in his two anti-papal tracts. In *Si sedes illa*, Henry VIII is praised for having defended the Church from heresies—i.e. for having written his *Defensio septem sacramentorum* (fol. 182 b). In the same tract, Gardiner emphatically asserts that England and her sovereign wish "to be fostered, fed and contained in that universal Church, outside the which there is no remission of sins" (fols. *164 a* : 192 b).

---

[1] Cf. Gardiner's two letters to Cranmer, June and July 1547, *passim*, in B.M. Add. MS 29546 and Harleian 417, and Bibliothèque Nationale, Latin MS No. 6051.

The words are significant: it is not only the universal brotherhood of Christians—a bond that can be made very loose—which is proclaimed here, but also the supernatural character and function of an united Christendom. Nor indeed does Gardiner anywhere, in his defence of the king's supremacy, contemplate the creation of a national Church, independent in its creed and its forms of worship. He does indeed use the words "Ecclesia anglicana" in one passage of *De vera obedientia* (fol. 11 b) but states quite clearly that it is nothing but "the gathering of the men and women, of the clerks and lay-people dwelling in the kingdom of England, and united in the profession of Christ". It is the Church in England, not the Church of England; there is no reason for local developments in belief and practice; each province of Christendom must still remain at one with the others; the common pattern for all is found in the tradition of the Church universal. Where that tradition is preserved Gardiner does not, for the present, venture to state. He grants indeed that the ecclesiastical body has its own proper part, which is to teach; a part which is not assigned to the hierarchy only, but also to the Holy See, if we are to credit his elaborate comparison of the Pope to a tutor in a family (fol. 27 a) or to a chaplain, who is superior to his master in the exercise of his spiritual function (fol. 27 b). But who is to determine what is to be taught? Either Gardiner shirks the problem, or its urgency has not struck him yet; nor apparently was it to strike him for many a year to come. Catholic tradition seemed to him so clear and evident as to need no definition. Meanwhile if the Church, and even the Pope, are to teach the flock which princes rule—a different sword, according to the old simile, being placed in the hands of either—a door is still left open for some sort of recognition of the Papacy in the future; not of papal jurisdiction of course, but at least of a primacy of honour, the visible expression of Christian unity. If there be such a thought at the back of his mind, the author of *De vera obedientia* will still appear to us as a time-server and an unscrupulous diplomat; yet it will give rise to less wonder, that within a few years of his anti-papal campaign he should have been on friendly terms with continental Catholics, and joined with them in fostering the cause of reunion.

Gardiner's efforts to effect a reconciliation between England and the Roman See at the Diet of Ratisbon stand, as we noticed before, in seeming contrast with his *Contemptum humanæ legis*, which he wrote at the same time. This tract, which placed on record his arguments to Bucer, in their debate on the power of kings over the Church, is not such at first sight as to attract much notice; it is an occasional writing, composed on the spur of the moment; it is rough and unpolished, with lengthy repetitions; it entirely lacks those ornaments of style which give the two anti-papal tracts a false Ciceronian air. Yet what it loses in literary perfection, it gains in forcefulness, sincerity, and interest, and deserves more attention than it has hitherto received. It is clear that the bishop of Winchester is now speaking his own mind, or at any rate doing his very best to persuade himself that he is doing so, while giving expression to the full-blown theory of Cæsaro-papism, in its most perfect and probably most extreme form.[1] Whether he was really true to himself in depriving the Pope of those powers which he now claimed for the king, there is some reason to doubt; yet though the Roman and Henrician conceptions of Church and State are in appearance exclusive of, and antagonistic to, each other, there is, behind Gardiner's variations, a deeper unity of temperament and purpose, which is manifested in the *Contemptum humanæ legis* more clearly than anywhere else. For here we find side by side his ideal of the Church—a flock respectfully attentive to the voice of its shepherds—and of the State—a people respectfully submissive to the guidance of its rulers. In either case the underlying principle is the same. Whether the Church have to submit to the State, or the State to the Church, the change is merely in the head; the rest of the body keeps on working in the same way, and according to the same spirit—the spirit of obedience.

We know Gardiner's memorandum to have been a private

---

[1] Strange to say, the question of the origin or justification of the prince's power is not once raised. He must be obeyed because he is the prince, but it does not seem to have ever struck Gardiner that a king's right to call himself so might possibly be disputed, or that his authority might depend on his legitimacy. This is the more surprising as the sovereign for whom Gardiner claimed such a plenitude of power had only a very questionable title to the English crown.

writing, not even composed with any view to a diplomatic understanding, hence more likely to embody its author's genuine
views and feelings. But its very tone would leave little doubt
as to its sincerity, or attempt at sincerity. It is plain, direct,
occasionally disdainful and haughty; little irony here, no
innuendos, no possible mistake as to the writer's meaning. The
bishop of Winchester steps out as what he had in fact been all
along, the champion of the old religion against Protestant innovations. As in *De vera obedientia*, he touches on the most
important of those, but in how different a vein! The "spirit"
is ridiculed; the populace, Gardiner scoffingly says, "nowadays
expound Scripture in the cross-roads, being inspired by the
spirit" (p. 270 of the MS). Exception is taken, in two different
places, to the use made by Protestants of the text, "In vain you
worship me with the commandments of men". Why should
Bucer lay such a stress upon it, if not to teach subjects to contemn the laws of their prince? (pp. 268 and 270). "Libertas
evangelica" is mentioned sarcastically, as an excuse for spurning
the laws of Church discipline (p. 262); justification by faith only
is a "paradox" (pp. 263–4) and a blind for gluttony and
Epicureanism (p. 265). Lastly, the reformers are found fault
with, for doing precisely what Gardiner had done in *De vera
obedientia*, namely for "making sport" of those who have taken
religious vows, and "declaiming against their unchastity and
adulteries" (pp. 273–4).

In respect to Gardiner's political thought, *Contemptum
humanæ legis* is strikingly akin to *De vera obedientia*, with the
very important difference though, that not a word is here said
of the Papacy, and that the prince's supremacy over the Church
is taken for granted. Obedience, we hear, is one of the forms of
the virtue of charity. He who contemns the superior powers
cannot be said to love God. Should the sovereign be a harsh
or unjust ruler, his subjects need not be concerned about it
since he cannot hurt their souls. If the prince be mild, let God
be thanked; if he be severe, brutal, wicked, let him none the
less be considered as a divine blessing, since patient sufferance
will gain us eternal life. We must, therefore, as Gardiner had
said in *De vera obedientia*, submit even to "an iniquitous rule"
(fol. 23 b). Will there be no exemption from such obedience?

lxv

Must individual conscience surrender all its rights? Here lies indeed the gist of the question, and it seems as if, in *Contemptum humanæ legis*, Gardiner were a trifle less positive as to the duty of absolute submission in all cases. We must "comply with the prince's laws", he says, "only in so far as they do not stand against God's precepts" (p. 255). By means of such a reservation, no doubt, was the bishop of Winchester able to plead conscience against the anti-Catholic legislation of Edward VI. Now, since the sovereign is the head of his people in the full sense of the word, since his rule and care extend to the religious side of their life as well, and since obedience is due to him, why should objections be raised against his laws, when he legislates on matters of Church discipline, and prescribes fast and abstinence, or the celibacy of priests? Such is Gardiner's curiously roundabout method for supplying the king with a substitute for the spiritual authority which in the Pope was held to be of divine origin, and therefore indisputable. It was a far more arduous task to justify it when transferred to Henry VIII. We notice, however, an important difference from *De vera obedientia*, in which Gardiner repeatedly asserts that the prince must attend to the moral life of his people. The Popes, he says in his earlier work, have "thus circumscribed the charge of the sovereign, that he need not trouble whether the citizens be good or not, that goodness being meant which is agreeable to the profession of Christ", unless they have committed unspeakable crimes (fol. 15 a). One main reason for withdrawing the kingdom from the Pope's obedience is that the king must fulfil his part as the guardian of his people's virtue. Now on the contrary in *Contemptum humanæ legis*, Gardiner no less forcibly affirms that the prince is not entrusted with the moral guidance of his people, that it would be mere imprudence on his part to proceed against sin as such, and that the sword placed in his hand need only be wielded against disturbers of the social order or public peace. His proper part is to hold together human society, not to avenge God's offences. May we not think that in assuming this new attitude, Gardiner, who hated sanctimonious cant of any sort, betrayed his dislike of what was soon to be Calvinistic theocracy, with the Bible set up in place of a code, and "godliness" in place of law-abiding citizenship?

At any rate, we find in *Contemptum humanæ legis*, if not an actual political theory, supported by a regular array of arguments, at least a clear expression of Gardiner's political temperament, both in regard to the Church and the State. For all that he may have transferred his allegiance from one power to another, he remains a believer in obedience for its own sake, as the necessary corollary of the principle of authority. Therefore "disobedience is the greatest and most infamous crime, which carries with it many other faults, and opens a door to all profligacy" (p. 258). Resistance to oppression is unlawful; only in extreme cases, when the subject is directly commanded to infringe God's commandments, has he a right to disobey; but then he must patiently bear the torments inflicted upon him. Thus pushing to an extreme some of the principles of the New Testament, Gardiner can feel but little sympathy with what we nowadays call the democratic spirit. His final summary (on p. 271 of the manuscript) will appear as especially striking: the people must not even be told that they are "entrusted to the prince's fostering care and protection", lest they should be tempted to inquire how the prince performs the part which God has assigned to him. An all-powerful sovereign, accountable to God only; silent, patient submission the main virtue, and the basis of human society; could the State, in such circumstances, view the opposite qualities of independence, self-reliance, initiative, with anything but deep suspicion? Gardiner's Protestant adversaries already insisted on the fact that Godliness goes hand-in-hand with thrift and economic prosperity. The community was to profit, in their view, by the exertions of its individual members, each of them being stimulated in his laborious activity by the thought that he was doing God's work as one of God's elect. If the English would lead godly lives, says John Hooper in one of his sermons, "they shoulde not only fynde grace at Gods hande, but also more healthe and soberness of bodye, more ryches in the cofer, more plentye in the Realme...".[1] On the contrary, Gardiner comes wholly to ignore the beneficial effect of individual righteousness, or the

---

[1] John Hooper, *An ouersight, and deliberacion vpon the holy Prophete Jonas...*, London, September 6, 1550 (sermons preached in Lent 1550 before King Edward VI). Second edition (B.M. G. 11850), fol. clvii *b*.

detrimental effect of unrighteousness, upon the general economy of the State: "slothful, sluggish and idle fellows spoil themselves by their laziness; they infringe God's law, yet they do not touch the commonwealth, nor do they disturb it... " (p. 273). The contrast between Hooper's notion of citizenship and Gardiner's is significant. It meant much for the future fortunes of Catholicism in England, throughout the next two-and-a-half centuries, that the most ardent champion of traditional belief and worship, together with his followers, should have staked their all on a theory of absolute submission to the prince, which left the individual wholly disarmed if the answering protection of his sovereign failed him; while their adversaries, being taught to rely upon themselves alone, and placing their mission as God's soldiers and prophets above any loyalty to the sovereign, developed the fighting qualities which were to lead them to victory.

Thus, as we pass on from one to the other of Gardiner's three tracts, we come finally to something deeper than the mere outward statement of ideas. From a confusion at first somewhat disconcerting the moral personality of the man gradually emerges; its underlying continuity asserts itself despite outward variations. Gardiner's contemporaries never fully grasped how the man who had rejected the Papacy could fight so pertinaciously in favour of the old religion. And yet while rejecting papal jurisdiction, he betrayed no partiality for spiritual independence. The Church must still be subjected to some supreme authority, whether in the person of the Pope or the king. Gardiner had written to Bucer: "You have not removed from the world the authority of Rome, but transferred it to Wittenberg" (p. 273). How crushing Bucer's retort might have been, if the Strasbourg reformer had used like words in his turn, he does not seem to have for one moment realized.

PIERRE JANELLE

STRASBOURG,
18 *January*, 1929

## ADDITIONAL NOTE

It has been thought better not to enlarge in the course of this introduction upon the value of the two sixteenth-century translations printed below for the history of the English language. A word must here be said of the spelling, which in the English version of *De vera obedientia* is on the whole remarkably consistent, and offers some interesting peculiarities. The present participle of verbs is generally in *-eng*, after a *y*, as for instance *denyeng, obeyeng, payeng, sayeng*. The verb *to stand* is generally spelt with an *o*, as *stonde, stonding, notwithstonding*. The sound *an* is in most cases represented by *aun*, as in *servaunt, ordinaunce*; and as a rule we find endings in *-ie*, not *-y*, and in *-cion* instead of *-tion*. Among noticeable spellings the following may be mentioned: *infidele, acknowlage, lauful* (but also *unlawful*), *neclecting* and *necligent, to stere* (stir), *maister* or *mayster, scrine* (screen). In regard to the use and value of diphthongs notice the spelling *sweorde* (sword), *speake* (spake), *hearde* (hard). It should of course be remembered that many strange spellings may be accounted for by the numerous misprints. In respect of grammar, the frequent use of *all one* meaning *one only* is worthy of mention.

## NOTE FOR THE READER

The following texts, whether manuscript or already printed, have been reproduced with the greatest possible accuracy, down to the minutest particulars. The spelling, punctuation, and even obvious misprints or slips of the copyist's pen, have been respected; the necessary emendations or elucidations will be found in footnotes, especially respecting the punctuation, misprints and copyist's mistakes. At the same time, all abbreviations or ligatures have been expanded, the letters supplied for that purpose being printed in italics.

In regard to the MS texts first published here, the following rules have been adopted to make the author's or scribe's corrections quite clear to the reader. Words erased in the original are placed between square brackets; words interlined in the original are followed each with an asterisk, and printed as far as possible in the position they ought to occupy, i.e., in general after the erased words which they are meant to replace. An asterisk in the body of a word refers to one letter only.

The numbering of the pages or folios of the printed or MS original is shown in the margin, "a" after a number meaning recto, and "b" verso. In the case of the first part of *Si sedes illa*, a double numbering refers respectively to Gardiner's draft and to the fair copy, the folios of the former being shown in italics. The end of a page in the original is denoted by the sign ‖. In the case of *Si sedes illa*, the end of a page of the draft is denoted by the sign |.

The pages referred to in footnotes are not as a rule those of the present volume, but those of the original texts, in the printed editions or manuscripts here reproduced.

# GARDINER'S ADDRESS
## TO THE LEGATES
### (1529)

## Gardiner's address to the legates
## (1529)

Postq*uam* in hac matrimonij causa discutienda definien-
daque controversia nihil quicq*uam* hactenus a vero
christiani principis officio alienum priuata autoritate
tentatum a nobis fuerit aut designatum. sed magnam ante
om*n*ia equitatis justicie, veritatis q*ue* rationem semper
habuerimus, tum multa religione Eccl*es*ie iudicio deferen-
dum vbiq*ue* censuerimus, freti sane innocentie huius
nostre conscientia, sperauimus fore Judices vt honoris,
conatum[1], consiliorum nostrorum optimos quosq*ue* adiu-
tores haberemus, potius quam vt huius tam pij animi
obtrectator, aut virtutis hostis, aut laudis invidus quisq*uam*
existeret. Q*uod* si esset futurum (neq*ue* enim sumus
ignari q*uam* multa prudentissimos quoq*ue*, eciam in reb*us*
suis, et republ*ica* fefellerunt), nunq*uam* tamen existimam*us*[2]
iudices Ep*iscopu*m Roffensem eam aduersum nos apud
tribunal v*estru*m accusationem suscepturum, que malor*um*
Ciuium, et sediciose concitate multitudinis odio, pocius et
furori, q*uam* ipsius virtuti et dignitati ‖ conueniret. Ex-
plicauimus hauddubie Judices huic Roffensi iam ante
aliquot menses non semel q*uam* non essent ille studio
quesite aut temere conficte rationes, que illegitimi et
incesti matrimonij conscientiam iam ante diu in nobis
peperissent.[3] Eas ipse Roffensis hactenus tunc approbauit
et tam graues tamque efficaces censuit vt citra S*erenissi*mi
domin*i* n*ostri* oraculum (quod sup*er* illis tum necessario
consulendum fore duxerat) pristinam illam animi tran-
quillitatem nobis restitutum iri non crederet Jam quum
idem sanctissim*us* dominus noster (non sine consilio tamen
et iudicio reu*er*endissimor*um* aliquot ap*osto*lici sedis
cardinalium aliorumq*ue* romane curie et dignitate et
eruditione prestantissimorum viror*um*) easdem rationes
matrimonij n*ostri* caus*am* adeo perplexam et ambiguam

---

[1] *Sic* for *conatuum*. [2] *Sic* for *existimavimus*. [3] This no doubt
refers to Wolsey's interview with Fisher shortly after July 3, 1527.
The Cardinal had been sent by Henry VIII to sound Fisher's disposition as to the divorce matter, and contrived to persuade the old

Since in this matrimonial cause now to be investigated, or in the controversy now to be determined, we have attempted or designed nothing, on our own authority, which were unsuited to the office of a true Christian prince; but on the contrary have always had regard before everything to equity, justice and truth, and have everywhere held that the judgment of the church was to be deferred to with great respect; relying upon our consciousness of this our innocence, we hoped, o Judges, that we should have all the best men as supporters of our honour, our efforts and our purposes, and hardly thought that there might come forth any one, to disparage such a dutiful mind of ours, show enmity to our virtue, and jealousy of our fame. If this was to be (and we are not ignorant how many things have deceived the very wisest,[a] even in regard to their own concerns, and to public affairs), yet we never supposed, o Judges, that the bishop of Rochester would take up before your tribunal that accusation against ourselves, which would rather befit the hatred, or better still the fury, of bad citizens, and a multitude seditiously roused, than his own virtue and dignity. Of a certainty, o Judges, we did unfold to this Rochester, and this already some months ago, and more than once, how far we had been from purposely seeking out or rashly devising those reasons, which long before had engendered in us scruples of conscience, in regard to this illegitimate and incestuous marriage. Which reasons this very Rochester thus far then approved, and deemed so weighty and powerful, that unless we applied to the oracle of our most serene Lord [the Pope] (which he then thought it necessary to consult upon those matters) he did not believe that our former peace of mind could be restored to us. Now when this same our most holy Lord (yet not without the advice and opinion of some of the most reverend cardinals of the apostolic see, and of other members of the Roman court, most eminent for their worthiness and erudition) has judged that these same reasons made the cause of our marriage so intricate and ambiguous, that only through

bishop for a time that the king's intentions were altogether honourable. Cf. Brewer, *Reign of Henry VIII*, vol. ii, pp. 194 sqq.   [a] How many causes of error even the wisest may meet on their way.

reddidisse iudicauerit, vt non nisi lectissimorum, et
sapientissimorum iudicum censura, satis pro dignitate
magnitudineque sua tractari, explicarique potuerit, quum-
que vobis Judices, vestreque religioni definiendam ||
167 a vniuersam meritissimo delegauerit, teque Reuerendissime
Campegi magnis quidem sanctitatis sue sumptibus tuis
vero immensis et periculis et laboribus per tot rerum
viarumque discrimina[1] non alio nomine huc destinauerit,
quid huic Roffensi in mentem venisse, aut quo tandem
spiritu adductum credemus Judices, vt huc tam im-
pudenter, tamque intempestiue prodiret[2] animi sui
sententiam nunc demum post tot menses ac non nisi in
tanto tamque celebri iudiciorum vestrorum consessu vobis
palam declaraturus[3] fuerat quid[4] constancie, quem olim
conscientie scrupulum merito concepisse nos putauerat:
nunc tandem publice topicis duntaxat (vt vocat) locis, et
argutijs in speciem tamen probabilibus, aliisque bractheatis
Rhetorum suasionibus minime tribuere. fuerat christiane
pietatis (si quidem multorum iam animorum[5] studio
consecutus fuisset vt quid in hac grauissima causa iustum,
quid verum, quid licitum foret, exploratissimum nunc
167 b haberet) nos eius iterum atque iterum || priuatim ad-
monuisse ac non illud publice tantaque cum confidentia in
magnam nostram conscientie suggillacionem invulgare.
fuerat officij, fidei et pietatis (que principi suo debet
quiuis bonus ciuis) nostram innocentiam a malorum
calumnijs tueri, vindicare, et quam[6] vehementer laborare
fluctuareque conscientiam nostram neutiquam obscuris
indicijs cerneret, modis omnibus eidem succurrere, fuerat
religionis et obseruantie, quam summo pontifici debet, vt
quum ille causam vehementer perplexam esse et ad
tuendam Regni huius nostri salutem imprimis necessariam

---

[1] Campeggio was suffering acutely from the gout, on account of
which he had to be carried in a litter from Paris to Calais. The delays
in his journey from Rome to England, though possibly due to the
Pope's wish to draw matters into length, seem to suggest practical
difficulties too. (*Ibid.* pp. 290–4.)    [2] The sentence is broken here
and a comma ought to be supplied.    [3] A new sentence begins here.
[4] *Sic* for *quidem*, which is no doubt the correct reading, though the

the ruling of the best chosen and most discreet judges could it be treated and set forth according to its dignity and magnitude; and when he has, most in accordance with your deserts, entrusted it to you, o Judges, and to your scrupulousness, to be wholly determined; and has sent thee here, o most reverend Campegius, for no other reason, to the great charges indeed of his Holiness, and to thy huge peril and travail through the dangers of so many things and ways; what shall we believe, o Judges, to have come into the mind of this Rochester, or by what spirit shall we think he has been led, to come forward here so impudently and so much out of season, in order to declare his own personal view of the matter, now at length after so many months, and even here before such a great and illustrious assembly as that of your court. It had been of constancy on his part, not to ascribe now at last in public those scruples of conscience, which he had once thought we were right in harbouring, to mere commonplaces (as he calls them), to subtleties only probable in appearance, and other gilded persuasions of rhetoricians. It had been of Christian piety (if indeed by the study of many opinions[a] he had succeeded in ascertaining thoroughly what in this cause was just, what true, what lawful), to have reminded us of it again and again in private, and not to proclaim it in public with such huge self-confidence, to the great blemishing of our conscience; it had been of his duty, of his faith and of his loyalty (which every good citizen owes to his king) to protect and vindicate our innocence from the calumnies of evil men; and since he saw, by tokens in no wise obscure, our conscience labour and fluctuate, to hasten to its help by all possible means; it had been of the pious reverence and observance, which he owes to the supreme Pontiff, when the latter had decreed that this cause was exceedingly intricate, and especially necessary to the preservation of this our realm,

---

"tittle" over *quid* is missing.    [5] *Sic* if the reading be right; *annorum* would be much more satisfactory; a slip of the writer's pen seems not unlikely with such letters as *n, m* and *i* in rapid succession. [6] *Quam* is here a relative pronoun referring to *conscientiam*, and conjugated with *eidem*. "That conscience of ours which he saw...to succour the same...."    [a] Or, more probably, "many years' study".

decerneret,[1] vt vobis potissimum iudicantibus, vniuersa estimaretur, eius sentencie acquiescere, pocius quam eius sanctitatem leuitatis publice arguere, quasi eam causam cognoscendam commisisset cuius sic esset omnibus obuia, facilis, dilucida et aperta veritas, vt stultum foret eam in questionem vocare. fuerat denique prudencie et modestie quum in hac vobis delegata causa iuxta iurisdictionis vestre amplissimam auctoritatem processissetis, liberum 168 a vobis iudiciorum ordinem[2] || permittere, non autem nouam quasi iudicandi formulam vobis prescribere vestrisque sententijs priuata sua autoritate preiudicium afferre.

Sed frustra in hoc Episcopo ista requirimus Judices cuius pectus animumque sic occupant, exagitant duo consultores pessimi Nempe immodica quedam arrogancia, nimisque confidens temeritas Nam vnde alioqui profecta ea vox Judices se solidis, et irrevincibilibus argumentis nudam in hac causa veritatem citra fucum, et pigmenta verborum ob oculos vestros, cunctorumque hominum statim positurum, et eam quidem se usque defensurum, et defensurum quidem usque ad ignes causamque nunc illi iustiorem adesse, vt dissolutioni huius matrimonii obsisteret quam fuerat illa olim diui Joannis baptiste contra Herodem O vocem omnis modestie ac grauitatis expertem. Quasi vero vnus omnium Roffensis sapiat et solus huius cause veritatem investigarit et illuminarit.[3] Et quid hic necesse fuit vt ignes, flammasque hoc nomine subiret, se paratum ostendere, quum de nostra clementia et veritatis tuende, non 168 b opprimende studio tam || manifestis argumentis illi consisterit[4]? Denique quam iniqua est illa collatio qua suam cum diue[5] baptiste causa componere nititur? nisi eam fortasse de nobis opinionem conciperet vt aut aliquem iam

[1] Whether these words are a quotation from some papal document we are not able to ascertain, but similar expressions are found in the conditional dispensation for the king to marry again, granted by Clement VII, December 23, 1527 (N. Pocock, *Records of the Reformation*, vol. 1, pp. 22–7), and in the commission to Wolsey and Campeggio to try the cause of the divorce (*ibid*. pp. 167–9), where the matter is said to be "magni gravisque momenti", and where a wish is expressed "in regno illo sedi Apostolicæ semper devotissimo, omnium dissentionum materiam extingui".    [2] *Ordo judiciorum* is the normal procedure, the normal development of the action, which is settled

so that he would weigh everything by yourselves judging supremely,—to acquiesce in his decision; rather than publicly to charge his Holiness with levity, as if the truth of the cause he had committed to you for investigation, was so obvious, easy, plain and open, that it would be foolish to call it into question. Lastly it had been of wisdom and modesty, when you had commenced in this cause assigned to you according to the most ample authority of your jurisdiction, to allow to you a free order of trial, and not to prescribe to you so to say a new *formula* for judging, and to bring forward of his own authority a pre-judgment before your sentence.

But it is in vain that we require those things in this bishop, o Judges, whose breast and heart are so filled and stirred up by two most evil advisers, namely a certain immoderate arrogance, and a too self-confident temerity. For else whence did these words proceed, o Judges, that he would by sound and un-answerable arguments, at once place before your eyes, and those of all men, the naked truth in this cause, without deceit and colouring of words; and that indeed he would defend it constantly, and defend it indeed as far as the stake; and that he had now a juster cause, in withstanding the dissolution of this marriage, than Saint John the Baptist had once had against Herod. O voice devoid of all modesty and gravity! As if indeed, alone of all men, Rochester was gifted with discernment, and alone had investigated and illuminated the truth of this cause. And what need was there for him to declare himself ready to endure fire and flame for that reason, when such manifest tokens gave him evident proof of our clemency, and our zeal to protect, and not to oppress, truth? And lastly how unjust is that comparison, by which he labours to couple together his cause and that of the holy Baptist! Unless perhaps he has conceived that opinion of ourselves, that apparently we were

beforehand, in Roman civil law, by the *formula* delivered by the magistrate to the judges. Here Fisher is found fault with for having so to say taken upon himself the part of the magistrate, and, by means of a novel kind of *formula*, prescribed the *ordo judiciorum* to the two legates. (Cf. W. W. Buckland, *A text book of Roman law from Augustus to Justinian*, Cambridge, 1921.)   [3] Such is our reading for a scarcely legible word, which looks like *colluuarit*; as the latter would give no sense, we have read the curious *c* as an &, and supposed that a "tittle" was missing above the second syllable, which is probably abbreviated.   [4] *Sic* for *consisteret*.   [5] *Sic* for *divi*, the mistake being no doubt due to attraction.

herodem agere aut aliquod facinus herodiano facinori proximum audere videremur Nobis plane Judices haud unq*uam* herodis arrisit,[1] impietas et certe in eo damnandum ex Euangelij regula Baptisteq*ue* voce didicim*us* q*uod* fr*atr*is sui sororem uxorem accepisset. Vtrumq*ue* vero de nobis sentiat Roffen*sis* ab huius sane crudelitate longissime semp*er* abfuimus si quid vnq*uam* seuere in eos statuerimus qui huic diuortio parum fauere sunt visi ac non pocius pro illorum virtutum ratione summis fauorib*us* sumus complexi.[2] Eat Roffen*sis* et nobis herodis tyra*n*nidem merito exprobret. Sed sit sane huius in nos principem suum maledicentie p*r*opria coerc*i*tio.[3] Illud vero Judices ne vobis fortasse tenebras posset effundere et iudicium ve*st*ru*m* remorari q*uod* veritatem ip*s*am se nunc tandem 169 a reperisse ‖ et e tenebris eruisse magno cum fastu contendat est nos gloriosam hanc, eius et plusq*uam* thrasonicam magniloquentiam[4] examinemus....

---

[1] Comma here in MS, but the sentence is obviously not broken in this place, *impietas* being the subject of *arrisit*. [2] This of course would scarcely apply to Fisher himself, who had received no favours from the king lately; but Gardiner may have had in his mind the case of Sir Thomas More, who as early as September, 1527, on the king's own request, had delivered to him privately his opinion on the divorce matter. That opinion was contrary to the king's wishes, yet

somehow playing the Herod, or daring some crime akin to the crime of Herod. To be sure, o Judges, never did Herod's impiety bear a pleasing aspect for us; and certainly we did learn from the rule of the gospel and the voice of the Baptist that this in him was to be condemned, that he had taken to his wife the sister of his brother. But whichever of the two things Rochester may think in regard to us, we were always far removed from Herod's cruelty. If ever we proceeded with any severity against those who appeared to look upon this divorce with little favour, and did not rather lovingly draw them to ourselves with the highest favours, in proportion to their virtues, let Rochester come, and justly cast Herod's tyranny in our teeth. But let this man's evil-speaking against us his prince be his own punishment. Yet, o Judges, lest you might be steeped in darkness, and lest your judgment might be hindered, by his assertion, uttered with great haughtiness, that he has now at last found the very truth, and plucked it out of darkness, it behoves us to examine this bragging, and more than thrasonical pomposity of words....

he continued to hold his chancellorship for several years, being left "free and used in other business", and retaining the royal favour (Bridgett, *Blessed Thomas More*, pp. 226–7).    [3] Our reading for a scarcely legible word, probably contracted, which looks like *coartio*. [4] From a character in Terence's *Eunuch*, Thraso, the bragging, bombastic soldier.

# THE POPE'S BRIEF
## TO FRANCIS I
### (July 26, 1535)

# The pope's brief to Francis I

## (July 26, 1535)

In fronte: Charissimo in Christo filio nostro Francisco, Francorum Regi Christianissimo.

P. PP. iii

Charissime in Christo fili noster Salute*m et* Apost*olicam* benedictionem. Cum expectaremus in dies audire liberationem bonæ memoriæ Ioannis Cardinalis Roffensis, quod illam et Majestati tuæ instantissime commendaueramus, *et* a tua excellenti probitate ac cum Henrico Angliæ rege auctoritate nobis promiseramus: ecce subito atroci nuntio perculsi sumus, dictum Cardinalem vltimo supplicio ab ipso Henrico a quo diu in vinculis habitus erat, fuisse affectum. Nec dubitam*us* quin tua Majestas pro sua maiorumq*ue* suorum inclita pietate, atq*ue* ea opera quam pro liberatione dicti Cardinalis alacrem, vt confidimus licet irritam præstitit, tantam sceleris atrocitatem dolenter *et* grauissime tulerit; cum intercessio tua, non solum liberationem non obtinuerit, sed etiam mortem dicti Cardinalis maturasse videatur. Nos vero fili *et* hæc Sancta sedes quid primum in tanto vniuersalis ecclesiæ vulnere deplorabimus? Innocentiamne *et* Sanctitatem illius viri, an celebrem *et* toto orbe diffusam pro fide Catholica doctrinam? an Episcopalem *et* Cardineam simul dignitatem eodem gladii ictu violatam? an genus *et* causam mortis? genus quidem ipsum crudele *et* noxijs ac sceleratis debitum Sanctissimo viro inflictum? omnia hæc quidem nobis maxime deflenda, sed causa mortis grauius deploranda est, Si quidem pro Deo, pro Catholica religione, pro Iustitia, pro veritate, vir sanctissimus occubuit, Cum non solum vnius tantum *et* particularis iura, vt olim B. Thomas Archiepiscopus Cantuariensis sed vniuersalis ecclesiæ veritatem tueretur. Itaq*ue* Henricus in hoc impietatis genere suos maiores non solum re-‖tulit, verum etiam ex causæ grauitate, *et* personæ dignitate superauit,

At the head: To our most dear son in Christ Francis,
the most Christian King of the Franks.

## Paul III. Pope

Most dear son in Christ, greeting and apostolical blessing.
Whereas we were daily waiting to hear of the liberation of John
cardinal of Rochester, of blissful memory, since we had most in-
stantly recommended his cause to your Majesty, and expected no
less a result from your surpassing uprightness and your influence
with Henry king of England; lo suddenly we were smitten with
the terrible news, that the said Cardinal had been condemned
and submitted to the last punishment by that selfsame Henry
by whom he had long been kept in chains. Nor do we doubt
but that your Majesty, considering your illustrious piety and
that of your ancestors, and the pains you took for the liberation
of the said cardinal, eagerly as we trust, though to no purpose,
bore such an atrocious crime with sorrow and great heaviness;
since your intercession, not only did not obtain the liberation
of the said Cardinal, but even seems to have hastened his death.
But as for us, o my son, and for this Holy See, what shall we
first mourn in such a wound of the universal church? The
innocence and holiness of that man, or his learning, both
famous and spread out throughout the whole world, for the
defence of the Catholic faith? The dignity, both of a Bishop
and Cardinal, violated with the same stroke of the sword? The
kind and cause of his death? The kind of death, indeed, in
itself cruel, and suited to culprits and criminals, which was
meted out to the most holy man? All those for certain we must
bewail, but the cause of his death is most to be lamented, since
this most holy man laid down his life for God, for the Catholic
religion, for justice, for truth, while he was defending not
merely the particular rights of one only man, as Thomas of
Canterbury formerly did, but the truth of the universal church.[a]
Therefore Henry not only took after his ancestors in this kind
of impiety, but even outdid them in respect of the weight of
the cause, and the dignity of the person, and to so many and

[a] The truth of which the universal church has the keeping.

atque ad tot et tanta suæ animæ vulnera, hoc postremum et atrocissimum adiecit. Quandoquidem non contentus censurarum a Clemente 7. prædecessore nostro in eum inflictarum contemptu, biennalique in illis insordescentia, non item adulterio notorio, et scandalum in tota ecclesia publice generante, non tot clericorum et religiosorum sacrilega cæde, non hæresi ac schismate, auulsioneque sui regni ab vniuersali ecclesia, non substractione eiusdem regni ab obedientia Romanæ ecclesiæ cui illud tributarium est, nouissime hunc sanctissimum præsulem a nobis ob doctrinam et sanctitatem in Cardinalium numerum relatum, pertentato prius illius animo, an se retexere, et veritati contradicere vellet, demum constantem et in ipso proposito usque ad vltimum persistentem, per carnificis ministerium,[1] et turpe genus mortis publice necari iussit, nece etiam citius accelerata et libentius inflicta, quod eum a nobis Cardinalem factum audiuerat, crimen læsæ Maiestatis præter multa alia crimina multipliciter committendo, pœnasque in tales a iure inflictas, præsertim priuationis ipso facto incurrendo. Nec uero dubitauit, quædam alia adjicere, his quæ commemorauimus non leuiora. Non enim ignoramus quæ ille nuper in proximo Calesii conuentu cum tuis tentauerit,[2] illa quidem ad vniuersalem tendentia pernitiem, ac prorsus indigna, quæ a te optimo ac pientissimo Rege peterentur, cuius inclytam pietatem Henricus teterrimis consiliis fœdare tunc

---

[1] This was misread by Gardiner "per carnificis *ministrum*". Cf. notes on *Si sedes illa* (fol. 174 a of the MS).    [2] An allusion to the assembly or "diet" held at Calais about Whitsuntide, 1535, between English and French commissioners or deputies. (Norfolk, Fitzwilliam and Foxe on the English side, Brion, Genouillac, Poyet and Bochetel on the French side.) The meeting was to begin on May 14 (*Letters and Papers*, vol. IX, nᵒ 606), was in progress on June 5 (*ibid.* nᵒ 826) and had come to its close by June 17 (*ibid.* nᵒ 909). Its main object—in which it failed—was the conclusion of a matrimonial alliance between the royal families of England and France, Francis I's son, the duke of Angoulême, becoming engaged to the princess Elizabeth. But there can be no doubt that Henry VIII's purpose was also to detach Francis I from Rome, and induce him to make himself the supreme head of the Church in France. The king's instructions to the duke of Norfolk and his colleagues (*Letters and Papers*, vol. IX, nᵒ 793) contain, it is true, no reference to church matters, except in connection with the general council, which Francis I must oppose with

grievous wounds of his soul, added this last and most atrocious one; since not content with contemning the censures inflicted upon him by Clement VII our predecessor, and living a foul life under them for the space of two years, not content with adultery, both notorious and engendering a public scandal in the whole church, nor with the sacrilegious slaughter of many clerks and religious men, nor with heresy and schism, and the tearing of his realm from the universal church, not with the withdrawing of that same realm from the obedience of the Roman church to which it is tributary; having latterly examined that most holy prelate, whom we for his learning and holiness had placed in the number of Cardinals, whether he would contradict himself, and gainsay the truth; and finding that he remained constant, and persisted to the last in his resolve, he ordered him to be publicly, and by the hands of the hangman, put to a shameful death; which death was also more quickly hastened, and more willingly inflicted, because he had heard that we had made him a Cardinal; thus committing in many ways, and beside many other crimes, that of *lèse-majesté*, and incurring from that very fact the pains inflicted upon such offenders by law, notably that of deprivation. Nor did he hesitate either to add some other misdeeds, no less grievous than those which we have rehearsed. For we are not ignorant of those things which he lately assayed with your envoys in the last meeting at Calais, things such indeed as to tend to universal ruin, and wholly unworthy, which were required of you, o excellent and most pious king, whose renowned piety Henry

---

all his power, if he wishes Henry VIII to agree to the proposed matrimonial scheme. But in a previous letter to Philippe Chabot, seigneur de Brion, the English king had very clearly suggested that Francis I should reject the authority of Rome, and enlarged on the reasons which should make it hateful to France in particular, in a style which strongly recalls that of Gardiner in *Si sedes illa* (*ibid.* vol. IX, n° 341). (Cf. *Si sedes illa*, fol. 178 a, and note on the same.) Paul III may have first obtained intelligence of the proceedings at Calais by a letter of his nuncio in France, Paolo da Carpi, bishop of Faenza, who wrote to him on July 3, 1535, an account of his last interview with Francis I. The latter, he said, told him that Henry VIII "non si essere vergognato di farli queste petitioni, che accettasse per nulla la sentenza data contra di lui, che con tutte le forze s'impedisse il Concilio, et che havessero mala et nulla ogni sentenza, che di nuovo li fosse data contra da la Sede Apostolica...". In his answer to the king, Carpi congratulated him that "Dio habbia tenuto la mano sul capo, che non habbi permesso che hora à Calais si sia venuto ad altro restretto con quelli" (Vatican Library, Nunziatura Gallica sub Paulo iii, vol. ii°, fol. 240 sqq.).

non erubuit. Quibus tamen a te merito repulsis, sicut egregiam tuam pietatem, ita pessimam illius volu*n*tatem deprehendimus. Itaq*ue* cum sicut Maiestati tuæ notissimum est, hoc toto triennio *et* vltra hæc S*ancta* Sedes tuæ quidem imprimis respectu Majestatis, tum deinde spe resipiscentiæ ipsius Henrici, tot *et* tanta ab eo patientissime tolerauerit, nihilq*ue* se profecisse videat, aut profecturam amplius speret cum veteres perferendo, nouas semper iniurias inuitauerit, iamque dei pene voce, omnisq*ue* iuris,

28 b  om-‖niumq*ue* hominum clamore ad vindictam excitetu[r][1] Nos maximo quidem cum dolore animi nostri, sed tamen extrema necessitate co*m*pulsi ad ea remedia cum venerabilibus fratribus nostris S*anctæ* Rom*anæ* Ecclesiæ Cardinalibus idipsum nobis vnanimiter suadentibus, venire decreuimus, quæ ius commune tam diuinum quam humanum[2] nobis iniungit, vt scilicet eundem Henricum, qui prius per rebellionem, per heresim *et* schisma, aliaq*ue* enormissima crimina, nouissime aute*m* per indignam cædem S*anctæ* Rom*anæ* Ecclesiæ Cardinalis *et* tot aliorum Clericorum ac Religiosorum Regno se ac regia dignitate priuauit, priuatum declaremus. Quamobrem pro certo habentes hæc tuæ Majestati vt Christianissimo Principi *et* Henrici dissimilimo vehementer displicuisse ac displicere, nec dubitantes quin maiorem Dei *et* Ecclesiæ tuiq*ue* officij rationem, quam ipsius Henrici non iam Regis, sed Regium nomen prorsus dedecorantis, tuaq*ue* coniunctione indigni habiturus sis, ad te suum Charissimum in Christo filium S*ancta* Rom*ana* Ecclesia confugit, solita semper ad tuos prædecessores in oppressionibus suis confugere, tuamque pietatem, beneuolentiam, amorem, studiose implorat, ac rogat, vt ha*n*c nostri officii necessitatem non solum æquanimiter ferrè[3] velis, verum memor quid tui maiores pro S*ancta* Rom*ana* Ecclesia olim egerunt, quantisq*ue* exercitibus iniurias eius vlti sunt iustitiam cum tempus erit, cumq*ue* a nobis requireris

---

[1] This letter dropped in Camusat.    [2] On the difference between *jus divinum* and *jus humanum* cf. the first part of the *Decretum Gratiani* (Migne, *Patrologia latina*, vol. 187) which is entitled: "De jure divinæ et humanæ constitutionis". The first distinction explains "in quo differant inter se lex divina et humana, cum omne quod fas est,

did not blush then to sully with his most sinister advice. Which being however deservedly rejected of you, we discerned as well your eminent piety, as his most evil-minded disposition. Wherefore since it is perfectly known to your Majesty, that for the whole of these three years and more this Holy See, first of all out of regard for your Majesty, then again hoping for the repentance of that same Henry, bore most patiently from him so many and such heavy offences; and that she sees she has gained nothing, and has no hope of gaining any more, since by putting up with old injuries, she still invites new ones; and that already she is, almost by the voice of God, and the clamour of all justice and of all men, incited to vengeance; we have decreed with a very great grief indeed of our soul, yet compelled by extreme necessity, upon the unanimous advice of our venerable brother Cardinals of the Holy Roman Church, to come to those remedies which common justice, be it founded upon the authority of God or man, enjoins to us; to wit that the same Henry, who previously through rebellion, through heresy and schism, and other most enormous crimes, and now latterly through the shameful slaughter of a Cardinal of the Holy Roman Church, and of so many other clerics and religious men, has deprived himself of his realm and royal dignity, should be declared of us to be thus deprived. Wherefore holding it for certain that those things vehemently displeased and displease your Majesty, as a most Christian king and one most unlike Henry; nor doubting that you will take more account of God, the Church and your office, than of that same Henry, who is no more a king, but utterly dishonours the royal name, and is unworthy to associate with you; the Holy Roman Church flees to you her most dear son in Christ, being accustomed to take refuge with your predecessors whenever oppressed; and warmly entreats and requests your piety, good will and love, that you may not only be willing to bear with an equal mind this necessity of our office; but remembering what your ancestors formerly did for the Holy Roman Church, and with what strength of arms they avenged her injuries, you will when the time comes, and when you are requested of us, enforce

nomine divinæ vel naturalis legis accipiatur, nomine vero legis humanæ mores jure conscripti et traditi intelligantur ". *Jus divinum* is really the moral law, founded on the nature of man and universal, *jus humanum* is founded on custom and is variable according to time and place.   [3] *Sic* for *ferre.*

contra dictum Henricum exequaris, sicut in tua bonitate speramus. Sed cum hæc scribi fecerimus venerabili fratri episcopo Fauentino Nuntio apud te nostro,[1] vt ea tuæ Maiestati particularius referret *et* explicaret, ad eius sermonem nos referentes, S*anctæ* Sedis Apost*olicæ* dignitatem *et* diuini honoris conseruationem, quæ maxime in hoc facto vertitur, tuæ Maiestati enixe com*m*endamus. Datum Romæ apud S. Marcum sub annulo piscatoris die 26 Iulii 1535. Pontificatus nostri anno primo. Signatum, Blosius

[1] The papal nuncio at the court of Francis I, Pio da Carpi, bishop of Faenza.

justice against the said Henry, as we hope in your goodness. But since we have had these things written to our venerable brother the bishop of Faenza our nuntio with you, so that he might relate and explain to your Majesty those things more particularly, referring ourselves to what he will say, we commend to your Majesty with all our might the dignity of the Holy Apostolic See, and the preservation of the honour of God, which is mainly concerned in these happenings. Given at Rome at Saint Mark's, under the Fisher's ring, the 26th day of July, 1535, the first year of our pontificate. Signed, Blosius.

# GARDINER'S TRACT
## ON
## FISHER'S EXECUTION

# Gardiner's tract on Fisher's execution

185 a *154 a*  Si sedes illa Romana que verbis iamdiu et app*ellatio*nibus sanctitatis cognomen sibi vsurpauit / rebus ip*s*is et factis vllam hactenus (quoad ultimo memoria n*os*tra repetere possit) sanctitatis vel speciem exhibuisset / que ex di*ctorum* factorumq*ue* constancia fidem orbi faceret probitatis et chr*isti*ane synceritatis ederet argumentum, Laborasset quidem multum se*renissi*ma Anglie ma*ies*tas dum famam et no*min*is (sui) integrita(tem)[1] ab illa sede nu*n*c subito convitiis (etiamsi muliebri quadam petulancia[2] impetitam *154 b* defenderet et conseruaret ‖ Quis e*nim* facile crederet in illa vocabulorum maiestate latere mendatium[3] / Nunc autem cum aperto Sileno[4] omn*i*a pateant.[5] videantq*ue* 185 b omn*e*s sanctam illam sedem nom*in*is app*ellatio*ne | contentam res ipsas et facta ex utilitate semper et com*m*odo non ex sanctitate et honestate metiri solere / nec ta*m* habere pensi quid dicant aut scribant ip*s*i nedum pollicentur[6] et faciant / q*uam* quid a*nim*i libidini satisfaciat / porro aut*em* virtutem probitatem fidem religionem ac pietatem / ignorantiam etiam et omniscientiam ijsdem *155 a* ho*min*ibus prout amici fuerint aut inimici ‖ p*er* vicissitudines desultoria quadam leuitate dent et auferant / ac mira quadam transformac*io*ne homines quos libet /

---

[1] Word and letters in brackets supplied from fair copy. [2] The sign ) missing here. [3] This clause, from *Quis enim* to *mendatium*, is a parenthesis. [4] The following explanation of this idiom is supplied by Erasmus in his *Adagia*, which were printed as early as 1500. "Σιληνοὶ ἀλχιβιάδου, id est, Sileni Alcibiadis, apud eruditos in proverbium abijsse videntur, certe in collectaneis Græcorum prouerbij uice referuntur, quo licebit uti, uel de re quæ cum in speciem, et prima, quod aiunt fronte, uilis ac ridicula uideatur, tamen interius, ac propius contemplanti, sit admirabilis, uel de homine, qui habitu, uultuque, longe minus præ se ferat, quam in animo claudat. Aiunt enim Silenos imagunculas quaspiam fuisse sectiles, et ita factas, ut diduci et explicari possent, quæ clausæ ridiculam ac monstrosam tibicinis speciem habebant, apertæ subito numen ostendebant, ut artem sculptoris gratiorem iocosus faceret error. Porro statuarum argumentum sumptum est, a ridiculo illo Sileno Bacchi pædagogo, numinumque poeticorum morione....Proinde Alcibiades apud Platonem

If the see of Rome which of long tyme hath vsurpyd in worde and saying the name of holynes had shewyd in hir acts and deds (so ferre as wee can remembre) anye apparance of holynes, the whiche by stedfastnes in saying and doyng, might prove to the world hir goodnes, and shew any token of Christian sincerite The kings maieste wolde haue laboryd myche to defende and [*conserve*] conserve the integrite of his good name and fame, the whiche sodeynly now of late is spitefully tochyd, by that same see.[a] Allthough it bee doon *with* a womanlyke scoldyng, for who wold lightly beleve any lyes to be hidden in that maieste of words, butt now thatt (the silenus beyng disclosyd) all thyngs ar manifest, and euerye man may [see] *per*ceyve that this holye see, contentyd *with* the only name of holynes, is wont to mesure all thyngs, and all doyngs by hir own utilite and profyt, and nott by holines in ded, or honeste, and thatt she regardyth nott so myche what she saith or wrytyth, yea *pro*misyth or doeth, as thaccomplishment of hir own pleasure, but doth attribute and take a way *with* an onstedfast lightnes, from the self same men, vertue, goodnes, faith, relligion, and piete, ignorance yea and also perfite knolege, as they bee, by turnes, other[b] hir frynds other foes, and by a maruelous ‖ transmutation is wont, to make all sorts 198 b of men now bests, and devills, now saynts and godds, as often

in convivio, Socratis encomium dicturus, eum Silenis hujusmodi similem facit, quod is multo alius esset propius intuenti, quam summo habitu uideretur" (*Sileni Alcibiadis*, per Des. Erasmum Roterodamum, separate print, Basileæ, April 1517, fol. 1 b). In other words a Silenus is a box fashioned as a statue of Bacchus' old tutor, or a box bearing some grotesque representation, which, being opened, discloses an object of far greater value. Cf. also the picturesque paraphrase of Erasmus in Rabelais' *Gargantua* (ed. Abel Lefranc, Paris, 1913, vol. I, pp. 3–4). It should be noted that Gardiner reverses the meaning of the idiom, since in the present case the Silenus bears a fairer appearance outside than inside, and contains inwardly nothing but the vices of the Roman court; also that Gardiner's use of the expression (cf. also *extra oleas versari* in *De Vera Obedientia*, fol. 24 b, and note) is a minor proof of his Erasmian training.     [5] The sentence is not broken here.     [6] *Sic* for *polliceantur*.     [a] The sentence is not broken here. [b] Either.

23

belluas ct demones / eosd*e*m rursu*m* heroas[1] et deos facere
186 a  soleant / v*idelicet* cu*m* id in a*n*imo sederit illi sedi **|** que
in certa firmitate veritatis nullam sedem (h*abet*)[2] sed super
arenam posita huc atque illuc p*r*out flatus venti impulerit
com*m*ouetur / hec inq*uam* hodie cum sint notissima /
[nihil] nihil veretur sacra*tissi*ma anglie ma*ies*tas quin apud
bonos et graues qui ex veritate [ut] vt\* par est sint de
155 b  eiusd*e*m **||** integritate apud se existimaturi nullum de causa
preiudiciu*m* faciant.[3] verba illa co*n*tumeliosa que paulus
aut verius Saulus spirans minarum et cedis in discipulos
d*om*ini ex illa sede sancta protulit / sed inditium solum et
argumentum iratum esse illum (nescio quid) co*m*motum
[ac] deniq*ue*\* ac vehementer affectum loquiq*ue* ac scribere
illum eas quas molestia / que alicunde illata atq*ue* inflicta **|**
186 b  dolet / voces expresserat / non que [res ip*s*as] reru*m*\*
ip*s*aru*m*\* que nulle sunt illiusmodi veritatem referrent /
156 a  Itaq*ue* ut vno verbo **||** dicam mendatijs plena sunt om*n*ia
multisq*ue* fictionibus referta / quas ad amplificac*i*onem et
exaggerationem docuerint aliquando Rethores pertinere /
Primum e*n*im [tentat] vt\* tentet\* a*n*imu*m* Chr*ist*ianissime
ma*iesta*tis et[4] / o\* [magnam]\* callida*m*\* astucia*m*\* in
liberando illo olim Roffensi E*pisco*po tandem suo merito
de proditione condempnato / quem isti scilicet post
mortem ut odium excitent om*n*iu*m* Cardinalium Cardinalem vocant / [et] operam ab illa Chr*ist*ianissi*m*a ma*iest*ate
cum chari*ssi*mo fratre suo Sere*n*issi*m*o Anglie Rege inter-

---

[1] This word is rendered as "saints" by the translator, no doubt
rightly.  Gardiner's use of a mythological expression in connection
with a Christian subject shows how little he had yet outgrown his
humanistic upbringing at Cambridge.    [2] Supplied from fair copy.
[3] No break in the sentence here, the subject of *faciant* being *verba
illa*.    [4] This *et* is obviously superfluous, and ought to have been
erased when *tentat* was replaced by *ut tentet*.    [a] Stronger than the
original, which says merely *breathing*.    [b] A distinctly Protestant
rendering for *discipulos domini*. This is one of the points which seem
to make it likely that the translator favoured the Reformers.    [c] Here
again the translation is stronger and more homely, *affectum* meaning
only "affected" or "touched".    [d] Heaviness of mind, sadness,
melancholy (*N.E.D.*); here more exactly: "annoyance".    [e] Inaccurate: "of the things themselves".    [f] Here ends the long rhetorical

as hitt shall please thatt se, which hath no seatt in any stedfastnes of trothe, butt beying buyldyd vppon the sande, is
mouyng now here now ther as the wynde bloeth. Wherfor
consideryng thatt those thyngs bee nowe openly knowen, the
king of Englonde his most sacred maieste dowtyth nothyng
butt thatt amonge good and sad men whiche *with* themselfs
shall wey his integrite by truthe (as reason is), those spitefull
words whiche paulus, or rather saulus hath spoken blastyng
and bloyng*ᵃ* owte threatnyngs and murdre agaynst the disciples of the lorde,*ᵇ* from thatt holye see, shall nothyng hinder
the matter, but rather they shall bee a signe and a playne
argument, thatt he is angry and movyd (I know nott for whatt
cause) and vehemently chafyd,*ᶜ* and thatt he spekyth and
wrytyth suche words, as pensyvenes*ᵈ* soomwhens inflictid
vppon him, dryuith owte, and thrustyth fowrthe, and nott
suche words as show the truthe of any thyng,*ᵉ* which bee none
suche in dede,*ᶠ* And to speke att a worde, all is full of lyes and
replenisshid *with* fictions, such as the rhetoricions haue tawght
to be mete for the amplifying or settyng ‖ fourthe of a matter,  199 a
ffor first to assaye*ᵍ* the mynde of the most Christian Maieste
(o subtyle crafte) concernyng*ʰ* the deliuerance of the late bisshop
of Rochester, beyng in thende for his onfeynyd deseruyng
condemnyd of treason, whom they after his deth (and God
will*ⁱ*) to excite the hatred of all Cardinalls, name a Cardinall,
he doth say that the labor of the most Christian Maieste inter-
posid *with* his brother the most noble Kyng of Englande, was
contemnyd sett att nowght and mockyd wher in ded no suche

period with which this tract, like *De Vera Obedientia*, begins. Its
obscurity is further increased by a break in the grammatical construction towards its close, and the order and succession of ideas may
not uselessly be summarized as follows: " If the Roman See had been
really holy, the king would have taken great pains to vindicate his
good name against the Pope's spiteful aspersions; but considering
that the Roman See can pretend to no real virtue, and only seeks her
own interest, the king feels certain that all wise men will take no heed
of such aspersions, and only consider them as lies uttered forth in
anger".    *ᵍ* To tempt, to try to gain over (*N.E.D.*).    *ʰ* Mistranslated; *in liberando* refers to *operam*. "He doth say that the labour of
the most Christian king, in attempting to procure the liberation of
the late bishop...."    *ⁱ* Not in the Latin text.

25

*156 b* positam / quam nu*n*quam interposuit[1] /‖ tanq*uam* con-
*187 a* temptam spretam atq*ue* | delusam [comemorat] pro-
ponit* / qua quidem fictione non contenta sancta sedes in
apertum se prouoluit mendacium / et falsissime infert
intercessionem Chris*ti*anissi*me* Ma*i*esta*t*is mortem ip*s*ius
Roffens*is* maturasse Testor in hac re conscientiam
Chris*ti*anissi*me* Ma*i*esta*t*is que quia cu*m* Amico a quo
nihil se no*n* [impetrat] impetrare potuisse sciebat nihil
egit / non modo mendaciu*m* istorum nunc videt mani-
festissime verum etiam pro sua prudencia facile ostendit
*157 a* proditionem om*n*em et inobedienciam ip*s*i in om*n*ibus ‖ sic
esse i*n*visam ut [nullius] nullu*m** aut are aut precatori[2] in*
ea* causa* locu[s]*m* fore putauerit / *u*t [res] Respublice*
suo statu cons*er*uentur Quacu*n*que certe ratione ab inter-
cessione abstinuerit Chris*ti*anissi*m*a ma*i*estas nu*n*q*uam*
*187 b* intercessit | quidem / nullum aliquando verbum ea de re
egit [vunsq*uam*] Nu*n*q*uam* vnq*uam* / [nunq*uam*] ei se rei
i*m*miscuit / quam sancta sedes bruiter[3] quidem sed aperte
eius intercessionem maturasse mentitur / Audistis iam
mendaciu*m* non dubium non obscurum / neq*ue* enigmate
aliquo tectum / sed certum / sed clarum atq*ue* nudum / eo
*157 b* solum ‖ munitum q*uod* a sancta sede processerat[4] ut illius
nimirum sanc*tita*tem nobis com*m*endaret / Nunc videte
queso rhetoricas eiusdem sedis lachrymas que tamen
adhuc* in ambiguo heret quid primu*m* aut potissi*mu*m in
eius morte qui debitas legibus penas luit / deploret / hicq*ue*
peruersam atq*ue* inversam in illa sede sancta vicem boni
*188 a* ac pii animi animaduertite / Nempe [illa] illa* sedes* | que
summ*o* cum gaudio de clade teterrima et morte crudelis-
sima triumphum in suis victorijs agere solet in quibus

---

[1] It is equally certain that the Pope did his very best to obtain
Francis I's intercession in favour of Fisher (*State Papers*, vol. VII,
no. CCCCXXV; *Letters and Papers*, vol. VIII, 779); and that Francis I,
while expressing unbounded devotion towards the Holy See, was
careful to refrain from any unadvised step which might give offence
to Henry VIII. Even after Fisher's death he was content to use the
Pope's brief in order to obtain better terms in the bargain he was about
to strike with the English king (*Letters and Papers*, vol. IX, Mr Gairdner's preface, p. iii); and before Fisher's death, his remonstrances, if
any, must have been of the mildest. However he declared to the papal
nuncio at his court, Paolo da Carpi, bishop of Faenza, "haver fatto
per la salute del Roffen*se* tutti quelli ufficii, che li sono stati possibili"

labor was made, And yett thatt holye see nott contentyd with thatt lye, makyth*a* a nother open lye, and most falsely bryngyth in thatt the intercession of the most Christian maiesti, hath causyd the sayd Rochester to dye the rather, in this matter I call to recorde*b* the consciens of the most Christian maieste, whiche, forsomyche as he neuer intermedled*c* with his frynd in this cause (of whom* he knowith*d* he may obteyn any* thyng that he desiryth) nott onlye doth see most manifestly now ther lyes, butt also (suche is his prudence) he hath playnly declaryd, thatt he hateth all treason, and inobedience, in so myche, thatt he thought, ther shulde bee gyven no place to altar ‖ [in suc] 199 b nother prayer, in suche case for the mayntenance of the comen wealth in his*e* estate / but for whatt so euer consideration he absteynyd from thatt intercession, of troth his most Christian maieste neuer made any desires*f* in this case, nother dyd speke any words of thatt matter, ne euer intermedlyd with thatt thyng, whiche this holye see, allthough brevely, yett nottwith-standyng playnely, sayth was hastyd by his intercession / yo haue now harde a lye, nott dowtefull, nott darke, not coueryd with any obscurenes but certayn, clear, [bather] bare, hauyng none other defence butt onlye thatt it procedith from thatt holye see, for to make vs perceyve*g* the holynes therof, Now beholde I pray yow the rhethoricall teares of the same see, whiche yett waloith*h* in miche ambiguite, whatt it shall chiefly and principally bewayle, in the deth of thatt man, whiche hath suffred the paynes due on to hym by the law, and in this place good and relligious herts beholde you the frowarde,*i* and in-verse chawnges, of this holy see, ffor the same see whiche with verye greatt Joye is wont to triumph of the most fowle slaghter, and most cruell deth, in hir victores, wherin infants, boyes,

which of course may not have meant much (Vatican Library, Nunzia-tura gallica sub Paulo III, vol. ii⁰, fol. 240).     ² That in such a case there is no place to be eaten either by the altar or the suppliant, i.e. there is no room for mercy.     ³ *Sic.* The fair copy has *breuiter.* ⁴ *Processerit* in fair copy.     *a* More accurately: "casts itself into". *b* I appeal to the king's perfect knowledge of the case and its character. *c* Stronger than the Latin text. More exactly: "He never took any steps...".     *d* Inaccurate: "He knew".     *e* Archaic for *its.* *f* More exactly: "Interposed, interfered".     *g* More exactly: "To commend to us".     *h* Stronger than the Latin text: "Which abides in ambiguity...". The meaning of the clause is as follows: "which cannot make up its mind as to what it shall chiefly bewail". *i* Perverse. (Etym.: "from-ward", contrary of "to-ward".)

27

*158 a* infantes pueri femine viri in*n*oxij || (ei)[1] illi* quidem* [fere] vere* innocentes ceciderunt hec nu*n*c sedes deplorat mortem iure inflictam proditori / de malorum morte luget sancta* sedes* de bonorum gaudet / sancta sanctitate fortasse affecta / que mortem nolit peccatoris[2] / Bonos vero qui eidem aduersentur sanctum putat deo obsequium ferro et igni in celum transmittere[3] ut terram permittant huic sedi possidendam que uniu*er*sum orbis ambitum conatur occupare / O sanctitatem vna sede dignam / ne

*158 b* a loco dimoueatur[4] / || Nempe sanctitas que orbem vniu*er*sum tot bellis concussit / vnius / si diis placet /

*188 b* mortem | legibus debitam ferre non potest quam ferro sine legibus suo iussu illatam in tam multis laudauit / Loquor de sancta sede quam paulus nu*n*c rethorice sibi adiungit in deplora*cione* / quasi qui theatrum com*m*overet que sedes* paulo quidem [antiquior] ip*s*o* no*n** paulo* antiquior* multa uidit et novit ab hoc qui nu*n*c affi*n*gitur affectu alie[na]nissi*m*a* / vidit quippe* illa vidit* et novit

*159 a* non unius sed multorum || et episcoporum et Cardinalium cedes exilia et carceres non modo sine fletu et singultu sed etiam cum gaudio / Vidit illa / ut alia preteream multa et[5] Italiam totam et ip*s*am imprime[6] Florenciam[7] multa et grauiter passam id*que* non mediocri cum alacritate / vidit

*189 a* et | audiuit, genera mortis crudelissima suo no*mine* infligi hijs qui nihil promeruerunt / nec est [deplorata tale] lachrimata* tamen / Illic prorsus sicca / hic ad fluminis modum in vniuersalis s*cilicet* eccl*es*ie vulnere irrigua facta est—lachrimisqu*e* plena / videlicet suis non tangitur sancta

*159 b* sedes / || sed o*mnium* no*mine* facile com*m*ovetur atqu*e*

---

[1] *Ei* is not erased, but does not appear in fair copy.     [2] A current phrase, from two passages of Ezekiel, which run as follows in the Vulgate: "Quia nolo mortem morientis, dicit Dominus Deus; revertimini, et vivite" (xviii, 32) and "Vivo ego, dicit Dominus Deus: nolo mortem impii..." (xxxiii, 11).     [3] The Latin text, with its biting irony, is here distinctly superior to the translation, in which the movement of the sentence is wholly destroyed.     [4] This clause is an exclamative parenthesis: "A fine holiness indeed, worthy of that only see—may it be left to stay where it is", or again, "Heaven forbid that it should spread to other places".     [5] This word not in fair copy.     [6] *Impune* in fair copy.     [7] This is an allusion to the siege of Florence, which, after an eight months' siege, was captured by the Imperials in August, 1530. Clement VII was particularly anxious

women, men withowte fawte, and verie innocents, bee slayn, that same see ‖ bewaylyth now, the deth iustly executyd vppon 200 a a traytor / This holye see bitterly wepith for the deth of Euyll men and reioysyth for the deth of good men, movyd of lyklihode with thatt holy holynes whiche will nott the deth of the synner, butt this nottwithstandyng[a] it doth reken hitt a holye sarvyce to God, to sende to heven by Iron, and fyre, suche good men as doo contrarye the same, to thentent they shall relinquisshe the erthe to be possessyd of hir, which studyith to haue in her said possession the hole circuite of the worlde, O holynes worthie thatt one seatt neuer to bee remouyd thens,[b] for thatt holynes which hath shakyd the hole worlde with so manye warres, now can nott (if hitt please god) abyde the lawfull deth of one man, And yett she hath praisyd the cruell[c] deth inferryd by hir commawndment, to many other, withowte any lawe, I speke of that holy see whiche paulus now adioynith to him, like a rhetoricion, in his lamentation, as thogh he shakyd the hole stage place, the whiche see nott a litle elder then [pau] the said paulus hath seen and knowen many thyngs, ferre wide from that affection whiche is now feynyd, she ‖ hath 200 b seen forsouthe she hath seen and also knowen the slaghters, exiles and emprisonments, nott only of one but of manye bisshops, and Cardinals, and thatt nott only withowte sighyng, and wepyng,[d] butt also with gladnes, she hath seen (I shall let passe many other thyngs) all Italye, and of very late dayes, the cyte of Florence, suffre myche hevynes, and yett she reioisyd nott a litle, she hath seen and harde many (whiche deseruyd nothyng) tormentyd[e] in hir name, with most cruell sorts of deth, and yett dyd wepe nothyng at all, she beyng then verye dric, is now here made all wete, and full of terys like a ryuer, (thatt is to say) for the wounde of the uniuersall churche, This holye see is nott towchyd for hir own causes, but she is very soone mouyd [fo] and doth mvrne, for the comen causes,[f] specially

to restore to his family (the Medici) the dominion of the city and therefore came to an agreement with Charles V at Bologna, with Francesco Sforza and with Venice; but towards Florence he was unrelenting (Cf. Pastor, *Geschichte der Päpste*, 1. bis 4. Auflage, vol. IV, 2, pp. 359–71).    [a] Mistranslated, *vero* meaning here "on the other hand".    [b] Cf. note on corresponding Latin passage. [c] More exactly: "the death inferred by iron".    [d] More exactly: "Weeping and sobbing".    [e] Stronger than the Latin text: "Upon whom most cruel sorts of death were inflicted".    [f] The translation here fails to render the ironical tone of the original, and may be improved as follows: "To be sure, it is not on account of her own interests that the Holy See appears to be concerned, but the interest of all is the pretext she gives for her emotion and mourning".

deplorat presertim si, quando id lubet[1] / alioqui vero quod
tandem vulnus vniuersali ecclesie inflixit vnius proditoris
mors ex legibus iure condempnati    Sanatur [quippe]
etiam* ecclesia proditorum morte non vulneratur / Sed
hec sedes est que contrariissimis omnia donat nominibus
ut cause inseruiat sue / Scelerosos Innocentes vocat / Innocentes scelerosos / Bene est quod non nisi vocabulo
189 b  tenus habeat | potestatem / que incredibilem alioqui nobis
160 a  sua inconstancia faceret || metamorphosim / Siquidem pro
deo inquit pro Catholica religione / pro Justicia / pro
veritate vir sanctissimus occubuit / quasi uero pro deo sit
adversari principi dei vicario / pro Catholica religione sit /
non prestare obedienciam quam eadem religio exigit /
pro Justicia sit violare leges legitime latas / pro veritate
denique repugnare veritati / Cumque in hijs omnibus
eatenus offenderet Roffensis quatenus secundum leges
160 b  mori debuerit / porro* autem* ex legibus || iure ac de more
convictus ac condempnatus sit mortuus / sic tamen libuit
190 a  sancte illi sedi verborum magistre | nominibus et appella-
tionibus veritatem invertere et falsissimis lachrimis
vniuersalis ecclesie vicem indolendo[2] Clarissimi et dignis-
simi principis famam suggillare. Nam illud ridiculum est
quod de genere mortis inter deplorandum meminit sancta
sedes / quod sane in acerba illa optione cum moriendum
esset fuit mitissimum [quoad] pro* rei conditione [patitur]
161 a  nobilissimum [et] || certe [id] eiusmodi*[3] quod preter
moriendi [metum] a natura metum* minimum quiddam
habebat sensus ac doloris / Non enim extinctus est veneno
quod quidam faciunt / non [equuleo] in* plumbo* [lente*
coctus*] coctus quod alicubi est solenne / non laqueo
suspensus quod proditoribus competit non igne extinctus /
190 b  non | tormentis lente exanimatus / sed subita vi gladij vita
priuatus / quod genus est mortis in illa acerbitate lenis-
simum / Et tamen Rethorculus hic quo deploracionem

---

[1] Si must here be understood as having a causative sense: "Specially
because at certain times it pleases her", hence, "whenever it pleases
her". Quando is here in the place of aliquando.    [2] Sic for in-
dolescendo?    [3] The preceding words stand as follows in the fair
copy: "et [quod] rei conditione [patitur] nobilissimum / [et certe
id] Certe eiusmodi"—which makes it certain that the fair copy

when it pleasyth hir, for ells, whatt wounde hath the deth of one trayter condemnyd by the law, inferryd to the vniuersall churche? The churche is heylyd, and nott woundyd, by the deth of a trayter, butt this see which geuyth contrarye names to euery thyng,<sup>a</sup> so thatt it make ‖ for hir purpose callith the good men euyll men, and the euyll good, it is happye thatt she hath no further power but only in woords, for ells, she wolde make by hir inconstance incredible chawnges amongs vs, for<sup>b</sup> (she saith,) for god; for the catholike relligion, for iustice, for the trothe,<sup>c</sup> the most holye man dyed, as though it war for god, to contrary his prince beyng the vicar of god, for the catholike relligion, nott to geve suche obedience as thatt same relligion requiryth, and asthough it war for Justice to breke the lawes lawfully promulgat, and finally asthough it war for the troth, to repugne agaynst the troth, And wher as Rochester hath so ferre offendyd in all the premisses thatt by the lawes he ou*ght to dye, And wher also hc 'is by ryght, lawe, and custome, convict, condemnyd, and putt to deth, yett it pleasyd thatt holye see hauyng store of woords so to inverte the truthe, by woords, and termes, and in lamentyng with thatt feynyd teares, the chawnce of the vniuersall churche, thatt by such meannes she blemashyth<sup>d</sup> the good name, of the most noble, and most worthye prince, And amongs other thyngs<sup>e</sup> this is to be laught att, thatt this holye see in the noombre of hir lamentations, makyth mention of the ‖ kynde of his dethe, the whiche of truthe, in thatt bitter choise (when a man must neds dye) was the most easye, and as the case requyryd, most noble, and suche as (takyng a way the naturall fear of deth<sup>f</sup>, had verie litle felyng, of any payne, he was nott kyllyd with poison, which thyng soom men doth vse, he was nott sod<sup>g</sup> in lead as the [custom] soleme<sup>h</sup> vse is in certayn places, he was nott hangyd in a halter, which best agreyth for [a] trayters, he was nott brent, he was nott putt to deth with lingeryng torments, butt lost his lif with a soden stroke of a swerde, the which sorte of deth, in suche bitternes is most easye,<sup>i</sup> And yett this nott with

201 a

201 b

was copied from this very draft. <sup>a</sup> The *est* in the Latin sentence is overlooked in the translation. <sup>b</sup> Since. <sup>c</sup> Truth. <sup>d</sup> It pleased that holy see...by such means to blemish.... <sup>e</sup> These last three words not in the Latin text. <sup>f</sup> The sign ) to be supplied here. <sup>g</sup> From *to seethe*, meaning "to cook by boiling". <sup>h</sup> This word here means, like the Latin *solenne*, "customary, habitual" (first instance of this meaning in N.E.D. dated 1616). <sup>i</sup> More exactly: "is easiest".

31

*161 b*  produceret in multa membra de genere sc*ilicet** ‖ mortis
minus q*uam* ridicule conqueritur  Habet e*ni*m hoc breue
quedam que Blosij[1] sunt non Pauli / sancte vero sedis
pleraque o*mn*ia / ip*s*ius vero Pauli quatenus idem numero
persona sit / qui olim farnesius[2] dictus sit non multa Illud
aut*em* a sede sancta manat q*uod* nunc maiores Sere*nissi*me
ma*iesta*tis in crimen vocentur / qui olim ab eadem sede
vt fuere elogijs suo merito com*m*endati / Sic e*ni*m solet
191 a illa sedes prout quisque eius glorie | ambitioni / questui
aut libidini patrocinatus fuerit aut* aduersatus* / ita ‖
*162 a* titulos a virtute mutuatos ei dare atq*ue* adimere eunde*m*q*ue*
uel in celum tollere vel infra orcum dimittere / Et videte
queso horum ho*min*um in perpendendis [vitasse] viciis*
iudiciu*m* [atq] atque censuram apud quos v*idelicet* grauius
sit multo atq*ue* atrocius ho*min*em [reu*m*] proditionis reu*m*
morte afficere q*uam* in adulterio viuere notorio / q*uam* in
heresim incidere / sic e*ni*m inferunt ipsi* conficta* cri*mina**

---

[1] In spite of inquiries at the Vatican, it has not been possible to
discover anything as to the identity of this Blosius, whom Gardiner
affects to consider as responsible for many parts of the papal brief.
In an early edition of the *Exercitia Spiritualia* of Ignatius of
Loyola (Dilingæ, apud Melchiorem Algeyer, 1620, p. 12) the
bull which grants approval to the work (July 31, 1548) is signed
"Blo. El. Fulginen." This can be no other than Blasius Palladio,
who was elected bishop of Foligno on Nov. 14, 1540, and for some
reason was never consecrated. He died on Jan. 1, 1547 (Gams, *Series
episcoporum*, p. 696). This Blasius may be the same as our Blosius, but
anyhow the point is of small importance. The signature at the bottom
of a brief is merely that of the secretary who brings the document into
shape, and Gardiner cannot possibly have believed that Blosius was
in a position to express any personal feelings.

[2] Alexander Farnese, born at Rome in 1466, was made cardinal of
SS. Cosmas and Damian (later of St Eustace) while yet a deacon, by
Alexander VI, in 1493; was promoted to the bishopric of Ostia and
Velletri in 1524. At the time of the divorce trial he was dean of the
sacred college. He was elected Pope on October 13, 1534, under the
name of Paul III. Gardiner here suggests and later asserts (fol. *162 b*-
191 b) that before he was raised to the papal throne he had shared
Henry VIII's view of the divorce matter. In so far as such an assertion
can be checked by means of the documents in *Letters and Papers*, it
appears to be ungrounded, and supplies a further proof of Gardiner's
continual bad faith. It is true that Farnese was supposed to belong to
the French party among the cardinals (*Letters and Papers*, vol. v, n° 782);
it is also true that in 1527, when the fortunes of the papacy were at
their lowest, he besought Henry VIII and Wolsey to come to the help
of the Roman See, and expressed warm devotion towards them (*ibid.*
vol. IV, 2, n° 3637; vol. IV, 3, n°s 5225, 5230) and even went so far as to
promise help in a general way (*ibid.* vol. IV, 2, n° 3156; vol. IV, 3, n° 5235),
but whenever he is said to lean to the king's side in the divorce matter

standyng, this yong Rhethoricion,[a] bicause he wolde prolong
his deploration, after dyuers wayes,[b] complaynyth more then
foolyshly, of the kynde of Rochesters deth, for this breve
hath many thyngs which bee of blosius and nott of paulus, butt
almost all together is onfaynydly of thatt holy see And of paulus
hym self, beyng the same man, which was soom tyme [ma]
namyd farnesius, nott many,[c] it procedyth from that holy see
that the [kings most noble] progenitors of the kings most noble
maieste, bee now blamyd,[d] the which soom tyme for ther
deseruyng, was[e] hyghly commendyd of the same see, ffor
suche is the vse of thatt see, as euery man doth other[f] aide hir
glorye, ambition, profitt or sensualite, or impugne any of them,
so doth [itt] it geve the || titles borowyd of vertue, or take them     202 a
away, extolle them above heven other[g] cast them down vnder
hell,[h] And I pray yow consider well the Judgement and censure
of these men in ther waying of vices, which doo reken it a
myche more heynous offence to putt to deth a man gilte of
treason, then to lyve in open adultery or fall in to heresye,[i] for

it is by Henry VIII himself or his agents, and nothing more is proved
than the sanguine hopes of the former, or the wish of the latter to please
their master (*ibid*. vol. IV, 2, n⁰ 3693; vol. IV, 3, nᵒˢ 5213, 6069). When
the divorce matter was at last taken in hand by the Roman See, Farnese
unhesitatingly sided with Catherine of Aragon (*ibid*. vol. VI, nᵒˢ 282,
311, 367, 369). It must further be noted that Farnese is not mentioned
in Gardiner's letters sent home in the course of his two diplomatic
missions to Italy in 1528 and 1529; hence the bishop of Winchester
can scarcely have had personal experience of the cardinal's inmost
feelings.     [a] Meaningless, for "this petty rhetorician".     [b] More
exactly: "into numerous sentences or heads".     [c] The Latin sentence
is obscure, and the translator evades the difficulty. The following
interpretation is suggested: "but of this same Paul, in so far as this
personage, modified by his numbering as a pope, is the same as when
he was called Farnese…".     [d] *To blame* means here "to charge, to
accuse" (*N.E.D.*), the translation being correct.     [e] *Sic* for *were*.
[f] Either.     [g] Or.     [h] The sentence is again obscure, and the
translation cannot claim to provide an accurate interpretation of its
grammatical difficulties. It is suggested that *ut* (*fuere elogiis*) and *sic*
(*enim solet*) are conjugated, the two related clauses forming an ana-
coluthon: "who as they were once deservedly praised by that same
see, so now this see is wont…to give them or to take from each of
them the titles…". *Titulos a virtute mutuatos*, here translated as "the
titles borrowed from virtue", probably means "the titles which they
(the kings) owe to their virtue only" and which cannot justly be taken
from them; the Roman See is exceeding her powers even in granting
titles which are not in her gift, still more in refusing to recognize them.
[i] An allusion to Henry VIII's first marriage, which Clement VII
finally declared to be legitimate, whereas in the King's own opinion it
was both sinful and heretical, since it disagreed with the prescriptions
of Leviticus.

ut occasionem arripient[1] cumulacius mentiendi / Quam-
quam certe quod de Adultero[2] notorio dictum sit / equidem
nunquam tribuerim paulo quem non adhuc putem sui
prorsus oblitum ‖ ac | memoria [iam] deposuisse / quomo-
do cum iam Cardinalis esset vnus inter omnes precipue
causam matrimonii pretensi Serenissime Maiestatis tam
aperte improbasset ut hoc presens legitimum matrimonium
Serenissime Maiestatis adulterium appellare nunquam
posset[3] / Qua in re tamen si respectus aliquis non ratio ab
eo tempore animum mutasset certe* debuisset [tamen] ille
vel saltem Blosius considerasse ut si verum legitimumque
matrimonium romano more que omnia invertit adulterium
appellare libuisset / abstinuisset tamen ab eo vocabulo

*163 a* scribens ad Christianissimum Regem / qui non ‖ ipse solum
sed omnes etiam consiliarij / intraque eius ditionem Aca-
*192 a* demie omnes / et inter has parisiensis | de alterius pretensi
matrimonii cum Catherina iniquitate* aperte pronun-
ciassent / et magna pars etiam constantis[4] matrimonij
legitimas ac perfectas esse vires comprobauisset[5] / Sed
hec haud perspiciunt isti qui non quid conveniat aut liceat
vere / sed quid libeat animadvertunt / Itaque heresim
obijciunt / obijciunt schisma / obijciunt avulsionem ab

*163 b* universali ecclesia / qua in re vincant verborum ‖ petulan-
cia / Tam est [enim] enim* honestum improbari a malis
quam a bonis laudari / promoveat deus nostram in christiana
religione quam* ipse* vocat* heresim / quo nomine christi
professionem homines Athei et* gentiles* cuiusmodi sunt

*192 b* isti | [et gentiles][6] semper donarunt / Abscidit deus a

---

[1] *Sic* for *arripiant.*    [2] The brief, which is here quoted, has
*adulterio.*    [3] On Farnese's real feelings in respect to the divorce
question, cf. note on fol. *161 b*:190 b above.    [4] As follows in fair
copy: "[stantis] presentis*".    [5] Gardiner here refers, with some
rhetorical amplification, to the opinions given from April to October,
1530, by six French universities on the lawfulness of Henry VIII's
first marriage (Orleans, April 5; Angers, faculty of theology, May 7;
Angers, faculty of canon law, May 7; Paris, faculty of canon law,
May 23; Bourges, June 10; Paris, Sorbonne (faculty of theology),
July 2; Toulouse, October 1; cf. Rymer, *Fœdera*, vol. XIV, pp. 391–8 for
most of these; and Dodd-Tierney, *Church History of England*, vol. I,
pp. 372–7). However, these opinions were not such as to justify
Gardiner's sweeping assertion. The question asked being whether the
Pope had a right to grant a dispensation for marriage with a deceased

so they bryng in feynyd vices, bycause they may haue the better
occasion to lye att liberte, And yett I can scarcely attribute
thatt to paulus *which* is spoken of the notorious adulterye,
whom I can nott thynk to haue holely forgoten hemself, and
scrapyd owte of his memorye, whow thatt he beyng butt
cardinall, one amongs all other chiefly disalowyd the cause of
the pretendid matrimonye of the kyngs hyghnes, so openly
thatt he can neu*e*r haue the face, to call this present mariage
of his most noble maieste adulterye, And in this matter all-
thought no reason, yett if any other respect, or consideration,
had chawngyd his mynde, sithens thatt tyme, yett he (or att
the lest blosius) shulde haue consideryd thatt if it had needes
haue*a* pleasyd hym (after the gyse of Rome w*h*ich turnyth
eu*e*ry thyng up *and* downe*b*) to call lawfull and iuste matrimonye, adulterye, yett he shulde haue absteynyd from thatt
terme, wrytyng to the most Christian kyng, w*h*ich, nott only
hemself, but all his cownsellers also, and all the vniu*e*rsities
w*ith*in his ‖ dominion, and amonge them parise, haue apertly      202 b
pronu*n*cyd thatt other matrimonye, with the ladye catherine,
to bee onlawfull, and a greatt parte of them haue allowed this
present maryage, to bee lawfull, and p*e*rfect, butt these thyngs
they foresee*c* nott, *which* regarde nott these thyngs w*h*ich bee
honest, and lawfull, but those only whiche make for ther own
pleasures, And so they cast to owr tethe heresye, they obiecte
[h] schismes, thei cast the separation from the vniu*e*rsall
churche, wherin they may well conquere in ther contumelious
words,*d* it is no lesse honestye to be blamyd, of euyll men, then
to bee praisyd of good men, I pray god further vs in thatt
christian relligion, which he callith heresye, by which name
suche gentiles, and godles men, as these bee, haue eu*e*r mis-
namyd the profession of christe, God hath disseueryd from vs

brother's wife and whether such marriage was lawful, the theological
faculty of Angers answered Yes; the others answered No, but the
faculties of canon law of Angers and Paris, and the university of
Bourges, made it clear that the case would be different if, as Queen
Katherine of Aragon persistently contended, the marriage had not
been consummated. Even with such a qualification, the King's agents
had great difficulty in obtaining the votes.    6 As follows in fair
copy, which was clearly copied from this draft: "et gentiles cuiusmodi
sunt isti [et gentiles]".    *a* *Sic.*    *b* Upside down.    *c* A somewhat
surprising use of this verb, which always implies some knowledge of
or provision for the future, even when it means "to see to or to
take care of beforehand" (*N.E.D.*). The Latin means "they do not
perceive, examine, acknowledge".    *d* They may well vanquish or
outstrip us in the impudence or sauciness of their words....

nobis que nos conturbauit illam sedem / quod schisma
etiam pro sua benignitate iubeat esse perpetuum / Avulsionem autem ab vniuersali ecclesia nullam nouimus /
utpote quam nunquam meditati sumus / sed christum in
164 a multis fratribus primogenitum agnoscentes[1] || in eum
numerum adoptari nos cupimus per illius gratiam / et in
vniuersali ecclesia foveri [et] ali et contineri / extra quam
non est remissio peccatorum / Non conabor hic convitijs
contendere aut Blosium maledicendo [superare] imitari* /
193 a Et tamen ut est in prouerbio qui que vuult[2] dicit | inter-
dum que non vult audiet / Itaque desinat si fieri potis est
sancta* sedes* maledicere maledicta ne noscat sua / discat
vera rerum nomina / et suis quidque appellare vocabulis /
Dehinc ne frustretur ipsa se illa sedes / aut sic cogitet ||
164 b defuncta sum / quod Germania nihil fere non dixerit /
quod in me merito dici posset Sunt enim sunt et alia
plurima / et parit semper illa venenosa sterilisque omnis
boni affrica / Romanam sedem dico [aliquid] aliquid* noui
monstri quod materiam indies suppeditet conuiciandi*
copiosam / Illud certe mendacium quod sequitur in quo
193 b regnum Anglie tributarium vocat Romane ecclesie | ex
eo consilio natum videtur quasi dicas [si hoc] hac* non
[successerit alia aggrediamur] successit* alia* aggrediamur*
via* / [Et iam si] Id* quod* etiamsi* ab honestatate[3]
165 a longissime remotum* || sit [id quod certe est de] de re
aliena movere controversiam / habet tamen ut ingenue
fatear ad victoriam exitum multo faciliorem quam si in
vindicando ex divina lege [primatum] primatu* quem sibi
[vsurpat] arrogat vsque insisteret / Nempe in hoc etiam
Colludentibus nobis nunquam vincet ex diuina videlicet
lege / competere primatum / In [ho] illo ad victoriam hoc
vnum suffecerat ut omnes et singuli id confiteamur[4] / Nam
alioqui bona fide contendentibus nobis* de certissima
regni libertate et unius principis in terris [imperium]

[1] Acknowledging Christ as the first-born of a great family in which
we are all brothers....    [2] Sic for vult.    [3] Sic for honestate.
[4] Fair copy reads here as follows: "ut id* omnes singuli confiteamur".
[a] More exactly: "since we never meant...".    [b] Condition means
here "character, disposition, temper" (N.E.D.).    [c] Possibly.
[d] I am safe, out of danger. The sentence, which is placed in the

36

thatt see, whiche of long tyme dyd troble vs, the whiche schisme I beseech his goodnes it may continue for euer, as for any separation from the vniuersall church, we knowe none, ne<sup>a</sup> euer meanyd any suche, butt wee knolegyng Christe, the first begoten amonge many brothern, desire to bee receyuyd in to thatt noombre, by his grace, and to be fed norishyd and conteyned within the vniuersall churche, withowte the whiche ther is no remission of synnes, I will nott contende with blosius ‖ in scoleding, nother folow his condition<sup>b</sup> *and* euyll 203 a spekyng, and yett (as the comen saying is) he thatt spekyth whatt hym listyth, shall hyre soome tymes suche thyngs as him list nott, Therfor lett this holy see cesse (if it may possible)<sup>c</sup> to say ill, lest it know hir evill sayings* agayn, lett her lern the true names of thyngs, and call euery thyng by hir own name, lett nott thatt see from hensfourthe deceyue hir self, or think thus. I am escapyd,<sup>d</sup> Germanye hath left nothyng onsayde, thatt myght bee sayd against me, ther bee forsowth, there bee, many thyngs more, And thatt affrike full of poyson, and baren of all goodnes, (I mean the see of Rome) bringyth fowrth all ways soom nue monstres, which maye geue sufficient argument to speke euyll, And thatt other lye whiche folowith, where he callith the Realme of Englonde tributary to the Roman churche, feinyth to bee broght in to his purpose,<sup>e</sup> as a man wold say; this way hath faylyd vs lett vs take better holde by a nother, and this thyng albehitt bee farre from honestye, to make claym to thatt thyng which apperteynyth to a nother man, yett (to saye the playne truthe) it is more easely obteynyd, then if he contynue, by the lawe of god to chalenge the primacye, for‖ in this poynte, all though wee colludyd<sup>f</sup> with him yett shall he 203 b neuer prove the primacye to bee his by the law of god. butt in thatt other matter, it war sufficient for his victorye, if wee all and euery of vs wold knoledge the same, for ells, if wee reason (with good feyth) of the most certayn liberte of this Realm,

mouth of the Roman See, ends with the words "against me". Rome thinks she is safe from any further denunciations, since Germany (i.e. the Lutherans) has said all that could be said; yet there are many more things to be brought forward.    <sup>e</sup> Mistranslated: "Seems to be brought in for this purpose, as though a man would say...".
<sup>f</sup> Even if we were privately agreed with him, even if we were secretly supporting him.

maiestatem\* agnoscenti[bus]s\* qui merum obtinet sine
*165 b* superiore impe‖rium / deum vnum [agnoscentis] habentes\*[1]
illo\* maiorem et [dominum] superiorem\* / nihil [......]²
*194 a* vnquam comminiscetur³ tam callide ǀ romana astucia [qud]
quod tributarium aut esse aut fuisse regnum Anglie con-
vincat apud Judices ex iustis rerum documentis pronun-
ciaturos / Atque hic ne quis de verbis nostris erret / Non
negamus quidem regnum Anglie romane ecclesie tribuisse
permulta / Tribuit enim Annatas non\* debitas\* tribuit
annuas [prestan] prestanciones non necessarias tribuit
venalium legum pretia⁴ idque temere / tribuit honorem
*166 a* non debitum [et] Postremo\* ‖ tribuit tot et tanta que nunc
demum peniteat tribuisse / neque tribuisse contenti⁵ etiam
ad alios vsus contribuimus interdum plurima que cum
multis preterea amicitie officiis nobis perierunt que si
regnum tributarium constituant / fuimus revera ante hos
tres annos eatenus tributarij / nunc demum dei benignitate / a qua melior in nobis sententia nata est / libertate
*194 b* donati et absoluti ǀ Alia autem racione regnum dici tributarium quasi romanam ecclesiam [agnoscant] agnoscat\*
patronum et tanquam [clientela] clientele\* iure illi sub-
*166 b* seruiat / calumnia est ‖ non levis sed que vt status questionem indigne mouet [sic vafram] sic\* vafram\* istorum
calliditatem palam ostendit An eo nunc scilicet confugient
ut ex annalibus suis / in rem suam conscriptis domesticisque
tabulis donacionem proferant Regni olim Anglie ecclesie
romane factam⁶ / [patris] paris\* fidei et auctoritatis atque

---

¹ Fair copy has "habentes" corrected to "habentis". ² A few
illegible words or letters erased in the draft. Fair copy reads: "nihil
comminiscetur", *unquam* being omitted. ³ *Sic* for *comminiscitur?*
⁴ An allusion to the various forms of papal taxation, which developed
especially from the latter end of the thirteenth century, and included
first fruits (*annatas,* fructus primi anni) to be paid on taking possession
of a benefice. "Annuas prestanciones", if taken literally, may refer
to the tribute which England was to pay in consequence of King John's
submission to the Pope; or again, in a loose way, to papal taxes collected
at regular intervals. "Venalium legum precia" seems more difficult
to explain, but may be merely a rhetorical expression for fees charged
by the Roman court for dispensations or administrative formalities,
e.g. the "common services" paid by bishops and abbots on their
appointment. Such payments might give rise to a charge of venality

knowledgyng the maieste of one prince in erthe, whiche hath
the high rule wi*th*owt any superior, and havyng only god above
him, and sup*er*ior to him, thatt Romishe crafte, can Imagyn
no thyng so craftely; wherby it may prove the Realme of
Englonde to bee or to haue byn tributarye, before any Juge,
which in his Jugement will folow due p*ro*bations, and here, by
cause no man shall bee deceyuyd in owr words, we denye nott,
butt thatt the Realme of Englonde, hath gyven many thyngs
to the Roman churche, it hath gyven annates, whiche neu*er*
werre due, it hath gyven many yerly prestations, nott necessarye, it hath gyven the price of many lawes, whiche haue byn
solde, and thatt onadvisydly, it hath giuen honor nott due,
and finally it hath giuen suche and so many thyngs, thatt it
now repe*n*tith the gifte of them, and nott contentyd to haue
giuen this, hath also contributyd many thyngs to dyu*er*s other
vses, the w*hich* w*ith* soundrye other acts of amite, wee haue
lost, ‖ the whiche things, if they make a Realme tributarye, wee   204 a
werre dowtelesse tributarye thus ferre, on to this iii yerys last
past, butt now att the last, by the benignite of god, who hath
gyven vs a better Jugement, wee ar losyd, and made free, butt
to call the realme tributary after any other fasshion, as though
it knolegyd the Roman churche, for his patrone, or as though
it shulde sarue hir as a clyent, it is no light calumniation, the
whiche as it towchith onworthily the state of the hole Realme,*a*
so it makyth manifest the craftye subtilite of those men, shall
they now take refuge to ther own cronicles, writen for the*r*
own profitt, and to ther own tables,*b* to prove the gifte of the
Realme of englonde, sometyme made to the churche of Rome?
whiche gifte is as true, and of as myche authorite, as thatt

against the Papacy.      ⁵ This word ends in the draft with a sign
that looks like an "f".      ⁶ Gardiner here evades the difficulty he is
placed in, by pretending to ignore the allusion in the Pope's brief.
King John's surrender of his crown to the Pope on May 15, 1213,
his grant to the Holy See of "the whole kingdom of England and the
whole kingdom of Ireland", which he was thenceforth "to hold as a
feudatory", are historical facts which could not by any means be
denied. Gardiner prefers to cast suspicion upon them indirectly by
putting them on a par with an undoubted historical forgery.      *a* As
it raises in an unworthy, unjust, revolting fashion (or against the
right) the question of the state of the realm....      *b* More exactly:
"Will they now fall back upon this, that they should bring out from
their annals, written to support their own cause, and from their own
private records, the donation of the realm of England...".

[ut] illa est qua*m* [Syluestro] Siluestro* a constantino[1]
factam fuisse perhibent sanctiss*ime* sanct*e* sedis monu-
menta / Vide queso per deum im*m*ortalem quousque se
proferat irrefrenata audatia? Vt nusq*uam* gradu*m* [sili]
sistit[2] ni cohibeat*ur* / Expediat primu*m* sancta sedes con-
*167 a* stantini ‖ donac*io*n*em* doceat illius Instrumenti de falso
suspecti veritate*m* Probet in eo fidem iam diu labefactatam /
ac tum demu*m* quasi ab *omn*i suspitione libera nouas si
non est aliud quod agat de alienis regnis moueat querelas /
facillimu*m* est intendere regnu*m* Anglie esse tributariu*m* /
si quidem sedi que in sessionib*us* suis[3] nihil aliud medi-
tatur / q*uam* quo pacto com*m*odas in rem suam co*n*cinnet
194 B a  lites Illud vnum peto si Regnu*m* **|** Anglie tibi o sancta
sedes / fuit tributariu*m* / cur id non vendicasti per amici-
tia*m* [q] cur quod tuu*m* esse putabas / non tu*m* id ab eo ‖
*167 b* dari audacter postulabas / a [quibus] quo* tam multa
indebite tibi[4] soluta animadu*er*teres / dices fortasse
Obediebat tum Regnu*m* Anglie mihi quod Vnu*m** tum
exigebam [prestitit] / neq*ue* aliud nu*n*c* requiro / Menda-
tiu*m* quide*m** etiam hoc [est] esset* sed verbor*um* Am-
biguitate contectum / Adeo sic* verecundius [mentitur]
mentiretur* sancta sedes Nam obedisse nos ut est certis-
simu*m*, Ita eam aliquando prestitisse obedienciam que
Regni tributarij causam referret est omnino falsissimu*m*
Obedimus quidem com*m*un*i* hominu*m* errore involuti vnde
*168 a* vix tandem licuit nos expedire / Ignorantiam ‖ in hoc
n*os*tram ingenue confite[a]m*ur* / Illud vero nu*n*q*uam*
ignorauimus principem diadematis gestamine insignitum /

---

[1] The "donation of Constantine", a document according to which
the Emperor Constantine granted to the Pope imperial honours and
full dominion over the lands of the West, was forged at Rome between
752 and 778, to support the Pope's claim to the Exarchate, especially
in his relations with the Frankish court, and used throughout the
Middle Ages to buttress up the temporal claims of the Papacy. Its
authenticity was first denied by the German Nicholas von Kues, in
his *Concordantia Catholica*, vol. III, c. 2, in 1432–3, then by Laurentius
Valla, whose *Declamatio* (*De falso credita et ementita Constantini
donatione*) was composed about 1440, and independently by Reginald
Pecock in 1450. When Gardiner wrote the above passage the donation
was not yet considered as a forgery by the Catholic party at large; the
first one among staunch supporters of the Papacy to agree to its
spurious character was Baronius, in his *Annales*, vol. III, p. 244 (1592).

gifte, which the most holy muniments, of thatt holy see witnessyth to haue byn made of Constantinus to Siluester, Marke I pray yow (for god his sake) how ferre this onbrydlyd boldnes stratchith it self, whow it neuer cessyth, except it bee repressyd, lett this holye see, first declare well the donation of Constantine, lett it shew the truthe of thatt instrument, whiche is thought fals, lett it prove the credence therof, which hath now of long tyme myche decayed, and then it may withowte suspicion, make chalenge to the kingdomes of || other men (if 204 b ther bee nothyng for it ells to doo) it is verye facill for that see to purpose in hir sessions that the Realme of Englonde is tributarye on to hyr, for in those sessions, she studyeth nothyng ells, butt whow she may forge nue debates, commodious for hir own profyt,[a] I aske this one question, if the Realme of Englonde, (O holy see) was tributary on to hyr?[b] whi didest thow nott freendly chalenge it, why didest thow nott aske boldly thatt thyng? whiche thow dydest thynk thyn own of thatt man, of whom, so many thyngs hath byn gyven the? Whiche werre neuer due / thow wilt say perchawnce, the Realme of Englonde then was obedient on to me, whiche thynge only I requyrid att thatt tyme, and as yett wolde bee content with the same, Certainly, this sayng werre also a fals lye, howbeitt well coueryd with ambiguous words, by this meannes, this holy see might lye the more honestly[c]; for as it is ondowtyd, thatt wee dyd ons obey, so it is most false, thatt we gave suche obedience, as shulde declare our Realme to bee tributarye, wee dyd obey, beyng att thatt tyme wrappyd in the comen error of other men, from the whiche, wee cowde scarsely now att the last delyuer owr selfs, wee knolege playnely owr ignorance in this behalf, butt in this thing wee neuer werre ignorant, || thatt the prince[d] 205 a

(Cf. Albert Hauck, *Realencyclopädie für Protestantische Theologie und Kirche*, article "Konstantins Schenkung".) [2] *Sic* for *sistat*. [3] Fair copy has: "in suis sessionibus". [4] Fair copy has: "tam multa tibi indebite". [a] The translation is hardly clear here, and may be improved as follows: "It is an easy matter to maintain that the realm of England is tributary, at any rate for that see, who in her deliberations meditates nothing but in what manner she may occasion new lawsuits, convenient for her own interests" (i.e. by putting forward new claims). [b] The MS has clearly *hyr* which is an obvious mistake for *thee*. [c] In such conditions, the lie of the Holy See would be covered up with a little more decency. [d] One clause forgotten here: "Whom the diadem he wears makes eminent among men".

41

alium non debere agnoscere in regni maiestate superiorem /
tantum abest ut romanus Episcopus / aut illa sedes que
sua sedendo [mon] tam diligenter cogitat de hoc aliquando
194 B b nobis | moveat controuersiam / nisi nunc tandem / cum
ceteris destituta iustis querelis ad calumnias comminiscen-
das irata deflectit [contensiosorum] contenciosorum*
pragmaticorum instar qui non tam ex materijs oblatis
actiones interdum formant / quam ne contenciones citius
168 b finiantur etiam || litibus conuenientes causas confingunt /
Si quid certe eiusmodi tibi iure* competisset o sancta sedes
petisses si non nuper per Clementem[1] qui animi semper
incertus fluctuabat in quo etiam nature excusares timidita-
tem, aut si non per Adrianum[2] quem mors subita atque
incerta extinxit / aut si non per leonem decimum[3] / qui sibi
ipsi potius quam tibi vivere dicebatur / petisses certe per
Julium[4] tuum in ecclesia tum et militanti et triumphanti
gloriosissimum imperatorem et [Bellicosis] bellicosissimum
Antistitem/sed diuersum equanimiter passus est Julius*/ ||
169 a obedientia nostra ab errore communi nata contentus atque
195 a ea | ad eum modum nostris legibus [tunc] tum* temperata
que tributarij regni questionem omnino extingueret / In
hac autem quid aliud / expendam Nam[5] / historias omnes*
suas [sco] sua temeritate suspectas reddidit sancta sedes /
testium nulla est memoria / Itaque*[6] extra causam non est
quod ad probacionem cum auctoritate afferatur / In causa

---

[1] Pope Clement VII, elected November 18, 1523, d. September 25,
1534. Gardiner here alludes to his "fluctuating" attitude in regard to
the divorce matter, in which he was always attempting to please
Henry VIII without fully committing himself: "fluctuations" due
mostly to the difficult position he was placed in, between the various
European sovereigns.      [2] Pope Adrian VI, elected in 1521, d.
September 14, 1523. He was a German, and during the few months
in which he sat in the Papal throne, evidenced reforming tendencies.
He was therefore obnoxious to the French and to the anti-reforming
parties, the members of which circulated a rumour that he had been
poisoned. The rumour was in all likelihood unfounded, Adrian VI
having presumably died of a nervous disease. Gardiner obviously
thinks that the "suspicious" character of his death in some way casts
a slur upon the Papacy. (Cf. Pastor, Geschichte der Päpste, I. bis
4. Auflage, vol. IV, 2, pp. 147–8).      [3] Pope Leo X, elected
March 11, 1513; d. December 1, 1521. He was greatly concerned
about the interests of his family—the Medici—and of his native city
—Florence. He showered favours upon his nephews, many of whom

owed to knoledge no superior, in the maieste of his Realme, miche lesse, the Roman bisshop, or thatt see, whiche in her seettyng so diligently remembryth hir own profitt, dyd eu*er* make any clayme for this mater,*ᵃ* on to thatt now att the last, she beyng destitute of all other iuste causes of complaynte, turneth hir self, in hir rage, to the feynyng of nue craftye calumniations, like the contencious lawer, whiche many tymes, doth nott so myche forme his action, accordyng to the cause, thatt he hath in hande, as he*ᵇ* goeth abowte to Imagyn nue matters, agreable, w*ith* the action dependyng, by cause he wolde haue the contencion endure the longer, If any suche title had apperteynyd on to the, forsoothe thow woldest.*ᶜ* O holy see, if nott by clement, who was all wayes of an onstedfast*ᵈ* mynde, in whom thow myghst excuse the timidite of nature, or if not by adryan, which was sodenly and oncertainly ded,*ᵉ* or if not by leon the xth, w*hich* was thought to leeve*ᶠ* more to hym self then to the, yet thow sholdest haue askyd hitt att the lest by Julius, thy most glorious capitane, and most manly bisshop, both in militant and also triumphant churche, butt Julius was well contentyd otherwise, requiring nothing ells of vs, butt only thatt owr obedyence, whiche procedy[th]d of a comen error, and yett thatt ‖ same obedience was so temperyd, by our own lawes, that it playnely apperyd this Realme nott to haue byn tributarye. In this purpose whatt shall I co*n*sider besyde the premisses?*ᵍ* for this holy see, by hyr temerite, hath made all historyes suspect, and ther remainyth no memorye of wytnes, and therfor no thyng is wyde from the purpose whiche may bee brought to prove w*ith* good authorite, In this

205 b

were raised to the cardinalate, and granted to countrymen of his every post of honour or profit in his gift, so that Rome was "overflowed with Florentines" (Pastor, *op. cit.* vol. IV, I, p. 371). Here as in regard to other contemporary characters, Gardiner's judgments, however prejudiced, betray no lack of clearsightedness.   **4** Pope Julius II, elected November I, 1503, d. February 21, 1513. His chief design was to free Italy from any foreign yoke, to which purpose he first made use of France against Venice, then turned against France and began against Louis XII a military and diplomatic offensive in which he was quite successful.   **5** These last seven words are placed in the margin.   **6** This word interlined in a Roman hand.   *ᵃ* More accurately: "Much less is it possible that the Roman Bishop, or that see who in her sittings attends so diligently to her own interests, should at any time make such a thing the matter of a debate with us, unless now at last, when, being destitute...".   *ᵇ* Not so much form his action...as go about....   *ᶜ* "Have asked" omitted.   *ᵈ* Unsteadfast.   *ᵉ* The cause of whose death was unknown, and therefore suspicious.   *ᶠ* Obsolete form for *leve, live*.   *ᵍ* In regard to this (debated point) what shall I further consider?

autem* nihil est [regni] quod consistit[1] / Adeo presidijs
destituta corruit intencio / et in vanitatis crimen facile
decidit / Non igitur in eo quod ipsum non subsistit [ins]
*169 b* insistam amplius sed pergam ad ‖ reliqua / Nouissime[2]
inquit paulus [ut] pauli illius*[3] longe dissimilimus [non
ille] qui ad romanos olim vere sanctissima scripsit / quippe
qui nunc e Romanis que ad causam faciant declamatoria
quadam / [sine] licencia sine* omni* pudore affingit
omnia / Sanctissimum enim inquit presulem a [nobis]
*195 b* nobis* ob doctrinam et | sanctitatem in Cardinalium
[numerum] numerum* relatum pertentato prius illius
animo / An se retexere et veritati contradicere vellet /
demum constantem et in suo proposito usque ad vltimum
persistentem per carnificis ministrum[4] et turpe genus
*170 a* mortis publice necari iussit[5] / primum enim ‖ paulum vel
sanctam illam sedem a britannis toto penitus orbe [den]
diuisis virum petisse qui ob doctrinam et sanctitatem in
cardinal[e]ium numerum* [cooptetur] cooptaretur* /
etiamsi per rerum naturam impossibile non sit / [Est] est*
tamen per illius sedis morem et consuetudinem incredibile
nisi fortasse aut huic nunc paulo nepotes desint aut liberi /
aut qui illam dignitatem ambiant hijs desunt pecunie /
Cum scriberet antehac Roffensis multa in illius sedis
aduersarios[6] / uiueretque* apud* suos* sine* querela*
tanquam ignotus et obscurus Domi [victitabat] miser*
victitabat valuit tum ratio quid nobis cum barbaris ultra-

---

[1] *Sic* for *consistat.*  [2] This is the first word of the sentence in the
brief which Gardiner goes on quoting a few lines below: "Novissime
hunc sanctissimum præsulem...".  [3] *Illius* interlined in a Roman
hand.  [4] The brief as printed by Camusat has "carnificis ministerium" which makes a different and far more likely meaning: "by
the hands of the executioner" instead of "by the executioner's
servant". Yet the mistake must have been Gardiner's.  [5] The
quotation ends here.  [6] The allusion is here to Fisher's controversial works against the Lutherans, several of which are specially
concerned with the defence of Papal claims. Such is the case for
*Assertionis Lutheranæ confutatio*, 1523, in which Luther's "articles"
or theses are dealt with one by one, and the Pope's supremacy by
divine right asserted and proved at great length; Fisher similarly
assails Luther in his sermon preached before Wolsey and printed
in 1521, in which he shows the Pope to be "*iure divino* head of the
universal church". (Cf. *The English Works of John Fisher*, ed. J. E. B.
Mayor, Early English Text Society, Extra series, vol. xxvii, 1876).

44

cause ther is nothyng that standith,[a] it is so nakyd from all aide that the hole intention therof, fallith to the grounde, and playnely apperith to bee a vayne crime,[b] and therfor I will stande no longer vppon that thyng, whiche standith nott it self, butt I will go fourthe to the residue, Att the last[c] sayth paulus, beyng ferre onlyke thatt paulus, whiche in tyme past dyd wryte to the Romans thyngs onfeynydly holye, butt this paulus from the Romans, withowte all shame, feynyth euery thyng that makyth to his purpose, with a liberte, after the orators fasshion, ffor those bee his words,[d] Thatt most holy bisshop, whom wee for his lernyng, and holynes, haue made a cardinall, his mynde beyng assayd to thuttermost, whether he woolde turne, and saye agaynst the truth, or nott, he hath[e] commawndyd, to bee putt openly to a vile kynde* of* deth, by the hangman his seruant, by cause he was stedfast, and contynuyd in || one mynde, to his last ende, ffirste of all all-   206 a though it bee not impossible thatt paulus, or thatt holy see hath chosen a man from Englonde, bcyng diuided from the hole world, to make him Cardinall, for his lernyng, and vertue, yett of troth (the vse *and* custome of thatt see well pondryd) it is very incredible, except perchawnce, this paulus lacke chyldern, or neuous, of his own, or ells thatt suche as covett thatt preferment, wante money, In tyme past, when Rochester dyd wryte, many thyngs against the aduersaries of thatt see, and in his own cowntre no man trobled him,[f] he then lyuyd miserably att home, like a man onknowen and litle spoken of, And then this was allowyd for good reason, of thatt holy see,

---

In his *Convulsio calumniarum Vlrichi Veleni* (1525) Fisher attempts to refute the theory according to which St Peter never came to Rome.
[a] The translator does not appear to have grasped the succession of ideas: "The Holy See has made all her histories (i.e. all her historical documents) suspicious: there are no witnesses whose memory might confirm them, and therefore, in the place of witnesses, any authoritative proof would be in point to serve the Roman cause. But in this cause there is nothing that stands, it is unsupported by any proof; its contention, pretension, falls to the ground".   [b] Mistranslated: "and plainly makes itself liable to the charge of vanity", i.e. may be considered as not being founded, as being an imposture.   [c] Cf. note on Latin text. These words in the brief introduce the last part of an enumeration of Henry VIII's crimes.   [d] The construction of the sentence is here destroyed: "Since he is this Paul, who, from among the Romans, now feigneth...fashion; that most holy bishop, he says...".   [e] "At last" forgotten here.   [f] Mistranslated: "Without giving occasion for any complaint".

45

196a *170b* montanis | Nunc autem cum in extremo vite || actu contra omne Jus tam diuinum quam humanum principi et dei ordinationi resisteret ac prodi[toris]tionis* reus carcere teneretur / dignus statim est habitus apud illam sedem qui cardinalis titulo donaretur Qua in re an non est cuiuis manifestum in hominis captiui calamitate lusisse sedem / non de illius liberacione bona fide [egisse] cogitasse* / Sic enim roffensis si viueret iure conqueri posset cum illa sede et eam ad hunc modum alloqueretur / Si* quid aliquando de te bene meritus sum [sancta] o sedes romana / si in
*171 a* tuam aliquando gratiam quicquam feci || dignum quod in memoria habeatur cur illa officia que [necessaria erant ad nostram] [meam]* [consolacionem et] ad* meam* liberacionem / quam te tantopere cordi habere dicebas necessaria* erant* pretermisisti et ea officii spetie vti* maluisti* que mihi nulla ratione prodesse multis vero modis nocere potuisset [vti maluisti] Que sola liberandi ratio erat ut per precatores a mitissimo principe veniam impetra[turos]
196 b retur[1] | facere non curasti / Annum et eo amplius in carcere cum fuissem nulle inquam vel a te vel a clemente preces oblate sunt ei qui solus liberare [posset] potuisset / Nihil
*171 b* egisti cum || Cesare / nihil cum Christianissimo[2] nihil cum ceteris principibus / aut si quid egisti illi non respiciebant aut cause se mee immiscere [voluerunt] noluerunt* / Ego meam felicitatem in te defendenda olim impendi / tu meam contra miseriam ad animi tui libidinem abusus es[3] / Nempe Inuidioso cardinalis titulo tum onerasti cum honorem mihi omnem et carcer et crimen eripuissent / Breuiter[4] non meam liberationem spectasti cum faceres quod mihi nullo modo profuturum sciebas / sed in infelicitate mea querebas quod aliquo tibi modo conducere

[1] The fair copy also has "Impetra[turos]retur*", which like other passages clearly proves that it was copied directly from the draft. [2] This is of course wrong since Paul III did his best to interest Francis I in Fisher's cause (cf. note on fols. *156 a:* 186 b). Besides Gardiner contradicts himself, since he alternately finds fault with the Pope for having sought the intercession of Francis I, and for not having sought it; which illustrates the character of this tract—a piece of declamation meant for the bar.    [3] This use of *abuti* with the accusative is an infrequent turn, to be met with mostly in the works of Plautus or Terence, and in the present case no doubt a piece of

whatt have wee to do *with* these rude and barbarous ultra-
montans? but now in the last ende of his lif, when he agaynst
all lawes as well of god, as of man, resistyd his prince, and
the ordinance of god, and beyng also*a* a traiter, was imprisoned
therfor, he was then inco*n*tine*n*tly estemyd of thatt holy see
worthye to bee a cardinall, wherby may nott eu*e*ry man see
playnely? thatt this holye see did rather worke*b* att the miserye
of thatt man, then *with* good fayth, go abowte hys delyu*e*rance?
for this might Rochester (if he war now on lyve) well complayne of thatt see and speke on to hir ‖ after this man*e*r, if 206 b
I haue eu*e*r deseruyd any thyng of the, thow see of Rome, if
I haue eu*e*r doon any thing for thy sake, worthye remembrance,
why didest thow lett passe those offices, whiche war most
necessarye for my delyu*e*rance, wherof thow didest shew thi
self very desirous, butt woldest rather vse thatt color of office,
whiche by no meannes might do me any good, butt soondrye
wayes hurte me, thow didest neu*e*r regarde*c* this (whiche was
the only way to my delyu*e*rancc) that my pardon might haue
byn purchased, of thatt most gentle prince, by intercessors,
And all be hitt I was in prison one hole yere, and more, yett
was ther neu*e*r any desyres made for me, other by the, other
by clement, to hem, whiche only had the power to delyu*e*r me,
Thow didest labor nothyng to the emperor, or to the most
Christian kyng, neither to any other prince, or if thow didest
make any such labor, they regardyd it not, or ells they wolde
nott intangle them self in my cause, I haue bestowed my
felicite in tyme past in the defense of the, and thow to the
contrary hast abusyd my miserye, to thy own pleasure, for
thow didest lode me *with* thatt odious title of a cardinall, att
such tyme, as nott only the prison, but my offensis also, had
taken all honor from me, And finally thow haddest none eye
to my delyu*e*rance, in the doyng of thatt, which thow didest
know cowde by no meannes doo me any good, but thow didest
rather ‖ by my infelicite speke*d* such thyngs, as dyd make most 207 a

humanistic affectation on the part of Gardiner, whose familiarity with
the Comics is in many places obvious.    ⁴ This word is struck out
in the fair copy.    *a* This word has no equivalent in the Latin text.
The meaning is rather "being thus a traiter".    *b* Mistranslated:
"To have made sport with the distress of that man in his prison".
*c* Mistranslated: "Thou didst never take those steps which only
might have led to his liberation, namely to obtain his pardon...".
*d* Possibly a mistake for *seeke*, which corresponds to the Latin
*querebas*.

posse putasti. / ‖ Quod Leo decimus Antecessor **|** tuus
per iocum morioni suo / ut cardinalis* post mortem [car-
dinalis tituli] tumuli* scilicet inscriptione haberetur[1] hoc tu
mihi afflicto et misero / quasi opere a me impense mercedem ridicule quidem aliis [vero] mihi vero* nimis serio
contulisti / Breuiter [ut] vt* dicam quod sentio tua*m*
causam egisti non meam cui carius [fuit] fuisset* priuatu*m*
viuere q*uam* mori cardinalem / Atq*ue* hec quidem diceret
Roffensis si mortu[u]is adhuc [Re] maneret[2] oratio Ego
vero etiam illud dico quotquot sunt reliqui in illo cardinalium ordine / si rem vere existim[ent]arent* non levi se
*172 b* affectos ‖ esse co*n*tumelia interpret[entur]arent*ur**
adscitum fuisse in suu*m* ordinem qui ipse in vinculis ex
crimine lese ma*iesta*tis adhuc detineretur / [Si] Adijcio*
aute*m** et* illud* q*uod** si* tanta sit prerogatiua Cardinalium quanta isti volunt nimirum ut in* principum
dominijs proditionis et inobedientie impunitatem pre-
ste[nt]t* De quo principes ip*s*i viderent / tollerabilius
197 b quidem **|** esset / ut venia sit lapso propter dignitatem
q*uam* ut ia*m* lapso dignitas conferatur ad veniam Sed
s*cilicet* promouit hanc sanctam sedem sanctitas atq*ue* adeo
sanctitas infamia carceris notata / sanctitas deniq*ue* ‖
*173 a* prodicionis conuicta / tantam vim h*abe*t invicem / rerum
congruentia et similitudo / Ex equo e*n*im gr*ati*a carne
sanguine et questu movetur hec sedes ut sanctitate / vnde
etiam que sit sanctitas[3] facile sit intelligere / Nimirum ea
non que in spiritu mentem dei gr*ati*a sanctific[a]e*t.[4] sed
que in [car] carne orationem vt ita hic loquar falsific[a]e*t /
et in verbis ac vocabulis ad alior*um* co*n*tumeliam prestig-
End of iu*m* facit / Ex qua quidem sanctitate domi in sede sua tam
draft longe ab Anglia **|** remota atq*ue* disiuncta co*n*iectura*m*

[1] Gardiner seems to be the sole authority for this inscription of a
cardinal's title on the tombstone of the Pope's buffoon; not a negligible
authority either since he had been twice at the papal court. Evidence
to corroborate his assertion has been vainly sought in early XVIth
century documents; and enquiries at the Vatican have been equally
unavailing. Leo X's love of buffoons has been dealt with by
many historians (cf. bibliography in Calvi, *Roma nel cinquecento*, i,
3019; Rodocanacchi, *Rome au temps de Jules II et de Léon X*, and
*Courtisans et bouffons*); but no one among them mentions the inscription on the tombstone. Nor is it found in Forcella's *Iscrizioni*.     [2] The
fair copy has "remaneret".     [3] Fair copy has "Que hec sit

for thi own profitt, thow hast giuen to me in my miserable afflictions, (hitt may bee to other a laughyng game, butt to me it is to ernest) thatt same rewarde for my labors, whiche leo the x^th thy predecessor, was wont^a in sporte to gyue to his foole, thatt he shuld bee a Cardinall after his deth, by writyng the title of a Cardinall, vppon his grave, And to say my mynde shortely, thow in making me Cardinall, didest sollicit thy own cause, *and* nott myne, for I had rather haue liuid a priuat person, then haue died a cardinall, and this wolde Rochester speke, if ded men might speke, And I say thys myche more, as many as yett remayn in thatt ordre of Cardinalls, (if they wold well wey this matter) they wold reken it, no litle contumelye, thatt suche one was chosen to ther ordre, whiche lay in the prison for treason.^b Wher on to I say more, if the priuilege of a Cardinall bee suche, as these men wolde haue it, thatt is to say thatt it may geve, in the realme of any prince, a saveness from punisshment, for treason and disobedyence (whiche thyng lette the princes them self well consider) [it] yett it war more tollerable, thatt the pardon shulde bee geuen for the dignites sake to hem w*hich* hath offendyd, all readye,^c then thatt the [pardon] dignite shulde bee geuen to him w*hich* is gylte to purchase his pardon, ‖ butt this holy see (and god 207 b will) was mouyd w*ith* the holynes of the man, and thatt such holynes as was spotted w*ith* infamye of the prison, and suche holynes as was coplyd^d w*ith* treason, the liklehode and agrement of thyngs to gether haue suche effect,^e thatt this see is as myche mouyd w*ith* fauor, fleshe, bloode, and profyt, as w*ith* holynes / wherby it is soone perceyuyd, whatt holynes this see vseth, forsowthe nott suche, as sanctifyeth the mynde, by the grace of god in spirite, but suche (if I myght so say, as falsefyeth the woords in flesh, and vseth jugglyng in woords, and termes, to the contumely of other, by the w*hich* holynes, this holy see in her seatt, so ferre from [Rome] Englonde, doth

---

sanctitas ". ⁴ Cf. a similar scriptural reminiscence in the *Contemptum humanæ legis*, p. 266 of MS. ᵃ An obvious mistranslation, the occurrence here mentioned (cf. note on Latin text) having taken place only once. ᵇ Exactly, for an offence against the sovereignty of the king. ᶜ This word is obviously misplaced here, and ought to be inserted in the latter part of the sentence between "which is" and "gylte". ᵈ Inaccurate: "Convicted of treason". ᵉ The construction of the sentence is not respected here and the meaning is altered; the clause "Tantam vim...similitudo" is an exclamative parenthesis, unconnected with what follows: "Such is the strength of a reciprocal agreement and similarity! For this see is as much moved...".

173 b  facile facit sancta sedes / quomodo nos ‖ hic in Anglia animum Roffensis pertentauerimus an se retexere et veritati contradicere vellet De quo etiam tanquam de re certissime gesta sancta sedes enunciat / libet enim hoc verbo vti propter eos qui in enunciatiuis verbis mendatio locum esse vel authoribus legibus affirmant[1] Roffensis in criminis quod ei obijciebatur disceptacione de more et legibus publice examinatus succubuit / Neque mos in extinguendis Rome Cardinalibus unquam probari nobis potuit / ut illis in carcere detensis et causis eorum ignoratis

174 a  orbi ipsi secretis iudicijs ‖ adiudicati intra parietes vitam deponant tormentis[2] Itaque publice accusatus Roffensis publice convictus et condempnatus / publice [eni] etiam* genere mortis apud nos in facino[rosis]ribus* nobilissimo mortis penas luit / atque adeo ipso qui pro carnifice tum deligebatur non eius ministro[3] id exequente / Neque enim est nobis Blosii in eo munere prefectus aliquis ac destinatus vt apud vos et alibi multis in locis / vnusquispiam enim a[4] carceratis prout res inciderit ad id conducitur[5] / vt appareat [te in] in hoc quemadmodum in reliquis multis non quod factum esse acceperas scribere proposuisse / Sed

174 b  quod causam exaggeret ‖ fierique potuerat non omittere /

---

[1] The sentence ends here. Gardiner means that in the text of certain laws, the word *enunciatio* is understood as meaning a statement of which the truthfulness is doubtful: " I choose to use this word, to take into account the opinion of those, who think that, by the authority of the laws themselves, what we call *enunciative words* may contain an untruth ".    [2] Allowance must here be made for Gardiner's customary use of rhetorical amplification. He certainly suggests wholesale slaughter; yet the only fact to which he can possibly allude seems to be the execution of Cardinal Petrucci in 1517. Petrucci had plotted with other cardinals against the life of Pope Leo X, and attempted to have him poisoned. The conspiracy was discovered and on June 22, 1517, its author was sentenced to degradation by a Consistory, and handed over to the secular arm. While his accomplices were pardoned, he alone was put to death in rather mysterious circumstances. The date of his execution was kept secret, and it is unknown whether he was beheaded or strangled. The official executioner was not employed on this occasion. The whole of the proceedings must have seemed suspicious to contemporaries, yet Petrucci had been tried regularly, and there could be no doubt as to his guilt, which he himself had confessed. (Cf. Pastor, *Geschichte der Päpste*, vol.i v, 1, 1. bis 4. Auflage, pp. 116–28.)    [3] Gardiner here makes a mistake as to the wording of Paul III's brief, and reads *ministro* for *ministerio*. Cf. note on fols. *169 b*–*195 b*.

coniecture, whow thatt wee here in Englonde haue assayd to thuttemost, the mynde of Rochestre, whether he wold turn, and say agaynst the troth, or nott, wherof, as of a thyng most certayn, this holy see makyth enunciation, wee thought it best, to vse this worde enunciation, for those which affirme by authorite of the lawes, thatt ther may bee a lye in the enunciatyve woords,[a] Rochester was openly examyned of the cryme layd to his charge, and accordyng to the lawes, and customes, he was convict.[b] wee cowde neuer allow, the maner of puttyng to deth of Cardinals in Rome, wher they beyng cast in to the prison, and ther cause nott knowen to the world, ar secretly Judgyd, and putt to deth,[c] within the walles of the prison, certainly Rochester beyng openly accused, openly convict, ‖ and condemnyd, did also suffre deth openly, and thatt suche a sorte of deth, which is with vs most noble, and execute by hem, which was all that tyme appoyntyd for hangman, and nott by his seruant, for wee haue none appoyntyd to thatt office (blosi) as ye haue, and in many other places, for with vs, soom one of the prisoners is hired to this office, after as it happeneth.[d] so thatt it apperith as well by this, as by dyuers other thyngs, thatt thy intent was to wryte otherwise then thow hardist to bee doon, and thatt thy mynde was to lett passe nothyng which myght sett fowrth thy cause, and was possible to haue byn doon, wherin thow doest playnely declare

208 a

[a] *Sic* for *e carceratis.*   [b] We have not been able to check Gardiner's statements from contemporary records. The following information concerning executions in the sixteenth century was kindly supplied by Prof. A. F. Pollard and Miss I. D. Thornley: "All matters connected with the 'execution' of justice and criminals came under the jurisdiction of the sheriff. In London there was a regular executioner and no doubt sheriffs elsewhere had the same. However, Gardiner here refers to prisoners put to death within the precincts of the Tower of London, and presumably either the Lieutenant or the Constable of the Tower would be responsible for the executions. Gardiner is probably right in saying that there was no permanent executioner for persons beheaded within the precincts of the Tower. In Anne Boleyn's case, a special executioner was brought over from St Omer; he was an expert swordsman who was paid a very high fee for the job". Gardiner also here refers in the case of Fisher, who was beheaded on Tower Hill, to a hired executioner, though one selected from among the prisoners.   [a] Cf. note on Latin text.   [b] Inaccurate: "Rochester, being publicly examined according to law and custom, was overcome in the discussion of the crime that was laid to his charge".   [c] "By torture" forgotten here.   [d] According to circumstances, as the occasion serves.

qua in re facile ostendis domini tui mores / qui hujusmodi fictionibus dilectetur / Vnde etiam adijcere nihil cunctatus es quam tu necem vocas / Roffensis acceleratam ac libentius inflictam quod eum ab illa sede cardinalem factum audiueramus[1] / denique ineptam illam consequentiam pari temeritate adiungis / crimen ese maiestatis multipliciter incurrendo[2] / : hic nunc cum sede agam illa sancta et queram ex quo tandem loco petitur argumentum morti[3] mulctasti id meritum Cardinalem. ergo minuisti Maiestatem romani Episcopi / aut[4] quomodo minuetur maiestas que

175 a nulla est / seruus vt est apud iurisconsultos capite ‖ non minuitur quia nullum caput habet[5] / Et seruus seruorum conqueritur de lesa maiestate / quod si vlla sit tibi vel tua opinione O paule maiestas / in eo videlicet constituta quod cardinalium numero constipatus auro atque bysso fulgens / tuoque diademate insignitus reliquorum occulis admirationem incutias / Vnde etiam num tibi in teipsum lese maiestatis accusatio competat / qui subditum alienum domino proditionis obnoxium et lese maiestatis crimine iam contaminatum tue quam vocas maiestati volueris adiungere / et in numerum Cardinalium cooptando tuam ipsius maiestatem eo facto contaminare quo [co] nomine

175 b certe iniurius tibi fuisti / et in eam ‖ quam te habere credis maiestatem contumeliosus / alioqui vero Serenissima Anglie Maiestas que maiestatem suam diuino iure subsistentem illesam conseruare studuit et in morte proditoris munitam restituere conata est / qui queso [pote] potuerit crimen

---

[1] There seems little doubt that such was indeed the case. Dr Hall, Fisher's biographer, states that the king said to Cromwell, in reference to the cardinal's hat sent to the bishop of Rochester: "He shall wear it on his shoulders, for head he shall have none to set it on". The imperial ambassador Chapuys wrote home on June 16, 1535, that Henry VIII "declared in anger several times that he would give him another hat, and send the head afterwards to Rome for the cardinal's hat". (Both documents in T. E. Bridgett, *Blessed John Fisher*, p. 359.)
[2] This clause is a quotation from the brief, and refers not to Fisher, but to Henry VIII, and his offences against the Pope's majesty.
[3] *Sic* for *morte*, the ablative being invariably used with *mulctare*.
[4] This second question refers to *queram*.     [5] We need not go into an unnecessary disquisition on the much-debated question of *capitis diminutio*, and the meaning of the word *caput*. Roughly speaking *caput* refers to the legal title which a citizen has to public or private rights; a title which he lost when he fell into *mancipium* or servitude.

the conditions*a* of thy lorde, which [delitith] delyteth mych in suche lyes: and therfor thow hast nott byn a frayde to say, thatt Rochester was putt to deth the more hastely, and the more gredely, bycause wee harde, thatt thatt see had made hym a Cardinall, and after thow doest adioyne w*i*th like folish boldnes, this consequent,*b* incurryng diu*er*sly the crime of the maieste offendyd or treason,*c* here now I will comen*d* w*i*th thatt holy see, and aske from whatt place she hath gatheryd this argument, Thow hast punishyd w*i*th deth a cardinall [deseruyng it] accordyng to his deseruyngs,*e* therfor, thow hast diminishyd the maieste of the bisshop of Rome, by whatt*f* reason may thatt maieste be diminishyd ‖ whiche is none, it is wryten w*i*th the lawes*g* thatt the state of a bondman can not be diminishyd, by cause he hath no state, and yett he w*hi*ch callith him self the bond man, of all bond men, complaynyth thatt his maieste is offendyd, And if thy conceyte sarve the so (O paulus*h* thatt thow hast a maieste, by cause thow, shynyng in gold, and bisse*i* and adornyd w*i*th thy imperiall crowne, and accu*m*panyd w*i*th a grete noombre of cardinals, doest make other men wonder vppon the,*j* take heed lest thou haue occasion to accuse thy self, of the hynderance of thy maieste,*k* w*hi*ch hast intendyd to adioyne to thy maieste, (as thow callest hitt) the subiect of a nother man, beying in his masters dawnger for prodition, and beyng also gilte*l* of the hinderance of the maieste of his m*aster*, and chosyng suche one to the noombre of Cardinalls, hast very myche spottyd thy maieste, and hast byn inivrious to thyself and also contumeliouse to thatt maieste which thow doest reken in thy self, for*m* by whatt meanes (I pray yow) myght the kyng of englonde his most noble maieste, in thatt, he endevoryd to maynteyn his said maieste, consistyng by the law of,*n* and in thatt he studyeth, to restore the hynderance therof by puttyng

208 b

---

It is clear that a slave could have no such *caput*. (Cf. F. Desserteaux, *Études sur la formation historique de la "capitis diminutio"*, Dijon, 1909.) *a* The manners or morals (*N.E.D.*), a suitable translation for *mores*. *b* *Consequence* (a term of logic): "You add that consequently, the king has made himself liable to a charge, etc.". *c* Cf. f. 207 a of English MS, note. *d* An obsolete spelling of *to commune*, meaning "to confer, discuss, debate" (*N.E.D.*). *e* This correction shows that the English text is in the translator's own hand, and possibly his draft or first copy. *f* Not clear: "and ask (that holy see) by what reason...". *g* More exactly: "in the works of lawyers". *h* The sign ) to be supplied here. *i* *Byssus* is supposed to be linen made from a fine kind of flax. Here no doubt the Pope's white vestments. *j* Look at thee in admiring wonderment. *k* More accurately: "On account of which, does not the charge of lese-majesty against thyself befit thee, who hast wished to annex, etc.". *l* Inaccurate: "Defiled with the crime of injuring his master's majesty". *m* Mistranslated: "On the other hand, by what means...". *n* "God" forgotten here.

53

incurrere / aut tuam in hoc facto vel maiestatem attingere
vel seruitutem / Nam hoc quidem verbo conuenientius
utereris vt qui qualemcunque te factis aliquando prebeas
verborum tamen appellacione non Regem aut Cesarem
quibus maiestas competit / sed magna vocabulorum
humilitate te infra seruos soleas nominare / Certe si
176 a maiestatem habeat sancta sedes / porro autem ‖ in eum qui
maiestatem leserit preter alias multas penas / proditoris
etiam appellacio omnino competat / Quis non iure ap-
pellauerit Cesarem proditorem qui romanam maiestatem
carcere per suos conclusit et detinuit / Nec nisi certis
conditionibus datis liberam dimisit[1] / proditor est christian-
issimus Rex qui iustis sepius ex causis bellum intulit
aduersus eandem maiestatem[2] Qua in re etiamsi a pena
iamdudum eos absoluerit eadem Maiestas / nunquam
potuit tamen omni sua indulgentia a culpa liberare / si
quam hujusmodi contraxisset / vt que nulla remissionis
spongia penitus unquam deleatur / Sed neque consistit vt
176 b qui ‖ dei maiestatem illustrare conantur in conseruanda
obedientia Christi maiestatem censeantur diminuere / qui
idem sit deus nedum eius qui se christi vicarium atque ad
illius Maiestatem defendendam sese reliquis prepositum
falso profitetur / Quare cum maiestas non sit que ledatur /
qui potuit ledi vlla in hoc maiestas / Quam tamen si con-
cederemus aliquam esse et eam prerogatiuam habere que
omnibus suis cardinalibus asylum prebeat et Immuni-

---

[1] The Pope was in fact only released from Castle St Angelo, where
the Emperor held him a prisoner, after he had signed an agreement,
according to which he promised to keep a neutral position between the
contending powers; to summon a general council for the reformation
of the Church, the uprooting of the Lutheran heresy, and the furthering
of the war against the Turks. The Emperor took six hostages and was
to occupy four towns of the papal States as security for the execution
of the treaty. On those conditions the rest of the papal States
was to be evacuated, as well as Rome. The Pope was also compelled to pay certain sums to the commanders of the imperial army.
[2] Francis I's main reason for making war against the Pope was his
wish to establish French supremacy in the Italian peninsula. We need
not enlarge here upon his Italian campaigns, the first of which took
place in 1515, and ended in the victorious battle at Marignano and the
taking of Milan; Pope Leo X was then a member of an Italian league
against France. In June 1521, the French invaded papal territory;

to deth a trayter,<sup>a</sup> by whatt reason I say doth he incurre any crime, or towche thy maieste[r] or rather servitute || for thow shuldest rather vse this worde, as he, w*hich*, (whatt so euer man*er* of man thow showest thi self in thy deds) in words thow are wont to name thi self,<sup>b</sup> [nother] nother kyng, nother emperor, to the which persons properly apperteyth<sup>c</sup> to haue a maieste, but w*ith* a grete humblenes in words, thow art wont to name thy self lawer<sup>d</sup> then bondmén, forsouth, if this holy see haue a maieste, and to hem whiche offendith this maieste, beside sondrye other paynes, apperteynyth the name of a Traiter, then we may lawfully call the emperor a traiter, which by his ministres<sup>e</sup> kept this maieste of Rome in prison, nother wolde delyu*er* it butt vppon certayn conditions, Then the most Christian king is also a traiter, whiche many tymes hath mad werre agaynst this maieste,<sup>f</sup> for the whiche causes, Allthough the same maieste haue long agon absoylyd<sup>g</sup> them from ther payne, yet it cowde nott w*ith* all hir indulging, delyu*er* them from the fawte,<sup>h</sup> for it is suche as may neu*er* bee taken a way w*ith* any sponge of remission, and these ij thyngs also can not stand togethers,<sup>i</sup> thatt those, w*hich* indevor them self to illustrate the maicste of god, in maynteynyng of obedience, shulde bee thought to diminish the maieste of Christ, bcyng onc god, and miche lesse* it can not hee thought, thatt the maieste of hem is diminishid w*hich* feynith hym self the vicar of Crist, and saith falsely thatt he is sett above others || for the defence of Christe his maieste, wherfor seyng ther is no maieste in this see whiche may bee offendyd, whow cowde his maieste be hynderyd,<sup>j</sup> And yett if wee shulde grawnte thatt ther war suche one, and had also this prerogatiue, to geve a sanctuarye, and immunite, to all his cardinals, in ther crimes and offens*es*,

209 a

209 b

Leo X sided with Charles V, and the united forces of the Pope and Emperor succeeded in recapturing Milan.     <sup>a</sup> Inaccurate and clumsy: "To restore and fortify it through the death...".     <sup>b</sup> The translator here suddenly changes from the third to the second person; the sentence ought to be altered as follows: "as he which (...) in words is wont to name himself...".     <sup>c</sup> *Sic* for *apperteyneth*.     <sup>d</sup> A Northern form for *lower* (*N.E.D.*).     <sup>e</sup> Somewhat inaccurate: "Who may not rightfully call the emperor a traitor, who...shut up and kept...".
<sup>f</sup> "For rightful causes" forgotten here.     <sup>g</sup> Assoiled, absolved. The sentence might be improved by substituting "from the which offences" to "for the which causes".     <sup>h</sup> "If they have contracted any such (guilt)" forgotten here.     <sup>i</sup> Obsolete form for *together*.
<sup>j</sup> The translation loses much of its previous quality in the present passage, and its clumsy lengthiness seems to imply greater haste or weariness on the part of the translator.

55

tatem in facinoribus adeo et sceleribus a maximis[1] non eousque tamen sese porrigat / ut etiam ad eos pertineat non modo qui iam sunt ante crimen admissum / sed etiam

177 a futuri sunt postea ad idipsum ‖ Cardinales ne commeritas penas ad exemplum persoluant / Nempe in similibus causis cum ius legationis[2] multa habeat priuilegia non competunt tamen ei qui legacionem ambiuerit ut fraudem faceret creditori / Quod si in* ea quam vendicat romanus Episcopus maiestatis pretextu prerogatiua eousque pertenderetur priuilegium / vt etiam ad futura pertineret / nouum genus aucupij uberrimique questus illi sedi nasceretur vt noxios vbiuis locorum liberent cardinaleo galero

177 b quem nemo [audeat] propter maiestatem ‖ auderet violare / Aliorum Maiestas est in conseruandis bonis istorum autem si que sit in tuendis a iusta vindicta malis / Egregia sane maiestas armis quidem per divitias et opes interdum armata / sed legibus ex diuina lege traducibus nusquam decorata vt de lesione iure et legibus conqueri haudquaquam possit / Nedum pene priuationis eo nomine infligi censeantur quales hec sedes meminit ipso iure inflictas et infligendas / Itaque ab illis nihil timemus / de eo autem

178 a nonnihil miramur / ‖ quo [tun] tandem modo sancta sedes noscere potuerit / ea tam indigna et abhominanda ac ad vniuersalem perniciem tendentia que a Sacratissima Anglie Maiestate per suos Caleti proposita ac a christianissima maiestate petita fuisse commemorat sancta sedes[3] / que

[1] The expression *sceleribus a maximis* lends itself to no ready interpretation. The meaning would seem to require not *a maximis* but *ad maxima*. Possibly *a maximis* may be referred to *immunitatem*; the meaning would then be: "immunity in regard to the highest powers". More probably *a* was interpolated by the scribe. In any case the translation does not agree with the text. [2] According to Roman custom, the ambassadors of nations which were on friendly terms with Rome were admitted to a number of special privileges; they were granted free lodgings and a regular allowance, a place of honour in public festivals, free medical attendance and a public funeral if they happened to die. As a civil lawyer, Gardiner would probably think of those prerogatives when writing the above passage, and stating that an ambassador's privileges did not include the right not to pay his debts. (Cf. Theodore Mommsen and Joachim Marquardt, *Le droit public romain*, Paris, 1889, tom. VI, pt ii, p. 214.) [3] Here as in other places Gardiner makes use of a display of rhetorical indignation to draw the attention of the reader from the real point at

bee they neuer so grete, yet it [exte] stratchith nott so ferre, thatt it may appertayne nott* only* on to those, whiche bee made all redy befor any offence commyttyd of them, but also those which after they haue offendyd, bee made Cardinals for this purpose thatt they* shulde not suffre punishment, accordyng to ther merits to the pernicious<sup>a</sup> example of others, for in like causes allthough ambassators haue by the lawe many privilegis yett, [yett] suche men as labor and make suetts for to haue thatt office of ambassaders to* defraude* ther* creditors* shall not enioye any of the sayd priuilegis, and if that prerogative which the bishop of Rome pretendith vnder the pretext of his maieste, shulde extende so ferre, that it shuld apperteyn to thyngs to coom, ther wolde arrise herof, a nue fashon and hawkyng;<sup>b</sup> and plentuous gaynes, to thatt see, for it might delyuer all sorts of offenders, in euery place, by sendyng to them the cardinals hatt, whiche no man durst violate, for fear of this maieste, The maieste of others consistyth in the conseruation of good men, the maieste of these men (if they haue any suche) standyth in defendyng of euyll men, from ther iuste punishments, fforsouth it is a noble maieste, armyd soomtymes, with goods, and riches, but neuer adornyd with any law, deriuid from god, so thatt it can nott complayne of hir hynderance by any lawe<sup>c</sup> ‖ nother any paynes of priuation can   210 a bee infligyd therfore, suche, as this see makyth mention, to bee infilct<sup>d</sup> all redye and to be like wise infligid in tyme cummyng, And therfor wee fear them nott, butt of one thing we maruell miche, bi whatt meannes this holy see might haue knowlege, of thos so onworthie, and so abhominable thyngs, tendyng to the vtter ondoyng of all the worlde, whiche this holy see reherseth to haue byn purposid,<sup>e</sup> by the ambasseders of the kyngs most sacred maieste, att Calеsc, and requiryd of the most Christian maieste, whiche thyng if they had byn

issue. How far grounded in fact Paul III's surmises were, in regard to the Calais "diet", appears from a number of contemporary State Papers. (Cf. note on the passage of the Pope's brief which Gardiner here confutes, p. 28 a of Camusat edition.)       <sup>a</sup> I.e. so that others may be terrified by the example of such ruin.       <sup>b</sup> More accurately: "a new fashion *of* hawking". *Hawking* must no doubt be understood here as "hunting birds with hawks". *Aucupium* means "bird catching, fowling, hence chase after something, or means of obtaining something, especially money". The phrase "hoc novum est aucupium" occurs in Terence (*Eunuchus*, II, 2, 16), its sense being: "This is a new means of gaining subsistence". Here we might translate: "New resources might hence accrue to the Roman See".       <sup>c</sup> So that it cannot take its stand on right or law to complain of any injury. <sup>d</sup> *Sic* for *inflict*. The brief here refers to the pains which the king, from the very moment he had committed his crimes, had incurred *ipso facto*.       <sup>e</sup> Proposed. Here, as in other cases, *to purpose* means "to put forward for consideration or for acceptance".

certe si fuissent reuera Caleti tractata / si rebus tam abhominandis cum consiliarijs Christianissime maiestatis questio incidisset / que in publicum non proferri aut propalari Serenissime Anglie Maiestatis interesset / magis tum ac magis augeretur admiratio / id potuisse expiscare[1] Romanum Episcopum presertim cum vt nos si quid ||

178 b eiusmodi fuisset honoris saltem nostri respectu secretum seru[i]assemus / ita etiam pari fide a consiliarijs Christianissime Maiestatis celata fuissent non dubitamus / Eam etenim amicitie synceritatem esse inter hos duos principes persuasissimum habemus / illis denique pactionibus et federibus communitam scimus ut consilia omnia communicata quecunque et apud alterutrum principem deposita in eodem secreti sinu reposita et collocata censeantur / Itaque si que talia aut proposita aut petita fuissent que

179 a feda et abhominanda || iudicarentur nunquam resciuisset Romanus Episcopus nunc autem cum nihil eiusmodi non modo non[2] dictum Caleti sed ne domi cogitatum quidem aliquando fuerit / nimis recte miramur / si spiritus mendatii qui semper ex proprijs loquitur illi videlicet sedi nimiumque familiaris / et iam hoc vt reliqua instillauerit ex quo nimirum liceat apercius deprehendere nobis quo spiritu vegetetur sancta sedes quibusque fictionibus ducatur ad iudicandum / Paulus in epistola ad Romanos christum docens de fratre iudicia temeraria prohibuit[3] /

179 b Paulus nunc e Romanis ad christianissimum || Regem scribens et Christi se in terris vicarium iactans / exemplo que certissima est doctrina et temeritatem in iudicando probat et apertam calumniam / Adeo in hoc loco non dissimulat cuius spiritus sit quemve agnoscat pro patre. vnde loquatur scribat dicat et faciat omnia / Nempe hoc eodem spiritu suggerente / false lachrimule oborte sunt / hoc

---

[1] *Sic* for *expiscari*, the mistake being perhaps due to a line in Terence (*Ph.* II, 3, 35): "Proinde expiscare, quasi non nosses", which may have left to Gardiner the impression of a transitive infinitive; more probably a mistake of the copyist. [2] *Sic*, the double negation being obviously a mistake. [3] An allusion to Rom. xiv, 13: "Non ergo amplius invicem judicemus, sed hoc judicate magis ne ponatis offendiculum fratri, vel scandalum". Cf. other passages in the same chapter. [a] Exactly: "to fish out", i.e. to search out, to find out.

treatyd att Cales in ded, if ther had any suche abhominable
matters byn in communication with the cownsellers of the most
Christian maieste, which, it war nott expedient for the kyng
of englond his most noble maieste, to haue talkyd att large, or
divulgat, I wolde maruell more and more, thatt the bisshop
of Rome cowde coom to any knolege therof,ᵃ specyally seyng
that wee, if any suche thyng had byn, wolde haue kept it
secrete for the regarde of owr honor, and in lyke maner, wee
dowte nott, they shulde haue byn kept, secret of the cownsellers
of the most christian maieste, for wee ar well assuryd thatt ther
is suche onfeynyd amite, betwen these ij princes, and wee
know the same to bee in suche wise confirmyd, with promises
and leges,ᵇ thatt all ther [secre] matters of cownsell which are
commoned betwen them, or sendᶜ from either to other, ar no
lesse secrete then if they had ‖ secretly remaynyd in one    210 b
bosome,ᵈ And therfor if ther had byn any suche thyng [haue
byn] purposyd or requirid which shuld haue byn thought so
fylthy, and abhominable, the bishop of rome had neuer
knowen them, butt now consideryng thatt no suche thyng
was spoken of att Calese, nother at any tyme* thought
vppon att home, wee maruell the lesseᵉ though the spirite of
lyeyng, whiche allways spekyth of his own,ᶠ and is to myche
familiar with thatt see, hath putt this in his mynde as he doth
manye other thyngs, wherby wee may playnely lerne,ᵍ by
whatt spirite this holy* see is quickened,ʰ and by whatt
fictions she is induced to geve her Jugements, Paulus in his
epistle to the Romans, [on to the Christian king] teaching
Christe, did prohibitt rasshe iugements of the brother,ⁱ And
now paulus writing from the Romans, on to the Christian king,
and bostyng him self to bee the vicar of Christe, in the erthe,
doth allowe by gyuing of example (which is the most certayn
teachyng) both rasshnes in iugements, and also manifest
calumniations, he dissimuleth nott in this place, of whatt
spirite he is, whom he knolegith for his father, whens he
spekith, writith, saith, and doth all things, fforsouth by the
motion of this spirite, those feynyd teares sprang owte, bi his

---

ᵇ Obsolete spelling for *leagues*.    ᶜ Obsolete form for *sent*.    ᵈ Misunderstood; the meaning is not "in the secrecy of the same bosom",
but "in the bosom (fold, hiding-place) of the same secrecy, in the
same deep secrecy".    ᵉ Inaccurate: "We marvel but too rightly".
ᶠ Through the mouth of those that belong to him.    ᵍ More accurately: "the more plainly gather".    ʰ From what spirit this holy
see draws its life.    ⁱ Forbade us to judge our brother rashly.

59

instigante conficti dolores quibus affectum se ea que ex voluntate temeraria facit / tanquam ex necessaria necessitate facere vult videri / hic idem spiritus se transformat in angelum lucis ‖ ut fucata et simulata verborum hypocrisi omnia pro pietate fecisse iudicetur / Nam et dei se voce ad vindictam excitatum affingit / O singularem impudentiam / deus qui christum misit affligendum et crucifigendum / eundemque opprobrijs contumelijs et iniurijs subiecit vilissimorum hominum / Idem nunc dicetur voce sua excitasse christi non ministrum / sed vt ipse quidem* iactat eiusdem vicarium ad vindictam / atque id scilicet ne veteres iniurias perferendo invitet nouas / video quo confugient et paulus et Blosius nempe ad aduerbium pene / dei inquient pene voce / neque dei vox vlla manauit sed ‖ pene / viderunt fortasse imminentem deum et ad sermonem labra componentem / facile diuinarunt quid voluerat dicere / Itaque pro modestia videlicet ne palam mentirentur / dei inquiunt pene voce excitati sumus ad vindictam / Seruus deinceps seruorum pene perpetuo habeatur vt dignus est qui cum aduerbii temperamento tam indignam deo vocem nihil sit* veritus attribuere / deus sibi seruat vindictam ad quam exercendam gladios porrexit et porrigit principibus / principes itaque vt scribit diuus paulus gladium gestant ad vindictam malorum / laudem vero bonorum[1] / hi vero qui pro ‖ christo legatione funguntur / et a vindicta priuata deterrere debeant omnes atque iniurias ipsi veteres perferendo nouas etiamsi que accesserunt hominum malicia et equanimiter ferre et vna cum veteribus pro thesauro repositas[2] tanquam preciosissimas et veras crucis christi reliquias amplecti et expostulari[3] / hoc enim docuit verbum patris Jhesus Christus cuius vox non pene sed clare exaudita est / vt pacientia ac humilitate in bono malum vincamus / A vindicta vero omni nisi quatenus eam deus

180 a

180 b

181 a

---

[1] The same words occur in *Contemptum humanæ legis*, p. 255 of MS. [2] Similarly compare this sentence with *Contemptum humanæ legis*, p. 267 of MS, § 5.  [3] *Sic* for *expostulare*.  [a] One line was forgotten here by the translator: "and namely lest by putting up with old injuries, he should invite new ones" (these words are quoted from the brief).  [b] To temper or moderate their words; a very accurate rendering of *modestia*.  [c] *Are* to be supplied here.

instigation, those lamentations war feynyd, by reason wherof he wolde haue [all] it appere. those thyngs to bee doon of mere necessitie which he doth in ded of his own rasshe selfwill, this same spirite transformyth it self in to the angell of light, thatt by his payntid ‖ and feynyd hypocrise of woords he may be thought to haue doon all thyngs for piete, for he feynith him self to bee stirred to revenge [him] by the voyce of god (O greatt onshamefastnes) god, whiche sende Christe to bee affliged, and crucified, and mad hym subiect, to the reproches, contumelies, and wrongs of the most vile men, shalbee saide now to haue stirred by his voice, nott the ministre but the vicar of Christ (as he bosteth him self) to vengeance,<sup>a</sup> I see to whatt refuge, Paulus, and blosius, will flee, doubteles to this aduerbe, allmost, they will say allmost by the voice of god, for god did speke nothing, butt he had allmost spoken, perchawnce they did see god att hand, bi them and preparyng his lippes to haue spoken, and they easely coniecturyd, whatt he wold haue said, and therfor for* a temperance<sup>b</sup> and bicause they wold nott lic openly, they say, wee<sup>c</sup> now allmost excited by the voice of god to revenge, from hensfurth lett him bee for euer the bondman of bondmen in payne,<sup>d</sup> as he is well worthie, which hath nott fearyd, with the temperament of this aduerbe to attribute to god so onmete a voice, God reseruith vengeance to hym self, and for the exercise therof, hath giuen and gyuith swerds to the princes, and therfor princes (as saynt paule saith) doth bear the swerde to the vengeance of euyll men, and to the commen- dation of good men, but thei whiche vse ‖ thoffice of a messanger in Christs stede, and owe<sup>e</sup> to fraye men from private vengeance, and suffryng olde wrongs, patiently to take also* the nue iniuryes. if any suche happen by the malice of men, and to embrace the olde with the nue, and [make] bee well contentyd with them,<sup>f</sup> as the most precyous and true reliques of the crosse of Christe beyng laide vp for a trea*sor, This was the teaching of the worde of the father Ihesus Christe, whose voice was harde not all- most butt clerely, thatt by pacience, and humblenes, wee may vainquishe the euyll with goodnes, and thatt wee shulde absteyne from all vengeance, butt onlye in suche cases wher

211 a

211 b

<sup>d</sup> An obvious mistranslation; it is clear that Gardiner is still playing upon the adverb *pene*; the meaning of the clause is: "let him be almost the bondman of bondmen for ever". A pun of the translator on *pene* and *pœnæ* seems far less likely than a mistake.      <sup>e</sup> "Have it as a duty or obligation to frighten men from...". *Owe* is the present of *ought*, obsolete in this sense.      <sup>f</sup> Inaccurate and weak: "to seek them, to ask for them vehemently".

181 b  per magistratus exercuerit abstineamus / ‖ Atque hec
quidem vox cum certa sit firma et inflexibilis sola digna
sit et ydonea cui reliqua consonent et quadrent omnia /
temerarios hominum clamores si vel spectat cum sint /
aut cum reuera non sint / fingit Romana sedes non repre-
hendam / facit enim se digna   Nam quemadmodum
scribunt de meretrice iurisconsulti.  quod licet turpiter
faciat corpore merendo / tamen meretrix iam cum sit / non
turpiter accipit / sic enim de hac sede sancta videtur
182 a  dicendum / quod licet turpissime ab illa ‖ prisca sanitate /
que olim viguit in hanc quam nunc vendicat sanctitatem
degeneravit / tamen postquam ita se questui palam ex-
posuerit ac se prostituerit mendacijs / nihil deinceps turpe
illi esse potest aut indecorum vt eam fabule partem peragat
quam sibi suscepit peragendam / Itaque in extremo actu*
huius tragico comedie quam sibi breui verborum compendio
complexa est.  misso videlicet breui ad Christianissimum
Regem pergit esse sui similis sancta sedes / et quem falso
per mendacia in crimen vocat / eundem pari temeritate ‖
182 b  condemnat / Quanti sit momenti huius vel sedis sententia
vel pauli ex causis et antecedentibus[1] facile est existimare /
Nempe si hereticus est qui christi religionem amauit
semper et coluit / atque ab heresibus defendit incolumem /
Si schismaticus qui summum in ecclesia christi vere
doctrine consensum et optauit et pro virili curauit[2] / Si
qui suam maiestatem illibatam conseruare studet / is cum
proditorem ne Maiestas minueretur plectendum cauit.
ficticiam Romane sedis Maiestatem ledit / aut si ledi
183 a  Maiestas que nulla est queat / ‖ denique si hec qui facit
Regno se suo priuat / tantum hoc allegacionis superit[3]
nobis vt paulum cum venerabilibus fratribus in sancta sede
licet vere / in re tamen aliena temere iudicasse dicamus /

---

[1] From the motives alleged and from past happenings, past actions.
[2] These two clauses are no doubt an allusion to Henry VIII's
*Assertio septem Sacramentorum*, composed in 1521 as an answer to
Luther's treatise *De Captivitate Babylonica* (1520), and to the controversy which followed, in which Fisher engaged on the king's side
(cf. note on fols. *170 a*–195 b of the MS). The allusion is also probably
to the steps taken under Henry VIII and in pursuance of his orders

god shall exercise it by the officers,[a] And seen thatt this voice is certayn, firme, and inflexible, it oweth alone to bee worthie and mete, to the whiche all other shuld bee agreable, and consonant! I can nott blame the see of rome allthough she regarde the rasshe crying owte of men, whan ther bee any suche, or though she fayne suche, when none suche bee in ded for therin she doth lyke hir self, for like, (as the lawers wryte of a whore) thatt allthough she doo filthelye* [onlawfully],[b] in that she playeth the whore, yet beyng ons a hore doth nott then [against] filthely* [the law][c] in takyng money therfor so it semith thatt wee may say of this holye see the whiche[c] nottwithstonding that it is verye shamefully degenerate from thatt olde holynes whiche was then lyvely in hir, in to this holynes whiche she || now takyth vppon hir, yett seen she hath openly exposid hir 212 a self to the getyng of money[d] and abandoned hir self to lyes, ther can bee from hensfourthe nothyng shamefull, or onmete for hir, butt thatt she may finisshe thatt fable which she hath taken vppon hir to bring to thende, And in the last pagent of this tragicall comedie, which it hath comprehendyd in a few words, in thatt bref sent to the most christian kyng, this holy see contynucth to bee lyke herself, and thatt man whom she by lyes falsely accusith. the same she condemnith, with like temerite. Of whatt importance the Judgment of this see, other of paulus, shuld bee, it is easely perceyuyd of these causes and antecedents, for if he* bee an heretike which hath allwayes louyd and wurshippyd the relligion of Christe and* defendyd* it* save* from* heresie* If he be a schismatike which hath allwayes desired and procurid to his power, a full consent of the true doctrine in the churche of Christe, If he that studyeth to kepe his maieste ontowchid, and providith the traitor to bee punisshid for thintent, his maieste shuld nott bee diminishid haue hurte thatt feynyd maieste of the see of Rome (if thatt maieste, whiche is none, may bee hurtyd) And finally if he whiche doth these || things depriuith himself of his realme, 212 b wee shall haue only this to allege for vs, though paulus with his venerable brethren in thatt holye see haue juged truely, yett wee may say they juged onadvisydly in a nother man his

to check the spread of Protestant doctrine, such as the burning of Luther's books, and the numerous trials for heresy which will be found related in the pages of Foxe.    [3] *Sic* for *supererit.*    [a] Magistrates.    [b] These words are not erased in the MS, but the corrections are interlined above them.    [c] The construction is defective: "We may say...that although it is very shamefully degenerate... yet...".    [d] For gain.

Nunc autem cum apertis mendacijs non obscuris fictio*nibus* manifestis s*er*monu*m* excessib*us* et a grauitate iudicior*um* alienissimis plena sint om*n*ia / nemin*em* puto futuru*m* qui chr*is*ti veritat*em* professus eius qui se chr*is*ti vicarium iactat me*n*dacijs com*m*oueatur Id quod quonia*m* anim*us* illi vt videtur presagit futuru*m* nimiru*m* vt mendax impudentia facile contemnatur / Arma tandem meditat*ur* et ex*er*citus / vt causa*m* cu*m* ceperit quo iure quaq*ue* [iur] 183 b iniuria per phas nephasq*ue* vincat obtineatq*ue*. || Sed fundati supra firma*m* petra*m*[1] verba impiorum non time-mus. / Qui habitat in adiutorio altissimi in protectione dei celi com*m*orabit*ur*[2] / Ip*se* liberabit nos de laqueo venantiu*m* et a verbo asp*er*o[3] / Scuto circumdabit nos*[4] veritas eius, qua*m* idem faxit vt om*n*es agnoscant / fucos pr*e*stigia et artes oderint ac detestent / deniq*ue* paul*um* a paulo / vicarium pr*e*tensu*m* chr*is*ti ab ip*so* chr*is*to internoscere norint atq*ue* distinguere / vt syncera*m* chr*is*ti doctrina*m* om*n*es implectentes verbis scriptis morib*us* et artib*us* eandem expr*im*am*us* / et referamus / vt paulini quidem no*n* pap*a*tici[5] sed eua*n*gelici om*n*es habeamur / et appareamus in conspectu dei qui nos filios eiusd*em* per || 184 a Ih*esu*m chr*is*tu*m* fieri / et no*min*is eius in baptismo professione in uni*ue*rsali chr*is*ti ecc*les*ia concludi et contineri / atq*ue* in eadem gloriari facit / Qui[6] sit honor in secula *etc.*

[1] Cf. Ecclus. xxvi, 24: "Fundamenta æterna supra petram solidam"; Matth. vii, 25 and Luke vi, 48: "Fundata enim erat super petram" (the house built on rock which is not carried away by a flood).

matter, now seen thatt all is full of open lyes, no darke<sup>a</sup>
feynyngs, manifest excesse of words, and ferre wide from the
gravite of any Jugements. I thinke ther will bee no man
whiche professith the truth of Criste that will bee mouyd *with*
these lyes of hym whiche bosteth hym self to bee the vicar of
Criste. And by cause his mynde gyueth hym (as it semith)
that it shall coom to this passe that his onshamefast lying will
bee lightly contemnyd, att the laste, he studieth to haue hosts
of men, and werre, to tinthent<sup>b</sup> he may ouercoom and obteyn
his purpose in that matter *which* he hath begon iustely or
iniustly, by right or wrong, butt wee beyng grownded vppon
the stedfast rock, fear nott the woords of the wyckyd, he thatt
firmely tristyth in the help of the hyghest god, he shall delyu*er*
vs from the snares of the hunters and from thatt sharpe worde,
his truth shalbee a buclar to vs, the whiche trothe I pray he
will cause may be knowen of all men. so thatt they may hate
and deteste payntynge ‖ Jugglyng, and crafte. and thatt they   213 a
may know paule, from paule, and putt a difference betwen thatt
pretendyd vicar of Christe, and Christ him self, so thatt wee
all embrasyng the synceie doctrine of Christ, may also expresse
the same, in words, wrytyngs, maners, and doyngs, thatt wee
may all bee taken folowers of paule, nott papisticall, butt
evangelicall, and thatt wee may so appere in the sight of god,
*which* grawnteth vs to be made his soonnes by Jh*esus* Christe,
and makith* vs* by the profession of his name in baptisme,
to bee concluded and [contey] conteyned in the vniuersall
churche of christ and to* glorye in the same to whom bee honor
for euer.

---

<sup>2</sup> Ps. xc, 1.   <sup>3</sup> *Ibid. v.* 3.   <sup>4</sup> *Ibid. v.* 5.   <sup>5</sup> *Sic.*   <sup>6</sup> Cui.
<sup>a</sup> Literal rendering of: "non obscuris fictionibus", obvious fabri-
cations.   <sup>b</sup> *Sic* for *thintent.*

# THE ORATION
## OF
# TRUE OBEDIENCE

# The oration of true obedience

## Stephan*i* Win*toniensis* Episc*opi* Oratio

Existimanti mihi, et cogitatione[1] mecum tacita con-
sideranti, præsentem in ecclesia Anglicana ordinum
statum,[2] in quo permulta quæ uel hominum, uel temporum
uitio iamdiu confusa, nonnulla autem labefactata, quædam
etiam collapsa, ac tantum no*n* funditus euersa essent, ad
pristina rursus diuini operis fundamenta, appenso uerbi
dei perpendiculo, reuocata, reposita ac restituta esse cum
uiderem,[3] Subibat animu*m* continuo meum, non sine
ueneranda quadam admiratione, diuinæ ueritatis inuicta
uis, et magnitudo, quæ nimirum licet humanæ interdum
persuasioni ruinas pergraues, ac diuturnas perpessa
uideatur, manet tamen ipsa solida semper, firma, atq*ue*
certa, ho*min*u*m* quidem no*n* nunq*uam* prestigiis, atq*ue*
fucatis artibus, ceu nebulis quibusdam paulisper obducta,
at tempore à deo præscripto, solis instar, tenebris tandem
discussis, et profligatis sese denuo proferens, atq*ue*
uindica*n*s: ut iustificetur deus in sermonibus suis, et
uincat cu*m* iudicetur. Neq*ue* uero dubito quin in hanc
eandem, aut certe haud multo dissimile*m* cogitatione*m*[4]
mecum multi, iiq*ue* docti, graues, ac boni uiri inciderint,
quibus inepta quadam, et inueterata superstitione im-
peditis, ueritatiq*ue* aliqua*n*diu reluc-||tantibus, ead*e*m hæc
cogitatio omnes dubitationis scrupulos prorsus ademit,
lucemq*ue* ueræ ueritatis, diuina operante gratia attulit,
atq*ue* adduxit.[5] Equidem autem ut de meipso ingenue
confitear[6] cum legis, *et* literæ[6] ut ita dica*m*, emulator, ac
propugnator essem acerrimus, nec quicq*uam* illibentius
unq*uam*, aut inuitius facerem, quam ut à receptis, qualia-

---

[1] The Strasbourg edition has *cognitione*, but the Hamburg edition
has *cogitatione*. [2] The organisation, constitution of the Church,
not the orders of the Church. [3] Marginal note in the Strasbourg
edition here: "Veritas non semper latet". [4] The Strasbourg
edition has *cognitionem*, but the Hamburg edition has *cogitationem*.
[5] Marginal note in the Strasbourg edition here: "Episcopus VVinton
ueritatem tarde agnouit". [6] Commas here in the Strasbourg edition.

68

An oracio*n* / made in Latyne / by the ryght reuere*n*de father in God / Stephan / byshop of Winchestre / now lorde chau*n*celour of Engla*n*de / touchinge true obedience / and now tra*n*slated in to Englishe etc.

As I co*n*sidered and secretely waied in my self *the* present state of ordres in *the* churche of Englande wherin / wha*n* I sawe *that* very many thi*n*ges, w*h*ich (whether it were lo*n*ge of*ᵃ* men or of times) haue bene of lo*n*ge season co*n*fusely io*m*bled together*ᵇ* somthi*n*ges blemished*ᶜ* / *and* somthi*n*ges decayed / *and* almost turned quite upside downe / were by *the* perfite*ᵈ* lyne *and* plu*m*met of Goddes worde / called again / layde a newe / *and* restored vnto *the* aucie*n*t founda*c*io*n*s of Goddes worke: ano*n* came in to my minde (eve*n* w*i*th a certai*n* revere*n*t admira*c*io*n*) the invincible power *and* excelle*n*cie of goddes vnfaili*n*g*ᵈ* truthe / w*h*ich (albeit it semeth now *and* tha*n* vnto ma*n*nes pe*r*suasio*n* to susteine ve*r*y sore *and* lo*n*ge enduri*n*g ouerthrowes) yet it remaineth euer hoole / co*n*stau*n*t and certay*n*: and though it be darkened w*i*th me*n*nes sleighty iugglinges / *and* cou*n*terfait craftes / as it were w*i*th certayn mystes for a while yet at the tyme of God appoynted / it bursteth out agayne and sheweth it selfe clearely*ᵉ* / like the ‖ sonne / wha*n* darkenes is bannished and chaced awaye: *that* God may be founde Juste in hys saie*n*ges / and haue the victorie wha*n* he is Judged.

And I doubt not / but many bothe learned / grave / and right good men were in the self same / or not muche vnlike thought that I was in: *and* wher they haue ben tangled with a certain folishe and cankred vile*ᶠ* supersticion / and haue wrastled against the truthe / of a longe time / this advised considera*c*ion hathe pulled awaye all their scrupulous doubtes / and by the workinge of Goddes grace / hathe conveyed and brought the*m* in to the light of the true veritie. And to confesse playnly of my selfe / wher I was a very earnest setter furthe and defendour of the lawe and of the letter / as I maye so saye and wher I coulde doo nothing with a worse will nor more against my mynde / than to shrinke from any thinge that I had ben

*ᵃ Longe of,* "alonge of", meaning "on account of". *ᵇ* A good instance of the translator's style, the English expression being much stronger and more picturesque than the Latin *confusa*. *ᶜ Blemished* is inaccurate for "shattered". *ᵈ* Not in the Latin text. *ᵉ* Inaccurate for "claimeth its own right". *ᶠ Cankred vile* is both inaccurate and too strong for *inveterata* which means "rooted". The translator is here carried away by the thought of superstition and makes Gardiner speak in a tone which he in fact never assumed.

cunque essent, discederetur,[1] quo quidem longius meum in ea re iudicium a ueritate recessit, hoc certe uehementius, atque acrius quiddam in ueritate agnoscenda passus uidebar. non aliter sane atque oculi tenebrarum caligine hebetes iam facti, ad subitum irradiantis luminis splendorem solent obstupescere. Mihi namque illud haud datum fuit, quod Diuo Paulo constat accidisse: qui simulatque à deo prostratus ceciderit, uocem obedientiæ protinus emisit,

Act. 9. dicens, Domine quid uis me facere? hoc enim electo illi uasi uberior dei gratia contulerat, ut uocem corripientis dei, et ab errore reuocantis confestim agnoscens, totum se deo committeret regendum, et ei in omni ueritate statim obediret, ac pareret in omnibus. Ego autem etsi ueritati semper, quæ omnis haud dubie a deo manat, obediendum statui, in ipsa tamen ueritate discutienda, atque examinanda, difficilior protinus non acquiescebam. Sed ita me

f. 3 a comparaui ut tanquam om-||nium sensuum iudicium exigendo, nisi ea prius me, et auribus audisse, et naribus olfecisse, oculis præterea uidisse, manibus denique contrectasse sensissem, haudquaquam satis spectatum putassem, ut ueritati quasi perspectæ, et cognitæ intelligentiæ meæ sensum submitterem, et captiuarem. Quam meam cunctationem, quæ aliquibus fortasse nimis quam pertinax reluctatio uisa est, non prudentiæ sane, aut grauitati uolo adscribere, ne quis me uelut bonis uicinis destitutum, quod dicitur, meas me ipsius laudes putet prædicare, sed dei plane in ueritatis traditione constantissime[2] uarietati, ut par est, tribuo, atque assigno. à quo omnes cum docean-

Ioan. 9. tur, qui uidelicet docentur, secundum illud: Et eritis omnes docibiles dei, ut quisque se in assentiendo ueritati senserit[3] affectum enarrare quidem licet, ac profiteri, causas uero cur hic citius, ille tardius, alius nunquam[4] oblatam a deo ueritatis cognitionem amplectatur, neque

---

[1] The Strasbourg edition has *discederem*, which seems more logical.
[2] *Sic* in the Berthelet and Hamburg editions. The Strasbourg edition has *constantissimæ* which seems the true reading, God's workings being varied in appearance only but constant in their purpose.
[3] The Strasbourg edition has a comma after *senserit*, which alters the meaning. Here as in other places it is clear that the translator followed

before persuaded in<sup>a</sup> / what so ever it were: the further that my Judgement swarved from the truthe in that behalfe / so muche the more vehementlye *and* eagrelie me thought I was astonied / wha*n* I knewe *the* truthe: even as a mannes eies bei*ng* dulled w*ith* darkenes / are wo*nt* to be amased at sodayne brightenes / wha*n the* light breaketh out. ‖ For I had not Sig. B vij a the gift / that Paule vndoubtedly had / who / as sone as God had ouer throwne him / fell downe / and spake the wordes of obedie*nce* / sayeng / **Lorde, what wilte thou haue me to doo?** Act. IX.

For that chosen vessell had so muche pleyntye of the grace of God / that he *co*nfessed by and by / it was the voice of God / that checked<sup>b</sup> him / and called him from his errour / and so commytted him selfe hoolly to the governaunce of God / and obeyde him in all truthe / and did after him in all poyntes without any more adoo. But as for me (albeyt my Iudge-me*nt* hathe bene alwaye / that the truthe ought to be obeyde / whiche doubtles dothe come all together of God) yet in the discussing and triall of the truthe / I did not so easely content my selfe. But I so framed my selfe / *that* / as it had be*n* in askinge the Iudgeme*nt* of al my senses onles I perceaved / *thut* Winchestre I furst of all hearde them w*ith* myne eares / smelled them at circum*spe*cte my nose sawe<sup>c</sup> / them w*ith* my eyes / and felte them with my in trye*ng* the handes / I thought I had not sene ynough: to the intent<sup>d</sup> truthe tha*n* I might submyt and captiuate<sup>e</sup> the wytte of my vnderstondinge to the truthe / as though I had throughly perceaved and knowne it. This my leasure taking / which some perchau*n*ce recken for a to muche obstinate rebelling / ‖ my my*n*de is not to Sig. B vij b ascribe vnto myne owne wisedome or grauitie / lest any man wolde thinke / I were fayne (as they saye) to praise my selfe / for lacke of good neighbours: But I doo most co*n*stauntly affirme and impute it (as right is) vnto the sondry working of God / in setti*ng* furthe the truthe / of whom / all men / whan they are taught which be taught in dede / according to this sayeng: **And ye shalbe all taught** of God: as euery one Joa*n*. IX. shall fele him selfe affected in assenting unto the truthe / so maye he talke and make playne mencion. But as for the causes / whye this man embraceth the knowlege of the truthe whan God offreth it / more spedily / that man more slowly / and an other man neuer in all his life / it is nether geuen to

---

the Hamburg edition of 1536. <sup>4</sup> The Strasbourg edition has a comma here. <sup>a</sup> The meaning is not clear, yet *recepta* seems rather to apply to traditional notions generally accepted by all men, than to ideas accepted by Gardiner personally. <sup>b</sup> I.e., rebuked, reproved. <sup>c</sup> *Sic* for the punctuation, which ought to be thus: "at my nose / sawe them...". <sup>d</sup> The meaning is: "not seen enough for me to submit...". <sup>e</sup> *Captivate* means here "make captive".

semper perspicere est datum, neque altius quam scripturis expressum est, permissum inuestigare. Tantum abest ut causam tarditatis meæ coner in præsentia reddere, aut cunctationem illam, ceu propriam animi mei dotem, mihi arrogare quod ipsum non solum apud homines stultitiæ nota, sed impietatis etiam apud deum crimine non uacaret.

f. 3 b  quin potius orbi rationem reddere nolui[1] || quid meam mihi sententiam tantopere mutarit, quidque me a meipso, ac meis antehac cum uerbis, tum factis tandem coegerit dissentire. Coegit certe (ut uno uerbo dicam) quod omnes cogit, cum ita deo uisum est, uis ueritatis: cui parent tandem atque obediunt omnia. Quod te oro atque obsecro benigne, candideque lector, ut me de uera obedientia uerba facturum læta fronte feras, quæque tua causa uel rhetorum, uel dialecticorum leges a scriptore exigunt, ut nimirum in ingressu te uel beneuolum, uel docilem, uel denique attentum reddam, cuiusmodi nihil hactenus præstiti, ea tu tamen mihi, quasi accepta referas, et quasi uere soluta acceptilatione remittas. Nam cum ego me uere obedisse sentiam ueritatem agnoscendo, non possum sane mihi temperare, quin de uera obedientia aliquid in medium proferam, eamque si non pro rei dignitate dicendo ualeam illustrare, at certe publice eam prædicare, ac profiteri contendam. Atque ut quod proposui statim aggrediar, nihil esse aliud puto uere obedire, quam obedire ueritati. Deus autem ueritas est, ut scriptura testatur, in qua etiam maxime prælucet nobis, adeo quidem, ut qui aliunde conquirant, et a cisternis, atque lacunis hominum non ab ipso limpidissimo, et syncerissimo fonte petant, hauriunt

f. 4 a  interdum, et referunt nescio quid turbidum, || et lutulentum certè ad restinguendam humanarum cupiditatum sitim, quod omnino ueritatis est proprium, inefficax atque inane. Solus enim ille est qui aquam nobis prestat ueritatis salutarem, de qua, qui fidei per IESVM CHRISTVM proditæ

Ioan. 4.  obediendo biberit, is etiam ueræ obedientiæ fructum feret, ut non sitiat in æternum.[2] Nempe deus etiamsi in ueteri

[1] The Strasbourg and Hamburg editions have *uolui*, which is clearly the right reading, *nolui* being a misprint. Here again the translator follows the Hamburg edition.     [2] In the Strasbourg University library copy of the Strasbourg edition, the whole passage from "Deus

72

men alwayes to perceave / nor premitted[a] to searche out / farther than is expressed in scriptures.   So that myne intent is not / persently[b] to re*n*dre the cause of my slackenes / or to clayme that advised leasure taking / as a propre inwarde gifte of myne owne / which were not only a token of folishnes with me*n* / but also a very wyckednes towardes God: but I wolde rather yelde acco*m*pte to the worlde / what it was / that chaunged myne opinion so muche / and what caused me now at leyngh / to dissent from my selfe / and ‖ from myne owne former wordes and dedes.   And in dede (to tell you at a worde) that compelled me / that compelled all men / whan God seeth his tyme / euen the myghtye power of the truthe / wherunto all thinges at leyngh obeye and doo ther after.

Nou I desire and hartely praye the / gentill reader / to beare frendly with me / in speaking of true obedience / and suche thinges / as for thy sake / the rules either of Rhetorike or Logike / require of a writer *that* is / *that* I shoulde / at *the* beginnyng / geue the occasion either to be lovingly bent / or fytte to be instructe / or elles to be atte*n*tyve / w*h*ich as yet I have nothing done / yet geve the*m* to me agayne / as if thou haddest received the*m* / and *f*orgeve me the*m* / as though thou were perfitly payed of them in dede.

For seinge I perceave that I have obeyed truly / in aknowladgeinge the truthe / I can not chose / but set furthe somthinge openly / touching true obedience / and though I am not hable to speake of it / according to the worthynes of the thinge / yet myne endeavour shal be to speake it openly / and open it plainly.

And to come spedely to my purpose: I thinke / that to obeye truly / is nothing elles / but to obey unto the truthe. ‖ And God is *the* truthe (as scripture recordeth) wher in he geveth his chief lighte vnto vs / so muche / that who so euer seketh it in any other place / and goth about to fette[c] it out of mennes puddles and quallmyres / and not out of the most pure and cleare fountayne it selfe / they drawe *and* bringe vp now and than / I wote not what / fowle and myrye geare / vneffectual and to no purpose / for the quenching of mennes thirstie desires / which perteigneth all together proprely vnto the truthe it selfe.   For it is only he / that geveth vs the holsom water of the truthe / wherof / he that drinketh / in obeyeng the faith which Jesus Christ hathe published / he shall also bringe furthe the frute of true obedience / so that he shall neuer be thirstye.   For albeit God in the olde lawe / whan

lege cum iam cultum sui syncerum *et* purum, quem nunc
ueri adoratores in spiritu et ueritate sint exhibituri in
uictimis et sacrificiis adumbrare et significare decreuisset,
ipsas ideo uictimas et sacrificia summo *in* honore haberi,
parique religione præstari præcepisset, ut ostenderet tamen
quanto habuerit semper cariorem obedientiam, eam
omnino omnibus et uictimis et sacrificiis etiam tum ante-
ponendam fore in quamplurimis[1] sacræ scripturæ locis
manifeste declarauit. Sic enim Samuel ex spiritu dei

I. Regum. 15.  loquitur ad Saul, Numquid (inquit) uult Dominus holo-
causta et uictimas, et non potius ut obediatur uoci domini?
Melior est obedientia, quam uictimæ, *et* auscultare magis,
quam offerre adipem arietum. Moyses etiam in deutero-

Deutero. ii.  nomio obedientiam populo commendaturus ait, En
propono, inquit Moyses, in conspectu uestro hodie benedictionem et maledictionem. Benedictionem, si obedieritis

f. 4 b  mandatis domini dei ‖ uestri, quæ ego hodie præcipio
uobis: maledictionem, si non obedieritis.[2] Diuus autem

Rom. i.  Paulus huius ueræ obedientiæ illis uerbis meminit, cum
ad Romanos scribens se gratiam, et apostolatum accepisse
refert ad obediendum fidei in omnibus gentibus *et*c. Fides
enim obedientiam exigit, uidelicet ut dei uoluntatem in
Christo, qui est uerbum patris agnoscentes, atque illius
merito gratiæ dei participes effecti, per eundem etiam
dominum nostrum, et obediendo credamus, et credendo
obediamus. Quisquis autem deo, atque in deum credendo
sperat, atque ab eo solo remunerationem expectat, neque
extra deum operum factorumque suorum fines porrigit,
sed illis limitibus circumscribit, ut tanquam a deo profecta, à quo omnia bona procedunt, etiam in deum referat,
illumque et initium unicum boni, et finem esse agnoscat.
hic certe est qui uere obedire dici potest, ueritatem uide-

---

[1] In the Strasbourg copy, the sentence is underlined by hand from
"habuerit" to "quamplurimis", while a manuscript note in the margin
insists on the same thought in the following words: "Obedientia
prestanda omnibus sacrificijs".  [2] Moses' words are underlined by
hand, from "En propono" to "obedieritis", in the same copy, the
stress being again laid by a contemporary Protestant reader upon
obedience to God as against obedience to the "ordinances of men".
[a] Inaccurate: "That even then obedience was to be preferred to
oblations..."  [b] Take heed.  [c] The translation is here definitely

he had determined in slaine sacrifices and offringes / to shad-
dowe and signifie / his owne syncere and pure service and
honour (which the true wurshippers should doo now in spirite
and truthe) and for that cause gave strait commaundement /
*that* those slaine sacrifices and oblaciones shoulde be had in
highe honour and devocion / to shewe / how muche more
dearely he estemed obedience / he hathe manifestly declared
in many places of the scriptures / *that* he setteth more by
obedience[a] / ‖ than by all oblaciones *and* sacrifices. For so Sig. C a
speaketh Samuel out of the spirite of God / vnto Saul: **Wolde** j. Regum xv.
**the Lorde haue offrynges and sacrifices** (saythe he) **and not
rather that the Lordes worde shoulde be obeyed? Obedience is better, than burnt offrynges, and to take heade,**[b] **is
more, than to offre the fatte of rammes.** Moses also in Deu. xj.
**Deuteronomio,** commending obedience vnto the people /
saythe: Lo (sayth Moses) **I set before your faces this daye,
blessinge and cursinge.** Blessinge, **if ye obey vnto the
commaundementes of the Lorde your God, which I
commaunde this daye: and cursinge, if ye doo not obey.**
 Of this true obedience Saint Paule maketh mencion / in Rom. j.
these wordes writing to the Romaines / where he saithe / he Faithe
requireth
obedience.
receaved grace and apostleship / that faythe might be obeyde
amonge all people. etc. For faythe requyreth obedience /
that is that we acknowlageinge the will of God in Christ / Than a true
faith maketh
which is the worde of the father / *and* beinge made partakers no reconyng
of the grace of god / by his merite / shoulde also / through of his owne
workes.
the same Christ our lorde / bothe beleue in obeyeng / and
obeye in beleving.  And who so euer putteth his perfite
belefe and hope in God / loketh for rewarde at his only
han-‖des / and without God compteth not vpon his owne Sig. C b
workes / and dedes[c] / but poynteth them their limites / so that
he rendreth them vnto God / as though they were done of
God / from whom al good thinges procede / and acknowlageth
God to be the only begynnyng and fynysshing of all goodnes:
that man is doubtles he / that maye be sayde / to obeye truly /
that is to saye / in folowing the truthe / and for truthes sake in

inaccurate and, we may add, dishonest, for it brings in the notion of
"justification by faith only" which is not to be found in Gardiner's
Latin text. The latter is rather vague and prosy, and the clause
"neque extra deum operum factorumque suorum fines porrigit"
should be translated almost literally, "and sets no other bounds to
his works and deeds but God himself", that is to say, makes God
his only motive and end. This rather general and harmless assertion
was altered by the translator so as to make it appear that Gardiner
had once professed the dogmatic tenets of Protestantism.

licet sectando, et præ illius amore omnia contemnendo, quæ fallax hic mundus et magnifacere solet, et ostentare. Quam quidem obediendi ueritatem ut dilucide, ac manifeste non auribus modo, sed oculis etiam cerneret, atque conspiceret mortalium genus, nempe ut ad eam consectandam *et* exterius, et interius a patre cælesti quotquot futuri sunt filii traherentur, à patre processit uerbum in ||

f. 5 a uirginem Christus Iesus: indutusque uero ac mortali corpore iam caro factus, idem deus et homo habitauit in

Ioan. i. nobis (gloria etiam eius in signis, et uirtutibus manifestata quasi unigeniti à patre) et quem nemo unquam uidit, deum nobis enarrauit, uerasque obedientiæ uias præiuit, et præmonstrauit, ut sicut per inobedientiam unius hominis

Rom. 5 peccatores constituti sunt multi, ita per unius obeditionem iusti constituantur multi: et superata morte, quam inobedientiæ peccatum induxerat, uera iam uita in Christo ex obedientiæ uirtute uiueretur. Fidere enim deo atque illi firmissime adhærere, quam iusti uitam appellat Scriptura[1]. hoc certe illi obedire est, et obedientiam exercendo corpus castigare, carnem in seruitutem redigere,[2] regnum peccati, quo ad licet, conuellere, à deo pendere, membra nostra in iusticiæ seruitutem mancipare, nostra contemnere, et dei amore quæ sunt aliena curare, deum ipsum pro premio sperare, nec absque deo, aut præter deum ipsum quicquam plausibile, aut iucundum ducere.

Exod. 20. Hoc autem est dominum diligere ex toto corde, qui uidelicet zelotes est deus, neminem ferens in amore communem, sed qui totum sibi exposcit hominem, nec in partes diuelli patitur, ut duorum dominorum præceptis subseruiat, sed se solum adorari uult, et sibi soli à suis

f. 5 b inseruiri. Cuius certe diui-||næ uoluntatis mysterium a seculis inscrutabili dei consilio absconditum, reuelauit nobis in fine temporum noster Christus, humani generis hostia, *et* piamentum, qui iustissimam dei iram placando,

i. Pet. 2. doctrinam obedientiæ factis ædidit salutarem, et pro nobis passus est, nobis relinquens exemplum, ut sequamur

---

[1] A comma is here rightly substituted for the full-stop in the Hamburg edition. [2] From I Cor. ix, 27. [a] *Sic* for *whom*. [b] The meaning of *fidere deo* is "to trust to God" and not "to believe in

contemnyng all thinges / that this deceaveable worlde / is wont bothe to make shewe of / and to magnifie.

And to thintent mankinde shoulde clearely and playnly / not only with eares / but also with eies / vnderstande and see this truthe of obedience / that is to saye / to thintent as many as are children / shoulde be drawne / both outwardely / and inwardely / of the heavenly father / to atteyne that truthe: the worde (Jesus Christ) proceded from the father in to the virgine / and taking vpon him a very true and a mortall body / became fleshe / and the very same / bothe God and man dwelt among vs / shewing his glorie in signes *and* power / as the glorie of the only begotten son of the father / and tolde vs playnlye of God / whom no man hathe sene at any time / and went before / and ‖ shewed vs the true wayes of obedience / that lyke as by the disobedience of one man / many became synners / so by the obedience of one / many shoulde be made righteous / and that / deathe (wom*ᵃ* the synne of disobedience brought in) beynge ouercome / men shoulde truly lyve in dede / in Christ / by vertue of obedience.    For to beleve*ᵇ* surely in God / and to cleave constauntely vnto him / which the scripture calleth a righteous mannes lyfe / is doubtles to obey him / and in exercising obedience / to chasten the body / to bring the fleshe in to seruitute*ᶜ* / to subdue the kingdome of synne / as much as lyeth in vs: to depende of God / to make our membres seruauntes of righteousnes / to set light by our owne commoditie / and for Goddes sake / to care for other mennes / to trust that God himselfe wil be our rewarde / and without God / or besides God / to compte nothing pleasaunt*ᵈ* or delectable.

This is to love the Lorde / with all our hearte / which is a gelous God / that can not awaye with any man / that serueth euery maister / but he requireth to have the man all holle to him selfe / and not to be hewen in peces / to serve two diverse maistres commaundementes / but he will be only worshipped / and ‖ he wilbe only served of them that be his.    This secret will of God / being (by his vnsearcheable devise) hidden from the begynnyng / is now in the ende of the world / reveled vnto vs / by our Christ / the slayne sacrifice and raunsom of mankynde / who in appeaceing the most iustly deserved wrathe of God / hathe declared the holsom doctrine of obedience in his dedes / and hathe suffred for vs / leaving vs an ensample / *that* we shoulde folowe his fotesteppes / w*h*ich if we will considre / we

*(marginal notes)*
Joan. j.
No man hathe sene God / at any tym.
Sig. C ij a
Matth. xxij.
Exo. xx.
Sig. C ij b
Goddes secret will reueled in Christ.

God". Here again the translator may have been tempted to bring in "only faith".    *ᶜ Sic* for *servitude.*    *ᵈ* Wrong translation, the meaning of *plausibile* being "praiseworthy, to be approved of".

uestigia eius; quæ quidem uestigia si considerabimus, reperiemus plane obedientiæ ueritatem eam demum esse, quæ uoluntatem dei in uerbo, qui Christus est, mortalibus proditam cæteris omnibus postpositis exequitur in mandatis, et à deo excitata, in deum etiam qui dat et uelle et operari pro bona uoluntate refert effectum, *et* finem.

Luce. 2. Itaque cum Christum iam in templo docentem, et in ueræ obedientiæ officio uersatum interturbaret mater, Nonne scis, inquit, quia in iis quæ patris mei sunt oportet me esse? ut ostendat manifeste etiam naturæ affectum diuinæ uoluntati parere oportere, nihilque prius esse debere,

Ioan. 14. quam præcepta diuina obediendo præstare. Sicut, inquit,
Mat. 15. mandatum dedit mihi pater, sic facio. Et alibi, Non sum missus nisi ad oues. *etc.*[1] innuens nihil esse petendum, quod ueræ obedientiæ officium uiolaret. Cum passionis hora iam appropinquaret, eamque orationis formam
Matt. 26. ædidisset Christus, quæ nostræ fragilitati in imminentis
f. 6 a mortis periculo maxime conueniret, orans, ‖ Pater, si possibile est, transeat a me calix iste. Subiecit tum, ut obedientiæ uictoriam faceret clariorem, Non sicut ego uolo, sed sicut tu uis. Cuius patris præceptis in mysterio redemptionis nostræ prorsus paruit deus filius, ut nobis quomodo pareamus ostenderet. qui ne uinum tamen parderemus[2] infusa, quod dicitur, aqua, et omnem obsequendi fructum amitteremus, idem suis uerissimis, atque certissimis uerbis nos alibi docuit, id quod factis etiam comprobauit, non suam se gloriam obediendo
Ioan. 8. quesisse, sed patris. Ego, inquit, gloriam meam non quero, sed patris. Si glorifico, inquit, me ipsum, gloria mea nulla
Matth. 5. est. Et alio in loco nos de hoc clarius admonens, Sic luceat, inquit, lux uestra coram hominibus, ut glorificent patrem uestrum qui in cælis est. Quod si ab hominibus laudem speramus, aut uanam gloriam consumpta hic mercede,
Matt. 25. uacuis olim uasis in conspectu altissimi tanquam uirgines fatuæ apparebimus, grauissimam ab adueniente sponso
Matth. 6. repulsam passuri. Itaque ne sciat sinistra quid faciat

---

[1] The complete text in Matth. xv, 24 is: "Non sum missus nisi ad oves, quæ perierunt, domus Israel." [2] *Sic* for *perderemus*. The mistake is corrected in the Strasbourg and Hamburg editions. [a] Stirred

shall playnly fynde / that to be true obedience / which (all other maters set aparte) executeth and practiceth the will of God / exprest to mankynde in the worde / which is Christ / and being stered vp$^a$ of god / ascribeth also the effecte *and* ende vnto God / which geveth the gifte / bothe to wil and to worke / according to his owne good will. Therfore whan Christes mother troubled him / as he was teachinge in the temple / and occupied in the office of true obedience / **Doest thou not knowe,** quod he, **that I must nedes be about my fathers busynes?** to shewe manefestly / that even the affeccion of nature / ought to obey the will of God / *and* that nothing ought to be done / before the commaundement of God / by obedience. **As the** | Joan. xiiij **father commaunded me** (saithe he) **so I doo,** ‖ And in an other | Sig. C iij a place / **I am not sent, but vnto the lost shepe of the house** | Mat. xv **of Israel**: shewing therby / *that* nothing ought to be desired / *that* shoulde blemyshe$^b$ the office of true obedience. Whan the houre of Christes passion drewe nere / and whan he had made that forme of prayer / that shoulde be most convenient for our weake frayltie / at the peril$^c$ of deathe / **Father, if it be possible, let this cuppe passe from me:** he added straight-wayes (to declare the victory of obedience / more playnly) **Not as I will, but as thou wilte.** Which his fathers com- | Matth. xxvj. maundements / God the sonne obeyed to the vttermost in the mysterie of our redempcion / to shewe vs how we shoulde obeye / and because (as the olde sayde sawe is) we shoulde not spill the wine with powring in water / and lose all the frute of obedience / he hathe also with his owne most true and most certayne wordes / taught vs in an other place (and perfourmed the same also in his dedes) that he sought not his owne glorie / through his obedience / but his fathers. **I** (saithe he) **seke not myne owne glorie, but my fathers. If I** (saythe he) **glorifie my** | Joan. viij **selfe my glory is nothing.** And in an other place / he geveth vs more playne warning of this / sayeng / **Let your light** (saythe he) | Mat. v. **so shine be-**‖**fore men, that they may glorifie your father,** | Sig. C iij b **which is in heauen.** Yf we trust vpon commendacion or vayne glorie at mennes handes / we lose our rewarde / and shall | Take hede appeare one daye before the presence of almightie God / with | of *that* be emptie vesselles like the folishe virgines / and shall suffre a | tyme ther most grevous repulse of the spouse at his comming. Therfore | fore. let not thy left hande knowe what thy right hande dothe: left | Mat. xxv.

---

up.    $^b$ This is a late meaning of *violare*, the sense being here more probably the classical one, "to be contrary to, to hurt".    $^c$ That is to say: "at the hour in which we are in peril of death".

dextra. Sinistrum est, obliquu*m*, et prauum quicquid est
carneum. Noli igitur co*n*spurcare et co*n*taminare diuina
Matth. 6. humanis,[1] sed seorsum a carne in abscondito obedias, et
deus in abscondito reddet tibi. Atq*ue* huc referri posse
puto, quod scribit diuus Paulus, inquiens, Non is, qui ||
f. 6 b in manifesto Iudæus fuerit, Iudæus est, neq*ue* quæ in
Rom. 2. manifesto carnis circuncisio fuerit, circuncisio est, sed qui
in abscondito Iudæus fuerit, is demu*m* Iudæus est, et
cordis circu*n*cisio est circuncisio, quæ co*n*stat spiritu, no*n*
Psal. 15. litera, cuius laus non ex hominibus, sed ex deo est. Sit
itaq*ue* dominus et pars et summa hæreditatis nostræ, qui
solus certam restituet hæreditatem. Nempe obediamus
deo propter deum, quæ sola uera obedientia est: quæ eò
regreditur unde cepit, et a ueritate profecta, in ueritatem
Colloss. 3. tendit, eodemq*ue* principio continetur, *et* fine. Quo
quidem temperame*n*to Diuus Paulus obedientiæ normam
proposuisse uidetur, cum seruis iuberet, ut dominis
propter deum forent obedientes, ostendens plane deum,
et illius iusti obsequii, quod a seruis præstatur carnalibus
dominis authorem esse, et remuneratorem. ut quicquid
illius nomine factum apparuerit, ratum id ab eo, atq*ue*
acceptum iri non dubitemus. In quam sente*n*tiam
Luce. 6. scriptum apparet in eua*n*gelio, Beati eritis, cu*m* uos
oderint homines. *etc*. propter filium hominis: gaudete, et
exultate, quoniam merces uestra multa est in coelo. Nam
i. Pet. 3. si debitam legibus pœna*m*, ut habet diuus Petrus, luentes
colaphizati patiamur, quæ nobis gratia? legibus etenim
hoc exhibetur,[2] non deo. quema*m*modum nec illud quan-
f. 7 a tu*m*-||uis specie pium ullam a deo mercedem promerebitur,
quod aliquid hic terrenum uenetur, aut gloriæ, aut
existimationis humanæ, quod hypocritarum est, quibus

---

[1] The words are almost the same as in the first sentence of the tract
*Contemptum humanæ legis*, but here the stress is laid upon the absolute
superiority of divine law, with a view, no doubt, to imitating Protestant
phraseology and enlisting Protestant sympathies. [2] This is literally
rendered in the translation, which retains both the Latin word ("is
exhibited" for *exhibetur*) and its meaning "to produce, to present,
to supply." [a] An obvious mistranslation, *sinistrum* being not a

hande mater is vngayne*a* / and wicked what soo euer procedeth of the fleshe. Doo not therfore defyle nor marre Goddes maters with mannes devises*b* / but obeye secretly from the fleshe*c* / and God shall rewarde the in secrete. And herevnto I suppose it maye be applyed / that S. Paule writteth / sayeng: **Not he that is a Jewe openly, is a Jewe: nether is the circuncision of the fleshe, that is done openly, circuncision, but he that is a Jewe secretly, is a right Jewe, and the circuncision of the hearte, is the circuncision, that consisteth in the spirite, and not in the lettre, whose praise is not of men but of God.** Let the lorde therfore be both our parte / and the hole summe of our enheritaunce / who only shall restore a sure enheritaunce vnto vs: that is to saye / let vs obey God for Goddes ‖ sake / which only is true obedience: which returneth thider / whence it came / and wher it proceded of truthe / it gothe in to truthe / and is conteyned of all one beginnyng and endinge. By this maner of ordre / it semeth that Saint Paule set furthe the rule of obedience / whan he badde seruauntes / be obedient vnto their maistres for Goddes sake / declaring playnlye / that God is the author and rewarder of that iuste obedient seruicc / that seruauntes doo vnto their bodily maisters: so that what so euer shall certainly appeare to be done in his name / we maye not doubte / but he will accepte and take it in good parte. And according therto / it appeareth to be written in the Gospell: **Blesshed*d* shall you be, whan men hate you, and persecute you etc. For the sonne of mannes sake, reioyce and be gladde, for your rewarde is great in heauen.** Forif wesuffre buffeting iustly for our faultes (as. S. Petre saithe) what gramercie is it to vs? For *that* is exhibited vnto *the* lawes *and* not vnto god / even as that is not worthy of any rewarde at Goddes hande / how godly so ever it seem in outwarde appearaunce / that hunteth after any earthy mater / glorie / or estimacion of man / *which* is *the* propretie of hypocrites / vnto

*Right margin notes:*
Mat. vj.
Defile not goddes maters *with* *the* deuyses of men.

Rom. ij.

Psalm. xvj.
Sig. C iiij a

Col. iij.

Mat. v.

noun, but an adjective, and an attribute of *quicquid* like *obliquum* and *pravum*. The meaning is "whatever is of the flesh is perverse, tortuous and corrupt". *Ungain* as an adjective means "not plain or direct" (*N.E.D.*).   *b* *Mannes devises* is borrowed from current Protestant phraseology, in which it refers to religious observances. Gardiner is here made to say more than he meant.   *c* That is to say "separating thyself from the flesh".   *d* *Sic* for *blessed*.

illa dei uox competit, Recepisti mercedem tuam: Sic enim
maledicetur homini, qui non obedierit deo: id quod
duobus modis contingit, uel cum dei præcepta aut am-
biendæ gloriæ, aut aucupandi questus gratia in speciem
apud homines exequimur, de quo superius nonnihil
diximus.

Cuius rei in singulis iudicium sibi deus seruauit
in diem iusti iudicii promulgandum, grauissime interdicens:
ne de cuiusquam in ea re animo temere pronunciemus,
etiamsi in uniuersum quod nos fecimus de hoc genere
peccati, ut de omnibus disserere non prohibuerit, aut in eo
de quo etiam hominibus pronunciare permittitur, cum
ueram obedientiam fucata obumbramus, et neglecto dei
præcepto aliunde in quibus exerceamur, accersimus, ad
illam seuerissimam diuinæ ueritatis sententiam obsurdes-
centes, Frustra colitis me in mandatis, et doctrinis hominum,[1] qui quidem mea uiolastis præcepta propter traditionem uestram.[2]

Quod ne fiat, prima nobis cautio esse debet, ut notam
certam illam, et digito dei obsignatam teneamus, qua
facile ab humanis diuina distinguamus, ne confundantur.
Primum itaque illud constet, elo-||quia dei, quæ in sanctis
scripturis ipso spiritu sancto dictante æditis continentur,
certissimam dei uocem ad nos referre, ut ex illis intelli-
gamus, discamusque uoluntatem eius, eiusdemque præceptorum, et dogmatum certitudinem, ut eam uiam
mandatorum edocti, ad patriam recta tendamus æternam.
In illis ergo quid tandem præcipitur? præcipiuntur
quidem multa, quorum in ueteri instrumento quædam
non ad animi præcipue iustitiam, sed ad populi conditionem relata, in hoc nouo populo in Christo renato,

---

[1] Strange to say, this hackneyed catchword of Protestant controversy
is not found in this form in the Vulgate, where the text runs (Matth. xv,
9): "Sine causa autem colunt me, docentes doctrinas et mandata
hominum". [2] The same remark applies to this text (Matth. xv, 3),
which runs thus in the Vulgate: "Vos transgredimini mandatum Dei
propter traditionem vestram". Both texts are underlined by hand in
the Strasbourg copy, and were obviously understood in a Protestant
sense. Yet Gardiner's concession to Protestant tastes is here purely
verbal; at any rate he was not long in taking exception to the
Protestant use of the very same texts, as will be seen in *Contemptum
humanæ legis*, p. 268 of the MS, and *passim*.     [a] The translation of

who*m that* sayeng of God is ‖ me*n*cioned: **Thou haste receaued thy rewarde.** For so shall the man be cursed / that obeyeth not God / which happeneth two maner of wayes / either whan we put the commaundementes of God in practyce in outwarde shewe before me*n* / or elles for ambicious vayne glorye / or vauntage sake / wherof I have spoken somthing allready before. As for the finall iudgement of this mater / God hathe particularly reserued it vnto him selfe / to be pronounced at the daye of his iuste iudgement / most earnestly inhibiting vs / that we pronounce not rashely of any mannes hearte in that behalfe / yea / though they doo al together as evil / as we have done in this kynde of synne / as he hathe not prohibited men to talke of all thinges / or in that / that men are permitted to iudge of*a* / whan we cloke true obedience with countrefait obedience / and neclecting*c* that / that God commaundeth we provide vs other ware to kepe vs occupied withall / turnyng the deafe eare to that most sore sente*n*ce of Goddes truthe: **In vayne doo you worship me, in the commaundementes and doctrines of men, seyng you haue broken my præceptes for your owne tradicion.**

The curse of god two maner of wayes

Goddes commaundement not to be cloeked*b* wi*th* mennes

Mat. xv

And to the intent we doo not soo / we ought furst of all to take hede / that we kepe surely ‖ that marke / which is certai*n* and is signed with the fyngre of God / wherby we may make a distinctio*n* betwene Goddes causes and mannes / that they be not shuffled together. Furst of all therfore / recken vpon this for a certaynti*e* / that the talke of God / conteyned in the holy scriptures / by the declaracion of the holy goost / doth reporte vnto vs the most certayn true worde of God / that we maye therby vnderstande *and* learne his will / and the certayntie of his commaundementes and doctrine / to the intent / being*c* instructe that waye of commaundementes / we may goo straight to the cou*n*trey euerlasting. Than Sir / what is commaunded in the*m*? Many thinges are commau*n*ded in them surely: wherof som thinges in the olde testame*n*t were chiefly spoken / not to iustifie the soule inwardely / but for the keping of the people in ordre / which in this newe people regenerate in Christ / are vanyshed awaye euen as it were by the light of

Sig. C v a

the sentence, from "ne de cuiusquam" to "accersimus", is simply meaningless, and the following rendering may be substituted for it: "(forbidding) that we should rashly pronounce on this subject in regard to any man's heart, though he have not forbidden us to discourse in general, as we have done, on this kind of sin as on all others—in so far at least as even men may be allowed to pronounce; a kind of sin which we commit when we cloak, etc.". The translator's misunderstanding of the text, as well as his obscurity, seem to show that he had no time to consider difficulties, and that his translation was a piece of hasty work.   *b* *Sic* for *cloaked.*   *c* *Sic* for *neglecting.*

tanq*uam* succedente tenebris ueritatis luce, euanuerunt. quorum tractatio superflua iam foret; et aliena, ut qui de iis dumtaxat præceptis dicere instituerim, que[1] no*n* uni Matthei. 5. populo deus, sed per unum populu*m* cu*n*ctis ge*n*tibus decreuerat significare, quoru*m* ne iota quidem unu*m*, aut apex præteriret. Quæ quidem præcepta a nonnullis moralia sunt appellata, quæ etiam cum ad sanctimoniam, casti- tate*m*que uitæ, ac morum pertineant, uim adhuc solidam, et integram obtinere censentur. id quod nos persuasum habeamus cum multis ex aliis locis, tu*m* ex illo præsertim euangelii, ubi Christus populu*m* docens tam aperte pro- nuntiat, non aliter ingressuros nos regnu*m* cœleste, nisi iustitia nostra, plus q*uam* scribarum, et phariseoru*m* abundauerit. Qua quidem sententia etia*m*si phariseorum f. 8 a iustitiam non ‖ omnino probauerit Christus, utpote humanam solum et carne tenus. i*d est*.[2] externa factorum hypocrisi consistentem, neq*ue* ab illo manantem fonte spiritus, quem sola dei gratia in eiusdem Christi meritis facit irriguu*m*: nobis tamen hac collatione iudicásse[3] uidetur et admonuisse de puritate moru*m*, qua*m* in scribis et phariseis lex exigebat, nihil per euangelii doctrinam re- mittere et relaxare ipsum, sed illa uerborum significatione etiam castitatis, et sanctitatis fines longius proferre eiusque augme*n*tu*m*, ac progressum in hac noua lege exigere uelle. Na*m* libertas, qua nu*n*c per eua*n*gelium donati sumus, quæq*ue* lege*m* Moysaica*m* sustulisse creditur, non eò pertinet, ut moralium etiam præceptorum obliti, dissolu- tam, ac turpem uitæ co*n*ditione*m* sequamur. sed ut uitiis liberi sanctitati seruiamus, et quod dei uoluntas ad sancti- moniam pertinere scripturis aliquando insinuauerit, id sequamur, id amplectamur, in eo pareamus[4] diuino præcepto, ut obedientiæ nostræ, ratio queat constare. quorum quidem moralium in ueteri lege præceptorum, ut

[1] *Quæ* in the Hamburg edition.    [2] Abbreviated to ".i." in the Berthelet and Hamburg editions, but in full as "id est" in the Strasbourg edition, and thus understood by the translator.    [3] Thus in the Berthelet and Hamburg editions, but corrected to *indicasse* in the Strasbourg edition. The translator also adopted this reading.    [4] These three words are omitted in the Hamburg edition, and consequently not

truthe succedinge darkenes / which it were superfluous / and not to the purpose / to treate of at this present / forsomuche as myne intent is to speake only of those preceptes / which God determined to signifie / not vnto ane only sorte of people / but by one sorte of people / vnto all nationes / wherof not so muche as ‖ one iote or one title*a* coulde be pretermitted.    And Sig. C v b these / of som men are called / morall preceptes / which / forasmuche as they perteigne also to holynes and chastitie of life and maners / thei are denied*b* to abide still perfitily in their full streynght *and* vertue.  And ther of we maye be persuaded / as well by many other places / as namely by this place of the gospell / wher Christ teaching the people / pronounceth so playnly / *that* we shall not entre in to the kingdome of heaven / onles our righteousnes excede the righteousnes of the scribes and Pharisees.  In which sayeng / albeit Christ did not altogether allowe the righteousnes of the Pharisees / because it was only a humayne and a carnall righteousnes / that is to saye / it consisteth in outwarde hypocrisye of dedes / and sprong not out of that fountayne of the spirite / whom the only grace of God (in the same Christes merites) causeth to spowte water: yet by this conference / we take it / that he shewed and admonished vs / the pure behaueour / which the lawe required in the Scribes and Pharisees*c* / and not to remitte nor to set it at lybertie by the doctrine of the Gospell / but by that significacion of wordes / to enlarge the limites of holynes and chastitie / and to require ‖ the encreace and gooing forewarde Sig. C vj a ther of / in this newe lawe of the Gospel.  For the libertie which is geuen vnto vs by the Gospel / and is thought to haue abrogated Moses lawe / perteineth not to that intent / *that* we may forgete the morall preceptes and haunt a light dissolute / *and* filthie maner of life / but *that* we shoulde be free from synne / *and* become the servauntes of righteousenes / and that / loke what the will of God / teacheth vs in the scriptures / to tende vnto godlynes / we shoulde haunte *that* / and embrace that / according to goddes commaundement / so as the state of our obedience maye be constauntly certayn*d* of the which morall preceptes in the olde lawe / to speake of som (for my purpose

aliquot commemorem, nam singula numerare non est
leuitic. 18.[1] huius instituti, Leuitica illa de uetitis, incestisque con-
iugiis[2] præcepta ad castitatem, puritatemque matrimoni-
orum attinentia, in quibus et humanæ uitæ consuetudo
f. 8 b tota continetur, et propagandæ so-||bolis origo consistit,
eiusmodi semper sunt habita, quæ Iudæis quidem tradita
primum, quoniam essent ad illustrandam naturæ legem
explicata, ad uniuersum ideo mortalium genus perpetuo
pertinerent. In quibus haud dubie et naturæ uox, et
diuina iussio in unum conuenientes, quod ab utriusque
conditione diuersum esset, prohibuerunt. Inter hæc
autem cum illud de non ducenda uxore fratris præceptum
contineatur, quid aliud debuit, aut potuit serenissima regis
Angliæ maiestas facere, quam quod cum summo populi
consensu, suæque ecclesiæ iudicio fecit? ut ab illicitis,
diuulsa federibus, licita, permissaque copula frueretur,
et dei præcepto (ut par fuit) obtemperans, relicta quam
nec ius, nec fas retinere permisit, casto, legitimoque
matrimonio indulgeret? Qua in re cum diuini uerbi
sententia suffecisset, cui omnes incunctanter parere
debent, grauissimorum uirorum suffragia tamen, et cele-
berrimarum orbis academiarum censuras adhibere, non
est grauata sacratissima regia Maiestas. Nempe ut quæ
facere, et posset, et deberet, ea eruditissimorum, et opti-
morum uirorum calculis, recte prorsus fecisse iudicaretur.
atque eiusmodi obedientiam in eo præstitisse, cuiusmodi
diuini uerbi ueritas ab omni pio, atque bono uidetur
f. 9 a exigere, ut et deo paruisse, et uere o-||bedisse merito
dici posset: de quo quoniam dicere aggressi sumus, id
quod commodum in hunc locum sese obtulerat, non
potuimus taciti præterire. Sed redeamus ad institutum,
quod in eo potissimum uertitur, ut ostendamus eum demum
uere obedire, qui ambulat in lege domini, nec a mandatorum uia discedit, sed humili promptoque animo diuinæ se
uoluntati committit, ut dei authoritatem nunquam de-
fugiat, sed et ei ipsi obediat, et omnibus, quibus ipse
iusserit obediendum propter se. Nempe deus pro sua in

---

[1] The Hamburg edition has "Leuitic viij", which is wrong.
[2] Misprinted as *conjugij* in the Hamburg edition.     [a] *Sic* for

86

is not to make present rehersal particularly of them all) the Leuiticalle preceptes / touching forbidden *and* incesteous mariages / as ferre as thei concerne chaste and pure wedlocke / wher in the hole custome of mannes life is conteyned / and the original fonntayne*a* of the encreace of people consisteth / are alwayes reputed to be suche sorte / that being in dede geuen furst to the Jewes / (because they shoulde be declared to advaunce*b* the Law of nature) they shoulde perteyne to all maner of people in the hole worlde for euermore.  Wher in doubtles / bothe ‖ the voice of nature and the commaundement of God / have forbidden / what so euer is contrarie to the condicion of them bothe.

☞ And amonge these / seing / ther is a commaundement that a man shall not mary his brothers wife / what ought or coulde the king of Englande his most excellent Maiestie haue done / other wise than .(·). by the hole consent of *the* people / *and* judgement of his churche / he hath done? that is / that he shoulde be dyvorced from vnlawful mariage / and vse laufull and permitted copulacion: and obeyeng (as mete it was) conformablye vnto the commaundement / he shoulde cast of her*c* / whom nether lawe nor right permitted him to retayne / and take him to chaste and lawfull mariage. Wherin / .C. for asmuche as the judgement of goddes worde might haue suffised / wher vnto all men ought to obeye without stopping or stayeng / yet the kinges most royal Maiestie was content to have the assisting consentes of men of notable gravitie / and the censures of the most famous .D. vniuersities of *the* world. And all to the intent / that men shoulde thinke / he did / that he bothe might doo / and ought to doo vprightely wel / seing *the* best learned and worthy good men haue subscribed / vnto it: and that he shewed such obedience in so do-‖ing / as the truthe of goddes worde / semeth to require of euery godly and good man / so as it might be sayde that he bothe obeyde God / and obeyde truly: of whom / forasmuche as I am purposed to speake / I could not passe ouer *with* silence / that / that occasion had commodiously offred / vpon this mater.

But let vs returne to the purpose / which chiefly standeth in this poynt / that / we shewe / that he obeyeth truly / which walketh in the lawe of the lorde and blenchet*d* not out of the waye of Goddes commaundementes / but with an humble and willinge hearte committeth him selfe to Goddes will / neuer to refuse the autoritie of God / and to obey bothe him and al them / whom God commaundeth him to obey for his sake.

In dede / God / according to his exceding great and un-

Sig C vj b

☞

The kinges mariage *with* lady Anne chaste and lawful / you say / and he coulde not by Goddes law haue the lady Katherine.

.(·). Than *the* bishop of Cantorbury was not all *the* doer / but *the* church *and* parliament.

Sig. C vij a

.C. If it were so by goddes worde than why doo you say nay now? Why dothe .D. Ridley lye *in* prison if this oracion be true? so by your double sayenges you are a double traitor *and* a very wethercocke

---

*fountayne.*   *b* Inaccurate for "to make clear" or "explain".   *c* Cast her off.   *d* *Sic* for *blencheth. To blench* means "to elude, avoid, shirk, to flinch from" (*N.E.D.*).

87

mortalium genus immensa, atque ineffabili bonitate ad augendum in nobis gloriæ cumulum, quo materiam nobis sisteret præsentem, in qua cum pietate, et merito nos ipsos exerceremus, homines substituit, tanq*uam* uicaria potestate obedientiam exacturos, quam illis nos pari cum fructu præstaremus propter deu*m*[1] ac si deo ipsi immediate, id quicquid esset honoris exhiberemus. Quo certe in loco pri*n*cipes posuit,[2] quos tanq*uam* ipsius imaginem mortalibus referentes, summo, supremoq*ue* loco uoluit haberi, eosq*ue* inter reliquas omnes humanas creaturas præcellere,

I. Pet. 2. ut scribit diuus Petrus. Seq*ue* authore eosdem principes
Prouerb. 8. regnare, ut prouerbia sacra testantur, Per me, inquit deus, reges regnant. adeo quidem ut secundum Paulum quis-
f. 9 b quis po-||testati resistit, dei ordinationi resistit: qui Paulus
Roman. 13 quod hic generaliter locutus, Tito explicans ma*n*dauit, ut
Tit. 3. admoneret uniuersos suis principibus obedire. Sunt porro et alii inter homines etia*m* a deo ad exigendam obedientiam constituti, sed ordine inferiori. Nam et marito uxor, et domino seruus, et quicunq*ue* quibuscunq*ue* subiecti sint, præpositis illis etiam obediant propter deum. Vnde certe accidere interdum hæsitatio solet, diuinæ legis sensum, non recte callentibus, quu*m* duorum præpositorum uno eodemq*ue* tempore ma*n*data dissideant, et inuicem collidantur, ac manifeste repugnent, utri primum, ac potissimu*m* sit obediendu*m*. Verbi gratia. Ma*n*dat dominus seruo id, cuius diuersum eodem tempore, eodemq*ue* momento imperat princeps: quibus utrisq*ue* cum obedientia propter deum debeatur ex uerbo dei, utriusq*ue* autem imperium uno, eodemq*ue* momento, ab uno eodemq*ue* homine obiri rerum natura haudquaq*uam* patiatur.[3] Hic ut ab aliquo fortasse, qui sensus non dum exercitatos habeat, subdubitari posset, cuinam seruus obedire primum, et potissimum teneatur: Ita ei qui in reliquis similibus causis animaduerterit, ita natura comparatum esse, ut inferiora superioribus sempe*r* sub-

---

[1] Comma here in the Strasbourg and Hamburg editions.   [2] Full-stop here in the Strasbourg edition.   [3] Comma here in the Stras-bourg edition.   [a] *Sic* for *hath*.   [b] The translator inverts two

speakeable goodnes towarde mankynde / to encreace habund-
aunce of glorie in vs / wherby he might establishe present mater
for vs / to exercise our selues godly and thankeworthyly in /
substituted men / who being put in autoritie as his vicegerentes /
shoulde require obedience / which we must doo vnto them with
no lesse frute / for Goddes sake / than we shoulde doo it (what
honour so euer it were) immediatly vnto God him selfe.‖

And in that place he hathe set princes / whom / as representours
of his Image vnto men / he wolde haue to be reputed in the
supreme / and most highe / rowme / and to excelle amonge all
other humayne creatures / as Saint Petre writeth: and that *the*
same princes reigne by his autoritie / as the holy Prouerbes
make reporte. By me (saythe God) Kinges reigne / in so muche /
that after Paules sayeng / who so ever resisteth power / resisteth the ordinaunce of God. Which Paule openyng that
playnly vnto Titus / which he speaketh here generallye / commaunded him / to warne al men / to obeie their Princes.

Sig. C vij b

Princes re-
present
Goddes
Image / *and*
excell all
men.
j. Pet. ij.
Pro. viij

And ther be other men appoynted also of God / to require
obedience / howbeit in an inferiour ordre. For the wife beinge
in subieccion to her husbande / the seruant to the maister /
and to whom so euer any man is in subieccion / they must also
obey their gouernours for Goddes sake. Wherof it chaunceth
now and than that som men / not vnderstanding *the* sense of
Goddes lawe rightly / stande in doubt / whan two gouernours
commaundementes geuen at all one self same tyme / varye /
and be contrary and manifestly repugnaunt one to *the* other /
whether of them ought furst and most principally to be
obeyde. ‖

As for example: The maister biddeth the seruaunt doo a
thinge / and the kinge commaundeth him to do a clcane contrary thinge / and bothe at one tyme / and in one moment.

Sig. C viij a

And forasmuche as they ought bothe to be obeide for goddes
sake / by the worde of God / the very nature of thinges / can
not admitte / bothe their commaundementes / to be applied
in at al one selfe safe time / and of al one selfe same man here
in like as it might perchaunce be doubted of som man that
hatheth[a] not yet his wittes / muche exercised / whether of
them the seruaunt is bounden chiefly and most principally to
obey / euen so vnto him / that marketh wel other like causes /
the solucion of suche a question shall anon playnly appeare /
that nature it self frameth the mater so / that *the* inferiours
must also serve and geve place to the superiours.[b] Therfore

clauses, and the sentence ought to stand thus: "Even so to him, who
observed in other like causes, that by the rule of nature itself, inferior
things should always be subjected to superior things—the solution,
etc.".

seruiant, ac locum de*nt*: h*uju*smod*i* questio*n*is enodatio
f. 10 a statim patebit. Itaq*ue* ‖ in exe*m*plo proposito no*n* dom*i*no
seruus pareat, sed pri*n*cipi, tanq*uam* dom*i*no illi[1] suo,
sup*er*iori, ut cui dominus pariter cu*m* seruo obedire teneatur. Quibus quide*m* seruo, dom*i*no, atq*ue* principe,[2] cum
unu*m* agnoscimus deu*m* superiorem, regem uidelicet
regum, et dominu*m* domina*n*tium, à quo omnia, per que*m*
omnia, in quo omnia[3] eius utiq*ue* præceptis omnes,
primu*m*, et ante omnia parere debent, seruus, dominus,
princeps: ut omnibus propter deum, nemini aut*em* extra
eum nedum contra eum obedisse uideantur. Itaq*ue*
laudatur etiam uxor marito morigera, sed usq*ue* ad aras,
Act. 5. ut est in prouerbio. Melius est enim deo obedire, q*uam*
hominibus. Ex his autem cum sit manifestum in obedientia ordine*m* esse seruandum, *et* ita cuiq*ue* nos primum
obte*m*perare oportere, prout is ordine alium ac prærogatiua diuinæ legis testimonio præcedat, operæ precium
uisum est, de ordinu*m* gradu necessario dicturum.[4] Illam
etia*m* hic attingere causam, quæ hodie ferme in manibus,
et ore omnium uersatur, et celebratur: Num iure[5] diuino
uniuersi populi Anglicani consensus imitatur,[6] quo in-
uictissimum, et potentissimum principem HENRICVM
octauum Angliæ et Franciæ regem, fidei defensorem, et
dominum Hyberniæ, summum in terris caput Ecclesiæ
f. 10 b Anglicanæ celebrat, et ueneratur, Eidemque in ‖ publicis
comitiis liberis suffragiis author fuerit, ut suo iure uteretur,
seq*ue* Ecclesiæ Anglicanæ caput no*n* minus nomine q*uam*
reipsa profiteretur. Qua in re nihil noui latum est, tantum

---

[1] The Strasbourg edition has the surprising reading *illo*.     [2] The
Hamburg edition rightly corrects this word to *principi*.     [3] Comma
here in the Strasbourg edition, full-stop in the Hamburg edition.
[4] Comma here in the Hamburg edition.     [5] The Hamburg edition
has *iuri*, both forms being equally classical.     [6] *Sic* in the Berthelet
and Strasbourg editions, rightly corrected in the Hamburg edition
to *innitatur*; the translator accordingly wrote "be grounded upon".
[a] *Sic* for *propounded*.     [b] The word is thus repeated by mistake in
the "Rome" edition.     [c] The present mistranslation seems almost
unaccountable, unless it be due to extreme hurry, since it contradicts the
translator's own marginal note, and spoils a text which makes entirely
for his own view of the relative importance of God's authority and
that of men. The text ought to be rendered thus: "Therefore a wife
is praised who obeys, but only as far as the altar, as the proverb says".
In other words obedience to a husband is only due so long as it does

in this propou*n*deth*a* example / the servaunt must not obey his maister / but the kinge / as his superiour mayster / as him / whom bothe / the maister and servaunt are bounden to obeye. And for asmuche as we acknowlage / that ther is one above bothe the servaunt / maister / and Kinge / even God / whiche is the Kinge of Ki*n*ges and Lorde of Lordes / of whom al thinges / ‖ thinges*b* / by whom all thinges / and in whom all thinges are: his co*m*maundeme*n*tes all men ought to obeye / principally and afore all thinges / bothe seruaunt / maister / *and* Kinge: that they may appeare / to haue obeide all men for Goddes sake / but noma*n* without God / nor against God. Therfore is the wife praised that obeyeth her husbande / yea / vnto deathe.*c* For it is better to obey God than men.

Sig. C viij b

All men ought to obey Goddes co*m*maunde-mentes though Princes co*m*maunde a contrary Act. v.

Thus in asmuche as it is manifest / *that* an ordre ought to be kept in obedience / and that our duetie is to obey euery one chiefly / after such sorte / as he excelleth other in ordre and prerogatyve by the testimonie of Goddes lawe: I thinke it requisite for me (seinge I am speaking of the necessarie degree of ordres)*d* to touche also in this place / that cause / which is co*m*monly in vre*e* / and spoken of at this daye almost in all mennes handes and in all me*n*nes mouthes: whether *the* hole consent of Englishe me*n* be grounded vpon Goddes lawe / in that they declare and honoure the most victorious and most noble prince Henry theyght Kinge of Englande and of Fraunce / defendour of the faithe / and Lorde of Irelande / to be in earthe the supreme headde of the churche of Englande / and is graunted vnto him / by autoritie therof / in the open courte of ‖ parliament / frely to vse his right / and to call himself supreme headde of the church of Englande / aswell in name as in dede.*f* Wherin / ther is no n'ewely invented mater

The Ki*n*ges supremacie grounded vpo*n* Goddes lawe.

Sig. D a

not come into conflict with obedience to God.     *d* Inaccurate: "It has seemed to us worth our while, that he who was necessarily going to speak of the degree of orders, should also touch..." or better: "it seems worth while for me, who am necessarily going to speak of the degree of orders, also to touch...".     *e* *In ure* (from French *œuvre*) means "in use, practice or performance". Rather a loose rendering here for *versatur*.     *f* The construction of the English sentence is both obscure and ungrammatical, and the text might be more clearly and more accurately rendered as follows: "whether the consent of the whole English people be grounded upon divine law, by which they declare and proclaim the most victorious...prince Henry VIII...to be in earth the supreme head of the church of England; and through which they gave him authority by free suffrage in the open court of Parliament, to make use of his own right, etc.".

significantiore uocabulo apposito, competentem principi iure diuino potestatem exprimi clarius uoluerunt, eo potissimum consilio, ut fucum illum a uulgi oculis amouerent, quem Romani episcopi ementita potestas, aliquot iam seculis obduxerat, non citra principis potestatem uehementer imminutam: quam saluam omnes, et ab iniuriis sartam tectam optare tenentur, et pro uirili præstare. Qua quidem in re certe non uideo, cur quenquam offendat, principem Anglicanæ ecclesiæ caput dici: magis quam regni Angliæ caput. Hic iam te appello candide lector, ut sepositis interim appellationibus, rem ipsam consideres. Neque enim ignoro utriusque appellationis uim[1] et ecclesiæ uocabulum non quamuis congregationem, nisi cum adiectione (ut odiui ecclesiam malignantium) significare: sed eam demum populi multitudinem, quæ Christiana professione unita in unum corpus coaluerit. Hoc enim usus obtinuit, ut ecclesiæ appellatio, alioqui communis, excellentioris tamen corporis propria efficeretur.[2] Regni uero appellatio latius patet, omnesque principis dominio subiacentes complectitur, qui-||cunque fuerint, et qualescunque Iudæi, Barbari, Saraceni, aut Turcæ, nedum Christiani. Cæterum cum in hoc, de quo agitur, ita se res habeat, quæ significetur, ut utrique appellationi ex æquo respondeat, atque ex eisdem hominibus hodie ecclesia constituatur Anglicana, qui sub regni uocabulo continentur, quorum caput dicitur princeps: sub appellatione regni Angliæ non erit, etiam[3] eorundem hominum caput cum ecclesia designantur Anglicana? Ita ne uero uerba, cum tantum eum usum habeant, ut sint rerum notæ, eatenus in hac causa ualebunt, ut etiam rerum ipsarum naturam in-

f. 11 a

---

[1] Comma here in the Strasbourg edition.  [2] That *ecclesia* was no common term, meaning simply "an assembly", or as the Protestants translated it, "a congregation", was Gardiner's contention in connection with the English version of the Bible, as early as 1541. At the convocation of the province of Canterbury held in that year "in the sixth session Gardiner publicly read a catalogue of Latin words in his own collection out of the Testament, and desired that for [on account of] their genuine and native meaning, and for the majesty of the matter in them contained, these words might be retained in their own nature as much as might be; or be very fitly

wrought / only their will was / to haue the power perteinyng
to a prince / by Goddes lawe / to be the more clearely expressed / with a more fitte terme to expresse it by / namely for
this purpose / to withdrawe that countrefait vayne opinion out
of the common peoples myndes / which the false pretensed
power of the bishop of Rome / had / for the space of certain
yeares / blinded them withall / to the great impeaschement of
the kinges autoritie / which all men are bounden to wishe /
and to their vttermost power / see kept safe / restored and
defended from wronges.    Wherin surely I see no cause /
why any man shoulde be offended / that the kinge is called
the headde of churche of Englande / rather than the headde of
the realme of Englande.  Here now I appeale vnto the[a] / gentill
reader / to set aparte the termyng of terme wordes[b] in the
meane season *and* to weyghe the mater selfe.  For I am not
ignoraunt / of the force of bothe the mamner[c] of speches / and
that this worde (churche) signifieth not euery congregacion /
but with and adieccion[d] (as / **I hate the malignaunt churche**)
but ‖ that only multitude of people / w*h*ich bei*n*ge vnited in
the profession of Christ / is growne in to one body.  For this
came in by custome / that this terme / churche / which elles
is a commo*n* terme / became (notwithstonding) the propre
name of a more excellent bodye.    But this worde (Realme)
is more playnly knowne[e] / and comprehendeth all subiectes of
the kinges dominions / who so euer they be / and of what condicion so euer they be / whether the[f] be Iewes / Barbarianes /
Saracenes / Turkes or Christianes.    Than / seinge in this
mater / which I haue in hande / the mater that is me*n*t by it[g] /
is of such sorte / that is[h] agreeth indifferently with bothe maner
of speches / and seinge the churche of Englande consisteth
of the same sortes of people at this daye / that are comprised
in this worde realme / of whom / the kinge his[i] called the headde :
shall he not / beinge called the headde of the realme of Englande / be also the headde of the same men / whan they are
named the churche of Englande? Shall the termynge of wordes /
inasmuche as they haue no*n* other vse / but to signifie the
thinges / be of suche force in this cause / as to turne the nature

All men
bou*n*de to
defe*n*de their
pri*n*ces
supremacie :
than he not
to suffre it
to be pulled
from the
crowne
though *the*
Quene wolde
forgoo it.

What *the*
churche is

Sig. D b

englished, with the least alteration...". The first of the list which follows
is *ecclesia*. (Fuller, *The Church History of Britain*, Oxford, 1845,
vol. III, p. 199; also in Wilkins, *Concilia*, 1737, vol. III, p. 861.)
[3] Punctuation in the Hamburg edition: "regni Angliæ, non erit
etiam...".    [a] Thee.    [b] Heavy and obscure for "to set aside for
the present the names by which the thing is called, and to consider
the thing in itself".    [c] *Sic* for *manner*.    [d] *Sic* for *with an adjection*
(with an epithet added to it).    [e] Mistranslated. "Regni appellatio
latius patet" means "the word *realm* has a wider meaning, a wider
extension, stretches farther".    [f] *Sic* for *they*.    [g] Obscure: "the
thing which has to be named".    [h] *Sic* for *it*.    [i] *Sic* for *is*.

uertant? ut pro nominum uarietate alius, atque alius homo in existendi ratione idem censeatur? Equidem non sum nescius relatione nominum nonnunquam mutari officia, atque eundem hominem prout alio, atque alio nomine afficiatur, partes etiam nomini conuenientes subire debere. Verum enimuero si princeps caput regni est, quod perinde est, ac si dicas, omnes quotquot intra regni ditionem sunt, tanquam uni corpori in existentes[1] adglutinatos habeat, ut illis pro capite præesse uideatur: an ullo modo fieri potest nominis mutatione, ut idem homo subsit capiti huic, et non subsit capiti huic in eodem genere subiectionis, nempe propter deum? Nam contra deum nulla est

f. 11 b  subiectio. Quam ridiculum igi-||tur illud, ut eundem hominem, quem si Ioannem libeat uocare, in Anglia commorantem, principi tanquam capiti subesse fatearis, hunc si uoces christianum eodem modo subesse neges? etenim quatenus in Anglia commoratur de regno est, quatenus uero christianus est in Anglia etiam commorans, de ecclesia anglicana esse censetur. Caput inquiunt princeps est regni non ecclesiæ: cum tamen ecclesia Anglicana nihil aliud sit, quam uirorum, et mulierum, clericorum, et laicorum in regno Angliæ commorantium, in christiana professione unita congregatio. Ecclesia uidelicet merito appellanda, quia communio sit christianorum, a loco uero, Anglicana, sicut et Gallicana, Hispana, atque etiam Romana. Itaque qui principem regni quidem caput fatentur, ecclesiæ tamen, si diis placet, in eodem regno congregatæ non concedunt (quæ est eorum siue inscitia, sive malicia) illud apertissime innuunt[2] principem caput esse infidelium, fidelium non esse. nisi ipse princeps sit infidelis, ut aut infidelis princeps fideli siue infideli populo

---

[1] The two words ought to be read as one: *inexistentes*. The misprint is corrected in the Strasbourg and Hamburg editions.   [2] Comma here in the Strasbourg edition.   [a] The sentence is obscure: "that one should be taken to be a different man in his manner of existence, according as he is called by different names".   [b] *Sic* for *being head.*   [c] Obscure: "which means no less than if you said that".   [d] *Sic* for *through.*   [e] Mistranslation: "to deny that he is subjected to the king in the same way".   [f] *Sic* for *the.*   [g] *Whereas notwithstanding* means here "and yet".   [h] Clause forgotten: "inhabiting

of the thinges them selues vp side downe? that one man shoulde be taken in his estate of beinge / and an other in his estate[a] / ‖ all one according to the diuersitie of names? I knowe wel ynough / that / by relacion of names / the offices are somtymes chaunged / and *that* the selfe same al one man / as he is called by this name or *that* name / must also doo the partes of office agreing to that name. But if the kinge be the headde of the realme / *that* is as muche / as a man wolde saye[c] / he hathe so many / as are within the dominion of the realme / vnited al vnto him selfe / as vnto one body / *that* they maye take him for their supreme headde / can it be by any possible meanes / throug[d] the mutacion of the name / for all one selfe same man / to be in subieccion to this headde / and not to be in subieccion to this headde / in all one kinde of subieccion / *that* is to saye / for Goddes sake? For ther is no subieccion against God. What a folye were it than / for a man to confesse that al one man (if ye lust to call him Iohan) dwelling in Englande / is in subieccion to *the* kinge / as vnto *the* headde: *and* if ye call him a christian / of *the* same sorte[e] / to saye *that* he is not a subiecte? For in *that* his abidinge is in Englande / he is of *the* realme / *and* in *that* he is a christian / dwelling in Englande / he is demed to be of the churche of Englande.   They[f] kinge (saye they) is the headde of the realme but not of the churche: whereas / notwithstonding[g] / *the* churche of Englande / is nothing elles / but *the* congregation ‖ of men and women / of the clergie and of the laytie[h] / vnited in Christes profession: that is to saye / it is iustlie to be called *the* churche / because it is a communion of christen people / and of the place / it is to be named / the churche of Englande / as is the churche of Fraunce / the churche of Spayne / *and* the churche of Rome.[i] So *that* they / which confesse the kinge to be supreme heade of the realme / and yet graunt him not to be supreme headde of the churche (on Goddes name[j]) beinge one congregocion[k] in the same realme (whiche is either their owne ignoraunce / or their owne malice) this is their playne meaning / that the kinge is the heade of the vnfaithfull / and not of the faithfull: except the kinge / him selfe be an infidele / that[l] either an infidele kinge dothe beare rule ouer a faithfull or vnfaithfull people / or elles the same kinge copuling[m] him selfe to the

Sig. D ij a

The king beinh head[b] of the realme must also be *the* head of *the* church

Sig. D ij b

*the* churche / is bothe of *the* laytie and clergye

the realm". [i] The rendering of the whole sentence is poor, the meaning being as follows: "It (the Church of England) is rightly to be called *a* church, since it is a communion of Christian people; and rightly to be called Anglican on account of the place in which it is situated, as also happens in the case of the Gallican church, the Spanish church, and even the Roman church". [j] Perhaps exclamative The meaning is "if such foolishness may be suffered to exist by the Gods". [k] *Sic* for *congregation*. [l] *So* that either the king, when an infidel.... [m] *Sic* for *coupling*.

imperet, aut idem princeps Christianæ se iungens ecclesiæ, omne deinceps imperium, et potestatem deponat. Quenquam reperiri, qui hoc innuat, satis certe mirari non possum, et tamen qui aduersantur, quid aliud dicant, non inuenio:

f. 12 a Fir-||mamentum aliud allegationis adferunt nullum, q*uam* quod nullo pacto consistat, et sibi constet. Caput inquiunt, regni est princeps, non ecclesiæ. O dictum absurdum, atque stolidum. Quasi uero quia populus iam cæpit fidere deo, iustissima causa sit, cur amplius non subsit principi, dei uicario, sed ab eius corpore omnino eximatur. At non ita docuit Paulus, qui dominorum ius in seruos Christi professione tradidit, non immutari, aut minui, sed integrum adhuc dominio conseruandum

Colloss. 3. admonuit, seruis præcipiens, uti carnalibus dominis sint obedientes propter deum. Vxoris ad fidem conuersio nihil detrahit imperio mariti, utpote qui caput adhuc manet uxoris, quæ etiam ne post fidei professionem, præposteri ordinis argumentum ædat, quod aliquorum animos abalienaret a religione, censuit Diuus Petrus, ut uxores fidem professæ, omisso prædicandi munere, quod uerbis exequerentur, lucrifacerent sine uerbo maritos per cast*am* co*n*uersationem. Ergo authoritas d*om*ini in seruum, et in uxorem ius capitis[1] marito religione non perit, et peribit principi? qui cum quandam dei imaginem in terris etiam infidelis dum est, refert ut caput, et dux populi dicatur, professione Christiana statu minuetur, nec

f. 12 b amplius caput illius populi, qui ecclesiam || constituit, dicetur, sed quò propius ad deum per fidem, qui unicus est aditus, accedit, hoc longius a dei imagine recedet, atq*ue* hoc minus populo uenerabilis esse incipiet, quo nomine uel maxime debeat honorari? Certe si caput est populi, idq*ue* diuina ordinatione, quod nemo non fatetur,

---

[1] Not the power of life and death, but the right of the husband to be the "head" of the wife, as in Eph. v, 23: "quoniam vir caput est mulieris". *a* Apparently not understood by the translator. The prince is the head of the state, which may be said to be his body. Hence if the people are withdrawn from his jurisdiction, they are "removed, taken away from his body", which is the meaning of the expression. *b* The whole of the passage is very poorly rendered and the translation will be amended in the following notes. "Through

Christian churche / geveth ouer (from thencefurthe) his autoritie and power. I wondre excedingly / that any suche one is founde / that can meane thus: and yet I can not finde / what thaduersaries haue to saye / for them selfes / but thus / As for any other sure and grounded allegacion / they bringe non / but suche as hengeth to gether in no pointe / nor agreeth *with* it selfe. The kinge (say they) is headde of *the* ‖ realme / but not of the churche. O what an absurde and folishe sayeng is that? As though / because the people begynneth now to beleve in God / it were a iust cause / why they shoulde be no more in subieccion to the kinge / Goddes lieftenaunt / but be exempte quyte from his body.[a] But Paule taught not so / which sayde / that *the* autoritie of maistres ouer their seruauntes sholde not be chaunged or dyminished through professing of Christ[b] / but warned them[c] to kepe it still in perfite autoritie / bidding servauntes / to be obedient vnto their bodily maisters for goddes sake. The conuerting of a wife vnto faithe / withdraweth nothing from thautoritie of her husbande / for he is the headde of the wife / still / and because she[d] / after she had professed the faithe / shoulde shewe no token of mysordre / wherby she might plucke the myndes of som from religion / Saint Petres minde was / that wives having professed the faithe / shoulde leave of *the* office of preaching / which they executed[e] by wordes / and winne (without *the* worde[f]) their husbandes through their chaste conuersacion. Therfore / the autoritie of the Maistre / towardes the servaunt / and the right of the husbandes superioritie ouer *the* wife / is not lost by *the* meane[g] of religion: *and* shal it be lost to *the* kinge? ‖ who / forasmuche as he (yea though he be an infidele) representeth / as it were the ymage of God vpon earthe / so that he is called the headde and the guyde of the people / shall his state be nypped of because of the christian profession?[h] *and* shall he be called no more the headde of the people / which is the churche[i] / but the nerer he draweth to God by faythe (which is the only meane to com to God[j] / shal he so muche the further goo awaye from Goddes ymage?[k] and shall he begynne to be had in so muche lesse reuerence with the people / for that names sake / that he ought most chiefly to be honoured for? Truly / if he be the headde of the people / and that by the ordinaunce of God / as

professing of Christ" means here "because the servant professes Christ". [c] *Them* is not in the text. "Paul gave warning, in general, to all men, that the authority of masters was to be retained." [d] In order that she…. [e] "Which they might execute." Grammar is not respected here. [f] Without words, without speaking. [g] On account of (the wife's) religion, for motives of religion. [h] Because he has professed Christ. [i] Which forms the Church. [j] The sign ) to be supplied here. [k] Shall he be less of God's image?

Sig. D iij a

If they beginne to beleue but now / than their belefe was no belefe / before now.

Col. iij.

Sig. D iij b

etiam tum cum populus simul, et princeps a deo per infidelitatem quam longissime disiunguntur: quanto magis nunc cum in unam fidei professionem, non sine diuina uirtute coeuntes, ecclesiam eo pacto constituerint, nomen capitis debeat retinere? ut ecclesiæ illius caput adhuc merito habeatur, dei iam uices multo clarius referens,

Roman. 13.   quam olim dum in tenebris infidelitatis uersaretur. Paulus sine distinctione, iubet iis obedire principibus, qui

I Pet. 2.   gladium gestant. Diuus Petrus de regibus loquitur

Matthei. 23.   nominatim. Christus ipse iubet tributum solui Cæsari, et discipulos increpans, quod de maioritate contenderent.

Matthei. 23.   Reges, inquit, gentium dominantur eorum. ostendens plane in tanta graduum, ac ordinum uarietate, quibus deus hunc mundum ornat, dominium, atque imperium ad solos principes pertinere. Sed dicet mihi hic aliquis: In eo laboras, de quo nemo dubitat. Nam principi esse obediendum quis unquam negauit? certissimum quippe est, eum qui principi non obedierit, morte esse multandum: ut ||

f. 13 a   in ueteri lege est comprehensum, atque adeo in noua[1] confirmatum. Sed uidendum, inquiet, est illud, ne terminos positos transilierit princeps, tanquam de finibus regendis adhibendus est arbiter. nam deberi obedientiam certum est, quatenus autem sese proferant obedientiæ exigendæ limites, totum quicquid esse poterit quæstionis continetur. Quosnam mihi limites dicis, cuiusmodi scriptura nullos dicit? sed generaliter de obedientia loquens, quam principi subditus, uel marito uxor, uel domino seruus præstare debeat, nullam uel sillabam exceptionis subiecit, præterquam quæ dei obedientiam integram conseruaret, ne ulli mortalium uoci contra deum auscultemus. alioquin plane indiffinita[2] oratio est, quæ mandat obedientiam[3] uniuersali ex æquo pollens, ut frustra mihi limites nomines, qui nullo Scripturæ testimonio comprobentur. Nobis quidem præcipitur, ut obediamus. In eo nostra functio est. quam si obire cum gratia dei, et hominum uolumus, animi humilitatem

---

[1] The Strasbourg edition misprints this word as *novo*.     [2] The Strasbourg edition had *indefinita*.     [3] Comma here in the Strasbourg

no man sayeth naye / yea euen aswell whan the people / as the prince be most ferre disseuered from God through infidelitie how muche more now / seinge they accorde through the power of God in one profession of faithe / *and* by that meanes are a churche / ought he to reteyne the name of supreme headde? And *that*[a] he maye worthily be taken for the headde of *the* churche still / he representeth the office that he occupieth[b] in Goddes stede, much more honourably now than before tyme / whan he wandred in the darkenes of infidelitie. Paule without difference / biddeth men obey those princes / *that* beare the || sweorde. Saint Petre speaketh of kinges by name / Christ him self commaundeth tribute to be payde vnto Cesar / and checked his disciples / for streyvyng / who shoulde be the greatest. Kinges of the naciones (quod he) beare rule ouer them / declaring plainlye in so great varietie of degrees *and* ordres / which God dothe garnyshe this worlde withall / that the dominion and autoritie perteyneth to non but to princes.

But here som man will saye to me: you trauaile about that / that no man is in doubt of. For who euer denyed / that the prince ought to be obeyed? it is most certayn / that he that will not obeye the Prince / is worthy to dye for it: as it is comprehended in the olde lawe / and also confirmed in the newe lawe. But we must see (wil he saye (*c* that the kinge doo not passe the lemites[d] appoynted him / as though ther must be an arbitrer for the ordringe of his limites. For it is certayn / that obedience is due / but how ferre the limites of requiring obedience extende / that is all the hole question that can be demaunded. What maner of limites are those / *that* ye tel me of seinge *the* scripture hathe non suche? but generally speaking of obedience / *which the* subiecte is bounden to doo vnto *the* prince / *the* wife vnto *the* husbande / or *the* seruaunt to *the* maister it hathe not added so muche as || one sillable of excepicion[e] / but only hathe preserued the obedience due to God / safe and hole / *that* we shoulde not hearken vnto any mannes worde in all the worlde against God. Elles the sentences / that commaunde obedience / are indiffinite / or without excepcion / but are of indifferent force vniuersally / so that it is but lost labour for you / to tell me of limites / whiche can not be proued by any testimonie of scripture / We are commaunded doubtles to obeye / In *that* consisteth our office / which if we mynde to goo about / with the favour of God and man / we must nedes shewe humblenes of hearte / in obeyeng

The Kinge befor in darkenes now in *the* true light.

Ro. xiij
Sig. D iiij a
j. Pe. ij
Matt. xxiij.
Luc. xxij

Sig. D iiij b
No mannes worde to be obeyde agaynst goddes worde.

---

edition. *a* So that.... The translator here wholly misunderstands the Latin sentence. *b* Representing the office.... *c* Sic for ). *d* Sic for *limits*. *e* Sic for *exception*.

exhibeamus oportet, imperia quantumuis grauia propter deum subeundo, non quid aliis imperare princeps, dominus, aut maritus debeat, aut possit inquirendo aut quæritando. qui si aliquid sibi amplius q*uam* æquu*m* et iustu*m* fuerit, aut ipsi arrogauerint, aut delatum sus-

f. 13 b ceperint, dominum habent, ‖ cui aut stant, aut cadu*n*t, et qui de illis sit olim iudicaturus. Attamen dicet aliquis, etiam de hoc dicere in initio es pollicitus, quod nunc reiicere conaris, propositi ut uidetur oblitus. Imo inqua*m* non reiicio, sed satis esse confirmatum asseuero ex superioribus, principi obediendu*m* esse ex præcepto dei; et obediendum quidem sine exceptione, ut pote cuius nulla fiat mentio in illa lege, cui si addideris quippiam, aut dempseris, impius sis. Quid igitur ultra quærimus? Nam si ad commodam interpretationem generalis illius de obedie*n*tia eloquii descendamus, et scripturam scripturæ conferentes collatione, et comparatione, uerum et genuinum scripturæ sensum elicere conabimur, id quod a sanctissimis, et doctissimis uiris fieri et solet et debet: non plane uideo, cur inferiores discedamus. Itaq*ue* consideremus, quid referant scripturæ, quæ ex aduerso proferuntur. Obedite præpositis, inquit Paulus ad Hebræos, quem locu*m*, et item caput decimumtertiu*m* ad Romanos de potestate pont*ificum* qua*m* uocant ecclesiasticam interpreta*n*tur quidam. Item in actis apostolorum, Attendite, etc. in quo uos posuit spiritus sanctus regere ecclesiam dei *et*c.[1] Ac ne quid prætermittamus, etiam illud non omittamus, quanquam alium se*n*sum habet, quod diuus Petrus

f. 14 a de regali sacerdotio loquitur. Nam ‖ illud, Quodcunq*ue* ligaueris, aliò pertinet, et illud: Pasce oues: præterq*uam* quod à Christi ore processerit, non amplius quicquam continet, q*uam* quod de regenda ecclesia mandatum fuisse iam indicauimus. Hæc et si qua su*n*t similia etiam eo sensu intellecta, quo isti uolunt, nimirum ut episcopis, et uerbi dei ministris in ecclesia obediatur, regiæ potestati

[1] The full text, from Acts xx, 28, is as follows: "Attendite vobis, et universo gregi, in quo vos Spiritus sanctus posuit episcopos, regere Ecclesiam Dei, quam acquisivit sanguine suo." *a* To empty your

autoritie / how grevous so euer it be / for goddes sake / not
questioni*n*g nor inquiri*n*g / what the kinge / what *the* maister /
or what *the* husba*n*de ought or maye commaunde other to doo.
And if thei take vpo*n* the*m* / either of their owne headde / or
whan it is offred them / more than right and reason is / they
have a lorde / vnto whom they either stande or fall / and that
shall one daye sitte in iudgement even of them.     Yet for al
this / som ma*n* wil saye: Yea but ye promised in the begynni*n*g /
to speake of *that* / *which* you are about now to avoide your
ha*n*des of*ᵃ* / having forgoten your purpose / as it appeareth.
No Sir / saye I / I avoide not my ha*n*des of it / but I saie / it is ‖
sufficiently confirmed / by these that we have spoken of before /
· that Pri*n*ces ought to be obeyed / by the commau*n*dement of
God: yea *and* to be obeied wi*th*out excepcion / as a thi*n*ge /
wherof ther is no mencion in that lawe / w*hi*ch if thou put any
thinge to / or take any thinge fro / thou arte a wicked man:
what wolde we have more ?

For if I must take in hande to interprete the generall doctrine
of obedience / as it ought to be *and* shall conferre and compare
scripture to scripture /. *and* searchc out the true *and* right
meani*n*g of the scripture / as the most godly and greatest
learned men are bothe wont and ought to doo: I see no cause
*in* dede / why I shoulde doo any lesse tha*n* they did. Therfore
let vs considre / what those scriptures saye / w*hi*ch are alleged
on *the* co*n*trary parte.  **Obey your rulers**, sayth Paule to
Hebrues: which place / and the xiij to the Romaynes / som
expounde of the Bishop of R*o*mes autoritie / whiche they call /
the ecclesiasticall power.  Also in the actes of the apostles / **Take**
**hede to your selues, and to the hole flocke, amo*n*ge whom**
**the holy goost hathe set you to be ouerseers, to gouerne the**
**church of God, whom he hathe purchaced, with his owne**
**bloude.**  And lest we shoulde passe ouer any thi*n*g / although
it is me*n*t to an other purpo-‖se / let vs not omitte that / that
Petre speaketh / concerni*n*ge *the* Royall priesthode.  For this
texte: **What so euer thou shal bynde in earth &c.** perteyneth
to an other mater / and this: **Fede my shepe:** besides that / that
Christ spake wi*th* his owne mouthe*ᵇ* / meaneth no more / but
that I haue already shewed / was commaunded / co*n*cerning
the gouernement of the church. These sente*n*ces and suche
like / though they be vnderstonden / as those me*n* wolde haue
them / that is / that Bishopes *and* ministres of the worde of God
in the churche*ᶜ* / are nothing against the kinges autoritie (but
that he maye be called *the* headde of the churche*ᵈ*) no more /
than the obedie*n*ce due to *the* kinge / is any thi*n*ge nypped or

hands of (*N.E.D.*), hence to get rid of, to set aside.     *ᵇ* Apart from
the fact, that Christ spoke them....     *ᶜ* The verb is here forgotten:"that
Bishops, etc....*should be obeyed...*".   *ᵈ* Nothing against his being called....

quo minus etiam ad capitis usque appellationem in ecclesia porrigatur, nihil aduersantur.[1] non magis certe quam principis obedientiæ detractum esse quippiam, aut diminutum in eo existimemus, quod uxor marito, et seruus domino obedire, sub generali quadam pronunciatione iubentur. Nam quemadmodum apud iurisconsultos, ut loquuntur ipsi, iurisdictiones interdum uariæ ab eodem manantes non se inuicem perimunt, sed mutuis auxiliis consistentes concurrunt. Sic quod apostolis, et iis, qui in eorum locum succedunt regimen ecclesiæ committitur, nulla in parte id quod antea a deo principibus commissum est, tollere. minuereue censeatur. Neque minor sane est parochi cura parochianorum, quod curare etiam debet episcopus, nec episcopi iurisdictio ideo nulla putetur, quod superiorem agnoscat archiepiscopum. Regit enim ecclesiam suo gradu atque ordine parochus, episcopus, archiepiscopus. Quemadmodum itaque in iis suo quisque

f. 14 b munere fungens, ‖ non detrahere sibi inuicem, sed auxiliari uidetur, sic quod apostolis, et qui in eorum locum succedunt, regimen ecclesiæ commissum reperitur, id quod antea a deo principibus commissum est, haudquaquam tollitur. Sed quum regimen multa opus habet, doctrinam in primis uidelicet, et præeminentiam secundum uariam distributionem donorum, aliis doctrinæ munus, et sacramentorum ministerium in eodem corpore mandauit

Roman. 13. deus, aliis uero præeminentiam, non ut aduersentur quidem, sed quemadmodum uaria in eodem corpore membra, sic in regimine congruenter consentientia sint, ac suum quisque munus obeat cum charitate. Sed audio hic obstrepentes quosdam, et magna quadam cum seueritate obiurgantes, quod noua potius distinctione uti maluerim, quam trita illa, quæ regimina tam commode, ut isti putant, secat principis uidelicet, et ecclesiæ, nimirum ut illud sit temporalium, hoc spiritualium. secundum quam distinctionem princeps tanquam luminare minus ea

---

[1] The Strasbourg edition has here in the margin: "Obedientia debita ministris uerbi, Magistratui non aduersatur". The point was apparently stressed by the Strasbourg Protestants, who did not wish to detract too much from the authority which the preachers of the

diminyshed / in *that* / that *the* wife is commaunded to obey her husbande / and *the* seruaunt his maister / as it were *with* generall speache of wordes.[a] For like as *with* the lawers / as they themselues terme it / ther be now *and* than sondry iurisdicciones *that* procede out of al one thinge / *and* yet they marre not one an other: but they consiste *and* concurre by *the* mutual helpe of one to an other: euen so in *that* the gouernement of the churche is committed to *the* apostles / *and* to those *that* succede in their rowmes / maye not be thought to abrogate or diminishe *that* / that God hathe committed vnto princes / in any condicion. The person / ‖ vicare or *the* parishe priestes cure of his Sig. D vj a parisheners / is neuer *the* lesse / because the bishop ought also to ouersee: nether maye *the* Bishoppes iurisdiccion be demed of non effecte / because he must take *the* Archebishoppe for his superiour. For *the* curate / *the* bishop *and* tharchebishoppe do gouerne *the* churche euery one in their degree *and* ordre.

Than like as euery one of them doing their office / seme not to hindre one an other / but to helpe one an other / euenso / in *that* we finde / the gouernement of the churche was committed to *the* apostles / *and* to those *that* succede in their rowme / *that* which beforehande is committed of God to princes / is in no wise taken awaye. But forasmuche as gouernement hathe nede of many thinges / especially teaching *and* preeminence occording[b] to *the* sondry distribucion of gittes / vnto som / God hathe committed the office of teaching / *and* *the* ministerie of *the* sacramentes in all one bodye[c] / *and* to som preeminence / not to be aduersaries / but as diuerse membres agree in one body / so in gouernement they shoude accorde together / *and* euery one goo about his owne office *with* charitie. But here me thinke / I heare som men startle / and as it were / wondrous earnestly chide / because I had rather vse a newe makinge of distinccion, than *the* olde accustumed **Hum trum distinccion**, which as those men thinke / dothe put a handesom ‖ difference betwene the gouernementes of a Sig. D vj b Prince / and of the churche: that is / that the Prince shoulde gouerne in temporall maters / and the churche in spirituall: after the whiche distinccion / the Prince / as the moone which is called the lesse light / shoulde haue charge of suche maters /

Word had gained, in their city as well as in Switzerland. [a] In a general statement of duties. [b] *Sic* for *according*. [c] I.e. "in one only society of men".

curet, quæ sunt noctis, cætera quæ sunt spiritus, et diei, soli soli relinquat perlustranda.[1] Caliginosa sane distinctio, et tenebrarum plena. Nam si principi Christiano regis adhuc nomen relinquis, ut dei uice in terris non præesse solum populo, sed ipsum etiam regere, atque adeo dirigere

f. 15 a teneatur: primum quæro, quam tan-‖dem uiam insistet regendo rex christianus, ut ducat populum christianum, ueritatis ne, quæ ducat ad uitam, an mendacii, quæ properet ad mortem? Nam media uia nulla inuenitur. si ueritatis? quam mihi solam curam narras rerum temporalium, scriptura clamante, Primum querendum esse regnum dei, cætera uero non quærenda, sed adiicienda dei benignitate? scilicet in priuata cuiusque solicitudine quærendum est Regnum dei, et in principis administratione negligendum, aut saltem non curandum? Illud est certe cum uererentur boni homines, ne quis aliquando rex nimium sanctus futurus sit. hic uidelicet ne uirtutis uestigia altiora imprimat, bello scilicet commento, cauendum putarunt principis quidem munus ita circumscribere, ut nihil ipse habeat pensi, sui ciues boni ne sint, an etiam non sint, bonitate quidem christianæ professioni congrua, modo non prorsus nephandis sceleribus, ac facinoribus sint ita infamati, ut ab hominum natura degenerasse uideantur. Itaque ne furentur, ne occidant, ne uim bonis inferant laici, id uero curet rex. Adulteria autem, et his deteriora, ac quæcunque faciant ii, quorum titulus, et uestis diuersa persuadeant, quantumuis enormia securus neglegat.[2] Sunt enim spiritualia, id est spiritualium hominum uitia, de quibus regem iubent esse securum: ut

f. 15 b cui ‖ satis sit populum in temporalibus regere, nec aliud præterea quicquam ad illius notionem pertinere, hoc uidelicet est regere ad interitum expeditissima plane uia, quam longissime ab illius munere diuersa, qui in regendo

---

[1] Marginal note in the Strasbourg edition a few lines above: "De eo quod Ro. Pontifex Sol, et Reges luna dicantur". [2] Marginal note here in the Strasbourg edition: "Immunitas ecclesiasticorum". [a] To be gone over, examined. [b] "Only" forgotten here. [c] The matter, the reason why those good people (the defenders of ecclesiastical supremacy) took this line, is that they were afraid.... [d] These latter

as are of the night / but the other / which be of the spirite and of the daye light / he must reserue to the sonne alone / to be discussed.[a] Forsothe a blynde distinccion / and full of darkenes. For if thou leave unto a christian Prince the name of a kinge still / so that his duetye is / not only to be the chief ouer the people / in Goddes stede / but also to gouerne them / and rule them: Furst I aske / what waye shall a Christian Prince take in gouernement / to leade christian people by: the waye of truthe / which leadeth vnto life / or the waye of lyes / which hasteth to deathe? For ther is no mydde waye founde. If he shall take the waye of truthe what[b] charge of temporall maters / tell you me of / whan the scripture cryeth: **Seke furst the king-dome of God, as for other thinges they must not be sought for, for Goddes liberalitie must geve them?** Must euery man in his owne priuate care seke *the* kingdome of god *and* must a prince in his administracion / neclecte it / or at least / not care for it? || This is the mater surely / because[c] the good men were afraide / lest any king shoulde waxe to holy and in this behalfe / lest he shoulde fall vnto vertue to earnestly / they invented a fine deuise / thinking it a wittie parte[d] / to appoynt a kinge his office / so as he take no thought / whether his people be good or not ( I meane / after *the* goodnes that is mete for the pro-fessiou[e] of christen men) so that[f] they be not notoriously cryed out vpon for abhominable impietie *and* wicked dedes / so as they seme not to become / more like beastes than men. Therfor it must be *the* kinges charge / to see / that they steale not /nor murther / and *that* the laye folke oppresse not the good people.

But as for all maner of horedomes / or worse than hore-dome and what so euer those men doo / whose title and rayment wolde make a man to thinke the contrary in them: though their behaueours be neuer so ferre out of ordre / the kinge must let it alone / and passe not on it.[g]

For those are spirituall maters / that is to saye / spirituall mennes synnes / which they bidde the Kinge / let them alone withall[h]: as though it were ynough for him / to gouerne his people in temporall affaires / *and that* it were not for him to knowe any further. This in dede is *the* most spedy waye to marre all / *and* ferre contrary from his || office that occupieth

*Marginal notes:*

by what way a prince shoulde gouerne his subiectes.

Note. Mat. vj

Sig. D vij a

They did not so wisely in-vent *the* deuise but you as subtelly folowe *the* same steppes.

Trustinge of prelates ouer muche marreth all.

Sig. D vij b

---

words added by the translator. A good example of his redundancy when he finds any chance for invective. [e] *Sic* for *profession.* [f] So long as they are not.... [g] More accurately: "the king may safely neglect them". *To pass on* means "to adjudicate, to pass sentence upon". [h] They bid the king set his mind at rest about those matters, make himself free from them, hence leave them to others.

populum in terris dei uicem referat. An hoc est pascere
2. Re. 5. populum? quo uerbo scriptura ad reges utitur. Multo
certe aliter cum summo applausu cura*m* principis in
moribus ecclesiæ corrigendis Dunstanus sanctissimus,
atq*ue* optimus uir,[1] Cantuariensis olim archiepiscopus
interpretatus est, qui eam regis uocem libe*n*ter amplexus
est, qua se gladium gladio copulaturum edixit: ut dissoluti
ecclesiæ mores ad rectam uidendi[2] norma*m* aptarentur.
Altero gladio ad illud alludens Pauli, quem uerbi ministri
docendo, et exco*m*municando exercent. Altero præeminentiam ostendens iure diuino concessam, cui omnes
parere, quotquot principis ditioni subiecti ecclesiam co*n*-
stituunt, omnino debent. Ma*n*datur enim principi, ut
populum regat: ipsosq*ue* principes officii commonefaciens
Psal. 2. alloquitur propheta, Et nunc reges intelligite, erudimini
qui iudicatis terra*m*. Quòdsi istoru*m* interpretationem
recipimus, hoc tantum intellegant, nihil aliud erudiantur
principes, quam ut negligant fere omnia, hoc est mediam
f. 16 a populi partem ne respiciant quidem, si nomine et ha-||bitu
domino mancipe*n*tur, in reliquam aut*em* partem eatenus
animaduertant, non ut ab omnibus facinoribus abstineant,
sed a quibusdam.[3] Ast longe alia est prophetæ *in*ter-
pretatio, quam subdit, Seruite domino in timore. hoc
nimiru*m* quid sit, nobis intelligendum est, atq*ue* ex ore dei
discendum. Os autem dei in sanctis tam ueteris, quàm
noui testamenti scripturis patet. De regis Salomonis

[1] Gardiner refers to the Anglo-Saxon kings, and the extensive
powers which they exercised over the Church. The king alluded to is
presumably Eadgar, and the words ascribed to him, which St Dunstan
is said to have approved, must have been uttered on some occasion
connected with the archbishop's schemes for Church reform, which
Eadgar favoured and supported with all his might. What particular
event is here meant does not appear in the *Memorials of St. Dunstan,*
published by Bishop Stubbs in the Rolls Series. It is indeed absurd
and somewhat dishonest on Gardiner's part to turn St Dunstan into
an ally in his attack against the Pope; yet the archbishop clearly took
no exception to the close union of the State and the Church which
prevailed in the tenth century, and the consequent increase in the
jurisdiction of the king. In a sort of proclamation issued in time of
plague, to admonish the people of their religious duties, Eadgar uses the
words "Ic ond se ærcebisceop" ("I and the archbishop"). (F. Lieb-
ermann, *Die Gesetze der Angelsachsen,* 1903, vol. I, p. 206, anno 962–3.)
Besides, according to one of his early biographers, St Dunstan pro-

Goddes rowne*a* in earthe.*b* Is this to fede *the* people? which
worde the scripture vseth to kinges? Naye / Saint*c* Dunstane
(which was a very holy and a right good ma*n*) somtyme Arche-
bishop of Cantorbury / did a great deale after an other sorte /
with great reioysing*d* / interprete the charge of a prince in
correcting the maners of the churche / beinge gladly well
apayed*e* of the kinges sayeng / whan he tolde him / he wolde
ioyne sweorde to sweorde / to thintent the light dissolute
maners of the **Holy Kirckemen,***f* might be framed in to the
right trade of lyfe. By the one sweorde / alluding to the sayeng
of Paule / which the ministres of the worde / exercice in preaching and excommunicating: by that other sweorde / shewi*n*g
a supremacie oppoynted*g* by the lawe of God / whervnto as
many as are the kinges subiectes (which is the congregacion /
that we call the churche) are all bounden throughlye to obeye.
For the kinge is commaunded / to gouerne the people: and
the prophet warnyng Princes of their duetie / sayeth to the*m*:
**Now you kinges get you vnderstanding,** *and* **be learned you**
**that are iudges of the la***n***de.** But if we admitte these me*n*nes
interpretacio*n* / tha*n* shoulde pri*n*ces hauc no more vnderstanding / nor be further learned / ‖ than to be negligent almost
in all thinges / *that* is to saie / they shoulde not meddle wi*th*
*the* one halfe of *the* people / if thei serve *the* lorde*h* in name *and*
apparail: *and* as for *the* rest of *the* people / they shoulde
correcte the*m* / not to refraine fro*m* al grosse synnes / but fro*m*
som. But *the* p*r*ophetes interpretacio*n* / is an other maner of
mater / which he bri*n*geth in afterwarde / saieng: **Serue the**
**Lorde in feare,** what this meaneth / we must vnderstande
and learne it of Goddes owne mouthe. For Goddes mouthe
speaketh playnly in the holy scriptures bothe of of*i* the olde
testament and newe. Touching kinge Salomons administracion /

Du*n*stane
a holi man /
*and* my
dogge other

fessed the duty of obedient service to princes, and justified their
supreme authority by some of the very texts of Scripture which
Gardiner quotes in various places (Rom. xiii, 1–7 and I Pet. ii, 13),
though he had no thought of using them against the Pope (*Memorials*,
p. 22). ² *Sic* for *uiuendi*. The misprint is also found in the Hamburg edition but corrected in the Strasbourg edition. ³ Marginal
note here in the Strasbourg edition: "Quod cura ecclesiastica ad
Reges pertineat". *a* *Sic* for *rowme, room*. *b* The translator
forgets the words "in governing the people". *c* *Saint* added by
the translator. *d* In the midst of great applause. *e* *To apay*
means "to satisfy, content, please" (*N.E.D.*). But the translation is
rather inaccurate and may be improved thus: "embracing, welcoming
those words of the king, in which he said...". *f* This satirical
expression is the translator's addition, the Latin text having nothing
stronger than "Ecclesiæ". *g* *Sic* for *appoynted*. *h* More accurately: "if they are made by their name and apparel the property of
the Lord". *i* *Sic*.

administratione sic refert scriptura: Constituit Rex Salomon iuxta dispensationem patris sui officia sacerdotum in ministeriis suis, et leuitas in ordine suo, ut laudarent, et ministrarent coram sacerdotibus iuxta ritum unius cuiusque diei, et ianitores in diuisionibus suis per portam, et portam. Audis hic Salomonem regem etiam sacra curasse, non temere, sed ex præscripto patris Dauid: de quo Deus per prophetam protestatur inuenisse se hominem secundum cor suum. Itaque etiam illa de Salomone historia contextum habet, quod sequitur, Sic enim præceperat homo dei, nec prætergressi sunt de mandatis regis quicquam, tam sacerdotes, quam leuitæ ex omnibus quæ præceperat. Quid hic commemorem solicitudinem regis Iosaphat, qui supremum illud in Hierusalem sacerdotum ac principum familiarum tribunal constituit?[1] || In qua tandem potestate fecit nisi regia? muneris sui ducens esse, diuina se potius curare debere, quam humana. Quæ denique audacia fuisset Ezechiæ regis, primo protinus regni sui anno, atque adeo primo mense, ita se diuinarum rerum administrationi immiscuisse, si non regii tum muneris à deo traditi disciplina id exigisset?[2] Vt uidelicet rex a deo constitutus, qui spiritus est æternus, spiritualia, et æterna potius, ac priori loco curaret, quam corporalia, et tempore peritura? Ezechias ergo ipse, de quo tam celebre extat elogium, ut non fuerit alius ei similis, qui seruaret omnia præcepta domini in cunctis regibus Iuda. Volens uidelicet requirere dominum in toto corde suo, id quod fecit, et prosperatus est, ut habent scripturæ uerba. 2. Pa. 29. hic inquam Ezechias quid fecit? In ipso sane primo anno, et primo mense regni sui, non modo instaurauit ualuas domus domini, sed etiam sacerdotes ipsos corrigere, atque adeo uiuæ structuræ ruinas reficere conatus est. Nempe sacerdotes in plateam orientalem congregatos, non solum admonuit neglecti officii, sed

---

[1] The full text from the Vulgate is as follows (II Paral. xix, 8): "In Jerusalem quoque constituit Josaphat Levitas, et Sacerdotes, et principes familiarum ex Israel, ut judicium et causam Domini judicarent habitatoribus ejus".   [2] *Sic*, corrected in the Strasbourg and Hamburg editions to *exegisset*.   [a] *Priester* as another form for "priest" is not quoted in *N.E.D.* and may be here a mere misprint.

this dothe scripture reporte: **Kinge Salomon, according to**
**his fathers appoyntment, ordained the offices of the**
**priesters**[a] **in their ministeries, and Levites in their ordre,**
**that they might geue thankes, and ministre before the**
**priestes after the ordre of euery day, and porters in**
**their diuisions gate by gate.** Here you do here[b] *that*
Kinge Salomon take cure also of holy or spirituall maters / ij. Parali.
not vnadvisedly / but by thappointment of Dauid his father / xxviij.
of whom god / by the prophet / protesteth / that he had
founde a man after his owne hearte. So that the same historie
of Salomon / speaketh of this sorte folowing: **For soo had**
**the man of God commaunded, ‖ nether did they omytte** Sig. D viij b
**any of the Kinges commaundementes, nether the priestes** ij. Par. xviij
**nor Leuites, of all that he had commaunded.** Wherto
shoulde I here make rehearsall of kinge Iosophat his care-
fulnes / that set vp the highe iudgement seate of the priestes
and levites householdes[c] in Hierusalem? By what autoritie
did he so / but by his Regall power? taking it to be his office /
rather to take charge concerning Divine maters than humane. ij. Par. xxviij
What a bolde dede had that ben of kinge Ezechias / euen the
very furst yeare and the furst moneth of his reigne / so to have
busyed him selfe with the administracion of divine maters /
if the discipline of his regall office / which he receaued of God /
had not required it? *that* is to saye *that* a Kinge ordayned of
God (which is *the* eternall spirite) shoulde take charge of
spiritual and eternall affaires / before and rather than corporal
maters / and thinges that shall perishe in time. This
Ezechias therfore / the scripture commendeth so highly / that
ther was non of all the Kinges of Iuda / which obserued all the
lordes preceptes like vnto him. For his will was to seke the
lorde with all his hole hearte / as he did in dede and prospered /
as the scripture testifieth. ij. Par. xxviij. What did this
Ezechias / I saye? In the very ‖ furst yeare *and* furst moneth Sig. E a
of his reigne / he did not only buylde vp the gates of the lordes
house agayne / but also gave diligence to refourme the priestes
them selues / and to repaire the lyuely buylding / that was
decayed. For he not only admonished *the* priestes / *that*

---

Yet it is found in the locution "Prester" or "Priester John".   *b* Hear.
*c* The translator's mistake about the meaning of this text is indeed
surprising, and is corrected by the Authorized Version, II Chron. xix,
8: "Moreover, in Jerusalem did Jehoshaphat set of the Levites, and
of the priests, and of the chief of the fathers of Israel", i.e. a tribunal
of the priests and heads of the families.

tanq*uam* potestatem etiam habe*n*s, Audite inquit, leuitæ et sacerdotes, sanctificemini et mundate domum domini dei uestrorum patrum, et auferte 'omnem immunditiam de sa*n*ctuario, *etc.*[1] Qui quæso potuit hic maiore cum

f. 17 a im-‖perio loqui? Neq*ue* enim more hortantis locutus est, quomodo inferiores, aut æquales solent seipsos, quò leuior sit oratio rei gerendæ communicantes, quod genus orationis pius interdum affectus etiam *in* aliena re exigit: ad quem modum si Ezechias loqui uoluisset, no*n* sanctificemini, sed sanctificemur, non mundate, sed mundemus, no*n* auferte, sed auferamus: aut si rei natura communionem non pateretur, a priuato illa optanda fuissent, aut indicanda, cui quidem certe neq*ue* exige*n*dæ rei se coniungere, ut exhortetur, neq*ue* pro imperio mandare licuisset. Cæterum Ezechias optimus princeps de regio officio cura, atq*ue* administratione à deo edoctus, oratione ad sacerdotes eiusmodi usus est, quæ loquentis authoritatem referet, et potestatem. Itaq*ue* imperandi modo, Audite, inquit, mundate, atq*ue* auferte. Illi etiam sacerdotes, ut in eodem loco habetur, tanq*uam* iustum regis mandatum exequentes, imperio paruerunt. Sic nimirum eruditi fuerunt reges illi, qui suum ex diuina authoritate munus in populo dei plene atque perfecte obierint. Quæ etiam a principibus deus nunc multo magis est exacturus: ut audita prophetæ uoce ad eruditione*m* huiusmodi amplectendam, exhortantis in regendo populo, domino seruiant cum timore, et tremore.

f. 17 b Vt populu*m* ‖ non qualemcunq*ue*, sed domino dignum, et acceptabilem, quo ad eius facere possunt, exhibeant,

---

[1] The whole text from the Vulgate is as follows (II Paral. xxix, 3–6): "Ipse anno et mense primo regni sui, aperuit valvas domus Domini, et instauravit eas. Adduxitque Sacerdotes atque Levitas, et congregavit eos in plateam Orientalem. Dixitque ad eos: Audite me Levitæ, et sanctificamini, mundate domum Domini Dei patrum vestrorum, et auferte omnem immunditiam de sanctuario". [a] Here again we find a surprising mistranslation in one who must have been familiar with Scripture, who might in any case have looked up the passage to ascertain the meaning. The Authorized Version (II Chron. xxix, 3–4) corresponds exactly to the above-quoted text from the Vulgate: "And he brought in the priests and the Levites, and gathered them together into the East Street". *Platea orientalis* is the open space in front of the porch of the Temple. [b] More exactly: "like a man having power to do so". [c] *Sic* for *felowe-like, fellow-like*; more clearly rendered

dwelt together on the east strete of the citie$^a$ / of their necligence in their office / but also like a man of autoritie$^b$ / sayde: **Hearken o ye Leuites and priestes: be ye sanctified and make cleane the house of the Lorde, the God of your fathers, _and_ put a waye all vnclea_n_nes fro_m_ the sayntuarie. &c.** I pray you / what coulde he speake more imperiously? For he spake not / as one / that exhorted the_m_ / as inferiours / or those that be folowe like$^c$ / vse to take in them selves with all / to cause the communicacion of the mater / to be the more easily taken. Which maner of talke is requisite som time in a gentill godly hearte in an others$^d$ ma_n_nes cause. And if Ezechias lusted$^e$ to haue spoken after that rate / he wolde not have sayde / **Be ye santified** / but let vs be santified: not make **you cleane,** but let vs make cleane: not put **ye awaye,** but let vs put awaye: or if the mater had ben suche / that it wolde not admitte feloweship / if a priuate man shoulde ha$^f$ wished or declared those cases / it had become ‖ him nether to make him selfe felowe like with the mater to be required / to exhorte them / nor to require it by the waye of commaundeme_n_t.$^g$ But the right good prince Ezechias / beinge taught of God / what his Regall office / charge and administracion was / vsed suche maner talke vnto the priestes / as shoulde declare _that_ autoritie and power of the speaker. Therfore he speaketh in the imperatiue mode: **Hearken, make cleane, and put awaye.** And the priestes them selues (as it appeareth in the same place) did / as _the_ kinge had iustly bidden them / and obeyed his commaundement.$^h$ Thus were those kinges learned$^i$ / that fully and entlerlye applied their office / by Goddes autoritie amonge Goddes people And these thinges will God require at princes handes / a great deale more in these dayes: that / they shoulde hearken / how the propheth exhortet$^j$ them / to laye hande vpon this maner of learning / to gouerne the people by / and to serue the lorde with feare _and_ trembling: and to cause the people / not to be suche as they lust them selues to be$^k$ / but a worthye and

Sig. E b

God wilbe angry _in_ these daies _with_ vnlearned Princes.

How ca_n_ _that_ be if

by "equals". Inferiors or equals, when exhorting others, include themselves in the exhortation.   $^d$ _Sic._   $^e$ Listed, list.   $^f$ _Sic_ for _have._   $^g$ The sentence as it stands in the translation is wholly unintelligible; it may be rendered as follows: "or if the matter had not allowed of the exhortation being thus placed in common (i.e. had not allowed him thus to include himself) those things should have been expressed as a wish, or as a hint, by a private person (i.e. he being only in that case a private person) who would not be allowed either to require the thing of himself too, in the way of exhortation, or to give orders in virtue of his power".   $^h$ More exactly "obeyed his commandments, as being just".   $^i$ This is a reference to "nunc reges erudimini". More clearly: "thus did those kings learn".   $^j$ _Sic_ for _prophet exhorteth._   $^k$ More exactly: "and to present their people [to God], not in an indifferent condition, but worthy and acceptable...".

III

sicque fideles dispensatores reperiantur in die illo, in quo rationem susceptæ administrationis sunt reddituri. Audiant itaque sapientem sapien. 6. Audite reges, et intelligite, præbete aures uestras uos qui continetis multitudinem, quoniam data est a domino potestas uobis, et uirtus ab altissimo, qui interrogabit opera uestra. Quare non tanquam pigri, negligentes, et ociosi uersentur principes, sed iugi in timore seruiant. Nam tanto magis solliciti esse debent ex munere dato, ut quidam scripsit, quanto se obligatiores esse conspiciunt in ratione reddenda. Magnum siquidem talentum est principibus à deo concreditum:[1] nempe ut populum non solum regant, sed recte etiam regant: non in una aliqua parte, sed in singulis. Sicque uineam domini, quam colendam suscepisse uidentur curare, ut non arceant solum, quod noceat, sed repurgent etiam, atque repastinent, nec ullum genus culturæ prætermittant, quo fructum proferat uinea uberiorem, a patrefamilias suo tempore repetendum. Quis[2] enim facultatibus sufficiat principibus illud cauere, ut cum ipsi

f. 18 a omnem in se regendi populi curam deo authore ‖ susceperint, pacisci deinde ipsis liceat ut partis maioris cura sit alterius, ipsi interim tanquam belle defuncti, in utranque aurem dormiant securi? Scilicet quam uocem præsentis reuerentia uirtutis, non ueritas potestatis aliquando expresserat, eam deinceps etiam si ab homine sic affecto emissam ad eludendam diuinæ authoritatis curam usurpabunt? Nempe illud Constantini dictum, Ego uos non

---

[1] An allusion to the parable of the talents (Matth. xxv, 14–30); the "talent" entrusted to the prince being his power over his subjects. [2] Contracted for *quibus*. The translator failed to realize that this was a contraction and consequently mistranslated the whole sentence. [a] *Sic.* [b] "In fear" forgotten. [c] *Sic* for *accompte*. [d] This is inaccurate, the meaning of *repastino* being to "hoe" or "weed" a field. Was the translator ignorant of this or was he carried away by his fondness for the picturesque? [e] Wholly misunderstood, the meaning being as follows: "By what means could it be sufficient for princes, to

an acceptable people vnto the lorde / as muche as in them were possible / *and* so to be founde faithfull stuardes / in *that* daye / whan they shal yelde accompte of *the* administracion / which they toke vpon them. ‖ Let them therfore heare what *the* wiseman saithe: **Heare o ye Kynges and vnderstande, marke with your eares, you that are rulers of the** **multitude, for power is geuen vnto yow of the lorde, and streynght from the highest, which shall enquire, what your workes be.** Therfore Princes must not passe the tyme / in slouthfnlnes[a] / necligence / and Idlenes / but continually serve the lorde.[b] For their duetie is / to be so muche the more carefull in the office that God hathe geven them (as one hathe written) as they see them selues the more bounden in yelding accompta.[c] For it is a great talent / that God hathe put princes in trust withall: that is / that they shoulde not only rule the people / but also rule them rightly / not in any one parte alone but in all particulraly: and so to loke vnto the lordes vineyarde / which men thinke they have taken in hande to kepe in good husbandrie / that they not only plucke out suche thinges as are noysom / but also trymme it and laye newe dong to it:[d] and to leave no poynte of husbandrye vndone / that the vineyarde maye bringe furthe frute more pleynteously / which the good man of the house shall require in his season.

For who is hable to save princes harmeles / or beare them out[e] / that / wher they have taken ‖ vpon them selues / all the hole charge to gouerne the people by Goddes autoritie / they maye compacte afterwarde / that the greater parte shall have the charge of the other[f] / and they in the meane while / as though thei had done their office gayly well / take their ease / and care for nothing?[g] And wher a worde was ones spoken / by cause of the reuerence of their present vertue / and not by the truthe of their autoritie:[h] shall men / though it were spoken of a man so affected / vsurpe it for that ende to mocke out the charge of Goddes autoritie? I meane / the saieng of Con- stantine: **I will not iudge you, of whom I my selfe ought to**

manage that, where they have, etc.". [f] An obvious and surprising blunder: "that some one else should have the charge of the greater part (of the people)". [g] A very flat rendering, curiously unlike the style of the translation as a whole, for "safely to sleep on both ears". [h] Unintelligible once more: "And those words (Constantine's, which will presently be quoted), which reverence towards the virtuous persons present, not truth concerning his own power, had forced him (Constantine) to utter; shall men...".

iudicabo, a quibus debeam ipse iudicari?[1] Deus generaliter loquitur, neminem excipit, populum credit principi interdum malum malo. Si bonum aliquando populum principi bono, certe tanto magis credit, ut uniuerso populo secundum dei præcepta, non uni populi parti secundum traditiones hominum præesse credatur. Qui populus una fide Christi conglutinatus, si ecclesiam constituat, quid habet absurdi, ut princeps, qui illius populi caput dicitur, ecclesiæ etiam, quam populus ille constituit, caput uocetur? Dices fortasse, solus CHRISTVS caput est ecclesiæ. omnes fatemur, qui quidem alioqui ne ecclesiam proprie constitueremus, nisi malignantium. CHRISTVM sane ecclesiæ caput agnoscimus, atque in cœlo regnantem cum patre, quem aduocatum habemus ad patris dextram as-||

f. 18 b sidentem, ac intercedentem pro nobis. Quatenus autem Christus mediator dei, atque hominum, ipse deus, et homo, caput ecclesiæ est, non recipit ea ecclesia adiectionem, cum neque Anglicana sola sit, sed etiam Gallicana, Hispana, neque non Romana, quippe nullo loco circumscripta, sed quocunque terrarum etiam apud turcas, sicubi suos sibi filios obsignauerit deus, à quo, ut est in euangelio, omnes trahuntur, quibus dedit potestatem suos fieri filios. Itaque sit hoc extra controuersiam, de quo uel contendere, ne dicam disceptare, sit impium. Atque ut hoc remoueatur, et ne qua causa calumniandi remaneat, et uerbo caput additur in terris, et uerbo ecclesiæ adiicitur Anglicanæ. Cuius quidem ecclesiæ Anglicanæ supremum in terris caput, quoniam id scripturæ, et rationes comprobant tanquam principis et regis appellationi inexistentem, rem

---

[1] Constantine's words do not seem to appear in any one of the early historians of the Church exactly in the form in which they are quoted by Gardiner. But there can be little doubt as to the allusion. Rufinus, who translated into Latin the *Historia Ecclesiastica* of Eusebius, adding two books of his own, tells us that at the beginning of the Council of Nicæa, the bishops requested the Emperor Constantine to arbitrate between them in regard to certain quarrels which divided them. The contending parties brought notes (*libelli*) of their respective grievances. But Constantine, taking up all the *libelli* and holding them on his knees, spoke thus: "Deus vos constituit sacerdotes, et potestatem vobis dedit de nobis quoque iudicandi; et ideo nos a vobis recte iudicamur. Vos autem non potestis ab hominibus iudicari, propter quod dei solius inter vos expectate juditium, et vestra jurgia quecunque

**be iudged.** God speaketh generally / he excepteth no man / he committeth the people vnto the princes charge / somtyme naughty people / to a naughtye prince. If somtyme good people to a good prince / than he puteth him so muche the more in trust / that me*n* maye surely thinke / he hathe the supremacie ouer all the people / according to the commaundementes of God / and not ouer one parte of the people / after the tradiciones of me*n* which people / being knyt together in one belefe of Christ / seing it is a churche: what absurditie is it / that a prince / which is called the headde of that people / shoulde not be called al-‖so the headde of the churche / which that people maketh? You will saye perchaunce / Christ only is the headde of the churche. We all confesse it / or elles we coulde not proprely coustitute*a* a churche / but the churche of malignauntes. In dede we acknowlage that Christ is the headde of the churche / *and* that he reigneth with the father in heauen / who is our aduocate / sitting on the fathers right hande / and maketh intercession for vs.

But as concerning that Christ*b* / the mediatour of God / and men / bothe God and man / is the headde of the churche / that churche hathe none addicion*c* / forasmuche as the churche of Engla*n*de / is not the churche / alone / but also the churche of Fraunce / of Spayne / and of Rome*d* / for the churche is not circu*m*scripte to any place / but where so euer it be in all the wide worlde / euen among the Turkes / wher God hathe sealed vp his owne children vnto him selfe*e* / who (as the Gospell saithe) draweth all / vnto whom he hathe geuen power to become his children. Therfore late*f* this be out of co*n*trouersie / about the which it were wickednes to co*n*tende / I wil not saye / Dispute. And to avoide this / that ther remayne no cauce of evil reporte of it / ther is to this worde / headde / added **in Earthe**: and ‖ to this worde / churche / is added / **of** **Engla*n*de.** Of which churche of Englande / the supreme headde in earthe / forasmuche as bothe scriptures and reasones doo allowe it / as a thing inexistent*g* vnto the name of a prince and

sunt ad illud diuinum reserventur examen. Vos etenim nobis a deo dati estis dii, et conveniens non est ut homo judicet deos, sed ille solus de quo scriptum est: Deus stetit in sinagoga deorum in medio autem deos discernit". Then the emperor ordered all the *libelli* to be burnt. (Rufinus' translation of Eusebius' *Historia Ecclesiastica*, ed. Mantua, 1479, Lib. x, cap. ii. This work was well known and easily accessible at the time of Gardiner's youth.) *a Sic* for *constitute.* *b* But in so far as Christ.... *c* No epithet should be added to the word "Church". *d* Mistranslated: "for this church is not only Anglican, but also Gallican, Spanish, yea, even Roman". *e* Wherever God has made men his own children by marking them with his seal. *f Sic* for *let.* *g* As a thing included in the name of a prince, being part of its very existence.

eam quoque uerbis apertis exprimenda*m* duxit populus Anglicanus uniuersus, plebs, patresq*ue* atq*ue* etiam ii, qui ab illa iurisdictione immunes, temporis, non ueritatis præscriptione habebantur. Quid ni enim consentirent ueritati? Neq*ue* profecto deterrere quicq*uam* potuit, aut debuit uerbi nouitas, et insolentia: postq*uam* enim re*m* ipsam, quæ nomine exprimebatur, non modo ueram, sed

f. 19 a  etiam ueterem fuisse appareret, Iudicii, ‖ non temeritatis fuit, ut insigne aliquod nomen proponeretur, quod oscitantes quorundam animos, languidaq*ue* iudicia ad ipsam ueritatis considerationem excitaret, ipsoq*ue* nomine admonere*n*tur subditi, principem totius populi principe*m* esse, no*n* partis, ipsumq*ue* populi corpus in ecclesiam coalescens non mancum esse, aut truncum, sed eodem principe tanq*uam* capite constare. cuius muneris sit non humana solum, sed multo magis diuina curare, cuiq*ue* uidelicet corporis membro commoda distributione suas functiones mandare: ut ipse oculis, auribus, et ore iuxta solicitudinem, qua dono dei præest corpori inseruiendo, et sui quem*que* muneris co*m*monifacie*n*do officiu*m* obeat eiusmodi, quod à christiano pri*n*cipe christiano populo præsidente, deus sit haud dubie olim exacturus. Atq*ue* hæc quidem de nominis nouitate.[1] Nam ipsa alioqui res, et multa, et grauissima habet exempla, no*n* ea modo quæ ueteri lege testata supra rece*n*suimus, sed pleraq*ue* etiam alia, non cum illis quidem pondere, et grauitate conferenda, quæ diuina authoritate nituntur: Verumtame*n* quoniam ad causam pertineant, no*n* omittenda. Itaq*ue* quis unq*uam* improbauit Iustiniani factum, qui leges ædidit de summa trinitate, et de fide catholica, de episcopis, de

---

[1] Marginal note in the Strasbourg edition: "Iustinianus se gessit pro capite ecclesiæ". *a Sic* for *prescription.* *b Exempt* forgotten. *c Sic* for *by.* *d* Inaccurate for "slumbering, languid". *e By* to be referred to the beginning of the sentence: "By which to stir up…". *f* Inaccurate, no doubt owing to the fact that there was some confusion in the translator's mind between the adjective *truncus* meaning

of a kinge / all Englishe people / thought it mete / to haue that
mater expressed *in* plaine wordes / bothe the commones / and
the fathers / yea / and euen those / that were reputed to be[b]
from that iurisdiccion / be[c] prescripcion of tyme / and not by
prescripcion of truthe. For / why shoulde they not co*n*sent
to the truthe? In dede the newnesse and unwont noueltie of
the worde nether coulde / nor ought make men any thinge
afrayde: For / after it appeared / that the thinge it selfe / which
was expressed by name / was not only true / but also auncient:
it came of aduised iudgement and not of temeritie / that som
notable name shoulde be set furthe / to stere vp the holowe[d]
heartes and feble iudgementes of som men vnto the co*n*sidera-
tion of the truthe by[e] and to aduertise the subiectes by that
name / that the prince is the hole Prince of all the people / and
not of parte: and that the same body of the people / growing
in to that condicion / to be called the churche / is not one
handed / nor cut of by the stumpes[f] / but that it consisteth
perfitly ‖ hole / the same Prince beinge as the headde: whose
office is / to take charge / not only of humayne maters / but
muche more of divine maters / that is / to distribute fitely vnto
eucry membre of the body / their propre offices / that he / with
his eies / with his eares / and with his mouthe according to the
care / wherby he hathe the gouernement / by the gifte of God /
in ministring vnto the body[g] / and chargeing euery one with
their duotie / he maye applye that maner of office / that God
shall doubtles / one daye / call for a reconyng of / at the handes
of a christe*n* Prince / havinge the gouernement of christen
people.    Thus muche towching the neweltie of the name.
For elles the mater it selfe / hathe bothe many and right
weightie examples / not those only / which I haue before
rehearced out of the olde lawe / but many other also / not com-
parable in dede with them (in that they are grounded vpon
Goddes worde) in grauitie and weightie importaunce: howbeit / forasmuche as they are pertynent to the cause / they are
not to be omitted.    Than Sir / who did euer disallowe
Justinianes facte / that made lawes / concerning the glorious
Trinitie / *and* the catholike faithe / of Bishoppes / of men of

prescrip-
ciu*n*[a] of tyme
is not
allowed but
prescripcion
of truthe.

wherfore
supreme
head is
written
in *the*
Kinges
stile

Sig. E iiij a
*The* office
of a prince
is to take
charge *in*
diuine
maters.

Justinianus

"truncated, mutilated", and the noun *truncus*, "a trunk or stump".
[g] The translation is obscure, a clearer rendering being as follows:
"That he, ministering unto the body (of the people) with his eyes, his
ears and his mouth, according to the solicitude, for the sake of which he
has been made the head by the gift of God, and charging...".

p. 19 b clericis, de hæreticis, et cæteris id genus?[1] Quas ‖ certe
leges aut frustra tulit, aut curam se etiam illius, quæ
purior, et sanctior esse deberet (id quod profitetur) populi
partis habere interpretatus est. Veritatis re uera iudicium
in hoc assecutus. Quoties autem legimus causas hæreseos
apud Cæsares et principes agitatas, ipsorumque examine
discussas fuisse? Si antiquas Anglorum retro principum
leges excutiemus,[2] quam multas reperiemus ad religionem,
et ecclesiam pertinentes ipsorum Regum iussu, et authoritate latas, promulgatas, ac demandatas executioni? Imo
tanquam defensores inquiunt ecclesiæ, non ut authores et
capita huiusmodi statuerunt. Quis igitur interim caput
fuit? quis præfuit? Cuius fuit præcipua solicitudo? Scio
quid respondebunt: Nempe Romani episcopi. post
uidebimus hoc. Interim certe concedatur necesse est
regiam dignitatem summis in Anglia episcopis semper
præfuisse, et sub nomine defensoris ecclesiæ[3] (quo titulo
Reges etiam donati sunt ab iis, qui minimum tribuerunt)
ea præstitisse, et exhibuisse, si non in omnibus, certe in
quamplurimis, quæ capitis dignitatem, atque officium in
ecclesia referrent. Defenderunt namque principes ecclesiam, quomodo caput tuetur corpus, atque defendit.
Cunque hodie passim accidere uideamus, ut rem ipsam in
f. 20 a multis negligentes: aliqui nomen tamen ‖ ambiant. Illi
principes contra, re atque officio tales, qui capita dici
merito debuissent, a capitis uocabulo tantum abstinuerunt.

---

[1] Gardiner here repeats the titles of the first chapters of the first
part of the *Codex Justinianus*, namely Chapter I, "De summa trinitate
et de fide Catholica, et ut nemo de ea publice contendere audeat";
Chapter III, "De episcopis et clericis, etc."; Chapter v, "De hæreticis
et Manichæis et Samaritis". (Cf. *Corpus Iuris Civilis*, ed. Mommsen-
Krueger, vol. II, *Codex Iustinianus*, Lib. I, art. i, iii, v.) Justinian's
code was promulgated in its later form—the one known to Gardiner
and to us—on November 17, 534. The pretensions of the great Byzantine emperor to absolute supremacy over the Church, not only in
regard to discipline but also in matters of faith, need scarcely be recalled here. He was the foremost exponent of the theory known as
"cæsaro-papism". Gardiner, as a doctor of civil law, must have been
thoroughly familiar with Justinian's legislation; but it is not a little
striking, both in regard to Henry V.III's own claims, and to Gardiner's
interpretation of the supreme headship, that the English sovereign
should here be likened to the Byzantine absolutist who made himself
a pope. The influence of Roman law on the development of political

the clergie / of heretiques / and others / suche like? Which ‖
lawes he either made in vaine / or elles he declared / that he
had the charge of that parte of the people also / which ought
to be of the greater puritie and of the more holynesse / as he
saythe him selfe he had / havyng perteyned in this behalfe /
vnto the iudgement of the truthe / out of all peraventure.[a] How
often doo we reade / that the causes of heresie / haue ben
debated before Emperours and Princes / and discussed by their
tryall? If we will boulte out[b] the auncient lawas[c] of kinges of
Englande in tymes past / how many shall we finde / concerning
religion and the churche / made / proclaymed / and bidden to
be put in execucion / by the commaundement *and* autoritie of
those kinges? Yea / saye they / they made suche statutes / as
defendours of the churche / and not as autours and headdes of
*the* churche. Who was headde than in the meane space? Who
had the gouernement? Who had the principall charge?
I wotte / what their answer wilbe: Mary Sir / the Bishop of
Rome. That shall we see here after. In the meane
while / it must nedes be graunted / that the kinges dignitie
hathe be*n* alwayes aboue *the* chiefest Bishoppes in Englande /
a*n*d that / vnder the name of **Defendour of the churche** (which
title was geue*n* vnto kinges / euen of them / that ‖ grau*n*ted
least) they did and exercised those thinges albeit not in all
thinges yet in most thinges that representeth the dignitie and
office of the headde in the churche. For princes were
defendours of the churche / euen as the headde maynteneth
and defendeth the body. And as we maye see it chaunce
almost in euery place at this daye / that som that be necligent
in many thinges[d] / couet the name for all that. And contrary
wise those Princes / which haue ben suche in dede and in
office / that they ought iustly to haue ben called headdes / haue
refrayned only / to be called headdes. For they haue made

Sig. E iiij b

Sig. E v a
How a
pri*n*ce is
defendour
of *the*
churche

thought in England at the time of the Renaissance appears here clearly;
and it will be worth remembering that Gardiner later appealed to
Henry VIII's judgment as final authority in the matter of justification.
(Cf. his two letters to Cranmer, June and July, 1547, in B.M. Add.
MS 29546.)     [2] Marginal note here in the Strasbourg edition:
"Angliæ Rex semper præfuit episcopis".     [3] Marginal note here in
the Strasbourg edition: "Defensor fidei". The allusion was therefore
clear to the Strasbourg editors. It was no doubt a piece of diplomatic
skilfulness on the part of Gardiner, not to remind Henry VIII too
brutally of the title which had been granted him by the Pope, while
hinting at it, so as to use it to the best advantage as an argument in his
favour.     [a] These latter words added by the translator.     [b] *Boulte
out* = "to bolt out, to sift, to pass through a sieve or bolting-cloth,
to search and try" (*N.E.D.*); here quite a literal translation for
*excutiemus.*     [c] *Sic* for *lawes.*     [d] More exactly: "that some,
neglecting the *thing* itself in many ways, covet the *name* for all
that".

Illi enim de hæresi, in qua prima, et præcipua functio est, sua authoritate, suisque legibus inquirendum statuerunt, quod et hodie est, et perpetuo us*que* ad hæc tempora fuit obseruatum. Iam uero episcopis ipsis, et clericis multa permiserunt, multas*que* illis immunitates concesserunt, quorum certe concessio abu*n*de magno argumento esse debet, aut frustra hactenus pri*n*cipes de re aliena rogatos fuisse, quæ nihil ad eos pertineret, dedisse*que* quod ipsi non haberent, quod plane absurdum est, aut eorum quæ concesserunt exercendi potestatem habuisse, atque ideo de suo iure eatenus discessisse, at*que* remisisse. Quæ cum ita sint, fuerunt reipsa quidem capita semper principes, etiam tum cum defensores dumtaxat appellarentur, si id est caput esse corpori præesse uniuerso, ac singulis eius membris, quod in usum cederet uniuersi mandare, remittere nonnunquam et indulgere, sicque singula moderari, et temperare, ut dei gloria fideique professio indies augeatur. At enim dicent isti, Romanum Episcopum tanquam uniuersalis ecclesiæ caput agnouerunt principes, huic honores supremo ‖ capiti pares habuerunt, huic se submiseru*n*t, huius authoritatem agnouerunt, hunc pro patre uenerantes, filios contra se ab hoc appellari gloriati sunt, ut si a factis ius estimemus, et ad iuris probationem satis fuerit facta docere, ut quicquid aliquando factum apparuerit, id etiam iure factum esse omnino fateamur: potior erit haud dubie causa Romanorum episcoporum. Nolim uideri à quo longissime absum tam uanus, aut impudens, ut dissimulem quæ facta sunt, nedum negem. *et* tamen cu*m* hæc concessero, quæ negari non possunt, uidetur mihi, q*uod* quemadmodum uirtus etiam tum cum maxime deiicitur, uiciis*que* obducitur, uim tamen suam alicunde ostendit, ut oppressam in præsentia, non plane extinctam intellegamus: Sic in mediis iis factis, quæ principis iuri, at*que* authoritati derogasse uideantur, uelut è longissimis te*n*ebris lux quædam ueritatis semper emicuit,

f. 20 b

---

<sup>*a*</sup> The word *now* here implies nothing as to time.    <sup>*b*</sup> *Sic* for *them*.
<sup>*c*</sup> A familiar locution meaning: "In point of fact, as a matter of fact, truly, really" (*N.E.D.*).    <sup>*d*</sup> More accurately: "If this be to be the head, to bear rule over the whole body".    <sup>*e*</sup> *Them* to be supplied

statutes by their autoritie and by their owne lawes / for to enquire of heresie / wherin consisteth the chief and principall poynt of office / which is yet still / and hathe alwayes ben obserued euen vnto these dayes. But now[a] have they permitted many thinges vnto the Bishoppes and clergie / and haue graunted them many immunities / the graunt wherof ought to be a wondrous great argument / either that Princes haue ben hitherto desired in vayne to graunt that / that is an other mannes / which ought to perteyne nothinge vnto him[b] / and that they gaue / that they had not them selues / which is a playne absurditie / or elles that they had power to exer-‖cise them selues / that they graunted to other: and that therfore / they remitted and departed in so dooing / with parte of their owne right.  Which beinge euen so / Princes haue ben allwaies headdes / mater in dede[c] / euen than / whan they were called only Defendours / if this be to be the headde vnto the body: to beare rule ouer all the people[d] / to commaunde / remitte / and somtyme to beare with all the membres therof / as muche as tendeth to the vse of al *the* hoole body / and so to ordre and modcrate euery thinge / that the glorie of God / and the profession of the faithe maye be advaunced from daye to daye.  But these men will saye: Princes haue acknowlaged the Bishop of Rome / to be the headde of the vniuersall churche: to him they haue geven condigne honoure / as to supreme headde / to him they haue submitted[e] selues / his autoritie they haue acknowlaged / reuerenceing him as their father / and reioyceing[f] that he called them sonnes / so that if we shoulde eotome the light by the dedes / *and* if it be ynough to teache dedes for the profe of the right / so as / what so euer is apparauntly done / we must confesse it to be done rightefully:[g] than doubtles the Bishoppes of Romes cause shalbe on the better hande.

I wolde not be reputed so vayne or so impudent ‖ a man (which is *the* formust ende of my thought)[h] as to clocke[i] or to saye naye / to those thinges *that* haue ben done / and yet whan I shall graunt to suche thinges as can not be denyed / me thinketh / that like as vertue / whan it is most throwne vnder fote / and soiled with vices / yet it sheweth his efficacie / by one shifte or other / that we maye vnderstonde it to be presently oppressed / but not vtterly extincte / euen so in the meane season / dedes[j] / which seme to dymynishe the right title / and autoritie of the prince / a certain light of the truthe

*the autoritie and im- munitie of bishoppes geuen by princes*

Sig. E v b

Sig. E vj a winchestre not im- pudent / no full lothe.

here.   [f] More exactly: "glorying".   [g] The translator here fails to render the ironical tone of Gardiner's sentence, especially in the last part: "so that, whatsoever appears to have been done at some time or other, we must confess it...".   [h] Which is as far removed as possible from my thoughts.   [i] To cloak.   [j] Unintelligible. Probably a misprint for "in the midst of deeds...".

ex qua propius, ac certius intuenti, licuit deprehendere, non fuisse hæc facta solida, integra, iustisque fundamentis innixa, sed speciosa magis quam uera, et honoris fœnerati, potius quam soluti argumenta. Etenim si illa unquam opinio principum animis penitus insedisset, Romanum episcopum Christi in terris uicarium fuisse, hoc est omnibus esse a deo caput constitutum, cui parerent omnia,

f. 21 a omnia o-||bedirent, sine quo nihil usquam sanctum haberi debeat, nedum sacrum, cuius benedictio prospera, maledictio semper aduersa daret, aut si hoc ipsis adeo Romanis episcopis sic se habere persuasum fuisset. Neque ipsi Romani episcopi quæsitis artibus et humano ambitu potius quam solido diuinæ ueritatis testimonio, si quod huiusmodi proferre potuissent hactenus in defendenda authoritate usi fuissent, neque principes illi suis quisque temporibus illam ipsam authoritatem, quam uocabulis, et appellationibus concedere uidebantur rebus ipsis, et factis non clam, sed aperte sic imminuere ausi fuissent, eorum certe principum, quorum summam in deum religionem, illis in sanctorum numerum relatis, orbis iam post funera colit, et ueneratur.[1] Nempe si episcopo Romano curam totius orbis a deo commissam maiores credidissent, quæ tandem audacia eos impulerit, ut tam multa statuerent curæ illi, et eius prætextu uenditanti se potestati aduersantia, atque contraria, et ut alia multa fecissent, illud certe quod tamen fecerunt, nunquam fuissent ausi facere, ut quem a deo speculatorem ad uidendum in eminentiore loco positum existimassent, huius oculos ne prouiderent impedire, obicemque opponere uoluissent. Aequum fuit credo tantam diligentiam in dei uicario improbare, qui cura

f. 21 b uide-||licet, ac solicitudine omnium ecclesiarum affectus,

---

[1] The allusion can only be to the Anglo-Saxon kings, several of whom were and are worshipped as saints, and who, in respect of jurisdiction, were in practice the heads of the Church in England, there being no clear distinction or boundary between Church and State. They frequently issued laws on definitely spiritual matters, and appointed, or deposed, archbishops of Canterbury and York. The latter went to Rome for the pall, which was readily granted to the king's nominees, the Pope allowing England considerable freedom in ecclesiastical matters.    *a* *Sic* for *marketh*.    *b* Than it is true indeed.    *c* And are tokens....    *d* Inaccurate: "Honour *lent* rather

hathe always peeped out / as it were / out of most depe darkenes / wherby he that marke it[a] more nerely and more surely / might perceave / that these dedes were not hoole nor perfite / ne grounded vpon iuste foundaciones / but had a greater appearaunce of truthe / than[b] true in dede / and[c] tokens of honoure rather borowed[d] than payde. For if that opinion had euer sonke in to Princes heartes / that the Bishop of Rome had ben Christes vicare on earthe / that is / the headde ordayned of God to be ouer all / vnto whom al thinges shoulde bowe / all thinges shoulde obeye / without whom / nothing must be reconed holye nor sacred / whose blessinge shoulde alwaies geve prosperitie / whose curse aduersitie / or if the Bissoppes[e] of Rome ‖ were persuaded / that it were so: the bishoppes of Rome wolde not haue practised straunge artes / and carnall fetches / rather than strong testimonie of Goddes truthe / if they coulde yet to this daye haue brough[f] out any suche / in the defense of their autoritie:[g] nether[h] durst the princes haue ben so bolde / euery one in his tyme / as to nyppe awaye that same autoritie (which they semed to graunt in wordes and termes of speache) after that facion in their procedinges / and doinges / not in corners but openly in the face of the worlde:[i] I speake of suche princes / whose excellent religious deuocion / the worlde now after their deathes / reverenceth and worshipp-eth: and reconeth them amonge the nombre of Saintes[j] verily if our elders had beleued / that God had committed the charge of all the hoole worlde / vnto the bishop of Rome / what wilfull boldenes caused them / to make so many statutes agaynst / and contrary to that charge and power aduaunceing it selfe / vnder that pretense? and as they wolde haue done many other thinges[k] / yet they durst neuer haue ben so bolde / to doo / that they did / to haue purposed to blyndefelde[l] him / from loking about him / and to stoppe his eies / whom they extemed[m] for a watcheman set of God / in the higher place / to see? I thinke / ‖ it was mete / to mislike so great a diligence in Goddes vicare / for that he beinge burthened with the cure and charge of all

Sig. E vj b

If *the* bis*hoppe* of *Rome* were christes vicar / he wolde not haue practised iuggli*n*ges

Sig. E vij a

than paid ".    [e] *Sic* for *Bisshoppes*.    [f] *Sic* for *brought*.    [g] More accurately: "would not hitherto have made use, in defending their authority, of strange arts, etc.".    [h] Neither.    [i] These latter words added by the translator.    [j] The sentence ends here.    [k] The sentence is here mistranslated, no doubt owing to the obscurity of the Latin text. The meaning seems to be as follows: "and supposing that they had done many other things, yet they would never have dared to do that which however they certainly did, namely, to have purposed...". [l] Blindfold.    [m] Obsolete for *esteemed*.

ne pastores deessent populo, triplici interdum substitutione prouidit.[1] In superiorem quidem, aut aduersus eum nulla legis latio legitima est. Inferiores enim non præscribunt iis qui præsunt: sed neque eorum administrationi quantumuis iniquæ, et graui, frena iure imponunt. Itaque maiores nostri retroque principes, qui maturo consilio in publicis consiliis cum ad consultandum de republica conuenissent, illam in Romanis episcopis oculorum aciem[2] ne prouisionem suam ad nos usque intenderent, æditis legibus arcendam censuerunt:[3] nec suæ interim conditionis inscii fuisse uidentur, nec illius potestatis originem, atque naturam prorsus ignorasse. quorum in ea re et iuditia, et facta episcopi Romani adeo non improbanda existimauerunt, ut principes ipsos, qui hoc et statuerunt, et obseruarunt non modo non reprehenderint, sed acceptam etiam cladem dissimulantes, a fide atque obedientia laudarint.[4] homines

[1] An allusion to the Great Schism and the Council of Constance. It will be remembered that there were at the time three rival Popes, Benedict XIII, Gregory XII, and John XXIII. English public opinion in all classes of the population was greatly concerned at such a state of things. As early as the Council of Pisa in 1408, the English delegates had done their best to put an end to the schism. At Constance (1414–17) it was the intervention of Henry Beaufort, bishop of Winchester, and uncle of Henry V, that decided the election of Martin V, in place of the three rival claimants to the Papacy. The order of ideas in the present passage would then be the following: " If our ancestors had acknowledged the claims of the Holy See, they would never have been bold enough to limit the authority of the Pope; but in fact they did not acknowledge them; and it was right (*æquum*) on their part to disapprove of the vicar of God who, lest the Church should lack pastors, substituted three Popes in place of one ". Of course it cannot be said that the vicar of God—i.e. any given Pope—actually appointed three successors to himself; and, at first sight, the sentence would appear more intelligible if " in conciliis " or " in cardinalibus " was substituted for " in dei vicario ". Yet it must be considered that the English disapproved of the three Popes themselves, and thus " in dei vicario " may be taken as a collective plural—or, again, as an equivalent for the Papacy, the papal institution in itself, rather than any particular Pope. The English objected to three Popes having substituted themselves for one, or to the Papacy having provided three Popes at one time. The translator entirely misses the point and understands the passage as if the Pope had created the orders of bishops, priests and deacons, which is of course absurd. The allusion to the Council of Constance is in keeping with other references to England's anti-papal past. It may be noticed that part of the English clergy were willing to grant the council an authority superior to that of the Pope.      [2] Comma here in the Strasbourg edition.      [3] An allusion to the various legal

124

churches / lest the people shoulde want shepeherdes / made prouision with iij. sortes of vnder sheperdes.[a] Against[b] the superiour / or against him / it is not laufull to make any lawe.

For inferiours prescribe not lawes to the superiours / nether doo they laufully make penalties[c] against their gouuernement / how wicked / or intolerable so euer it be. Therfore our elders / and princes / that were before tyme / whan they assembled together to counsail vpon maters of the common weale / taking deliberate advisement in their open counsailes / haue by statutes and lawes determinately thought it mete put out that quicke sight in the bishoppes of Romes eies / that it shoulde not serve them to loke ouer / so ferre as vnto vs: yea / those princes seme that they knewe owne right autoritie[d] / and that they were not al ignoraunt of the originall begynning and nature of the Bishop of Romes power; and yet the bisshoppes of Rome thought it good to allowe bothe their iudgementes and doinges / in *that* behalfe / so muche / that they haue not only / not founde faulte with those Princes / which bothe made suche statutes and kept them / but also ‖ dissembling the foile that they had taken / commended those Princes / for their fidelitie and obedience. Yea Mary Sir / the bishoppes of

A wylie foxes.

Sig. E vij b

enactments which were put in force at different times during the Middle Ages, in order to restrain the jurisdiction of the Holy See, such as the Constitutions of Clarendon (1262) which forbade appeals to Rome, the Statute of Provisors (1350) which did away with apostolical reservations, the Statute of Præmunire (1353) which again made all appeals to Rome penal offences.    [4] The above-mentioned anti-papal legislation was never fully enforced. King and Parliament in the fourteenth century publicly denied the Pope's right to reserve to himself the collation of benefices in England; but nevertheless, when the king wanted to confer an ecclesiastical dignity upon one of his own favourites, he often appealed to the Pope for his support, thus implicitly acknowledging his authority. It needs scarcely be wondered at, therefore, that some of those very kings in whose reign anti-papal statutes were enacted or re-enacted, should have found favour in the Popes' eyes. Such favour was obviously not equivalent to a renunciation of papal pretensions, or an acknowledgment that they were ungrounded; and thus Gardiner's reasoning, though founded on fact, is really valueless.    [a] Mistranslated: "It was right in them, I think, to disapprove of such diligence in the vicar of God (or rather the Papacy) who, inclined thereto by his care and solicitude for all churches, lest the people should lack pastors, provided those by substituting three (popes) for one". Cf. note on corresponding Latin passage.    [b] A typical instance of the slipshod character of the translation, *against* being twice used in succession, first to translate *in* and then *adversus*. Yet the meaning is not the same, and the difference may be expressed as follows: "it is not lawful to pass legislation bearing on the superior, or directed against him".    [c] More exactly: "place a curb on".    [d] Probably "their own right and authority".

125

nimirum cauti, et prudentiores in generatione sua, callidos in hoc negotiatores imitantes, qui ex inutili stipulatione cum dimidium uix auferant, discedunt tamen quieti, id omne lucro quod acceperint, deputantes, cum nihil iure potuissent uendicare. Maiores autem nostri cum Romanorum Episcoporum authoritatem ex fructibus depre-||

f. 22 a  hendissent, nec dei uicarium iudicassent, ita putauerunt, tollerandam præcariam illam authoritatem quidem cum moderamine, sic enim ratio tum ferebat[1] non abiiciendam, sensisse certe nobiscum se, æditis factis apertissime significauerunt. Cæterum ut est cuiusque animi magnitudo, ita uel suum uendicat, et præsente animo utitur, uel oblata utilitate contentus, cætera dissimulat animi securus. Quæ cum ita sint, nihil est quòd moueant reliqua facta quantumcunque in specie aduersantia, quibus iuri diuino haud potuerunt derogare, suamque potestatem temeritate minuere, aut negligentia. Appellarint sane episcopos Romanos patres, appellarint capita, ornarint quibuscunque præterea nominibus, ueritas certe rerum erroribus gestorum[2] non uitiatur. Fuit olim Romana ecclesia uel sanctimoniæ specie, uel potestatis amplitudine non modo magni nominis, uerum summæ etiam authoritatis. quum authoritatem dico, Tullii[3] sensum sequuor,[4] qui in testimoniorum pondere ingeniosis, et opulentis propter uulgi iudicium, etiam si interdum non rectum, ut ipse ait, tamen quia non facile mutatur, tribuit authoritatem. Nam alioquin authoritas, quæ diuino iure censeretur Romano episcopo nulla est apud nos quidem, quemadmodum nec

---

[1] Comma here in the Hamburg edition.    [2] *Sic*, but corrected to *gestarum* in the Strasbourg edition.    [3] It has not been possible to determine exactly which one of Cicero's sayings or works Gardiner is here alluding to. Merguet's *Lexikon zu den Schriften Ciceros* has been consulted in vain.    [4] *Sic* for *sequor*.    [a] The translator does not seem to realize that the Latin comparative implies no real comparison here and is equivalent to "very".    [b] Of the same hair (*N.E.D.*).    [c] Who, when they scarcely obtain one-half of the price they had in vain asked for, bargained for, yet....    [d] *Pick-purse* is very much in the translator's style for *borrowed*. *Cum moderamine* is not translated: "must be borne withal with certain temperaments".    [e] More exactly: "the state of things (when considered)".    [f] The translation is rather obscure here; the sequence of ideas may be better expressed as follows: "Our ancestors tolerated the authority of the bishop of Rome; but there is reason to think that they agreed

Rome were circumspecte / and the more wittye men<sup>a</sup> in their generacion / folowing in this case the example of subtyl marchauntes / that of an vnthriftye bargayn<sup>c</sup> / whan they haue scant halfe / yet they holde them content / reconyng it all wonne that they had / because of right they coulde haue claymed nothing. As for our elders / whan they perceaued the bishop of Romes autoritie by his frutes / and iudged him not to be Goddes vicare / they thought / that pykepurse autoritie must be borne withall<sup>d</sup> / and not cleane cast out (for so reason<sup>e</sup> permitted at *that* tyme) but their expressed dedes doo most manifestly declare / that they were of the same iudgement / that we are of. Neuertheles / as euery mannes hearte serueth him / so dothe he either clayme his owne / *and* vseth it / like a stowte hearted man / or elles beinge content with the commoditie that is offred him / letteth the rest alone / and wotteth what he thinketh.<sup>f</sup> And seing the mater stondeth euen so / ther is no reason / why the rest of their doinges shoulde trouble them / how contrary in outwarde appearaunce so euer they seme / by the which they coulde nyppe a-‖waye nothing from Goddes lawe / and dymynyshe their power / through temeritie or by necligence.<sup>g</sup> Let men<sup>h</sup> call the Bishoppes of Rome / fathers: let theym call them / headdes: let them ad-vaunce them with what names / they lust: yet the truthe of thinges / is not impeched by errours of thynges mysdone.

The churche of Rome / was in the olde tyme / either by reason of outwarde holynes or by mightie power / not only of great fame / but also of highe autoritie: whan I speake of autoritie / I folowe Tullies meaning / who / in *the* weightie importaunce of witnesse bearing<sup>i</sup> / attributeth autoritie vnto such as be wittye and wealthye men / because of the common peoples iudgement / though it be not alwayes a right<sup>j</sup> / as he saithe / yet because it is not easily altred. For elles the autoritie / that the bishob<sup>k</sup> of Rome shoulde be thought to haue by Goddes lawe / is non autoritie with vs in dede / like as no maner of

*(margin)* you are a whelpe of *the* same heare<sup>b</sup>

*(margin)* *the* neclig-ence *and* temeritie of princes putteth not away *the* autoritie *that* god geueth them. Sig. E viij a errours of mysdoinges hurteth not the truthe of the thinges

*(margin)* *the* churche of Rome godly in the olde tyme. Autoritie after Tullies minde *etc.*

with us. Besides, in cases in which a man's right is contested, he may, according to the greatness of his soul, either claim everything, and exert his own right with a resolute heart, or being contented with the advantage offered to him, keep silent as to the rest, sacrifice the rest, being safe as to his right in his own heart, drawing safety from his inner certainty of his right".　*<sup>g</sup>* The translation is obscure, and may be improved thus: "Things being so, there is no reason why any other [past] actions [of our princes], however contrary [to their present claims] in appearance, should trouble them, for it was not possible for them to take away from divine right by their doings, or to lessen their power through temerity, or negligence".　*<sup>h</sup>* Mis-translated: "They (the princes) may well have called...etc."　*<sup>i</sup>* In regard to the weight of evidence....　*<sup>j</sup>* The adverb *aright*, referring to *judgment*.　*<sup>k</sup>* *Sic* for *bishop*.

cuiusqua*m* externi episcopi. Neq*ue* hic ueritati afferat
f. 22 b praeiudicium, quod uariis consiliis ‖ antehac homines in
speciem fecerunt. nempe uel inseruientes suæ utilitati,
uel tempori cedentes, aut ignorantia occupati. uincat modo
ueritas diuini uerbi, quæ si istis Ro*manis* episcopis nihil
concedit amplius, q*uam* cæteris episcopis, uidelicet ut
commissam in sua diocesi plebem diuini uerbi, et sacra-
mentoru*m* ministratione alant, et pascant, ne præscribatur
tempore, ueritati diuinæ, nec iudicentur principes, aut
populus ignorantia occæcati, calliditate circumuenti, aut
utilitate rerum capti, aut denique quouis alio respectu
inducti fecisse, quod facere nullo facto debuissent, aut
potuissent. An quia consulere episcopum Ro*manum* in
rege*n*da ecclesia moris fuit, illo id propterea inconsulto
nihil agere liceat? et quia principes eos a suis consuli per-
miseru*n*t, propria eo pacto iurisdictione se exolueru*n*t,[1]
quam a deo commissam no*n* licet abdicare? Quæ præteritis
temporibus confusa sunt, reuocentur ad amussim uerbi
dei, expendantur utriusque potestatis fundamenta, et
quemadmodu*m* principis amplissimam potestatem non
corrogatis, aut eblanditis populi suffragiis quæsitam, sed
a deo collata*m* diuini uerbi testimonio supra ostendimus,
etiam num idem deus episcopo Romano aliquam potestatem
concesserit, quæ supreme*æ* principum potestati debeat
f. 23 a derogare consideremus. Qua in re ‖ non est quod in
scruta*n*dis ueteris testamenti scripturis detineamur, in
quibus sacerdotes summis principibus subditos fuisse, et
supra nonnihil attigimus, et multis aliis locis est mani-
festissimum. An non Aaron Moysen pro domino agnouit,
Exod. 32. quæ est appellatio imperium agnoscentis? Nunquid
eode*m* subiectionis uocabulo usus est Achimelech summus
1. Regu*m*. 22. sacerdos, cum loqueretur ad Saul rege*m* Israel? Nonne
3. Regum. 2. Salomon in summum sacerdote*m* Abiathar etiam capitali

---

[1] *Se exsoluerunt.*    [a] *To florishe out,* "to flourish out = to orna-
ment, to adorn, to decorate, hence to embellish" (*N.E.D.*). The
translator understands *species* as meaning "beauty". The real meaning
is "to give things a certain appearance in order to obtain an advantage", more simply, "to deceive".    [b] Put to shame.    [c] *Sic* for
*spiritual.*    [d] Let no prescription of time avail against God's truth.
[e] Another instance of the translator's carelessness or haste. The
meaning of the text is as follows: "Nor let it be judged that princes or

forayne bishop also hathe autoritie among vs.    Nether let it / in this case / be preiudicall vnto the truthe / that men haue done here to fore in sondrye counsailles / to florishe out the mater withall :[a] that is to saye / either seruing their owne turne / or geving place to *the* tyme / or elles blinded through ignoraunce. Let the truthe of ‖ Goddes worde haue the victorie now / which if it geue no more autoritie vnto these Bishoppes of Rome / than to all other bishoppes / that is / to fede *and* bring up the people / within their diocese committed to their spirttual[c] charge / with the ministracion of the worde of God / and of his sacramentes : let not tyme prescribe against Goddes truthe[d] / nether let it be iudged / that the Pri*n*ces or the people were blinded[e] *with* ignorau*n*ce / circumve*n*ted with subtiltie / or gredy of gaines / either induced through any other respecte / to doo / that they nether ought nor coulde possiblye by any meanes haue done.  Because men haue vsed / to aske the Bishop of Rome counsail in gouerning the churche / is it not lauful therfore to doo any thinge without his counsaill?  And because Princes haue suffred their subiectes / to aske his counsaill[f] / did they by that meanes geue ouer their owne autoritie / which / because it is committed vnto them by God / it is not laufull for them to put awaye?  Let the maters / that haue / in tymes past / ben made a myngle mangle / be called agayne to the true square of Goddes worde : let the groundes of bothe their powers be wayed / and like as we haue by testimonie of Goddes worde shewed before / that a Princes mightie power is not ‖ goten by flattery / or by priuilege of *the* people[g] / but geue*n* of God / let vs also considre / whether the selfe same God haue geuen any power to *the* bishop of Rome / that ought to hindre the supreme power of princes.  And in this mater / we nede not to make much a doo in searching out the scriptures of the olde testame*n*t / wherin we haue aswell touched somwhat all ready as also it is most manifest in many other places / that the priestes were in subieccion to *the* high princes.  Did not Aaron take Moyses for his soueraigne lorde / which is the maner of speche of him that acknowlageth superiour autoritie?  Did not Achimelech the high Priest vse the same worde of subieccion / whan he spake to Saul / the kinge of Israel?  Did not Solomon put Abiathar the high priest to deathe? what did

Remembre this lesson your selfe / elles ye wilbe she*nt*[b] one day.

Sig. E viij b

Tyme may not pre-scribe against truthe.

Pri*n*ces may not put awaye their supremacie / because they haue it of God.

Let maters amyse be called home agayn to *the* line of Goddes worde.
Sig. F a

Examples *that* high priestes were subiectes to pri*n*ces.

Exo. xxxij.

j. Reg. xxij

iij. Re. ij

---

people, when blinded by ignorance, deceived by guile, carried away by the hope of gain, or impelled by any other motive, ever performed what it was neither permissible nor possible for them to perform ". In other words whatever princes or people may have done against their own right, they could not possibly alienate it.      *f* More exactly: "suffered them (the Popes) to be consulted by their subjects". *g* More exactly: "by the suffrages of the people, obtained by begging or flattery".

sententia animaduertit? Quid quod Alexander rex, ut est
in libro Machabeorum, scripsit Ionathæ, dicens? Nunc
constituimus te hodie summum sacerdotem gentis tuæ.[1]
An non hæc satis indicant superiorem principum esse,
etiam summis sacerdotibus, potestatem? Omitto, quod
Demetrius Simoni summum sacerdotium contulerit, ac
deinde aliis.[2] Præetereo etiam alia quamplurima. Non tam
enim confirmationis uim habeat ex diuina lege exemplorum
multitudo, quam ostentationem.[3] Hoc nanque[4] interest
diuina et humana, quod illa constantia, hæc uanitati, ac
proinde uarietati semper sint subiecta. In illis itaque
nunquam non est uerum, quod exemplo semel pro uero
proditum est. ut ad probandam supremam principum
potestatem, atque authoritatem unius Ezechiæ exemplum
diuina historia testatum, ac nobis com-||mendatum merito
suffecisset. Relinquitur ergo ut Romanus episcopus aut
noui instrumenti tabulas proferat, aut nullas. Primum
autem ut de noua lege in uniuersum loquamur, qui potest
illius auctoritati ulla in Christi uerbis syllaba suffragari?
cum idem Christus tam aperte sit, et uerbis, et factis pro-
testatus, non terrenum se regnum quæsisse, aut huiusmodi
regnum arrogare se unquam uoluisse, sed manente
ordinum statu, cælestis conuersationis formam, et in-
testinæ mentis iustum per dei gratiam imperium tradere,
atque docere, quod non in fastu, et dominatione, sed contra
in humilitate, et rerum humanarum contemptu consistere
factis luculentis, dum pro nobis acerbissimum, et crudelis-
simum mortis genus pateretur, clarissime declarauit. Cuius
profecto uices sunt, si quis eas bona cum fide obire uelit,
non præesse, sed subesse, non principibus imperare, sed
eorum potestatem, atque imperium agnoscere. idque non

---

[1] I Mach. x, 20.    [2] I Mach. xiv, 38: "Et rex Demetrius statuit
illi summum sacerdotium". The kings here placed by Gardiner on a
par with Saul and Solomon belonged to the dynasties which shared
among themselves the remnants of the empire of Alexander the Great.
Those princes were not Jewish; what is more, they were heathen
despots holding the Jewish people in subjection, and Gardiner's
reasoning, in the present case, would tend to prove that even a foreign
and non-christian prince can exercise supreme authority in spiritual
matters.    [3] Marginal note in the Strasbourg edition: "Exempla
non probant sed ornant".    [4] Namque.    [a] Probable misprint for is.

KingeAlexander (as it appeareth in the boke of Machabees) write
to Jonatha / sayeng? **Now haue we this day ordayned the**
**to be the high priest of thy people.** Doo not these sayenges /
sufficiently declare / that the power of Princes / as*ᵃ* aboue euen
the highest priestes of all? I speake nothing / that Demetrius
gaue vnto Symon the office of the highe priest / and so to others
after him. I passe also ouer many other moo. For the multitude of examples out ‖ of Goddes lawe dothe not so strongly
confirme as shewe*ᵇ* the truthe. For this is the difference betwene Goddes lawe / and mannes:*ᶜ* Goddes lawe is constaunt /
but mannes lawe is euer subiecte vnto vanitie / *and* so vnto
varietie. In Goddes worde*ᵈ* therfore / it is alwaies true / that
is ones set out by example for truthe*ᵉ* / as / to proue the supreme
power and autoritie of princes / the example of Esechias alone /
which is regestred in Goddes boke / and commended vnto vs /
might iustly haue suffised. It remayneth tha*n* / that the bishop
of Rome / must ether bring out the tables of the newe testament / or non.*ᶠ* But furst / to speake vniuersally of the newe
lawe / how can any sillable in Christes wordes / helpe his
autoritie / seing the selfe same Christ / dothe so openly protest
bothe in wordes and in dedes / that he sought not a*ᵍ* earthely
kingdome / nor wolde clayme any suche kinde of kingdome /
but (the state of ordres remayning still) he set furthe and
taught the forme of heauenly conuersacion / and the iuste
gouernaunce of the inwarde mynde / through *the* grace of god /
which he by his open doinges most playnly declared / to
consiste / not in highe ruffling estate nor in ruling the rost / but
contrary wise / in humilitie and contempte of wordly*ⁱ* thinges /
wha*n* ‖ he suffred *the* most bitter *and* cruell ki*n*de of deathe for
our sakes. And *the* pointes of office / of him that is his vicare /
if he doo his office faithfully / are / not to beare rule / but to
be in subieccio*n* / not to comma*u*nde princes / but to acknowlage him selfe to be vnder their power *and* comma*u*ndeme*n*t /
not only whan they co*m*maunde thinges indifferent / and easily
to be done / but also whan they commaunde thinges not in-

j. Mach x

j. Mach. xiiij.

Sig. F b

Goddes
lawe
co*n*staunt /
mannes
vayne *and*
variable

Christ
altred not
the state af*ʰ*
ordres

Sig. F ij a
*the* office
of him *that*
occupieth
christes
rowme.

---

*ᵇ* The translator seems to have misunderstood the sentence: "It is
not necessary to give so many examples for the sake of proof, it would
rather savour of ostentation". The marginal note in the Strasbourg
edition seems to adopt the same meaning. *ᶜ* More exactly: "between things divine and human". *ᵈ* More general in the Latin
text: "In God's matters" (*Illis* refers to *divina*). *ᵉ* That is always
true, which one example has shown to be true, so that to prove....
*ᶠ* Or none at all. *ᵍ* Sic for *an.* *ʰ* Sic for *of.* *ⁱ* Misprint or
rather erratic form for *worldly.*

solum cum æqua imperent, et facile obeunda, sed iniqua
etiam modo impia non sint, in conuiciis, in plagis, in
uerberibus usque ad mortem, et mortem quidem crucis.
Hæc sunt certa Christi uestigia, atque adeo hæc in Christo
dominandi maiestas: hæc inquam, est Christi uera potestas,
et admirabilis nobis, ac summe salutaris: per quam data

f. 24 a est nobis etiam potestas filios || dei fieri. hanc factis docuit,
atque expressit, de regno Israel. Somniantes discipulos
semper increpauit: neque aut Cæsaris tributo, aut cuiusquam potestati quicquam factis aliquando derogauit.
Atque hæc cum ita se habeant, iam fecimus opinor, manifestum, si Christi facta consideramus, quæ mutari non
possunt, nec ullam ambiguam interpretationem recipere,
reperiemus plane omnia cum his ex dyametro pugnare,
quæ tanquam Christi uicarius sibi uendicat episcopus
Romanus. Superest igitur tantum hoc, ut ad uerba ipsa
confugiat euangelistarum, de quibus quidem ipsis (utcunque
in interpretatione sit uariatum) ut sunt tamen in contextum relata inter omnes satis constat. In iis autem quid
quærit? Nimirum hoc. Num dixerit aliquando Christus
uia ueritas, et uita, in quo a factis nonnihil dissentiret suis?
ut quam nunquam apud homines exegerit ipse authoritatem, eam nihilominus Romano episcopo tanquam suo
uicario commiserit usurpandam. Hæc est certe quæstionis summa, uerbis quidem (ut proponitur) blasphema,
et impia, sed quæ rem profecto ipsam exprimit quæ
tractetur. Nam cum in cæteris omnibus cæpit[1] Iesus, ut
euangelista testatur, facere et docere, et quod factis præstitit, doctrina exprimere: hac una certe in re, de qua
nunc agitur, si quid docuerit eius, quod hodie christi

f. 24 b titulo || sibi arrogat Romanus episcopus uidelicet ex
uerbis Christi principibus præesse, confitendum omnino
erit docuisse Christum uerbis id, cuius nullum in seipso
exemplum non modo ædidit, sed cuius longe diuersum in
perpetuo uitæ cursu præmonstrauit. Maneat itaque hoc
in causa, Christi facta a nobis stare, quæ nulla hominum
interpretatione queant torqueri, Tantum in Christi uerbis

[1] *Cœpit.*   [a] We shall find plainly, that to be clean contrary
to the above [teachings of Christ] which the bishop of Rome....

different / so they be not wicked: in checkes / in scourginges / and beatinges vnto deathe / yea euen to the deathe of the crosse. In dede / these are Christes fotesteppes / *and* this is the maiestie of rule bearing in Christ: This / I saye / is the true power of Christ / vnto vs bothe wonderous / and exceding holsom: by the which also is power geuen to vs / to become the children of God. This he taught and expressed in his doinges / touching *the* kingdome of Israel. His dreaming disciples he alwayes rebuked: but he neuer hyndred Cesares tribute / nor any mannes autoritie / one iote by his dedes. And seing it is so / I wene / I haue made it manifest / if we considre Christes dedes / which maye not be altred nor doubtefully interpreted: we shal finde playnly / that all is cleane contrary*a* / that the bisshop of Rome chalengeth to him self / as Christes vicare. This therfore only remayneth / that he || flee to the wordes of the euangelistes / which (how so euer men haue varied in the interpretacion) all men knowe well ynough / how they stande in the texte. But what loketh he for / in them? Mary Sir / this. Whether Christ / the waye / the truthe and the life / spake euer any thingh / wherin he shoulde disagree from his owne dedes? *that* wher he never sought autoritie among men / he gaue it notwithstonding to the bishop of Rome / to vse as his vicare. This in dede is the summe of the question / in wordes (as it is propounded) blasphemous / and wicked / but yet it paynteth out the mater / that I haue in hande. For wher in al other maters / as *the* euangeliste reporteth / Jesus begane to doo and to teache / *and* to teache that he did: And in this one only maters*b* / which we now treate of / if he taught any whitte of that / which the bishop of Rome claymeth at this daie to him selfe / by Christes title / that is / to be aboue Princes / by Christes wordes / we must nedes confesse / that Christ taught in wordes / that wherof he not only shewed no example in him selfe / but shewed cleane contrary in all the hole course of his life before. Let this therfore remayne still in *the* cause*c* / that Christes dedes stande on our side / which maye not be wrested by no mannes interpretacion: only the que||stion is in Christes

Christes
wordes and
dedes agree.

---

*b* *Sic* for *matter*.    *c* Let this point be settled once and for all in our favour, let this remain as a gain for our cause.

133

quæstionem esse, quæ humana interpretatio interdum audet uiolare. Quanquam etiam cum ipso Romano Episcopo hac in causa congressurus, in eo primum posset insistere. Nullam de ipso Ro*mano* episcopo in scripturis sacris syllabam reperiri, ut quancun*que* uerborum Christi interpretationem confirmauerit, extra oleas quod dicitur uersari[1] uideretur. Nam quæ tandem consequentia est? Petru*m* uoluit Christus pri*n*cipibus præesse, id quod nun*quam* etiam uoluisse uidetur, ergo etiam et episcopum Roma*num*. An scilicet quia est successor Petri? utina*m* esset, nihil a*m*plius dico. quo casu præesset omnibus non dubio, si non eminentia potestatis externæ, cuiusmodi haud dubie nullam habet, at certe admiratione, ac ueneratione internæ uirtutis, quo nomine, ipsis etiam imperatoribus uoluit Christus suos prælucere, ac primatum obtinere.

f. 25 a Vtpote quibus, tanq*uam* legatione pro se fu*n*-||gentibus, claues etiam tradidit regni cælorum, et in iis Petro, qui omnium nomine confessionem primus emiserat tam salutarem, ut Iesum agnosceret filium dei uiui. Quam quidem confessione*m* ut caro et sanguis non reuelauerat, ita nec carni in Petro, aut sanguini data est prerogatiua, quæcu*n*que est data, sed potiori eius parti, qui spiritus

Primatus erat, nimirum ut uberiore gratia a deo donatus, in uirtute,
Petri. ac uerbi dei potentia regendorum*que* affectuu*m* potestate primatu*m* obtineret. q*uod* si Christi uerba sic interpretaremur, ut externam aliquam in dominando potestatem,

---

[1] This curious and apparently mysterious idiom occurs again in another one of Gardiner's woɪks in a slightly different form: "Extra oleas vagari" (*Annotationes in Œcolampadium*, Lambeth Library, MS No. 140, p. 51). It is not to be met with in the usual repertories of classical or medieval Latin, but Erasmus supplies the following explanation in his *Adagia* (*Erasmi Roterodami...adagiorum chiliades tres...*Basileæ, mense Augusto, 1513, fol. 125 b) ῎Εκτὸς τῶν ἐλαιῶν φέρεται. Extra oleas fertur, ubi quis terminos præscriptos transgreditur, aut aliena nec ad rem pertinentia facit, dicitve. Aristophanes in Ranis, μή σε ὁ θυμὸς ἁρπάσας ἐκτὸς οἴσει τῶν ἐλαιῶν. Ne te correptum ira extra oleas auferat. Interpres adagium hinc natum ait. Stadia in quibus currendi certamina peragebantur, oleis per seriem positis utrinque sepiebantur, quas præterire non licebat, proinde, qui præterisset oleas, extra stadium currere videbatur'." The expression clearly means here: "to look for reasons where there are none, to be on a wild goose chase", and the translator wholly mis-

wordes / which now *and* than / ma*n*nes interpretacion is so sawcye as to blemyshe.   Albeit he that shall stande*ᵃ* with the bishop of Rome in this cause / might furst of al / sticke fast in this poynt: that ther is not fou*n*de in the holy scriptures/ so muche as one syllabc / of *the* bishop of Rome / so *that* what interpretacion of Christes wordes so euer he wil stande to / he might seme to lose his accion*ᵇ* / as they saye.   For what is the consequency*ᶜ* than?   Christ wolde haue Petre to be aboue Princes / as it appeareth it was neuer his mindc.*ᵈ*   Ergo he wolde haue the bishop of Rome to be so to.   Why / because he is Petres successour?   I saye no more / but I wolde he were. And than / in that case / I doubt not / but he shoulde be aboue all me*n* / though not*ᵉ* in hault estate of worldly power ( as out of doubt he hathe non suche) yet in admiracion and reuerence of inwarde vertue / and in that poynt / Christ wolde haue those that his be / to excelle and be ring leaders euen aboue emperours: as those / vnto whom / bei*n*ge his Embassadours / he gaue the keyes of the kingdome of heaue*n* / and amo*n*g them / vnto Petre / which in all their names / had*ᶠ* spoken so holsome a co*n*fession / to acknowlage Iesus / to be the sonne of the living God.      Which confession / like as fleshe and bloud had ‖ not reueled / euen so was ther no prerogatiue geuen vnto fleshe and bloud in Petre / what so euer was geuen / but to the chiefer parte / which was the spirite / to *the* intent / that beinge endued the more pleynteously with the Grace of God / he shoulde be the ring leader in vertue *and* mighte of the worde of God / and in the power of ruling affecciones.   If we shoulde so interprete Christes wordes / as if they ment som externe power / in rule

Petre spake one for the*m* all.

Sig. F iij b

---

understands the passage. Gardiner was given to a free use of proverbial locutions; and he himself was to indulge, while a prisoner in the Tower, in the then fashionable pastime of making collections of Latin *adagia*. Several phrases belonging to this class are met with both in *De vera obedientia* (fol. 33 b) and *Contemptum humanæ legis* (pp. 266, 267); we have not been able to trace their origin, but the *aperto sileno* in *Si sedes illa* (fols. *154 b*–185 a) may very well have been borrowed from Erasmus. (Cf. note on the passage.)      *ᵃ* The translator's mistake on the sense of the word *congressurus* makes the whole passage unintelligible. The meaning is as follows: "Although he that would *engage, fight with*, the bishop of Rome in this cause, might first of all take his stand on this point...".      *ᵇ* See note on the corresponding Latin passage.      *ᶜ* The succession or logical order of ideas.      *ᵈ* The latter clause is a parenthesis.      *ᵉ* If not. *ᶠ* The translator omits *primus*, "had *first* spoken", which is surprising, for that is precisely the alleged ground of Peter's primacy.

135

quam reliqui omnes agnoscerent mortales, atq*ue* in iis etia*m* principes, licet antea ab eodem deo in superiori loco collocati, ut nihil aliud afferatur, qui consisteret illa Christi se*n*tentia? Non est discipulus maior domino suo, si præsertim discipulus exemplo Christi imperium no*n* pateretur, sed supremam illam potestate*m* exequeretur ipse, quam dominus nunq*uam* uoluit sibi arrogare. In scripturis de primatu Petri nulla facta est mentio. et Eusebius in ecclesiastica historia refert Clementem in sexto dispositionum libro asseruisse Petrum, Joannem, et Jacobu*m* post assumtionem saluatoris, quamuis ab ipso fuerint omnibus pene prælati, non sibi tame*n* eos primatus gloriam uindicasse, sed Iacobum, qui iustus appella-||batur, apostolorum episcopu*m* esse statutum.[1] Verumtamen propter authoritatem eoru*m*, qui a uerbo primatus non abhorruerunt, uerbum ipsum non perinde refugio, sed ad illam eius uerbi interpretationem confugio, quæ cum genuino eua*n*gelii sensu, in Christi factis depicto, queat conuenire. Fuerit igitur Petrus primus, habuerit etiam primatu*m* a Christo, quid tum postea? an simul cu*m* primatu regnum, aut dominium collatum est, aut præeminentia? An quia iussus sit fratres confirmare in fide, datum est idcirco in fratres exercere imperium? Nullum huius generis uocabulu*m* nouit Christi humilitas, nedum rerum.[2] licet enim Christus deus erat æqualis patri, apud quem erat in principio, et in omnibus quæ ab eo creata, dicta, aut facta sunt, una cum spiritu sancto cooperator

f. 25 b

Iacobus
episcopus
apostoloru*m*.

---

[1] This sentence is almost literally quoted from an early Latin translation of Eusebius' *Historia Ecclesiastica*, that of Rufinus, where the passage runs as follows: "Sicut Clemens in sexto dispositionum libro asserit dicens. Petrus enim inquit et Iacobus et Ioannes post assumptionem salvatoris quamuis ab ipso fuerint omnibus pene prelati. tamen non sibi uendicant primatus gloriam, sed Iacobum qui dicebatur iustus. apostolorum episcopum statuunt". (Edition published at Mantua by Johann Schall in 1479, without a title, Lib. 2, cap. i.) It is of interest to compare the above with the original text, which Gardiner, considering his great familiarity with the Greek fathers, can scarcely have ignored: "Κλήμης δὲ ἐν ἕκτῳ τῶν Ὑποτυπώσεων γράφων ὧδε παρίστησι· 'Πέτρον γάρ φησι καὶ Ἰάκωβον καὶ Ἰωάννην μετὰ τὴν ἀνάληψιν τοῦ Σωτῆρος, ὡς ἂν καὶ ὑπὸ τοῦ Κυρίου προτετιμημένους, μὴ ἐπιδικάζεσθαι δόξης, ἀλλ' Ἰάκωβον τὸν Δίκαιον ἐπίσκοπον Ἱεροσολύμων ἑλέσθαι'" (Migne, *Patrologia Græca*, vol. 20,

bearing / which al other folkes / shoulde acknowlage them selues to be vnder / yea euen Princes to<sup>a</sup> / albeit the same selfe God haue set them in the superiour rowne<sup>b</sup> / so that nothing elles coulde be alleged / how coulde that sentence of Christ stonde together? The disciple is not greater than his maister, namely if the disciple wolde not be content to be in subieccion / as Christ was / but execute the supreme power him selfe / which his lorde wolde neuer take vpon him. In scriptures / ther is no mencion made of Petres supremacie / and Eusebeus in Ecclesiastica historia / reporteth / that **Clemens in sexto li.** Dispositionum, affirmed / that Petre / Iohan / and Iames / after the ascension of our saueour / although he had set them almost aboue all the apostles / yet they toke not the glorie of supremacie vpon them / but that Iames / which is cal-‖led / Iustus<sup>c</sup> / was ordayned the bishop of the apostles. Notwithstonding for the autorities sake of them / which haue not misliked the worde of supremacie<sup>d</sup> / I doo not so muche refuse the worde selfe / but I flee to the interpretacion of the worde / that it maye agree with the right propre meanyng of the Gospell / expressed in Christes dedes. Admitte / that Petre were chief / admitte he had the supremacie of Christ<sup>e</sup> / what of that? was a kingdome / lordeship / or preeminence geuen him / with the supremacie? Because he was bidden to confirme his brethren in faithe / was it geuen him / to beare rule ouer his brethren / therfore? Christes humble estate knewe no suche kinde of speache / nor mater. For though Christ (as touching his Godheadde) was equal vnto the father / with whom he was in the begynnyng and in all thinges / which he created / speake / or did / he was always / together with the holy goste / the indivisible worker

Joan. xiij

Iames
Bishop of
the apostles.

Sig. F iiij a

Supremacie
may be
taken
diuersely.

col. 136, v. 86–7). James is here only said to be, according to the Latin translation in Migne, "Hierosolymorum episcopum", bishop of Jerusalem, which scarcely warrants Gardiner's argument drawn from the passage. The Clement here mentioned is Clemens Alexandrinus, and the *Hypotyposes* from which Eusebius quotes are not now extant.
<sup>2</sup> The sentence is ungrammatical and presumably contains a misprint or a slip of the writer's pen; we ought to read either: "nullum huius generis vocabulum, nedum rem", or "nullum hujus generis vocabulorum, nedum rerum", nothing of those words or even less of those things.   <sup>a</sup> Too.   <sup>b</sup> *Sic* for *room.*   <sup>c</sup> Or rather "the Just". See note on corresponding Latin passage.   <sup>d</sup> The word *supremacy* now implying some measure of power, the Latin *primatus* should be rendered in a modern English translation by the corresponding word *primacy*, both here and throughout the whole passage.   <sup>e</sup> From Christ.

indiuiduus (una uidelicet trium personar*um* in diuinitate
essentia) semper fuerit, licet inqua*m* secundum hanc
maiestatem, omnem potestate*m* habuerit semper, qua
subiiceret sibi omnia: uixit, uiuit: uiuetq*ue*: regnauit,
regnat, atq*ue* regnabit per secula deus omni tempore: pro
imme*n*sa tamen sua in humanum genus misericordia,
seipsum exinaniuit, formam serui accipiens, habitu
inuentus ut homo,[1] atq*ue* adeo inter homines secundu*m*
prophetam, opprobrium,[2] ut faceret planu*m*, atq*ue* aper-||

f. 26 a tum, ea quæ summo apud homines in præcio[3] haberentur,
imperia, dominia, et præemine*n*tias tanq*uam* impedi-
menta quædam ad æternam fœlicitatem assequendam,
abiicienda potius, et contemnenda esse, q*uam* cum studio
quærenda, ambiendaq*ue*, imo nec amplectenda quidem,
si se ipsa offerant, nisi ea cautione adhibita, ut tanq*uam*
materiam, in qua exerce*n*dæ pietatis causa uersemur,
unusquisq*ue* in uocatione sua a deo oblatam accipiamus.
quæ, quo maior ac numerosior fuerit, eo certe difficilior sit
expeditio, quam nemo eorum sibi exoptat, et quærit, qui
ad patriam bona fide contendunt æternam. Tantum abest,
ut de primatu aliquo externæ administrationis sensisse
Christum intellegamus, qui milites suos, quos uelut in
acie aduersus mundi, carnis, et Sathanæ fraudes, prælia,
et perpetua bella instruxit, eos demum primos, et in
ipsa fronte quasi antesignanos collocauit: quos quasi ad
frangendos maiores impetus hostium fide robustiores
nouerat, nulla alia cura externarum rerum occupatos,
atque impeditos: quique cæteros infirmiores, ut nomina
huic militiæ darent, constantiæ exemplo animarent, alli-

---

[1] Quoted from Phil. ii, 7 (Vulgate): "Sed semetipsum exinanivit,
formam servi accipiens, in similitudinem hominum factus, et habitu
inventus ut homo".    [2] Presumably a reference to Jer. vi, 10: "Ecce
verbum Domini factum est eis in opprobrium, et non suscipient
illud" (Vulgate).    [3] *Pretio*.    [a] The sentence is misunderstood
and mistranslated, possibly owing to the change in tense and mood
from *erat* to *fuerit*. The meaning is as follows: "If it be therefore
true that Christ, as being God, was equal to his father, in whom he
was from the beginning, and although he have been at one with the
holy ghost his inseparable co-operator, in all that has been created,
said or done by him (since the essence of the three persons is one in
the Godhead); although I say...".    [b] More exactly: "He emptied
himself (divested himself) of his godhead".    [c] Once again the

(one substaunce of three persones in divinitie)although I saye<sup>a</sup> /
according to his maiestie / he hathe alwayes had all power / to
subdue al thinges vnto him selfe: he was alyve / he is alyve /
*and* he shall lyve: he hathe reigned / he reigneth / *and* he shall
reigne God for euer more: yet for his exceding mercie towardes
mankinde / he made ‖ him selfe of no reputacion<sup>b</sup> / taking the
forme of a seruaunt / being in apparaill founde as a ma*n* / and
a very opprobrie / as the prophet saithe: to make it plaine and
open / that those thinges / w*h*ich were highely estemed with
men / as empires / dominiones / and highe autorities / being /
as it were / stoppes and impedimentes to the atteyning of
eternall felicitie / are rather to be cast awaye and contemned /
than to be gredily sought for / and ambiciously coveted / yea
they are not to be receaved though they offre them selues / but
vnder this condicion / that we receaue the*m* / as mater offred
of God / to trauaile in / for the exercise of Godlynes sake /
euery one in his vocacion.   Which / the greater it is / and the
moo thinges it is tangled withall / the harder it wil be to doo it
so well / as euery one wolde be glad and fayne to doo / that
faithfully contendeth to com to the countrey that euer shall
endure.<sup>c</sup>   So that we must vnderstande / that Christ me*nt*
neuer a worde<sup>d</sup> of any supremacie of wordly<sup>e</sup> administracion /
but he appoynted his souldiers / whom he furnished / to en-
countre as it were in the vawarde<sup>f</sup> against the co*n*tinuall
fraudes / perpetuall / bataill and warres of the worlde / the
fleshe and the dyvell / to be the forewardest / *and* as it were the
enseigne bearours<sup>g</sup> / in the very ‖ formost ranke. Whom he
knewe / to be of better courage in faithe / to breake the more
daungerous raye<sup>h</sup> of thenemies / because they were not tangled
nor letted with any charge of worldly maters / and might by
their example of constance / encourange<sup>i</sup> / allure / and provoke other of the weaker sorte / to become souldiours of *that*

Sig. F iiij b
Phil. ij.
A preacher
shoulde not
receyue
lordship

meddli*ng*
wi*th* many
offices
marreth a
preacher.

Loke to
your selfe
therfore.

What
shouldiers /
preachers
should be.

Sig. F v a

translator utterly misunderstands the text, which may be rendered as
follows: "Which matter, the greater and the more abounding it is,
certainly the more difficult will be the performance (literally: *the
campaign*), which no one wishes and seeks for himself, who in good
faith strives to attain the everlasting home". In other words, worldly
power may be an occasion to exercise one's piety, yet is in itself so
contrary to godliness, that no one who really wishes to save his soul
will wish to encounter such a trial.   <sup>d</sup> More exactly: "Far be it
from us, therefore, to understand that Christ ever meant a word...".
<sup>e</sup> Misprint or erratic form for *worldly*.   <sup>f</sup> Vanguard.   <sup>g</sup> *Ante-
signanus* is properly the soldier committed to the protection of the
ensign, he who walks before the ensign, hence an instigator or even
a chief, a ringleader.   <sup>h</sup> Array.   <sup>i</sup> *Sic* for *encourage*.

cerent, et prouocarent. qua in militia, quod CHRISTVS
suorum faciens delectum[1] primam, stationem Petro inter
f. 26 b fratres contulerit, nihil mirum: ‖ cum ita eum ipse
armauerat, ut etiam si aliquando hosti pro tempore
cessurum, rediturum tamen eum ad pugnam, nec prorsus
succubiturum, sed acriter fortiterque pro ueritate asser-
enda dimicaturum præcognouerat. Primus ergo Petrus
fuit? id nemo negat. primus enim confessus est Christum
uerum filium dei uiui. Petrus etiam in eadem ueritate defend-
enda nemini unquam fuit animi constantia, atque firmitate
secundus. primus post Christum docuit Iudæos. In
conuentu etiam apostolorum cum necesse esset unum
loqui omnium nomine, aliquando, cum ita res ferebat,
primas obtinuit in dicendo partes. Non igitur refragabor
argumento, quod uocant a coniugatis,[2] quo minus diuus
Petrus tot modis, atque rationibus primus, etiam primatum
inter apostolos habuisse censeatur. Quemadmodum enim
sapienti quatenus est sapiens adest sapientia, sic etiam
primatus adest primo. quid ergo? qui primus medicorum
omnium habetur, an non habet etiam primatum inter
medicos? quid ni etiam habeat? In pictoribus rursum, si
quis hac tempestate Appellem æquaret, aut Pyrrasium,[3]
et primus ideo pictor appellaretur, an non eum primatum
inter pictores obtinere diceremus? planissime. In academiis
autem si omnium consensus in hoc conueniret, Lutetiam
f. 27 a parisiorum tanquam doctissimis ui-‖ris refertissimam, ac
frequentissimam[4] primam, appellare orbis academiam,
An non etiam eidem, inter alias academias primæ, primatus
appellatio competere posset?[5] certe. Sed propius adhuc

---

[1] Comma here in the Hamburg edition, and none after *primam*, the
correction being clearly justified.     [2] A proof of Gardiner's logical
training. Cf. the fifth treatise on logic of Petrus Hispanus, which
Gardiner certainly knew (*Tractatus duodecim Petri Hyspani*, Argentine
1511, Tractatus quintus, § de locis mediis, sig e$_b$, or better *Com-
pendiarius paruorum logicalium...per...*Chunradum Pschachler, Vienne
Austrie, 1512, p. 131) "vniuocum vel principale seu abstractum quod
idem est: dicitur coniugatum cum suo denominatiuo: vt iustitia et
iustum: albedo et album...Quicquid conuenit vni coniugatorum conuenit et reliquo: et si vnum coniugatorum inest et reliquum inerit."
[3] *Sic*, corrected in the Strasbourg edition to *Parrasium*, in the Hamburg editicn to *Parrhasium*.     [4] Comma here in the Strasbourg
edition; also in the Hamburg edition, which has none after *primam*.

bande also.    In which kinde of warrefarre / though Christ / making choise of his owne / gaue the vppermost standing to Petre / among the brotherne / it was no marvaill: seinge he had so armed him / *that* he knewe before hande / though he wolde geve backe from the enemye perhappes for a tyme / yet he wolde not geve it ouer so / but to it agayne stotaly[a] / and fight like a tall felowe for the defense of the truthe.   Ha / was Petre the chief than?   No man saithe naye.   For he confessed Christ / to be the very sonne of the lyvyng God / furst.   And Petre was of as constaunt and stedfast myndes / in defending of the same truthe / at all tymes / as any man was.   He was the furst after Christ / that taught the Iewes.   And in thassemblye of thapostles / whan one shoulde nedes speake in all their names / Petre / somtyme as the mater required / was chief in the tale telling. Therfore I will not saye naye to the argument / which they call : ‖ **Argumentum à coniugatis**, but Sig. F v b that Saint Petre / beinge by so many wayes and reasones / the furst / might also be thought to be chief among thapostles. For like as the wise man hathe wisedome / in that he is a wise man: so hathe the chief man *the* chief place or supremacie. What than? he *that* is chief of all *the* Phisicianes / hathe not he also the supremacie among Phisicianes?[b]   For why shoulde he not?   Among Paynters also / if ther were any in these dayes / as connyng as Appelles or Pharrhasius[c] was / and were called therfore *the* head Paynter / wolde we not saye / that he had the supremacie among paynters? yea doubtles.   In vniuersities / agayn / if it were agreed by all mennes consentes / that Lutetia of Parrise / as being a vniuersitie most playnteously furnished and occupied with great learned men / shoulde be called the headde vniuersitie of the worlde / might not *the* name of supremacie be fitte for it / being chief among other vniuersities / yes doubtles.   But let vs come nerer to the mater.   If a man /

[5] Gardiner's praise of Paris University may be due to its compliance with the king's wishes in the divorce matter. On May 23, 1530, the faculty of canon law (*facultas decretorum*) declared that the Pope could not grant a dispensation for marriage with a deceased brother's wife, if the former marriage had been consummated, and on July 2 the Sorbonne (*theologi*) gave a similar "determination", in which, however, no mention was made of the consummation (Rymer, *Fœdera*, Hagæ Comitis, 1746, tom. vi, part ii, p. 155). Such an attitude would of course greatly add to the merits of Paris university in the eyes of Henry VIII. Cf. note on *Si sedes illa*, fols. *163 a–192* a of MS.
[a] *Sic* for *stoutly*.    [b] It should be kept in mind that here the Latin word *primatus* implies no *supremacy* in the modern sense of the word, i.e. no superior power; hence where the translator uses *chief*, we should substitute *first*, where he says *supremacy* or *chief rule*, we should substitute *first rank*, throughout the passage. The inaccuracy is the more surprising, as it goes against the translator's own purpose.
[c] *Sic* for *Parrhasius*.

accedamus. Si quis cum unum uniuersæ familiæ regendæ
præposuisset, in qua magnum numerum iuuenum cum
haberet, quos bonis artibus imbui, atque instrui cuperet,
multosque præceptores asciscendos curaret, ac in his unum
præter cæteros egregie doctum uirum, quem tanquam
inter alios eminentem, præceptorum omnium quos
asciuerat primum uocaret, cuique quos habet charissimos
erudiendos committeret: An non hic, præceptor primus
cum sit, primatum obtinet? maxime. Neque sane primus
quauis in re non habere potest primatum: sunt enim
primus, et primatus coniugata non solum uocabulo,
uerum etiam re. Cæterum illud quæri potest is, de quo
diximus, Primus præceptor in hac familia si quid ibi
inciderit de moribus, aut ordine controuersum: utrius
prior potestas haberetur, eius ne cui familia commissa sit,
an eius qui ad erudiendam iuuentutem asciscitur? qui
primus, ut diximus, appellatus est, atque ideo habet primatum. Quis dubitat, quin illius cui commissa sit familia?
quid ita? nempe manifestissima est ratio, uidelicet quia
f. 27 b  ordo nonnunquam relatione mutatur? et quod ‖ in una
relatione primum, et supremum est, in alia uel diuersa
inferiorem interdum locum, etiam sæpenumero ultimum
tenet. Itaque deus filius æqualis patri secundum diuini-
tatem, minor est patre secundum humanitatem. Item deus
filius quatenus quidem deus in principio est, atque principum[1] ipsum, quatenus uero dei filius, secunda numero
persona est, licet sine omni consideratione temporis deo
patri semper coeuus. Sed è rebus inferioribus ut petamus
exempla: An non domi uidemus eundem hominem diuersis
muneribus functum, Arithmeticarum figurarum instar,
nunc primum, deinde secundum, tandem tertium occu-
pare locum, interdum etiam inferiorem, prout causæ, in
qua uersatur, et loci, ubi conuenitur, ratio postulat?
Nunquid uidere est eum, qui in iudicum consessu primus
est, et eo nomine etiam primus iudex appellatur, cum

---

[1] *Sic*, rightly corrected to *principium* in the Strasbourg and Hamburg
editions.  [a] *Sic* for *called*.  [b] Inaccurate. The sentence should stand
thus: "Who doubts, but his (authority will be considered superior),
to whom the family is given in charge".  [c] By the relation between
the man and his charge, and the circumstances in which he is placed.

whan he had set one man to gouerne the hole householde /
wherin inasmuche as he had a great sorte of yong men / whom
he wolde fayne haue taught and instructed in good artes / and
wolde provide many scholemaistres / and among ‖ other / ther
were one man excellently wel learned aboue the rest / whom /
as a notable man among other / he wolde call the chief of all
the scholemaisters that he had gotten: and to whose instruccion
he wolde committe / those that he setteth most by: hathe not
he / seing he is chief scholemaister / the supremacie? yes. For
the chief person can not chose / but haue chief rule in any
mater: For these two wordes / **Primus**, which is furst / principall / or chief / *and* **Primatus**, which is chief rule / preeminence /
and is here rightly englished / supremacie / are **coniugata**, that
is to saye / lynked to gether / the one depending of the other /
not only in speache / but also in mater.    Neuertheles this
question maye be asked: he / of whom I spake / *the* chief
scholemaister in this householde / if ther should fall any
controuersie / touching maners / or ordre / whether of their
autorities shoulde be estemed aboue the other / his / vnto
whom the householde was committed / or his / that is callad<sup>a</sup>
to instructe the youthe? he that is called the chief / as I saide /
and therfore he hathe the supremacie.    Who doubteth /
but his rowme is the greater / that hathe charge of the householde?<sup>b</sup> why so? For it stondeth most with reason / because
ordre is somtyme chaunged by relacion.<sup>c</sup> And that / ‖ which
in one relacion is supreme and chief / in an other or in a contrary relacion / hathe somtyme an inferiour place / and often
tymes the lowest place of all. And so God *the* sonne / is equal
with the father / after his divinitie / but he is lesse than the
father / after is<sup>d</sup> humanitie.    Also God the sonne / in that
he is God / is in *the* begynnyng / and is the begynnyng it selfe:
but in that he is the sonne of God / he is the seconde person in
nombre: albeit without all consideracion of tyme / he is without
begynnyng as God the father is. But to sette examples / out<sup>e</sup>
inferiour maters: Do we not see all one man to vse diuerse
offices at home / like Arithmeticall figures<sup>f</sup> / now to occupie
the furst and chief rowme / than the seconde / afterwarde the
thrid / *and* somtyme a lower rowme / as the cause / wherin he
is occupied / and place / wher company meteth<sup>g</sup> / doo require?
Doo we not see him<sup>h</sup> / that sitteth highest among iudges / and
for that cause / is called / the chief iudge / whan he is required /

<sup>d</sup> *Sic* for *his*.    <sup>e</sup> The text as it stands is obscure. Possibly *of* may
be supplied between *out* and *inferior*.    <sup>f</sup> This refers to the following
clause.    <sup>g</sup> I.e. "where the parties concerned meet".    <sup>h</sup> Exactly:
"Is it not in some respect possible to see, is it not a possible thing
to see, does it not happen that we see...".

extra ordinariis iudiciis adesse rogatur, quod non raro fit, in tertio aut quarto loco post alios collocari? Quin in diuinis quæso functionibus, quantum, ut ita dicam, primatum obtinet Sacellanus in dominum, dum interest diuinis, quem tamen cum loco, et ueste mox deponit. Neque id sane mirum. In hoc enim ita se res habet, ut qui primi, ac primatus nomen cupit retinere, ab eo non discedat oportet, cui illa fuerat appellatio apposita, atque af-‖fixa. Itaque ut ad exempla redeamus. Medicus quidem habeatur in medicina primus, hoc est scientia cedat nemini, sicque quoniam etiam id res ipsa postulat, retineat primatum, cæterum tantisper dum uersatur in re medica: In administratione autem reipublicæ quoniam alia est functio, sua sit classe etiam secunda contentus, nec aliis contendat imperitare, quia primus sit medicus: sed nec cæteris quidem medicis imperandi sibi arroget authoritatem, quippe quæ in primatu collata nulla est, non quia non potuit conferre etiam hoc, qui eum sic prætulit, sed quia non collibuit conferre, quia sic ratio non ferebat: uel quod grauissimum est dicere, quia id non fecit, utpote qui eum non absolute primum, sed primum medicum appellauit. Sit etiam pictor egregius pictorum primus, et in eo contendat retinere primatum, ne si alius superarit arte, superet etiam nominis dignitate. Academia parrisiensis non tam de honore glorietur uocabuli, quam studeat præstare quod est appellatione tributum. Denique hic præceptor, qui ad liberos erudiendos ascitus est, quia non hominis personam, sed latentem sub persona uirtutem honore primatus donandam censuit paterfamilias, meminerit etiam atque etiam se non tam honorari hoc nomine, quam onerari, studeatque potius secundum nominis rationem in exhibendo docendi munere, se primum præstare, ‖ quam uano appellationis titulo abuti, et tanquam absolute primus esset, neglecto officio, et eo pacto amisso

f. 28 a (margin, opposite "af-‖fixa")

f. 28 b (margin, opposite "stare")

---

*a* *Quin* rather seems to mean here: "What is more". *b* *His gear*, i.e. his ecclesiastical vestments. More clearly: "and has cast off his gear". *c* *Sic* for *name*. *d* The translator fails to see that the series of examples here is merely the repetition and conclusion of the examples two pages higher up: "Let the physician be first in medicine, that is, let him be second to none by his science, and thus

to be present in extraordinarie iudgementes / as it is often sene / placed after others in the thrid or fourthe rowme? But*a* in divine offices / I pray you / how great a supremacie as I maye to call it / hathe the chappelayne ouer his maister / as long as he is in divine ministracion? And yet ‖ whan he is out of the place / and cast of his gaire*b* / he leaveth his supremacie behynde him.    And it is no marvail.  For in this cace / the mater stondeth so / that who so mindeth to reteyne the name of the chief person *and* chief office still / must not swarve from the thinge / whervnto *the* nvme*c* was applyed and setto. Therfore to returne vnto examples.  Admitte / ther were a famous chief Phisician / that is to saye / were as conning in Phisike as any man / and so / because the mater so requireth it / he kepeth still / his preeminence / yea Sir / but while he meddleth with Phisike*d*: But forasmuche as there is an other maner of office in the administracion of *the* common weale / let him be conte*n*t also with his seconde forme*e* / *and* stryve not to beare rule ouer other / because he is the chief Phisician: nether let him take autortie*f* vpon him to be a co*m*maunder of the rest of the Phisicianes / which is not geuen him in his preeminence / not because he coulde not geue it hi*m* / which so preferred him / but because it was not his pleasur to geue it hi*m* / for it was no reason why he shoulde: or elles which is the sorest thinge*g* to speake of all / why he did not: Mary Sir / because he made him not absolutely chief / but he called him the chief Phisician.    Admitte also a curious connyng ‖ payntour*h* / to be chief payntour / let him stryve also to continue still in his chief payntourship / lest an other passe him in connyng / and so have the name of chief payntour from him / because he is more worthy than he.  Let the vniuersitie of Parrise reioyce not so muche of the honour of the name / as to studie to make it good / that is attributed by the name. Finaly let this scholemaister / which is called to teache children / because the good man of the house thought not the person of the ma*n* / but the vertue hidden vnder the person / whorthye the honour of chief scholemaister / remembre and remembre again / that he is not honoured / but burthened with *the* name / and let him study rather according to *the* the intent*i* of the name / to shewe him selfe chief / in the office of teaching / than to abuse the vayne title of a name / and as though he were chief absolutely without condicion / yet neclecting his office / and

Sig. F vij a

Sig. F vij b

---

...keep the primacy, at least while...".    *e* Inaccurate: "But in the administration of the commonwealth, since the function is a different one, let him be content with his rank, though it be only the second one".  *Second form* is here the school term for *secunda classis*. *f* *Sic* for *autoritie*.    *g* More accurately: "the most weighty thing to say".    *h* Mistranslated: "let the eminent painter be the first of painters, and let...".    *i* *Sic* for *to the intent*.

primatu, de nomine tamen atque uocabulo cum his qui
uerum obtinent primatum, atque absolutum, tanquam
regendæ familiæ præpositis contendere, et digladiari,
sacraque et prophana miscere, ut quo iure, quaque iniuria
uincat, ac pro libidine obtineat, nihil præterea de functione,
atque officio habens pensi: sed totus in hoc. Id quod
multo iam tempore plane fecisse uidentur Episcopi
Romani qui ea, quæ primatui Petri adiecta fuerunt, nihil
curantes, atque primatus nomen certis quibusdam functionibus annexum ipsi absoluentes, quippe qui absoluunt
omnia, nudum orbi uocabulum proposuerunt, ut primi
haberentur, atque ipsis primis priores: nihil interim
cogitantes, quam sint in cæteris, infimis quibusque inferiores. Non confero hic, in quo mihi latissimus pateret
campus, hominum uitia cum causæ conditione. non
semper boni præsunt scio, nec authoritati tamen quicquam
derogat hominis malicia, etiam illud scio, omnes pec-
cauimus, et egemus gratia dei. Quod autem causæ annexum est, sileri non potest, ne quis mihi obiiciat illud
Pauli, quod in quo aliis prædico, ipse reprobus reperiar.
Quam enim non satisfaciam mihi in meo munere, conscius

f. 29 a  mihi ipse sum. Fidelis autem dispensator quis inuenie-||tur?
secundum Paulum qui in eodem loco subdit, Nolite ante
tempus iudicare. Itaque nec ego hac in re latius, ampliusue
uersabor, quam postulat causa, Nempe ut eum qui se
primum uocat immerito, quam modestissime cum ueritate
refellam, eique si nihil aliud, illud saltem optem, ut iisdem
titulis primus sit, quibus primus esset[1] debet is, qui
primus merito appelletur, quibusque fuit ille, unde sibi
tanquam successione primatum uendicat. Quamobrem
præcedat modo alios Christum confitendo, et primus
eatenus inter omnes, etiam iure diuino, merito censeatur,

---

[1] *Sic* for *esse debet*. The misprint is repeated in the Strasbourg
edition.     [a] The sentence is wholly misunderstood by the translator
and the sarcastic intention found in it remains unsuspected. The
meaning is as follows: "who not fulfilling those duties, which are
attached to the primacy of Peter, and of their own authority absolving
(i.e. detaching, loosing) the name of primacy from certain functions
which are annexed to it, as men who absolve all (in virtue of the
power to bind and loose), they have propounded...".     [b] This refers

so losing his supremacie / to contende and stryve / about the name and terme of it / with them / that as being set in autoritie to gouerne the householde / haue the true and absolute supremacie in dede: and to myngle Goddes maters / and the worldes maters together / so that he maye ouercome / by right or by wrong / and haue it as him lusteth: as for his function *and* ‖ office / he taketh no more thought for / but is holly bent in that.　As it appeareth now for a great while / that the bishoppes of Rome haue done / which not regarding those thinges / that were added vnto Petres supremacie / and accomplishing the name of supremacie being annexed vnto som certain poyntes of office / as they accomplishe all thinges*a* / they haue propounded the bare name vnto the worlde / that they might be taken for chief / yea / and chiefer than the chiefest: not remembring in the meane tyme / how / in all other maters / they are inferiour to the lowest that is.　Here I doo not compare / the faultes of the men with the condicion of the cause*c* / wherin I might haue very large mater to speake / I knowe / they are not alwayes good men / that beare the swinge / and yet the naughtynes of the man dothe not hyndre his autoritie. I knowe this also / *that* we haue all synned / *und* nede the grace of God. But as concerning / *that* which is annexed vnto the cause*d* / can not be kepte in silence / lest any man caste this sayeng of Paule in my dishe / that / in the same I preache to others / I my selfe be founde to blame.　For how great lacke I fynde in my selfe in myne owne office doing / myne owne conscience knoweth. But who is it / that shalbe founde a ‖ faithfull stuarde / as Paule saithe? who also in the same place speaketh further: **Judge not before the tyme come.** Therfore will not I wade in this mater / any broader nor further / than cause requireth: the*e* is / as modestly as I can with that*f* truthe / to refelle him *that* calleth him selfe chief vntruly / *and* to wishe him this at least / if nothing elles / *that* he maye be chief in those titles / wherin he ought to be chief / that he might worthily be called the chief / and wherin Petre was / by whom he claimeth the supremacie to him self / as by succession. Wherfore let him now excelle othters*g* / in confessing Christ / *and* let him so ferre be worthily taken for chief amonge all men / euen by the lawe of Godde: which if Boniface had perceaued /

Sig. F viij a

and as you
do yet
except it be
*with the*
poyson of
popish
heresies*b*
good men
haue not all
way *the* rule.
*that* is as
true as the
Gospell: for
you are as
badde as
nedeth to be.
For so*the*
you haue
amended the
mater gayly
sithence
*that* tyme.

Sig. F viij b

to "As it appeareth…that the bishoppes of Rome have done". The meaning is "as you are still bent on acquiring worldly power by spiritual means, except when you apply yourself to the spreading of popish heresies".　　*c* Mistranslated: "I do not compare the vices of men with the condition of their rank".　　*d* Similarly misunderstood: "What is attached to their rank cannot be left untold".　　*e* *Sic* for *which*.　*f* *Sic* for *the*.　*g* *Sic* for *others*.

id quod si Bonifacius sensisset, non fuisset ei opus idipsu*m* suffragiis a Phoca imperatore, tanq*uam* mendicando impetrare, quod sibi ipse, dei opitulante gratia, per se conquirere potuisset.[1] Præterea primus ante alios doceat, et prædicet Christu*m* episcopus Ro*manus* et tantisper ante alios obtineat eius functionis primatu*m*. Quam uero illud ridiculu*m*, ut multis in stadio curre*n*tibus, unus quispia*m* à spectatoribus magno cu*m* ambitu cupiat impetrare, ut ipse ad curre*n*du*m* quidem inter cæteros designatus, cu*m* ia*m* aut culpa sua claudus, aut aliter ad cursu*m* ineptus factus sit, alios ta*men* om*nes* etia*m* tu*m* cursu anteuertisse, ac primus omniu*m* meta*m* attigisse dicatur, quu*m* præterq*uam* q*uod* uestitu ad cursu*m* apposito p*r*odierit, sederit *i*nterim inter spectatores ociosus, nulla*m* alia*m* precu*m* suaru*m* ratione*m* afferen*s*, q*uam* q*uod* ab iis (si diis placet)

f. 29 b ortus et ‖ prognatus sit, qui olim optimi cursores, atq*ue* ideo primi sunt appellati. Egregia sane ratio, et eo sane digna, qui uanis, ac falsis appellationibus gaudeat, et adulationem plusq*uam* Gnatonicam[2] æquo animo ferat. Quemadmodu*m* aut*em* huic sanus amicus, si quis adesset, no*n* modo mente*m* optaret meliorem, uerum ab illa etiam inepta petitione, recta si posset admonitione auerteret. indicans nimirum, q*uam* sit stultitiæ plenum, uelle uerbis dici, et appellari, quod reuera non sis. Ita quoq*ue* ego sane cuperem Romanis episcopis, quos simili quodam affectu,

---

[1] The Boniface here referred to is Pope Boniface IV, who sat in the pontifical chair from 608 to 615. The above passage seems to be a rhetorical and wholly unwarranted amplification of the one fact known in regard to his relations with the Byzantine Emperor Phocas, namely that the latter granted him the Roman Pantheon, which he transformed into a church dedicated to the Virgin Mary and All Saints. Gardiner's source was probably Bede's *Ecclesiastical History*, in which we read: "Hic est Bonifacius, quartus a beato Gregorio Romanæ urbis episcopo, qui impetravit a Focate principe, donari ecclesiæ Christi templum Romæ quod Pantheon vocabatur ab antiquis, quasi simulacrum esset omnium deorum: in quo ipse, eliminata omni spurcitia, fecit ecclesiam sanctæ dei genitricis, atque omnium martyrum Christi" (Migne, *Patrologia Latina*, vol. 95, col. 87; lib. II, cap. 4 of the *Historia*). Bede's *History* was no doubt well known to Gardiner and had been published at Strasbourg in 1473, 1483 and 1500, at Spires in 1490, at Hagenau in 1506. The same event is referred to in the *Liber Pontificalis* in the following words: "...Eodem tempore petiit a Focate principe templum qui appellatur Pantheum". (Ed. Vignolius, p. 238; ed. Duchesne,

he nedde not to haue goten that / by priuilege of Phocas themperour / as it had ben by begging / which by *the* assistence of Goddes grace / he might haue wonne to him selfe by him selfe. Moreouer let the Bishop of Rome be chief in teaching and preaching Christ a fore other / *and* so longe let him haue the supremacie of that kinde of office. But what a folye were it / whan many are runnyng in a race / that som one shoulde winne by his ambicious importnuitie[a] muche fauour of the lokers on[b] / wher he / being appointed in dede to runne amonge others / whan he ‖ is now either made lame through his owne faulte / or otherwise vnmete to runne / yet shalbe reported / that he ouerrunne them al / and came furst of all to the pricke[c]/ wher as saving that he came out in apparail made to runne withall / he sitteth him downe amonge the lokers on / *and* clowteth a toorde[d] as for any other consideracion of his requestes / he allegeth non / but that he was borne *and* bredde of them (on Goddes name ) wher[e] in tymes past were the best runners / and were therfore called the chief. A goodly reason forsothe / and worthye of him / that is ioyous of vayne and false titles / and contenteth him selfe / to be flattred / aboue measure.[f] But like as a sure frende / if he had any wold not only wishe him better minde / but also wolde turne him / if he might by right admonicion / from that folishe desire of priuilege: and tell him / what a very folye it is / for a man[g] / haue a minde to be named *and* called that in wordes / which he is not in very dede.    euen so wolde I also wishe vnto the bishoppes of Rome / whom[h] it is manifest / haue ben in like

tom. I, p. 317.) In neither case is Gardiner's *tanquam mendicando* at all justified by the text, though it is clear that in the seventh century the Popes were not yet full sovereigns at Rome (cf. also Vacant et Mancenot, *Dictionnaire de théologie catholique*, tom. II, p. 990, and Philippus Jaffé, *Regesta Pontificum*, 1st edn. p. 155).    [2] From the name of one of the characters in Terence's *Eunuchus*, "Gnatho, parasitus Thrasonis—(a γνάθος, maxilla, quod sit edax)".    [a] *Sic* for *importunitie*.    [b] Inaccurate: "that he should wish to obtain from the spectators, by currying favour with them, that he, being..., yet should be declared to have outrun them all...".    [c] *Prick* first meant a target for archery, hence that at which one aims, and finally the winning-post (*N.E.D.*).    [d] A typical instance of the translator's coarseness, these words being far more than a rendering of the Latin *ociosus*. To *clowt*, "to clout = to wipe with a cloth" (*N.E.D.*); *toorde* = "turd" (*N.E.D.*).    [e] *Sic* for *who*.    [f] And bear with an equal mind flattery worse than that of Gnato.    [g] "To" no doubt forgotten here.    [h] *Sic* for *who*.

(uolo rem uerbis temperare) laborasse constat, atque adeo in præsentia ab inueterato (ut audio) non desistere, consultum ab aliquibus fore, ut ne contenderent primos dici, quòad consisterent in postremis: Sed si nominis appellatio delectaret, uiderent potius quibus rebus parta, quibusque rebus proprie fuerit attributa. Vt enim in ciuitate bene constituta qui primi sunt in diuitiis, non sunt ideo authoritate primi: sic nec in ecclesia Christi aliis præsunt ii, qui fastu, pompa, diuitiis antecedunt.[1] Ideoque si in munere, atque officio prædicandi uerbi dei, si in illustrandi nominis Christi cura, et solicitudine, si in prompta ad ueritatem tuendam, et fidem Christi ab hæresibus uindicandam animi magnitudine magno olim cum consensu orbis, Romanæ ecclesiæ primatus stetit, id quod illis temporibus

f. 30 a   maxime patuit, cum Romani ‖ iam episcopi, et fere soli, in ipso nascentis ecclesiæ primordio furori tyrannorum in Christianos seuienti, cum sanguinis profusione mederi curarint: Neminem puto hodie christianorum principum, qui Romanos episcopos, si uiderent de illo primatu contendere bona fide, nimirum ut alios omnes quotquot habet ecclesia christiana quaqua uersum dispersa, episcopos pietate, fide, religione, pia quadam emulatione uincere, et tam longo anteire interuallo certarent, ut in cursu hoc primi merito dicerentur. Hæc inquam principes, si uiderent, haud grauatim facerent, ut quod oculis cernerent, ueris nominibus donarent: et quem primum animaduerterent, in eo certamine etiam primum appellarent, ac in primatu honore uirtuti debito, uenerarentur. Qua quidem opinione inducti uidentur maiores, quæ etiam opinio ad nostra tempora durauit, ut operam sibi conducerent Romanorum episcoporum, qui se seruos seruorum dei, non tam nomine, ut nunc, quam reipsa tum profiterentur.

[1] A surprising description of the Papacy, after Gardiner's journey to Orvieto in 1528, when according to his own description, he had found the Pope in a miserable condition. In his letter to Wolsey from Orvieto, March 23, 1528 (Nicholas Pocock, *Records of the Reformation*, 1870, vol. I, pp. 88–9) he states for instance that "for the pope's bedchamber, all the apparel in it was not worth twenty nobles, bed and all". Even by 1535, the splendour of the English court might have been a fitter subject for sarcasm, complaint or indignation.   ᵃ I.e.

sorte affected (I will not ouershote my wordes<sup>a</sup>) *and* yet still at this present (as I heare) surcesse not their olde cankred<sup>b</sup> minde: that they were<sup>c</sup> counsailed of som bodye / not to contende to be called supremes / as longe as they ‖ are still postremes:<sup>d</sup> But if their delight were to be so called / they should see / by what thinges that title was gotten / and by what thinges / it was proprely attributed. For like as in a well ordred citie / those that are chief in riches / are not therfore chief in autoritie: euen so in Christes churche / they are not put *in* autoritie aboue other / that excede other in pompe / lordely estate and riches. And therfore if the supremacie of *the* churche of Rome in tymes past / with great consent of the worlde / stode / in *the* office of preaching Goddes worde / if in advaunceing the cure and charge of Christes name if *in* prompte valeauntnes of mynde / to defende the truthe / and to kepe *the* faithe of Christ from heresies / as it is most playne that in those dayes it did / whan the bishops of Rome (yea almost non but they) at the furst begynning of the spring of the churche / were diligent to heale<sup>e</sup> the furour of tyrannes rageing against christian people: I wene / ther is neuer a christen prince in the worlde / but if he sawe the bishoppes of Rome / contende about that supremacie faithfully / that they might godly and zelously passe all other bishoppes (that *the* churche of Christ / wher so-euer it is scattred / hathe) in godlynes in faithe / and religious deuocion / and wolde stryve to goo so ferre before / that in ‖ this race they might be worthily called *the* furst. If the princes / I saye / might see this in them / they wolde with good will / call them by those true names / that they sawe with their eies:<sup>f</sup> *and* him that they spied to be furst / they wolde call chief / in that matche game: and in that kynde of supremacie / they wolde reverence him with due honour / according to his vertue. And with this opinion / semeth our elders were induced (which openion also dured vnto our tyme) *that* they wolde geue *the* bishoppes of Rome wages / for their paynes<sup>g</sup> / which called them selues the **seruauutes**<sup>h</sup> of **Goddes Seruauntes**, not only in name / as they doo now / but mater indede in those

Sig. G b

Nou he bringeth *in* hresies *and* so doo you w*ith* your pestilent masses *and* other such.

Sig. G ij a

Loke how hipocrysie ca*n* begile men of simple wittes.

"I shall say the thing in temperate words—not to use a stronger expression". ᵇ *Cankred* (added by the translator) = "infected with evil, corrupt, depraved" (*N.E.D.*). ᶜ That they should be. ᵈ As long as they remain among the least. ᵉ The translator forgets *cum sanguinis profusione*, "while shedding their blood". ᶠ They would be far from unwilling to give their true names to the things which their eyes should see. ᵍ More exactly: "Hire the services of the bishops of Rome". ʰ *Sic* for *seruauntes*.

151

Cæterum serui appellatio ministerii rationem notat. Neque enim seruus operas suas locandas imperat, sed tanquam in medio promptas sistit, ut alliciant conductorem. Qua in re aliqui tamen diligentiæ, ac fidei commendatione sic operas ostentant suas, atque desiderabiles reddunt, ut multos efficiant competitores, atque eos ita afficiant, ut quum domi negotium et melius, et expeditius absolui f. 30 b potuisset, illis tamen inconsultis ‖ nihil aut præclari, aut recti geri posse existimetur. Id quod in uariis opificum generibus, atque minimis quibusque rebus cum indies accidere uideamus, non est mirum si in religione, in qua ad absolutissimum quodque exemplar, omnia componi omnes optant. in quo tamen nonnulli suis ingeniis partim diffidunt, partim in eo corruptis utuntur, quod peregrina domesticis anteponant,[1] non debet inquam cuiquam mirum uideri, si splendor nominis Romanæ ecclesiæ, claris tum uirtutibus illustris, etiam omnes fermè orbis partes in sui admirationem excitans, attrahensque uirtutis amore, quod est uinculum firmissimum, sibi adglutinauerit omnes, effeceritque, ut eam ecclesiam, quam omnes tot uirtutibus tum temporis conspicuam cernerent, inter alias tanquam primam, ac præcipuam uenerarentur. Pii[2] quoque homines iis etiam nominibus ornarint, quæ hodie tanquam diuinis oraculis prodita orbi iactant Romani episcopi, ut primatum defendant non uirtutis, sed potestatis atque huius quidem terrenæ, externæ, atque carneæ, qualem nec exercuit Christus aliquando, nec unquam exercendam commisit, quatenus ex sacris quidem literis licet colligere. E quibus tamen cum aliqua decerpserint aliqui, quibus id confirmarent a Christo esse mandatum, atque constitutum, in quod sua sponte populus, ac principes, uirtutis ui, tanquam a

---

[1] By accepting the authority of the bishop of Rome in preference to that of the national sovereign. [2] *Ut* is understood before *pii*. [a] Inaccurate: "to be hired". [b] This difficult expression (not found in *N.E.D.*) may perhaps be explained as follows: *keen* properly means "sharp, pungent, affecting the senses sharply"; hence *sale-kene* may mean "which affects people in such a way that it may be sold, which induces people to buy". [c] Inaccurate: "though in religion...". [d] *Sic* for *corrupte*. [e] More accurately: "It is

152

dayes. Howbeit the name of a seruau*n*te / signifieth a seruice. For a seruaunt commaundeth not his labours to be set out*ᵃ* / but he setteth them asale / as it were in an open place / to provoke som body to hyre him.   Wherin notwithstonding / som make such a shewe of their labours / in commending their diligence and fidelitie / and make them so sale kene*ᵇ* / that they cause many to be desirous of them: and bringe them in that mynde / that / whan their busynes might bothe better and more spedily be dispatched at home / yet they thinke / nothing can be comly nor well done / without their counsail. ‖   And forasmuche as   Sig. G ij b
we see that dayly chaunce / in sondry kindes of craftesmen / *and* in euery trifling mater: it is no marvaill / though it be so*ᶜ* in religion / wherin / all men wishe / that all thinges were ordred / according to the most perfite example / wherin for all that / many men partly distrust their owne wittes / partly vse currupte*ᵈ* wittes / in that / they esteme strau*n*ge ware more than domesticall stuf: no man ought / I saye / to thinke it any marvaill / though the glorious name of the churche of Rome / beinge at that tyme famous in excellent vertue / drawing and alluring almost all the partes of the worlde / in to admiracion of it / for vertues sake / which is the most sure bonde / knyt all men to it / and caused that churche / whom al men might see so notably vertuous / to be reverenced / as the chief *and* principall churche among other.  And*ᵉ* Godly me*n* beautified it also with those names / w*hich the* Romishe bishoppes make boast of to the worlde / as though they were set furthe by oracle from God / to the supremacie withall*ᶠ* / not the supremacie of vertue / but the supremacie of power / and that earthly / an externe *and* a fleshly power / such a one as Christ neuer exercised / nor committed it at any tyme to any manne to exercise / as ferre as we maye gather out of holy scriptu-‖res. Wherout*ᵍ*   Sig. G iij a
notwithsto*n*ding / seing som men haue piked out som thinges / wherwith they wolde confirme it to be commaunded and ordayned of Christ / whervnto the people and *the* princes / wolde euen of their owne voluntary will / because of their great vertue / wherwith they were allured / as it had ben me*n* drawne vp with an admounde ston*ʰ* / wolde haue graunted

---

no marvel that...and that godly men should have beautified...".
*ᶠ* The translation is obscure and possibly mutilated. The sense is as follows: "...by oracle from God, so that they might defend the primacy not of virtue, but of power, and that earthly...".   *ᵍ* Out of which.   *ʰ* From the latinized French *adamaunt* (*N.E.D.*, which has the forms *admont* and *adamounde*). The meaning is "loadstone or magnet".

magnete attracti concessissent, nempe ut ecclesiam illam Ro*manam* et in ea præsidentem episcopum, non modo colere*nt* ‖ ac uenerarentur, sed iis etiam appellationibus exornarent, quæ pietas fingere, atq*ue* exprimere solet (qua in re pius nonnunq*uam* est error bonorum hominu*m*) Tame*n* æditis in hoc multis multoru*m* libris, mutuaq*ue* conflictatione impetentium, ac defendentium, cum sit plusq*uam* manifestum illa scripturæ loca, ad eam authoritatem defendendam, a uero, ac genuino se*n*su detorta esse, no*n* putaui operæprecium actam rem agere, et illa repete*n*do, quasi scrinia aliena compilasse uideri. Cum interim ego etiam ne omnia omniu*m* scripta uidear reiecisse, de primatu non ita multum contendo, modo ne ultra id proferant, q*uam* cui[1] uidetur ab initio fuisse appositu*m*. Id autem pernego fuisse episcopum Ro*manum* in absoluta aliqua externa potestate primu*m* a deo co*n*stitutu*m*: de hoc est questio, in hoc causa co*n*sistit. Qua in re planum fecimus (opinor) facta Christi a nobis stare, nec primatus uocabulum a patribus usurpatum obstare, eam aut*em* appellationem co*m*moda interpretatione adhibita potestati, qua*m* nu*n*c sibi uendicat episcopus Ro*manus* nihil suffragari. Nihil præterea, causæ episcopi Romani patrocinari prærogatiuas, quas deus sua in Petro dona coronans eidem contulit: quæ uidelicet non carni, et sa*n*guini, sed ad insigni[2] illius fidei professionis testimonium su*n*t collatæ. Cuiusmodi adhuc deus, qui etiamnum inexhaustam habet bonitate*m*, istis ipsis ‖ Ro*manis* episcopis sit daturus, si fide*m* Petri fuerint imitati. Quod si adhuc perga*nt* Romani

f. 31 a (margin)
f. 31 b (margin)

---

[1] *Cui* (for *alicui*) is not rendered in the translation: "that they carry the thing no further, than it may seem to one...". [2] *Sic*, rightly corrected to *insignis* in the Strasbourg edition. [a] The whole sentence is clumsily and carelessly translated and ought to stand thus: "Out of which, however, as some men have culled out a few things, by which to confirm that power to have been ordained and established by Christ, so that both princes and people should of themselves agree in it, attracted by the force of virtue as by a magnet, namely that they should not only...". [b] For it. [c] *Sic* for *places*. [d] *Sic* for *thought it not meet*. [e] The whole passage is involved and obscure, even in the Latin text, the succession of ideas being the following: "Since on the one hand texts of Scripture have been produced to support the Pope's authority...but since on the other hand it has been proved by previous controversies that those texts had been mis-

them[a] / that is / that they wolde not only honour and reuerence
that churche of Rome / and the bishop therof / but also advaunce
them with those titles: which godly affeccion is wont to diuise
and vttere / wherin good men doo somtyme erre: yet forasmuche / as bycause many men haue set furthe many bokes
touching this mater / and by reason of mutuall conflicte of men
reasonyng with it[b] and against it / it is more than manifeste that
those place[c] of scripture / are wrested from their true and
propre meaning / to defende that autoritie / I though it not
mete[d] / to doo that is done already / and in making rehersall .
of them / to make men thinke / I had geuen them a pigge of
an others mannes sowe.[e] Wherin[f] the meane space / lest I
shoulde seme to cast awaye al mennes wrytinges / I doo not
so muche contende about the supremacie so[g] they racke it
out no further / than it appeareth to be ment from the begin-
ning. || But this I vtterly denye / that God ordayned the bishop
of Rome to be the chief / as touching any absolute wordly[h]
power: of this is the question / in this point the hole cause
consisteth.    In this mater / I wene / I haue made it plaync
ynough / that Christes dedes stande on our side / and that the
name of supremacie vsurped of our elders[i] maketh nothing
against vs: and that the title / having a right interpretacion
ioyned vnto the power[j] / which the bishop of Rome claimeth
now to him selfe / maketh nothing for his purpose / and
moreouer / that the prerogatiues / which God gaue vnto Petre /
crownyng his owne giftes in him[k] / helpe the Bishoppe of
Romes cause nothing at all: which: prerogatiues were not
geuen vnto fleshe and bloud / but to be a testimonie of that
excellent profession of his faithe.    And such wolde God
(whose liberall goodnes dothe neuer waste) geue yet still / vnto
these bishoppes of Rome / if they folowed thexample of Petres
faythe.
But if the bishoppes of Rome goo about / to kepe in state still

You are a
good sone
for teaching
your father
so good a
lesson as
nether of
you taketh
hede to.

interpreted, I refrain from repeating known arguments". The second
part of the sentence is clumsily translated and may be improved thus:
"Yet since it is more than manifest, from many books published on
that subject by many men, some attacking, some defending, in their
mutual conflict, that those places of scripture have been wrested
from their true and natural meaning, I did not think it worth while
to do that which is already done...".    [f] Sic for where in, the
meaning being as follows: "While at the same time, lest I should...
etc."    [g] As long as.    [h] Obsolete for worldly.    [i] I.e. "from our
elders".    [j] Misunderstood by the translator who wrongly referred
potestati to adhibita: "and that the title, if properly interpreted, in
no wise supports that power, which...".    [k] Crowning in him the
gifts made to him.

episcopi male constructæ, atque ideo iamdiu nutantis potestatis ruinas fulcris et pedamentis, ab humano ingenio fabrefactis, in suo fastigio sustinere, potiusquam ne casum patiantur grauiorem ad eum usque modum demittere, quem ueritas tueri ac defendere posset, nolo grauius quicquam ominari. Tantum animaduertant uincere tandem in omnibus ueritatem. Iam tenebris successisse euangelii lucem. lucem autem arguere quæ non sunt probanda. Vident omnes quid sibi uelint ea euangelii uerba, Tu es Petrus, et super hanc petram ædificabo ecclesiam meam. Cernuntur mysteria, et trinæ interrogationis domini ad Petrum, et trinæ eiusdem negationis, ac solutionis didragmatis[1] pro eodem. Intelligitur hodie, quid sit apostolorum esse primum: quid denique oues pascere concreditas a deo, hæc passim obuia in ore sunt omnibus. Clamant etiam aliqui fucum, et imposturam. Alii uero aliis, ut fert natura, atque ingenium, parcius loquuntur, atque moderatius. Sunt etiam qui, quoniam se animi tamdiu falsos fuisse animaduertunt, præ pudore quoad licet tacent. omnes plane constantissimo consensu in hoc conuenerunt, docti pariter, atque indocti tum uiri tum feminæ, nihil ei cum Roma esse negotii, quem Anglia genuit, et educauit.[2] omnes summo consensu ueritatem amplexantes, atque exosculantes principem, supremum in terris ecclesiæ caput ||

f. 32 a  agnoscunt, colunt, et uenerantur. Iubere ualere episcopum Romanum cuius operam utcunque receptam aliquando, ita hoc tempore inutilem atque incommodam non magis religioni habent, ut in quo nulla sit religio, quàm a se illum sacellanum inuitum dimittere, qui ad diuina peragenda conductus, aut rogatus, non seipsum officio, fide, ac diligentia probauerit iis, a quibus operæ præstitæ mercedem deberet expectare. Maluit enim reipsa seruum in

---

[1] The miracle through which Christ enabled Peter, and Peter alone, to pay tribute money (Matth. xvii, 24–7) was considered throughout the Middle Ages as one of the proofs of the superior position of Peter in regard to the other apostles. This had been again asserted by Fisher only a few years before, in his *Assertionis Lutheranæ confutatio* (ed. 1523, p. ccclxi): "Quinta subinde prærogatiua non parui ponderis est, quod in soluendo didragmati, Christus Petrum solum, præ cæteris omnibus apostolis, sibi tanquam parem adiunxit. Quæ res tam apertum indicium, cuiusdam præeminentiæ fuit in Petro futuræ, ut

and holde vp *the* decayes of their power (whose buldin-g*a* was naught / and therfore hath wryed on the one side longe a goo)*b* *with* proppes and stayes / divised by mannes braine / rather the*n* to let it shrynke downe to that state / ‖ that the truthe were hable to defende *and* beare out: well / beware lest they catche a sorer fall / I will gesse no sorer a thinge. Only let them co*n*sidre / that at leynght truthe hathe the victorie / and that the light of the Gospell / is now come in place of darkenes: and that the light reproveth the thinges that are not allowable.

Sig. G iiij a

It were best for you to take this cou*n*sail also.

All me*n* see / what these wordes of *the* Gospel meane. **Thou arte Petre, and vpon this rocke will I buylde my churche.** Men perceave the misteries / bothe of Christes three tymes asking of Petre / of Petres thrise denyeng / and of the payeng of tribute money for him / It is vnderstande*n* at this present / what it is / to be the chief of the apostles: *and* what it is / to fede the shepe / whom God geueth charge of: this gaire almost euery body hathe in their mouthes. Yea / som crye out / that they haue ben iuggled withal and deceaued. And (as their nature and disposicion is) som speake lesse / and more temper-atelye than som. and som ther be also / which / perceaving they haue ben so longe / falsely beguyled / a*s* muche as they can refrayne / saye neuer a worde for shame. Wel / al sortes of people / are agreed vpon this poi*n*t / with most stedfast consent: learned and vnlearned / bothe men *and* women / that no maner of person / borne and brought vp in ‖ Englande / hathe ought to doo w*i*th Rome. Al maner of people / receavi*n*g and embracei*n*g *the* truthe / doo with one hole co*n*sent / acknow-lage / honour and reuerence the kinge for the supreme hcade of the churche vpon earthe. They bidde the bishop of Rome farewell. whose labour / how so euer it hathe ben receaued in tymes past / euen so now as vnprofitable and discommodious / they haue no more deuocion to it / as a thing / wherin a man shoulde haue no deuocio*n* / but*d* to turne such a chappelayn / out of the dores / will be nyll he / as*e* bei*n*ge hyred or prayed to ministre divine service / hathe not shewed him selfe faithfull and diligente / in his office / vnto them / that he shoulde haue loked to haue rcccaued his wages of / for his paynes taken. For a man had rather haue a faithfull seruaunt to ministre in

Mat. xvj: *the* light of *the* Gospell came in / whan *the* bisho*p* of Rome was drynen out.*c*

Sig G iiij b

Than as many as receaue *the* truthe haue not a doo w*i*th the bisho*p* of Rome.

---

inde mox inter cæteros (ut apud Matthæum patet) [Matth. xviii, 1] oborta quæstio fuerit, quis futurus esset maior in regno cœlorum". ² Marginal note here in the Strasbourg edition: "Tota Anglia Roma*m* reiecit". The unanimity of the English nation in rejecting the Pope's authority was one of the points which Henrician propaganda attempted to place beyond doubt, and statements to that effect were of course greeted with joy by continental Protestants. *a* Obsolete form for *building*. *b* Inaccurate: "to maintain a power ill-built, and which therefore has long been tottering, threatening ruin...". *c* *Sic* for *dryuen* (driven). *d* Than. *e* Who.

ministerio fidelem, in cuius nomine certa rerum nota, qui uocabulorum est usus deprehendatur, quam serui loco factis quidem[1] uenditantem, sese dominorum dominum, qui interim sese appellet seruorum seruum. Cui tamen pro christiana charitate bene præcantur, et optant omnes, inter quos etiam ego uel maxime: nimirum ut nunc qui Paulus est, ita cæteros antecessores superet diui Pauli dotibus. Vt quemadmodum hic una ad Romanos epistola uniuersa nostræ religionis mysteria complexus est: sic ille e Romanis ea nunc scribat iis, qui ei auscultant, quæ ueram CHRISTI gloriam sapiant, et ad fidem illustrandam pertineant, uerius quam quæ superioribus his annis ab archiuis illis, et scriniis in orbem emanarunt.[2] Breuiter uiuat, et ualeat in Domino fœlix. Ego uero redeo ad institutum: Nempe ut omnes cohorter ad obedientiam, quæ

f. 32 b in dei præceptis, ac propter deum sola ‖ nos efficit fœlices, ac beatos. Præcepta autem dei lucida, quæ oculos illuminant, ne in tenebris offendamus, sunt iusta, sunt honesta, sunt denique tum animæ tum corporis perpetuæ uitæ non utilia modo, sed necessaria, eademque nec grauia obseruatu aut difficilia. habent quidem iugi rationem quod detineant, et contineant in labore, sed cum suauitate. onus autem sunt, sed leue. Nempe illud præstat dei gratia, quæ per Iesum Christum facta est, ut quæ carni sint impossibilia, per spiritum præstentur cum alacritate. diffusa namque charitate in cordibus nostris per spiritum sanctum, qui datus est nobis, ac renouati spiritu mentis nostræ, iamque spirituales effecti cum simus, dicere licebit cum diuo Paulo, Omnia possumus in eo qui nos confortat Christus. Non est igitur quod rei grauitate deterreamur, quæ Christi beneficio, morte eius preciosissima, et gloriosissima interueniente, facillima effecta sit iis, qui

---

[1] Comma here in the Hamburg edition, which has none after *uenditantem*.      [2] Compare this passage with several places in the tract on Fisher's execution, in which Gardiner makes use of the same comparison between the writings of the Pope and those of St Paul, but to quite a different purpose. The contrast is striking between the affected goodwill of *De vera obedientia* and the sarcastic tone of the tract, and it is clear that the two works were meant for different purposes. (Tract on Fisher's execution, fols. *169 b*–195 a and 179 a–b.)
[a] Whose name is the sure sign of the realities it expresses—according

dede / in whose name / the true token of doing / which is the right vse of calling*a* / maye appeare: than in stede of a seruaunt to haue one / that taketh vpon him to be lorde of lordes / in his doinges / though in the meane space / he calleth him selfe **seruaunt of seruauntes.**

And yet all men / for christian charites sake / praye for him and wishe him wel / amonge whom I am one specially: that Paule *that* now is / may so excelle his predecessours in Saint Paules gi-‖ftes / that / like as Saint Paule hathe comprehended all the mysteries of our religion / in one only epistle / to the Romaynes: so this Paule maye now write from Rome / to them that be vnder his obedience / suche thinges / as tende to*b* the true glorie of Christ / and concerne the advauncement of faithe*d* / rather than such ware / as hathe crept*e* into *the* worlde / these yeares past / from those highe potentates and stoare houses.*f* To be shorte / God sende him good life / and well to fare in the Lorde.

Sig. G v a

*the* same we wolde pray for you / but that your obabstinate*c* wilfulnes maketh vs afraide to pray for you.

But I wil returne to my purpose: that is / that I maye move all men to obedience / which only in *the* commaundementes of God / *and* for Goddes sake / maketh vs happie *and* blessed. And commaundementes of God / are cleare / *and* lighten our eies / *that* we stomble not in darkenes: they are righteous / they are honest / they are also not only profitable alwayes to the life bothe of soule and body / but also necessarie / and not sore nor hearde*g* to be observed / for they haue a respecte vnto the yoke*h* / *that* they deteyne and kepe still in labour / yea but with a sweatnes / they are a burthen / but yet a lighte one. For it commeth to passe by the grace of God / which is made by Iesus Christ / that thinges impossible vnto the fleshe / are accomplished by the spirite with chearfulnes / by love / ‖ that is powred in our heartes / by *the* holy goost / which is geuen vs / and seing we are now renewed in the spirite of our mynde / and become spirituall: we may saye with Saint Paule: **We are hable to doo all thinges in him, that streynghtneth vs,** that is to saye / Christ. Ther is no cause than / to make vs afraude*i* / of the weightye importaunce of the thing / which through the benefite of Christ / by meanes of his most precious and most glorious deathe / is made most easie / to them / which acknow-

Goddes worde pure than truthe maketh not men heretiques but kepeth them from heresye.

Sig. G v b

Mennes interpreta- cions not to be folowed

---

to the true use of words.     *b* More exactly: "that savour of…". *c* *Sic* for *obstinate*.    *d* Mistranslated: "that tend to place the faith in its full light".    *e* More exactly: "flowed into, come out into". *f* Mistranslated. According to du Cange, "*archivum* = scrinium, locus ubi asservantur chartæ publicæ". The meaning is "from their archives and cabinets". The translator probably did not know the word *archivum* and made a wild conjecture as to its sense.    *g* Hard (*N.E.D.*).    *h* They are like unto a yoke, in that they….    *i* Misprint or erratic form for *afraid* (not in *N.E.D.*).

carnis imbecillitate*m* agnosce*ntes*, diuinæ se totos fidei, cu*m* certa in deu*m* fiducia obediendo committunt. Ergo accingamur obedire deo in præceptis eius, quæ ut difficilia non sunt, ita nec numerosa. Qui diligit proximum, ait Paulus, legem impleuit: quid dici breuius potest, aut maiore cum compendio? Quoniam autem dilectionis uerbum interpretationem habet, eam sequamur ante f. 33 a om*n*ia oportet, quæ in scripturis ab eo pro-‖dita est, qui legem ædidit, et promulgauit. Ordinem deniqu*e* seruemus à deo præscriptum, nec ab eodem constituta, atqu*e* diuisa commode corporis ecclesiæ membra, ut unus in ecclesia doceat, alius præsit, id quod principibus est attributum, nostra interpretatione confu*n*dere conemur, atqu*e* per-uertere. Quinimo relictis, atqu*e* neglectis, quæ ho*minum* siue prudentia, siue calliditas adinuenerit, ipsam sequamur ueritatem. Huic pareamus, huic obediamus, quæ sola co*n*stituit ueram obedie*n*tiam. Atqu*e* hic quidem claudere sermonem potuissem, ni me ineptæ quorundam uoces, tanqu*am* pone præhensum resupinassent, mequ*e* de meipso rationem reddere coegissent, quo tandem fretus de obedie*n*tia quacunqu*e*, nedum uera, uerbum ædere ausus sim, qui interim obedie*n*tiam docere professus, meam detego inobedientiam, et in eius potestate*m*, atqu*e* authori-tatem impetum facio, cui defendendo patronus olim ascitus su*m*, atqu*e* adeo iureiura*n*do adactus, ut eam pro uirili tuerer, et propugnarem? ubi inquiunt, iurisiura*n*di religio? ubi fides? quid credas his temporibus? aut cui credas? Etenim episcopus quidam Romani episcopi suffragio in episcoporum ordinem cooptatus, et eius mandato consecratus, atqu*e* inter sacra ipsa ecclesiæ Roma*næ* iura defendere iuratus, quæ om*n*ia uolens, ultro et sponte subiuit, atqu*e* pollicitus est præstare. En in-f. 33 b quiunt, ‖ idem ipse deterrimo præuaricationis exemplo fidei datæ, atqu*e* iuramenti oblitus, aut si non oblitus, certe quod deterius est, iureiurando ac fide spretis, atqu*e* con-

---

*a* *Sic* for *interpretacion.*     *b* Inaccurate: "of any manner of obedi-ence, and still more of true obedience".     *c* Inaccurate: "A certain bishop, admitted and consecrated by the privilege...".     *d* Inac-curate: "to the most horrible example of prevarication, forgetting

lageing their weakenes of fleshe / committe them selves holly
to Goddes trust / through obedience / with a sure confidence
in God. Let vs therfore make vs / ready / to obey God in his
preceptes / which / as they be not harde / so they are not many
in nombre. He *that* loveth his neighbour (saithe Paule) hathe
fulfilled the lawe: what can be spoken more briefly / or knitte
vp in lesse rowme? And because this worde (love) hathe an
interpretacion / we must nedes afore all thinges / folowe that
interpretacion / which is set furthe in scriptures / by him / that
made the lawe and published it.   Let vs than folowe the
ordre / that God hathe prescribed / and not goo about with
our interpretacton[a] / to confounde and peruerte the membres
of his body the churche / which he hathe set ‖ in ordre *and*
disposed in particulares accordingly / that one in the congregacion shoulde teache / and an other haue the preeminence /
which is appointed to princes / and forsaking and neclecting
those thinges / which either mennes wisedome or subtill brayne
hathe invented / let vs folowe the truthe it selfe: let vs obey it /
let vs doo after it / which only maketh true obedience.
And here I coulde haue made an ende of my tale / had not
som folkes folishe wordes ben / *that* had almost pulled me downe
backewarde and enforced me to rendre accompt of my selfe /
what caused me to be so hardye / as to write one worde / concerning any maner of obedience / namely[b] true obedience /
seing I neuertheles / entreprising to teache obedience / disclose
myne owne disobedience / and geue the onsette against his
power and autoritie / for whose defense I was called ones to
be a patrone / and bounden by myne othe to defende and main-
tene his autoritie to my possible power? wher is the keping of
othes become / saye they? Wher is fidelitie? What maye a man
beleve now a dayes? Whom maye a man trust? For he was
made a bishop[c] and by the priuilege of the Bishop of Rome /
admitted in to the ordre of Bishoppes / and consecrated by
his commaundement / and sworne vpon the ‖ holy euangelistes
to defende the rightes of the churche of Rome: all which thinges
he willingly and with al his hearte obeyde / and permised to
performe. Lo / saye they / euen the very selfe same man / to
the most horrible example of breache of his fidelitie[d] / and
forgotting[e] the solemne othe / he made / or if not through
forgotefulnes[f] / yet (which is the worse of the twoo) having
contemned and defied[g] his othe and fidelitie / he professeth

*Marginal notes:*

I beseche
god / kepe
his worde
frely
amonge vs
*and* than
your
mysordre
shalbe
spied well
ynough.

Sig. G vj a

Loke how
good coun-
sail *the*
traytour
geueth *and*
yet will
nether folowe
it him selfe
nor suffre
other.

Sig. G vj b

his pledged faith and his oath…". 	[e] Misprint or erratic form for
*forgetting* (not in *N.E.D.*). 	[f] Misprint or erratic form for *forget-
fulness* (not in *N.E.D.*). 	[g] More accurately: "having rejected and
spurned his oath…".

temptis, Romanæ ecclesiæ apertum se hostem profitetur, ac, quo tela in illam uenenata securius iaciat, tanq*uam* ab obedientia hastam mutuatus, quasi tectis lateribus delitescere se credit, cum interim omnibus pateat apertus, et nudus, pari cu*m* stultitia atq*ue* improbitate. Hæc qui dicturi sunt, iis me ut¹ satisfacere possim, nonnihil uereor, atq*ue* pertimesco. Afferen*t* enim fortasse ad causam nescio quid, animo præiudicatum, quo repletus ia*m* animus, id quod a me dicetur, non aliter respuet, q*uam* uas quodcunq*ue* aqua iam plenum, superfusum liquorem non admittit. Qui uero hæc audient, ac uacuo deinde, liberoq*ue* animo, aut saltem non su*m*mo tenus pleno, nostra uicissim cum æquitate legere uoluerint: his nihil dubito ostensurum me, atq*ue* adeo persuasurum uerba hæc quantumuis specie grauia, quippe periurii, et infamiæ accusationem continentia, conuitii dumtaxat crimine alligare eos qui proferunt: me uero, in quem dicu*n*tur, no*n* magis mouere debere, q*uam* e dolio reddita tonitrua,² quod habet prouerbiu*m*.² Neq*ue* eni*m* in dictis iuratis, aut promissis spectari potius debet forma, quam materia. Quinimo dicas, jures, aut promittas sanctissime id, quod facere, et exequi non debes, no*n* ‖ uincent pacta rerum natura*m*: nec in his forma mutabit materiæ conditionem, sed persancte iuratu*m*, si malum sit, aut non rectum, sanctius omittitur, q*uam* iuramenti prætextu, quasi uinculum sit iniquitatis, efficiatur, atq*ue* præstetur. nisi fortasse persuasu*m* habeamus in malis, atq*ue* peruersis laudandam esse constantiam, uitioq*ue* potius dari deberi de media uia recurrere, q*uam* semper currere male. Ad quam rem clarius demonstrandam illud mihi exemplum uisum est accommodatissi-

f. 34 a

---

¹ *Ut* stands here for *ne non*: "I am afraid that I shall not be able to satisfy them". The translation, in which *ut* is taken to mean "how", is obviously impossible and ungrammatical. In any case, *me* appears as superfluous, and may be considered as an error, presumably due to the presence of an erased *ne* in the MS.    ² It has not been possible to ascertain the origin of this *proverbium*; but *dolium* is "a jar", and the phrase therefore means, not "the blombling of an olde barel", as the translator renders it, but "the noise of thunder imitated by blowing or shouting into a hollow jar", which swells the sound. This may not inappropriately be likened to two passages of Horace, in which tragedy is said, whether properly or figuratively, to

him selfe an open enemye of the churche of Rome / and to
shote his poysoned shaftes the more surely again*st* it / he
boroweth a pece of artillary as it were of obedience / and
thinketh he lyeth closely in covert / as though his sides were
ouerhilled / whan for all that / he lyeth open and naked to al
mennes sightes / bothe like a fole and a naughty man. Such
me*n* / as wil talke on this sorte / I am afraide / *and* in great
doubt / how I shall satisfie them. For they will allege perhappes / to amende the mater withall*ᵃ* / a certai*n* preiudice of
soule / I wote not what / wherwith their mynde being blowne
full / they will spue out that that I shall speake / euen as it
were a vessell being toppe full of water / that receaveth no
more liquor / wha*n* it is poured vpo*n*. But they *that* shall heare
these mennes talke / and than on the other side will indifferently reade ‖ my saieng / with an emptie and free minde / and
not all*ᵇ* ready brynke full: I doubt not / but I shall shewe vnto
them / and persuade them so / that their wordes as weyghtie
as men thinke them (in dede they accuse me of periurie and
slaundre(*ᶜ* co*n*demne them for false reporters / *that* speake
them: and that they ought no more to move me / against whom
they be reported / than the blombling*ᵈ* sounde of an olde barel /
as they saye. For in othes or promises / the forme ought not
so muche to be respected / as *the* mater. But*ᵉ* let a ma*n* / saye /
sweare / or promise as faithfully*ᵍ* as he can / that thing that he
ought not to doo nor performe / *the* promise shall not be aboue
the nature of the mater selfe: nether shall *the* forme in these
cases / chaunge the condicion of the mater / but the faithfully
made othe / if it be starke naught / or not good / is better broken /
than vnder pretense of the othe / as though it were the bo*n*de
of widkednes*ʰ* / it shoulde be perfourmed *and* kept: onles we
must be persuaded / that constauncie is commendable in
naughtie and and peruerse*ⁱ* maters / and that it is a greater
faulte to turne agayn in the mydde waye than still to runne
always naught. And for the more cleare demonstracion of
this mater / I take this to be the most fitte example. A certain

Sig. G vij a

vnlaufull
othes not
to kept.*ᶠ*

How shoulde
folishe or
vnlaufull
vowes be
bounde*n* to
be kept
whan such
othes are
not?

---

swell its voice and give it a solemn tone, by speaking into a jar, *ampulla*
being here used in place of *dolium*, and in the same sense: "An tragica
desævit, et ampullatur in arte" (*Epist.* III, 1. 14); "Projicit ampullas et
sesquipedalia verba" (*Ars. poet.* 97).     *ᵃ* Mistranslated: "For they
will bring to the cause (i.e. to the judgment of the cause) I wot not
what already prejudged in their minds, wherewith…".     *ᵇ* More
accurately: "or at any rate not brimful…".     *ᶜ* *Sic* for ).     *ᵈ* This
form is not found in *N.E.D.*, which gives *blumbering* (John Heywood,
1556) as meaning "a rumbling, lumbering noise".     *ᵉ* More accurately: "What is more…",     *ᶠ* *Sic* for *to be kept.*     *ᵍ* Inaccurate:
"with the most holy, sacred or religious oaths".     *ʰ* *Sic* for *wickedness.*     *ⁱ* *Sic* for *naughtie and peruerse.*

mum. Maritus quidam cum iustissimis argumentis credidisset primam uxorem nusquam inter uiuos extare superstitem, Authore ecclesia, quasi a coniugio liber, mulierem quandam uirginem creditam, specie quidem egregiam, cum consensu parent*um* superinduxit uxorem, ex qua post aliquot annorum cohabitationem liberos cum sustulisset, en rediit tan*quam* postliminio[1] prior uxor inexpectata. hæc repetit uirum secundis nuptiis male colligatum. Vir autem ipse re pene incredibili percitus, atque perculsus, primum negare eam ad se pertinere, dein signa querere, postremo quoniam se ab illa, quam posterius duxisset, ægre admodum auelli pateretur, quoad[2] poterat dilationibus procrastinare, tandem uero ad iudicium prouocare, in iudicio autem, quod secundæ uxoris causam

f. 34 b   tueretur, nihil omittere. At uictus || tandem ueritati cedit, ac priori uxori ex ecclesiæ iudicio se adiungit. hic nunc si ea mulier, quæ secu*n*do loco ducta merito expellitur, aut ea per tristitiam, et merorem tacente, parentes eius, aut amici exclamare*n*t: O mores, o tempora, atq*ue* in hu*n*c hominem similem qua*n*dam orationem haberent, atq*ue* in me dicere uidentur isti, Quid tu pessime, fædi-frage, nequam, an hanc nunc deseris, atq*ue* destituis, cui tu olim tam sancte inter ipsa sacra, cum deus testis adesset, dedisti fidem? An exciderunt memoria uerba illa, quæ in corona hominu*m* celeberrima, ministro dei recitante, in ipso templo protulisti, muliere quam nunc turpiter abiecisti, tum præsente, et stipulante, atq*ue* inuicem etia*m* promitte*n*te? An no*n* orasti nos olim de hac, et illius nuptias multis precibus ambiuisti, atq*ue* æditis pactis iurasti seorsum[3] nobis, ha*n*c te tan*quam* matre*m*familias semper habiturum, neq*ue* te uiuo deserturum? an etiam no*n* pudet, quu*m* hæc te patrem fecerit

---

[1] The Hamburg edition misprints this word as *postlimino*.   [2] The Hamburg edition misprints this word as *quod*, yet the translator who used that edition rightly amended the word to *quoad*.   [3] This word is not rendered in the English version: "To each of us in particular, separately to the father and mother".   [a] *Postliminium* is the right to return home from exile and resume one's former rank and privileges. The translation is here somewhat fanciful.   [b] Another mistranslation; *negare* is here a narrative infinitive, and is not connected

ma-‖ried man / whan he thought by most iust likelyhodes /
that his furst wife had ben vndoubtedly deadde: as a man that
had ben free from mariage / by the autoritie of the churche /
toke another woman / which was a faire damoysell / *and*
thought to be a mayde / to wife by consent of her parentes: by
whom / after they had dwelt a fewe yeares together / and he had
children by her: Lo / his former wife vnloked for / came
againe / as it were peeping behinde the post.[a] Well / she requireth to haue her husbande agayn / that had done evil in
marieng an other woman. Than *the* man being astonyed at
that / as a mater allmost incredible / and dryven at the furst
to denie her to be his wife:[b] than to aske her what tokens she
coulde tell him / and last of all / because he was wonderous
lothe to be divorced from her / that he had maried the later /
to make as longe delayes as he coulde: and at leinght to cal her
to the lawe / *and* ther to make al the shifte he coulde / to defende his seconde wifes cause. But whan he was cast[c] / he
gaue place to the truthe / and taketh his furst wife to him agayn
by the iudgement of the churche. In this cace now / if the
woman / that he maried last be iustely put from him / or for
sorowe and heavines speaking neuer a worde / her Parentes or
frendes wolde crye ‖ out:[d] Out vpon mennes maners? out
vpon it / what a worlde is this? *and* after this sorte wolde make
suche a like wondrement[e] / as these men seme to vse against me:
thow helhounde / thou wicked couenaunt breaker / doest thou
forsake and cast of this woman now / vnto whom thou madest
ones so faithfull a promise in the open face of the churche /
whan God him selfe was a present witnesse? hast thou forgoten
the wordes which thou spakest in the temple / the ministre of
God rehearsing them vnto the / in the presences of so many
people / this woman / *that* thou hast now shamefully cast vp /
being present / *and* making covenaunt *and* promise to the in
like sorte agayne. Diddest not thou ones desire vs for her /
and madest muche entreatie to haue her to thy wife / and
promisedest vs vpon thy othe / *that* thou woldest vse her as
the good wife of thy house for euer / and neuer to forsake her
during thy lyfe? Arte thou not ashamed / seing thou hast suche
children by her / to cast her of now / as though she were an
whore? and now whan thou leavest her to take her parte / that

with *perculsus.* The meaning is: "The husband, first...greatly stirred
and struck dumb...denies her to be his wife...". [c] *To cast* = "to
throw on the ground, to overthrow, hence to defeat in an action at
law" (*N.E.D.*). [d] The sentence is misunderstood, the meaning
being as follows: "Now, if this woman, who having been married
second, is rightly put away; or if, she being silent in her sadness and
grief, her parents or friends, should exclaim...". [e] *Against him*
should be inserted here.

talium liberoru*m*, illam nunc turpiter tanq*uam* meretricem
abiicere? atq*ue* adeo illam cum deseras, eius qui te ab hac
euicit partes tueri? ubi iurisiurandi religio? ubi fides?
Quid credas his te*m*poribus, aut cui credas? Maritus
deserit uxorem. Quæ quidem orationis ipsius forma, ut
mulieris dolori co*n*cedi posset, tum propter graue*m* præsentis calamitatis se*n*sum, tu*m* etia*m* propter sexus in-
f. 35 a   firmitatem, ita certe ab aliis pro-||lata, qui quidem grauiter
uideri uellent dicere, extremæ stultitiæ æderet argumentum, quamq*ue* in contione ridere*n*t omnes, in ipsis iudiciis
ferret nemo. Mulieri autem ipsi post aliquod te*m*poris
i*n*teruallum si quis respo*n*deret, No*n* recte accusas mulier
eum, quo nunc iure cares marito, et defensore. Quid enim
in eo nunc improbas? Nempe quamdiu aberat prior uxor,[1]
te amauit, te coluit, te habuit pro uxore. atq*ue* adeo primæ
redeunti, qua*m* non superesse putauit, illi non temere
credidit, no*n* protinus assensus est: nihil amplius tua causa
facere potuit, q*uam* fecit. Si a te eum meretricis amor
abalienasset, fuisset aliqua tua querela. Nunc autem quid
exprobras fidei uiolationem ei, qui ut eam seruaret, à te dis-
cessit, et mulieri adhæsit, qua*m* iure antea desponsauerat?
quid adhuc co*n*querereris? cederet opinor mulier: certe non
haberet quod co*n*quereretur. Quæ quidem si non uirgo,
ut credebatur, fuisset, sed corrupta, quæq*ue* priorem huius
uiri uxore*m* ideo curauerat ipsa in extremas aliquas insulas
ablegandam, ut fide*m* interim huius sibi obstringeret, et
quo minus alteri in matrimonio seruiatur efficeret: utrius
tandem culpa maior censeatur? huius uiri qui bona fide
contraxit, nulla: callidæ certe mulieris maxima, ut quæ
alieno matrimonio delectaretur. Atq*ue* hæc si quis co*n*-
sideret, an non tanq*uam* in speculo cernet in me huius
f. 35 b   mariti || ueram imaginem, qui scilicet quum eam obedientiæ
ueritatem nusq*uam* extare crederem, aut saltem requisitam
non inuenissem, secundis me fœderibus ei copulaui bona

---

[1] The word *uxor* omitted in the Hamburg edition.     [a] *Sic* for
*communicacion*.     [b] That you now lack as a husband and defender.
[c] Held herself away.     [d] *I ween* = "I think".     [e] She would have.
[f] The translation is very free here, the meaning being thus: "to
fasten unto herself the faith of that man, and prevent him from being

caused the to be divorced from her? Wher is the keping of othes become? wher is fidelitie? what maye a man beleve now a dayes? whom maye a man trust? The husbande forsaketh the wife. ‖ Which maner of communictcion[a] / as it maye be borne withall in the womans heavynes / bothe for the great grief of her present calamitie / and because she is the weaker vessell / euen so whan it is spoken of other mennes mouthes / which wolde haue folkes to thinke / they speake pithily / it wolde make men thinke / they were starke foles / and in open company / euery body wolde laughe at them / and in triall of lawe noman coulde abyde them. But after a certain space / if a man wolde answer *the* woman : and saye : woman you doo not well to accuse him / that you want now to be[b] your husbande and defendour : For what faulte fynde you now in him? For as longe as the farther wife helde her[c] awaye / he loved you / he honoured you / he vsed you as his wife : yea so muche / that whan the furst wife came agayne / whom he thought had ben deadde / he was not rashe in geuing credence vnto her / nor sodaynly assented vnto her : he coulde doo no more for your sake / than he did. If he had fallen to whores / and so forsaken you / your querell had ben somwhat. But now / what cast you him in *the* tethe / with faithe breaking / which to kepe his faithe / departed from you / and kept him to that other wife / that he had laufully maried before? Why doo you complayne still? the ‖ woman / I wene[d] / wolde geue ouer : in dede she had[e] no cause to complayne. Yf she had not ben a mayden / as she was taken for / but an evill disposed woman / *and* had occasioned this mannes first wife / to be sent in to some ferre ylondes / to haue this man to her husbande in *the* meane tyme / *and* caused *the* furst mariage to be broken:[f] whether shoulde be thought to be more in the faulte? this man / *that* maried (as he thought) rightly / were in no faulte : and the subtyll woman were in *the* greatest faulte / as one *that* delighted to haue an other womans husbandc. And if a man wolde considre this gaire / shal he not see / as it were in a glasse / *the* very ymage of *that* husbande in me. For in dede I / seing I beloved / *that* no suche truthe of obedience / had ben / or if it had ben sought for / I wolde neuer haue founde it:[g] I coupled myselfe in seconde couenaunt / *and* therto plighted my trouthe / with

Sig. G viij b

Sig. H a

Saye you true doo you loue chaunge of women / as he did?

Some thinketh you forgote it now agayne.

enslaved to another woman in marriage". [g] Mistranslated; to be corrected thus: "For indeed I, believing that not such truth or obedience was in existence anywhere, or at any rate not having found it when looking for it; I coupled...".

fide, cum qua mihi cohabitationem interdictam non putaui, redeunti ueritati, quæ prima est uxor omnium hominum, utpote in baptismo desponsata, et quæ primam fidem ab omnibus exiget, ei acquieui, ei adhæsi: a secunda copula, tanq*uam* nulla, ecclesiæ meæ iudicio recessi. Et æquum cuiq*uam* uidebitur, quia ueritati pareo, appellari mendace*m*? quia in obediendo principi, deo inseruio, sacrorum contemptorem dici? aut iurisiurandi uiolatorem? Et quod ridicule obiicitur marito post diuortium, qui fide*m* no*n* præstitit, quam dare non debuit: id mihi in hac causa grauiter, et serio obiicietur, qui grauissimo quidem ueritatis iudicio ab illa Romana ecclesia, qua*m* mihi retinere non licuit diuulsus, sponsam ueritate*m* tandem postliminio redeunte*m* cogor agnoscere, atq*ue* illi firmiter adhærere? Si docere posset no*n* esse ha*n*c ueritatem, quam pro uxore, fidem primam repetente, amplexus sum, quod nunq*uam* faciet, me quibus uolet, uocet nominibus. Sin hoc omisso de iuramento aget, uerendum est, ne odisse incipiant omnes eam calliditate*m*, quæ iuramentis contra ueritate*m* innitatur. Itaq*ue* remoueatur a causa iurame*n*tum, quod
f. 36 a ueritati subseruire, non autem præiu-||dicare possit, aut debeat. Qui iurat illicita, haud recte facit: qui uero illicita iurauerit, et ea exequi perseuerat, altius, atq*ue* altius sese immergit; unde nisi retrogradus queat nunq*uam* euadere. Quamobrem nimis absurtum foret, ut, in quo quis resipiscere laboret, in eo crimen contrahere, et sese dehonestari, ac deturpari uideatur. Secundum quam rationem fit, ut ne in ciuilibus quidem legibus ulla sit turpium obligatio: uidelicet ne in criminibus perseuerantiam potius, quam resipiscentiam probasse uideantur. In ecclesiasticis uero sanctionibus, nullo eum teneri nexu, qui illicita iurauerit, diffinitum est, cum iurame*n*tum non sit uinculu*m* iniquitatis. Superest tantu*m* hoc, ut ab illa impetitione depulsi, qua

---

*a* With whom I thought I might lawfully dwell....   *b* Or rather "promised in marriage, betrothed".   *c* Misprint or erratic form for *effect* (not in *N.E.D.*).   *d* The meaning seems rather to be: "think it equitable, fair".   *e* Foolishly.   *f* To *trump* means "to sound a trumpet, hence to proclaim, celebrate" (*N.E.D.*).   *g* Sic for

whom I thought I had laufully dwelt *and* kept laufull company withall:[a] But whan the truthe came / which is euery mannes furst wife / maried[b] to him in baptisme / which will require the furst promyse / at all mennes handes to her I applyed / to her I cleaued: *and* from my seconde knotte / as of non affecte[c] / by *the* iudgement of my churche / I departed. And shall any man thinke it indifferent[d] / that I shall be called a lyer / because I obey the truthe? Because I ‖ serue God / in obeyeng my Prince / *then* I shalbe reported to be a contemner of the sacramentes / or an othe breaker? And that / that is fondly[e] layed to the husbandes charge / after he is divorced / because he perfourmed not his promyse / that he ought not to haue made: shall that in this cause be grevously and earnestly tromped[f] in my waye / because I am by most graue iudgement of the truthe / diuorced from the churche of Rome / which it was not laufull for me to kepe still and am compelled to take my wyfe **Truthe** to me / whan she commeth agayne at leynght peeping behynde the scrine[h] / *and* to cleaue constauntly vnto her? If he coulde teache me / *that* she is not the truthe / whom / I haue reccaved for my wyfe / clayming againe[i] my furst promyse (as he shall neuer doo it) let him call me by what names he will. But yf he will let that passe / and make a doo about the othe / it is to be feared / lest all men will begynne to abhorre that subtyltie / which is grounded in makyng of othes agaynst the truthe. Therfore take aweye the othe from the cause / for the othe ought to be a seruaunt of truthe / *and* can not nor ought to be preiudiciall vnto the truthe. He that by his othe promiseth vnlauful thinges / dothe not right: but he that ma‖keth an vnlauful othe / and gothe on stil to put it in execucion / thrusteth downe him selfe deper and deper / from whence he can neuer escape / except he com out arsewarde. Wherfore it were to great an absurditie / that a man shoulde be compted to doo a notorious crime / and to dishoneste and shame him selfe / in that point / wherin he goeth about to doo better. And according to this consideracion / it is decreed / that not so muche as by the ciuile lawes / a man is bounden to perfourme vnhonest or vnlaufull promyses[j] / lest it might be though[k] / that these lawes doo rather commende perseueraunce in crymes / than repentaunce. And in the ecclesiasticall decrees / it is also established / that no man is bounden to perfourme an vnlaufull othe / seinge an othe can not bynde a man to wickednesse. This only remayneth / that whan these men / which accuse me of periurie / are driuen backe / that they

I pray you lose it not / now it is founde to your hande.

**Sig. H b**
and so doo maried priestes goo from their seconde knotte *and* folowe *the* iudgement of Goddes wrode[g] / wherby his churche is gouerned: which sayth To avoide fornicacion let euery man haue his owne wife. Hearken to your owne reason my lorde / Doctor dubbleface.

**Sig. H ij a**

They are lesse hurtefull than you / for they only speake euil / but you both say euil *and* do worse. Me thinketh you shoulde be ashamed to

worde.    [h] Cf. note on the word *postliminium*, sig. G. vii *b*. *Scrine* = "screen" (*N.E.D.*).    [i] Mistranslated: "Reverting to...". [j] Somewhat beside the meaning, which is: "Which is the reason why, not even in the civil law can a man be bound to keep any dishonest promise...while in the canon law...".    [k] Sic for *thought*.

periurii notarent, temeritatis mihi notam inurere conten-
dant, qui iuraui ea, quæ præstare non licuit. At licuisse
putaui, no*n* solus, sed cum iudicio multorum. Nam
ueritatis uox, iamdiu tum sepulta, haud impedire uidebatur.
Nunc autem cum domum redierit ipsa, et tam multis se
iudiciis mihi eam ipsam esse confirmauerit, Quid ni
amplectar ueram sponsam, quæ fidem meam habet sibi
obnoxiam, ipsam nimirum ueritatem, in cuius obsequio
nulla est culpa, nedum crimen? Tantum abest, ut aliorum
conuitia pertimescam, dum huic uni mea probem officia,

f. 36 b  et secundum eam principi ‖ supremo ecclesiæ Anglicanæ
in terris capiti obediendo, alias simul obedientiæ ueræ
partes obire contendam, quæ sunt hominis proprie
Christiani, ut emensis in obedientia, et ueritate huius uitæ
spaciis, potiri ualeam æterna uita, Cuius Author est, et
dator Iesus Christus, qui ut omnes ad patre*m* traheret,[1]
patri per omnia factus obediens mortem pro nobis obiit
salutiferam. nec facto minus, q*uam* uerbo eam docuit
obedientiam, quæ ueritatis plena cum sit, ad ipsam omnes
quotquot in fide adhæserint, tandem euehet ueritate*m*,
qui est deus benedictus in secula. Amen.

*FINIS.*

[1] The Hamburg edition misprints this as *trahere.*

ca*n* laye no more periurie to my charge / they wil go about to
burthen me w*ith* vnadvised temeritie / for promising by mine
othe / *that*ᵃ was not lauful for me to perfourme.  Well Sir /
but I thought it had be*n* laufull / and not I alone / but w*ith the*
iudgeme*n*t of many men.  For *the* worde of Truthe / lyeng
tha*n* buried a lo*n*ge season / was thought to be no let. But now
wha*n* she is come home agayne / *and* ha-‖the confirmed her
selfe vnto me by so many proues / *that* it is euen she / why
shoulde I not embrace mine owne true wife / euen **Dame
Truthe** her selfe / vnto who*m* I plighted my trouthe / *and* in
*the* accomplishment of *the* same / ther is non offense / muche
less any notorious cryme? well / ther is no cause*ᶜ* / why I shoulde
be afrayde of other folkes euil reportes / as lo*n*ge as I doo my
duetie to her alone / *and* according to her mynde / obeye my
pri*n*ce / *the* supreme headde in earthe of *the* churche of
Englande / *and* tha*n* doo myne endeuour / to accomplishe the
other partes of true obedience / w*h*ich belong proprely to a
christen man / so as wha*n* I haue passed ouer *the* pilgrimage of
this life / in obedience *and* truthe / I maye obteyne eternal life /
*the* autor *and* gever wherof / is Iesus Christ / who / to drawe
al vnto *the* father / obeie*n*g *the* father in al thi*n*ges / suffred
deathe for our saluacio*n* / *and* bothe in worde / *and* dede taugt
obedie*n*ce w*h*ich / forasmuche as it is full of truthe / shal at
leingh*t* pr*o*mote all *that* faithfully sticke vnto it / to *the* very
truthe selfe / w*h*ich is God blessed for euermore Amen.

speake
against
priestes
maiage*ᵇ* / if
this reason
be true / as
it is *in* dede /
*that* ye
make here.
Sig. H ij b

Than a
ma*n* may
make an
vnaduysed
vowe / after
xxj yeares /
being
vnlearned
sci*n*g you
a mischeuous
wel lerned
ma*n* / made
an vnaduysed
othe of
your age.

---

ᵃ That which.     ᵇ *Sic* for *marriage.*     ᶜ More accurately: "Still
less cause is there why…".

# GARDINER'S ANSWER
## TO BUCER

Corpus
Christi
College,
Cambridge,
MS. No. cxiii

p. 255
Wyntoniensis
ad Bucerum

# Gardiner's answer to Bucer

Contemptum humanæ legis iusta authoritate latæ grauius *et* seuer*ius* vindicandum q*uam* diuinæ legis qualem*cu*nque transgressione*m*.

Nimis inuidiosu*m* foret co*m*mittere humana Diuinis, nedu*m* anteferre quæ sunt humana. Itaq*ue* animaduertendu*m* est, contemptu*m* legu*m* humanaru*m* ad diuinæ Maiestatis iniuria*m* pertinere, quaten*us* voluit homine*m* homi*n*i parere oportere: *et* sublimioribus potestatib*us* omne*m* anima*m* subiecta*m* esse debere. Adeo ut q*ui* homine*m* potestate preditu*m* spernat, non homine*m* spernat sed Deu*m*:[1] *et* qui fratre*m* que*m* videt no*n* diligit, Deu*m* quem non videt, quo*modo* pote*st* diligere? Non diligit aut*em* qui sup*er*ioris auctoritate*m* non agnoscit, sed violat per contemptu*m*, quod du*m* facit, et*iam* diuinam Maiestatem grauissime offendit, sub cui*us* manu humiliari nos oportet, quæ gladiu*m* principib*us* porrexit ad vindicta*m* maloru*m*, laudem uero bonoru*m*.[2] Quæ ta*me*n laus apud homi*n*es nonnu*n*qua*m* obscurat*ur* ea quidem, sed magno bonor*um* co*m*modo *et* foenore in diem illu*m*, quo iustus iudex reddet vnicuiq*ue* secu*n*du*m* opera sua in iustitia *et* Veritate. Atq*ue* hoc doceant*ur* quoru*m* officiu*m* est parere, ut intelligant nullo legu*m* humana*rum* pondere opprimi se posse, ut damnu*m* aut iacturam vllam faciant, si forte nimia legu*m* seuitia aut facultates, aut et*iam* vitam amiserint, quæ duo Deus esse voluit in hominum potestate, neq*ue* timeam*us* eos q*ui* occidu*n*t corpus.[3] sed honore*m*

---

[1] I Thessal. iv, 8.  [2] The whole of this passage, though not quoted directly from Scripture, is a clear allusion to the beginning of Rom.xiii,*v.*2:"Itaque qui resistit potestati,Dei ordinationi resistit…"; *v.* 3, "Nam principes non sunt timori boni operis, sed mali…"; *v.* 4, "Dei enim minister est tibi in bonum. Si autem malum feceris, time; non enim sine causa gladium portat. Dei enim minister est, vindex in iram ei qui malum agit". The words here used by Gardiner already occur practically in the same form in the tract on Fisher's execution, Latin text, fol. 180 b of the MS.  [3] Matth. x, 28.  *a* A distinction should be made between *gravius* and *severius*, which can hardly be emphasized in an English rendering of the sentence. *Gravius* refers to the weight or rigour of the punishment in itself,

The contempt of human law, made by rightful authority,
is to be punished more heavily and more seriously[a]
than any[b] transgression of the divine law.

It were too odious to place on a par things human and divine,
and still more to give the first place to those which are human.
Therefore it must be observed, that contempt of human laws
implies injury offered to the majesty of God, in so far as he
deemed it necessary that man should obey to man; and that
every soul should be subjected to the higher powers; to such
an extent that whoso despiseth a man endowed with power,
despiseth not man, but God: who does not love his brother
whom he sees, how can he love God whom he does not see?
Now he does not love, who does not acknowledge the authority
of his superior, but injures it through contempt; which while
he does, he also offends most grievously the divine Majesty,
under whose hand we ought to humble ourselves, who held
out the sword to princes for the punishment of the evil, but
also for the praise of the good. Which glory however is sometimes obscured among men, but to the great advantage and
gain of the righteous, in view of that day, on which the upright
judge will reward every man according to his doings, in justice
and truth. And let this be learnt of those whose office it is to
obey; so that they may understand, that no weight of human
laws can possibly oppress them so heavily, that they should
suffer any damage or peril, if by any chance they should lose,
through an excessive harshness of the laws, either their property
or even their life, which it was the will of God to place in the
power of men; nor let us fear those which kill the body, but

severius (severus being a doublet of serius) to the importance that must
be attached to the crime: "The contempt of human law...must be
considered as more serious and therefore punished more pitilessly...".
[b] It is difficult to find a satisfactory rendering for the adjective
qualiscunque, which Gardiner uses in the second part of his comparison
in reference to transgressio. From Gardiner's own words (p. 263 of
the MS.) it is clear that he considers qualiscunque as somewhat less
strong than quilibet. The latter is to be taken in a more universal sense,
meaning "any whatsoever", whereas qualiscunque merely means "un-
distinguished by any particular feature"; qualiscunque transgressio would
best be translated by the French "une transgression quelconque",
i.e. a transgression not otherwise notable, an ordinary, current transgression, which therefore must necessarily be of a minor kind.

illis *et* obedienciam impendentes, *et* omni animi humilitate
eorum legibus quatenus Dei preceptis, non aduersentur,
ex fide *et* conscientia bona obtemperantes, Deum solum
timeamus, qui potest corpus *et* animam mittere in gehennam ignis.[1] neque animi christiani argumentum est, subditum de principis sui legibus, seueræ ne sint an remissæ,
esse sollicitum. iussa ille capessat *et* faciat, *et* dominis
etiam discolis[2] obediat propter Deum. Si principem tamen
mitem, agnoscat in Principe Dei clementiam, sin seuerum,
p. 256 disciplinam misericordiæ ‖ Domini interpretetur, inuitantis
populum ad poenitentiam. Atque hæc doctrina laqueum
non inijcit homini christiano,[3] sed hanc induisse persuasionem illi conducibile est, ut sub imperio principis
grauiori discat mundum contemnere, *et* concupiscientias
eius.[4] Interdicit princeps esum carnium sub pœna capitali,
quid id mea refert, qui scio regnum Dei (quod vnum
quæro) non esse escam et potum.[5] et utcunque caro
moleste ferat priuari cibo delicatiori, animus tamen in hoc
uero Dei cultu lætatur *et* gaudet: ut in pace obediat
principi propter Deum, qui cultus est Dei verissimus *et*
gratissimus: neque ijs mandatis hominum Deus frustra
colitur: sed pie *et* utiliter a christianis adoratur, ut gentes
contemplantes conuersationem nostram bonam, Deum
glorificent qui est in coelis. Quamobrem etiam in scrip
obedite, sed turis nulla frequentior vox est, quam (obedite) ut nemo
mandatis<br>Dei ægre ferat contemptum legum humanarum, cum Dei etiam
ipsius contemptum contineat, grauius *et* seuerius vindicari
deberi,[6] quam diuinarum legum qualemcunque transgressionem, quarum iustam vltionem Deus tardius interdum
*et* lenius in hoc sæculo dispensat, sed ut ille ait, tarditatem
supplicij grauitate compensat.[7] Cum autem hanc doctrinam
defendam quæ vera enim *et* salutaris, ac etiam vnicuique
tum priuatim, tum etiam publice admodum vtilis, cuperem
tamen principes sui vicissim officij meminisse, ne hac ipsi
doctrina abutantur, sed omnia ad Dei gloriam etiam ipsi
referant, *et* tum in legum æditione, tum etiam modo

---

[1] Luke xii, 5.   [2] From the Greek δύσκολος, ill-humoured, morose.
[3] Expression borrowed from I Cor. vii, 35.   [4] Words borrowed

granting them honour and obedience, and in all lowliness of mind, complying with their laws, in so far as they do not stand against God's precepts, with good faith and conscience, let us fear God alone, who has power to cast both body and soul into the hell of fire; nor is it a token of a Christian mind, for a subject to be troubled about the laws of his prince, inquiring whether they be severe or mild: let him understand and execute his orders, and for the sake of God obey even ungentle masters. If however his prince be mild, let him acknowledge in the prince God's clemency; if he be severe, let him consider this as a lesson mercifully taught by the Lord, who invites his people to penitence. And this teaching does not cast a snare upon a Christian man, but it is behoveful to him to have embraced this belief, so that when the prince's sway is more heavily felt, he may learn to despise the world and the lusts thereof. The prince forbids the eating of flesh on pain of death, what matters it to me, who know that the kingdom of God (which alone I seek) is not meat and drink? And however the flesh may be vexed at being deprived of a daintier food, yet the soul takes joy and gladness in that true manner of worshipping God; so that it obeys its prince peacefully for the sake of God, which way of worshipping is the truest and most acceptable to God; nor is God worshipped in vain through obedience to those commandments of men, but piously and usefully adored by Christians, so that the nations beholding our good conversation, may glorify God who is in Heaven. Wherefore in the Scriptures also, no word is more frequent than "obey"; so that no one may take it ill that the contempt of human laws, since it includes the contempt of God himself, should be punished more grievously and severely than some transgression of the divine laws, the just revenge for which God dispenses in this world sometimes rather late and leniently; but as the saying goes, he makes up for the delay of the torment by its grievousness. However, while I am defending this doctrine, which is indeed true and salutary, and altogether useful also to every man, both privately and in public affairs, I should at the same time wish princes to be for their own part mindful of their charge, lest they should abuse the doctrine; and themselves also to refer everything to the glory of God; and as well in the framing of laws, as in the mode of enforcing

Obey, but God's commandments.

from I John ii, 17. [5] Rom. xiv, 17. [6] *Sic for debere.* [7] This phrase is not scriptural and *ille* can scarcely refer to God.

vindictæ non priuatos affectus exerce*n*t. sed Deu*m* præ
oculis habentes, eius no*min*is sanctificationi studeant, ut
boni ab iniurijs tuti vitam transigant quietam: *et* mali ac
morigeri poenæ ipsius formidine arceant*ur* a vicijs, *et* ad

p. 257 moru*m* honestate*m* tuenda*m* compellantur. ‖ Diuinas leges

Diuinæ leges
non acrius
vindicandæ
vide
rationem contemni non sinant principes, sed ne acri*us* etiam vindicent omnes, ne male loquant*ur* fidei aduersarij, religione*m*
chri*s*tiana*m* non tam charitate mutua consistere q*uam*
principu*m* cohercione. In initio nascentis ecclesiæ Petrus
mendaciu*m* mulctauit morte,[1] sed hoc exemplum non est
secuta eccle*s*ia, nec Deus voluit nostra*m* excommunica-
tione*m* esse tam grauem. Est hodie mitior in corpus
sententia, etiamsi excomm*un*icat*us* tradat*ur* Satanæ in
interitu*m* carnis, ut spirit*us* saluus fiat in die Domini.[2]
Itaq*ue* princeps du*m* in vindicanda lege diuina non semp*er*
gladiu*m* exerit, ostendit non se illa negligere, sed relin-
quere vindicanda diuinæ vltioni, nisi crime*n* aliquod
eiusmodi sit, quod spectet ad diuulsione*m* corporis
ecclesiæ, *et* violationem societatis humanæ. Itaque in
hæreticos *et* homicidas, *et* fures, atqu*e* adulteros principes
animaduertu*n*t, in illos, gladio ut extinguant, ne quid
*con*tagio inficiant: in hos poena mitiori ut comm*o*nefaciant.
auaros aut*em*, ebrios, mendaces, segnes, superbos, in-
uidiosos, iracu*n*dos, denique alios in*n*umeros fere p*re*ter-
mittu*n*t, non quod hæc vitia non detestent*ur*, *et* maxima

·Ebrietas *et*
helluatio*n*es ducant, sed quia ut exemplo pernitiosa esse queant, ad
pernitie*m* tam*e*n vniuersæ congregationis non pertinent,
illos relinquu*n*t disciplinæ ecclesiæ, quæ testificat*ur* quia
vltor est Deus in ijs omnib*us*.[3] Quod si Princeps Dei

Dei gloria in
adiaphoris gloria*m* *et* ecclesiæ conseruatione*m* spectans, aliquid p*ro*-
hibuerit alioq*ui* adiaphoron,[4] esu*m* verbi gratia, carniu*m*

---

[1] The allusion is here to the incident in Acts v, 1–5, in which
Ananias, having lied in regard to the price of a piece of land which he
had sold, was upbraided by Peter, and fell down dead.    [2] These
words are borrowed, from *tradatur* onward, from I Cor. v, 5. The
passage refers to the condemnation of the man who had committed
incest.    [3] Possibly from Jer. li, 56: "Quia fortis ultor Dominus
reddens retribuet".    [4] This word is here translated, according to
sixteenth-century practice, by "indifferent". By "things indifferent"
is generally meant in sixteenth-century controversy such ceremonies

them, to refrain from following their own private affections, but having God before their eyes, to apply themselves to the hallowing of his name, so that the good may be safe from injury, and spend a quiet life; and the evil, or those who show complacency to them,[a] be hindered, by the very fear of punishment, from falling into vices; and be compelled to maintain honesty in manners. Let not princes allow divine laws to be contemned, but let them not avenge them all too sharply, lest the enemies of the faith should slanderously say, that the Christian religion is not maintained so much by mutual charity, as by the constraint of princes. In the beginnings of the newborn church, Peter punished lying with death, but the church has not followed that example, nor did God want our excommunication to be so grievous. The sentence against the body is to-day milder, even though the excommunicate be delivered up unto Satan for the destruction of the flesh, that the spirit may be saved in the day of the Lord. Therefore the prince, while in avenging breaches of the divine law he does not always bare his sword, does not thereby show that he neglects such things, but that he leaves them to the divine vengeance to be punished, unless some crime be of such sort, as to tend to the tearing asunder of the body of the church, and to the overthrow of human society. Therefore princes chastise heretics, and murderers, and thieves, and adulterers, the former, so as to extinguish them by the sword, lest they should corrupt anything by their touch; the latter, by means of a milder penalty, so as to give them a warning. But as for the covetous, the drunkards, the liars, the slothful, the proud, the envious, those given to anger, and lastly others almost numberless, they almost pass them by; not that they do not detest those vices, and consider them as things of great importance; but while they may be baneful by their example, yet their effect does not extend to the ruin of the whole community, and so they leave those men to be taught by the church, which testifies that God is the avenger in all such things. If that the prince, having regard to the glory of God and the maintenance of the church, forbid some otherwise indifferent thing, for example the eating

*Divine laws not to be enforced too sharply. Mark this reason.*

*Drunkenness and gluttony*

*The glory of God in things indifferent.*

or rules of discipline as are not prescribed by the word of God, yet are not forbidden either.　 [a] The Latin word *morigeri*, which means "complying, obedient, obsequious", appears at first sight to contradict the meaning of the clause; it seems that its place ought to be occupied by a word meaning "disobedient" or "evil-disposed". The translation given above seems to solve the difficulty, *morigeri* being those who do not resist evil, who bear up with it, who are favourably disposed towards wickedness, without having actually fallen into it as yet. In Plautus (*Casin.* v, ii, 20), *morigerus* means "compliant in carnal intercourse".

certo die, in sancienda pœna non rem imperata*m*, quæ seorsim considerata minimi est momenti, sed pacis, quietis, *et* obedientiæ conseruatione*m* spectabit, in quo populi more*m* *et* ingeniu*m*, rei prohibitæ illecebram, pro-

Cur no*n* et qui adulteriu*m* com*m*iserit pensione*m* *et* procliuitate*m* co*n*siderabit, ut ad tuendu*m* imperiu*m*, *et* ad constituenda*m* authoritatem ualeat illa vox: qui no*n* obedierit principi, morte moriat*ur*.[1] Quod

p. 258 si quis exclamare velit, O rem indignam, ‖ Princeps à Deo constitut*us* sua mandata gladio vlciscit*ur*, diuina negligit, carnis esus morte vindicat*ur*,[2] ebriu*m* aute*m* *et* gulosu*m*

Perq*uam* ridicule nemo accusat, hic sane perq*uam* ridicule fecerit, Quasi uero res cu*m* re conferenda sit, ac non potius reatus cu*m* reatu, qui a malitia æstimatur *et* intemperantia. Quod si fiat patebit statim longe graui*us* deliquisse, qui per contemptu*m* vetita comedit volens *et* sciens, interim uidelicet peccans *et* in Deu*m*, qui mandauit obedientia*m*, *et* in proximu*m* dupliciter, tu*m* malo exemplo in om*n*es *et* pernitioso, tu*m* grauissima in Principe*m* contumelia, cuius edicta sacrosancta ducere, *et* sarta tecta habere debeat. Q*uod* si quis conquerat*ur* Manliana[3] imperia, *et* nimiu*m* stoica decreta quasi om*n*ia peccata sint paria, *et* nihil referat gallu*m* gallinaceu*m* quis occiderit, an patre*m*, adeo ut esus carniu*m* etia*m* morte mulctet*ur* *et* maxima poena in re minima consumpta, nulla sit reliqua, quæ in maiora crimina competat, ut pro criminis qualitate sit plagaru*m*

Inobedientia mod*us*: Dico inobedientia*m* esse maximu*m* *et* flagitiosissimu*m* crime*n*, quæ multa secu*m* trahit crimina, *et* aperit fenestra*m* ad omne*m* nequitia*m*. Itaque prima principi cura esse debet, ut ad Dei gloria*m* cui*us* vicem sustinet obedientia*m* tueatur, nec se contemni patiat*ur*, ne frustra-

---

[1] This precept is modelled on those which are found in Exod. xxi 17 ("Qui maledixerit patri suo, vel matri, morte moriatur"), but is not found among them. [2] This is not a statement of fact, but an assumption brought in for the sake of argument. Henry VIII apparently never put to death, or even punished, any man for infringing the law of abstinence; yet he may have considered himself as entitled to enforce it, since he asserted his right to dispense from it, as from "a mere positive law of the Church" (cf. proclamation in Foxe, *Acts and Monuments*, ed. Pratt, vol. v, pp. 463–4, which dates back originally to March 1538, as shown by *Letters and Papers*, xiii, 385, and is earlier than Gardiner's tract).

of flesh on a certain day, when enacting a penalty he will not have in view the thing ordained, which considered in itself is of very small moment, but the maintenance of peace, quiet and obedience; in doing which he will take account of the customs and humour of the people, the attraction, propensity and proneness they feel towards the thing forbidden; so that for the protection of his dominion, and stablishing of his authority, the following words may have force: who has not obeyed his prince, let him die the death. Should any one now be inclined to exclaim, O what a shameful thing, the prince appointed of God enforces his own ordinances with the sword, and neglects those of God; the eating of flesh is punished with death, but no one calls to account the drunkard or glutton;— such a man would handle the question most ridiculously; as if the comparison should be made between fact and fact, and not rather between guilt and guilt, the latter being measured by the degree of malice and insolence. The which being done, it will straightway be plain, that he has offended the more grievously by far, who through contempt eats forbidden things, with full will and knowledge; meanwhile, as it appears, sinning both against God, who enjoined obedience, and doubly against his neighbour, as well by setting an example evil and baneful for all, as by most heinously affronting his prince, whose edicts he should consider as sacred, and reverently follow. If that any one should complain that such a rule is worthy of Manlius, and that those decrees are too stoical, according to which all sins appearing as equal, it would matter nothing whether a man had killed a poultry-cock, or his father; since they go so far as to punish with death even the eating of flesh, so that the heaviest penalty being used up for a trifle, none will be left to be suitable for greater crimes, and to allow the stroke to be measured by the nature of the offence:—I say that disobedience is the greatest and most infamous crime, which carries with it many other faults, and opens a door to all profligacy. Therefore the prince's first care must be, for the glory of God in whose place he stands, to maintain obedience, and not to suffer himself to be contemned,

*Why not also: who has committed adultery[a]*

*Utterly ridiculous*

*Disobedience*

---

[3] The adjective *Manlianus* refers to L. Manlius Torquatus, a dictator, and his son, T. Manlius Torquatus, a consul, who on account of their severity, received the surname of *Imperiosus*. The expression is borrowed from Cicero, *De finibus*, II, 32: "Vide, ne ista sint Manliana vestra, aut maiora etiam, si imperes quod facere non possim". [a] This is no question, but a statement of what is going to be proved, namely for what reasons disobedience should be punished with death, and not adultery.

toria *et* illusoria sit iurisdictio. In contumaces *et* morigeros[1] quacu*n*q*ue* in re, quæ legi Dei non repugnet, gladiu*m* a Deo datu*m* stringere potest, citra cui*us*q*uam* iniuria*m*. Neque t*ame*n author esse velim, ut omni edicto prohibitorio eande*m* poena*m* adijciat: sed ut antea dixi, cu*m* deliberatu*m* fuerit, *et* post maturu*m* consiliu*m* statutu*m* reipublicæ admodu*m* expedire, ut hoc aut illud edicatur fieri, non fieriue, ne quod Labeo[2] in irridenda iniuriarum lege docuit mediocris poena arcendæ populi temeritati haud sufficeret. Equidem sane contenderim p*re*stare edicta sanguine q*uam* aqua scribere ne poenæ neglectu populus discat contemnere: cu*m* interim poenæ

p. 259 atrocitas pro || disciplina multis in causis fuit, nec authoritatis maiestate*m* *con*seruasse solu*m*, sed etia*m* populo vtilem *et* com*mo*da*m* extitisse exempla comprobant, atque adeo cogitationib*us* ho*minu*m illos temerarios conatus euellisse, *et* eradicasse, in quos si poena mitior fuisset multis illecebris pertrahi *et* pe*r*pelli potuisset.[3] Et si ab effectu vtilitas æstimanda e*st*, ea mihi lex etia*m* vtilior videtur *et* mitior, quæ exerta in vnu*m* aut alteru*m* seueritate, reliquos omnes deterret, q*uam* quæ p*ro*posita leuiore poena quæ poterat contemni, multos p*er* mandatu*m* capiat *et* reddat obnoxios. Sed hoc cure*n*t principes quos imperare Deus voluit: populus aut*em*, cui parendi incu*m*bit necessitas, non quo*modo* imperet Princeps, cogitet, sed quo*modo* ipse ad Dei gloria*m* diligenter sine o*mn*i murmure, aut conquestione pareat, *et* obtemperet nihil ducens graue, quod ab ho*mini*b*us* homini Christiano inferri queat.

(*The bottom half of this page is blank*)

p. 260 Facile est perspicere quo moueantur qui istam oratione*m* non ferunt, *et* in ea interpretanda calu*m*niari malint *et* sophistica ludere, q*uam* quod res est ingenue confiteri. Dicis cu*m* mecu*m* dissereres de iusta legis latione nihil

[1] Cf. note on p. 257 of MS. [2] Marcus Antistius Labeo, a celebrated teacher of the law in the time of Augustus, was born about 50 B.C. and died between A.D. 15 and 20. None of his extensive works is at present extant but he is frequently quoted in the writings of other jurists, notably in the Pandects. A complete collection of

lest his jurisdiction should be a mere deception, and scoffed at. Against the obstinate and those who show complacency towards them, in any thing that is not repugnant to the law of God, he may unsheathe the sword given to him by God, without doing wrong to any one. Not that however I should advise the prince to attach the same penalty to every one of his pro- hibitory edicts: but as I said before, when after due weighing of the matter, and mature consultation it has been decreed that it is altogether expedient for the commonwealth, that this or that thing should be ordained to be done, or not done; for fear, as Labeo taught in regard to the law of injuries which was set at naught, a moderate penalty should hardly be sufficient to hinder the rashness of the people; forsooth I should main- tain that it is better for edicts to be written in blood than in water, lest being able to overlook the penalty the people should learn to contemn; while, at the same time, the direness of the penalty has been in many cases a teaching, and examples attest that it has not only preserved the majesty of authority, but has also been for the people useful and behoveful, and even plucked and rooted out of the resolutions of men those rash attempts, to which, had the penalty been milder, they might have been drawn or driven by many lures. And if usefulness is to be judged from the effect, this law seems to me more useful and milder, the severity of which being displayed in the punishment of some man or other, frights all the rest from evil; than that which, a lighter penalty being offered, which may be despised, ensnares many by its very prescriptions, and draws them into guilt. But let the princes look to those things, whom God appointed to reign; as to the people, that must of necessity apply themselves to obedience, let them not revolve in their minds how the prince governs, but how they them- selves may obey and show compliance, for the glory of God, diligently and without any grumbling or complaining; deeming that nought that is inflicted by men can mean real oppression to a Christian man....

It is easily seen whither those tend, who cannot bear this speech, and in interpreting it prefer to pervert it and play with sophistical arguments, rather than ingenuously confess the truth of the matter. You say that when you argued with me,

the fragments or references thus preserved is found in Otto Lenel, *Palingenesia Iuris Civilis*, Lipsiæ, 1889, vol. 1, col. 501 to 558, but Gardiner's quotation is not found there, and possibly he may have been wrong in ascribing it, from memory no doubt, to Labeo.
[3] *Sic* for *potuissent*.

fuisse dictum.[1] Quod non concedo. Quum tamen de contemptu legis queritur. An non hujus verbi notio iustam etiam lationem continet? Quum lex dici nulla potest quæ iniuste feratur. An tu leges eas dices proprio vocabulo quæ iniustæ sunt? Quales omnes profecto sunt quæ iniuste latæ sunt. Libertatem mutandi verba nec probo nec sequor. Interpretationem uero eam ab omnibus exigo, quam res ipsa postulat, et quam hominum de rebus tam serijs disputantium candor et ingenuitas prestare solet apud bonos et graueis. Sed quomodo tractes hanc sententiam videamus. Dicis propositionem non consistere. Primum quia maior est authoritas diuinæ legis quam humanæ. fateor: ergo et seuerius vindicanda. Concedo. Sed hoc est sophistam agere: cum ego statim subieceram in contemptu humanæ legis, etiam diuinam legem de obedientia violari. Ego non oppono hominem Deo, nec humana Diuinis, sed Diuinæ legis partes inter se confero, et humanam legem dico, quam diuina authoritate homo fert, quæ et ipsa eatenus etiam diuina est. Paulus cum docet eum qui diligit proximum, legem implere,[2] non ideo proximum Deo pretulisse putandus, sed ostendisse Deum in proximo querere dilectionem. Quemadmodum etiam in legibus ab homine latis obedientiam. Itaque Paulus diserte ait, non hominem (inquit) spernit, sed Deum.[3] Et uter tibi grauius peccare videtur, qui in Deum peccat et hominem, an qui in Deum solum? Si poteris contemptum legis humanæ ab offensione in Deum distinguere, ac separare, equidem tibi manus dabo, et me temere hæc dixisse fatebor. Sin illud non poteris, uide quam non syncere

p. 261    a te tractatus ‖ est hic locus, dum colligis ex propositione mea sequi contemptum legum humanarum seuerius vindicandum quam contemptum diuinæ legis, et eleganter ludis in verbo (qualiscunque) cuius verbi vim hanc vis esse, ut cum in comparatione hunc locum occupet, et verbo adiungatur molliori, complectatur ·tamen omnes species etiam eas quæ sub altera parte comparationis continebantur. Secundum quam dialecticam etiam illud sequere-

---

[1] The word *dicis* must be understood as referring to Bucer's own writing or memorandum, which Gardiner is now closely following in

no mention was made of justice in the declaring of a law. Which I cannot grant: for since after all the question in debate is contempt of the law, does not the idea expressed by that word also imply justice in the declaration of the law? since no law can be called a law, if unjustly made. Do you for one properly apply the name of laws to such as are unjust? which all those are, that have been unjustly made. I neither commend nor imitate your liberty in altering the sense of words. But I demand this interpretation from all, which the thing itself requires, and which the frankness and ingenuousness of men disputing of things so serious, are wont to provide among good and sober people. But let us see how you handle this opinion of mine. You say that the proposition cannot stand. First, because the authority of divine law is greater than that of human law: which I confess; and because it must therefore be enforced more severely: which I grant. But this is playing the sophist: seeing I had immediately added, that in the contempt of human law, the divine law of obedience is also violated. I do not, for myself, oppose man to God, nor human things to divine, but I compare the different parts of divine law between themselves, and call human law, that which man proclaims by the authority of God, which itself to that extent is also divine. When Paul teaches that he who loves another hath fulfilled the law, we must not think therefore that he places our neighbour before God, but that he shows to us God seeking our love in the person of our neighbour; and the same applies to obedience, in the case of laws made by man. Wherefore Paul expressly says: he despiseth not man, but God. And whether seems to you to sin more grievously, he who sins against God and man, or against God alone? If you can make a distinction and separation between the contempt of human law and displeasure given to God, I shall yield to you, and confess that I was rash in uttering such things; but if you cannot do so, see with how little sincerity this matter was handled by you, when you gather from my proposition, as a necessary consequence, that the contempt of human law is to be avenged more severely than the contempt of divine law; and gracefully banter with the word "any",[a] the strength of which you want to be such, that when it is placed as it is in the comparison, and is adjoined to a gentler word, yet it should embrace all kinds, even those which were contained in the other part of the the comparison. According to which dialectics

his discussion of its contents.     [2] Rom. xiii, 8.     [3] I Thessal. iv, 8.
[a] Cf. note on the title of the present work.

tur: vincit o*mn*es eruditione, *er*go vincit etia*m* se ipsu*m*
eruditione. Superat omnes cursu, ergo seipsu*m* superat.
Opponu*ntur* in mea pro*positio*ne contemptus *et* Transgressio. Nam alio*qui* in hac pr*edi*catione Diuina lex ab
humana re non omnino diuiditur: Sed demonstrationis
causa distinguu*ntur* potius, cu*m* alioqui, ut sæpius dixi,
in humana lege est diuina authoritas qua princeps nititur.
At cu*m* transgressio generale verbu*m* sit, contemptus
aute*m* transgressionis species: ego cu*m* veritatis insinuandæ
causa contemptu*m* oppono transgressioni. Tu ex signo
vniuersali apposito o*mn*es species contineri vis, atq*ue* adeo
illa*m* repetis qua*m* antea in collatione expresseram / quasi
dicerem, Contempt*us* Dei est seuerius vindicand*us*, q*uam*
contemptus Dei. In contemptu *enim* legis humanæ
semper pono contemptu*m* Dei, quod semel hic dictu*m*
volo, ne cogar toties idem repetere *et* inculcare. Non est
ista profecto dialectica, sed matæologica. Q*ui*d appellas
religiosu*m* animu*m*, ut tibi auscultet du*m* rem vna*m* *et*
simplicem in plures notiones diuidas, *et* contemptu*m* a
contemptu distinguas qui semper est idem, videor subolere
vestra mysteria. Non habet proprie contemptus errorem
sed scientia*m* quæ inflat, *et* malitia*m*, neq*ue* semper qui
legem violat ea*m* contemnit aut etia*m* latorem. Qui uero
contemnit, quid hic aliud q*uam* in diuina*m* po*tes*tatem sese
erigit, *et* cu*m* Deo pugnat, qui talem posuit principem, *et*
illi permiserit talia *et* tam dura ferre, ne liceat vesci carni-
p. 262 bus in feria ‖ sexta[1] ut tot dies nobis inutiliter pereant in
quibus non liceat ut libitu*m* fuerit indulgere genio. Hic
scilicet vir religiosus, *et* pius, qualem tu nu*n*c compellas
de libertate Euangelica diligenter, frequentib*us* videlicet

[1] There is a break in the sentence here, which the punctuation ought
to make clear. "Ut tot dies" etc. refers not to the preceding clause,
and to the action of the prince, but to that of the contemner: "et
cum deo pugnat...ut tot dies nobis inutiliter pereant...".     *a* The
sequence of ideas is hard to follow in this purely logical passage,
yet Gardiner's demonstration can easily be summarized as follows:
Bucer intentionally misunderstands his proposition, which he takes
as if the contempt of human law was opposed to the contempt of
divine law. But that is impossible for two reasons: first, divine law
is not opposed to human law, since what is called here the contempt
of human law is also contempt of the divine law of obedience; the
words human law are only used here for the sake of clearness, because

the following reasonings would be true: he surpasses all men by his erudition, *ergo* he surpasses even himself. He outstrips all men in the race, *ergo* he outstrips himself. In my proposition contempt and transgression are opposed. For else in this my contention divine law is not altogether separated from human things; but they are rather divided for the sake of demonstration, since otherwise, as I repeatedly said, in human law is contained the divine authority, on which the prince takes his stand. Now since transgression is a general word, but contempt only one kind of transgression; and whereas I, in order to bring in truth more easily, oppose contempt to transgression; you, from the fact that a universal expression is attached to the latter word, want it to contain all kinds, and you bring in even here that kind which I had mentioned in the first part of the comparison, as if I had said: the contempt of God is more severely to be avenged, than the contempt of God. For in the contempt of human law I always place the contempt of God, which I want to state here once and for all, lest I should be compelled to repeat it and force it in over and over again. Indeed these are no dialectics, but mere empty talk. Why do you appeal to reverend minds, and bid them give heed to you, while you divide a thing which is one and plain into several notions, and distinguish contempt from contempt, though it be always the same?[a] Meseems I begin to smell out your mysteries. To contempt does not properly belong error, but knowledge which swells man with pride, and malice; nor does he who breaks the law always contemn it or its maker. But he who contemns, what else does he do but rise up against the divine power, and fight with God, who placed the prince in such a position, and committed it to him to make such laws and of such severity, to forbid the eating of flesh on Fridays; so that those days are now rendered useless and of no avail to us, on which we are not permitted to indulge our tastes to our full content.[b] Certainly this reverend and pious man, to whom you earnestly appeal on behalf of Gospel freedom, instructed by frequent sermons in regard to this trifling matter,

that law is declared by man, though being actually divine; so that the real opposition is between some ordinary transgression of divine law through weakness, and contempt of the divine law of obedience. Secondly, it is absurd to understand the word *transgression* as if it also included *contempt*; it is true that contempt is one form of transgression, but then since it is opposed to transgression in Gardiner's proposition, the latter must obviously be taken as meaning a transgression other than, or rather lesser than, contempt. The whole passage casts a light upon the logical training that Gardiner must have undergone at Cambridge.    [b] In other words, days which previously were sanctified by abstinence, are rendered spiritually useless to the man who contemns the laws made by the prince in that respect.

contion*ibus* edoctus in hac re minima, magno supercilio legem contemnet, *et* se hanc legem contemnere inter fratres præsertim, qui (quu*m omnia omnibus* licere putent) in nullo offendu*nt*, audacter iactitabit, et hic ia*m* contemptus opinor apud tuos religiosos, minimus dicitur, id est, in re minima. Nam alioqui que*m* contemptu*m* minimu*m* voces, non intelligo. Et nisi aliam huic verbo notione*m* subijcias, q*uam* alij hactenus tribueru*nt*, fatearis oportet, contemptu*m* aliu*m* manifestiore*m et* apertiore*m* esse, atq*ue* ideo et*iam* grauiorem, ut habeat quo augeatur, et crescat, quo minuatur aut*em* a gradu, ut dicatur mini*mus* contemptus, non video. Nam in reb*us* minimis, et facilib*us* est maior, *et* ubi error est ignoratio aut infirmitas, adeo non minuitur contemptus, ut ne subsistat quidem. Quum, ut antea dixi, nemo contemnit, nisi qui firmus in corde non habens necessitate*m*, sed p*r*oprie volu*n*tatis pot*es*tatem, decreuit in corde suo[1] se no*n* obtemperaturu*m* illis aut illis præceptis principu*m*, scilicet ne per obedienti*am* fraudem faciat libertati euangelicæ, hunc ego appello contemptorem.

Tandem post aliquot verba temerè p*r*ofusa, donas s*cilicet* mihi transgressionem intelligi de ea transgressione, quæ ex infirmitate accidit. Sed ea concessione transitu*m* facis ad aliud sophisma, ais e*nim* necesse esse, ut quu*m* inter se conferantur lex humana *et* diuina, ex vi locutionis ea*m* humana*m* legem intelligere, quæ non sit diuina. Alioqui fateris etia*m* ipse contemptu*m* maiestatis principis ad diuina*m* legem pertinere. Sed vrges videlicet verba, *et* exigis sensu*m* simplicem, nimiru*m* ut verba mea de lege humana, significent lege*m* quanda*m* humana*m* quæ cu*m* p. 263   diuina pugnet. Alioqui vero, si legem humana*m* ‖ intelligo illa*m*, quæ diuina subsistat *et* nitatur, nulla (ut tibi videtur) est hic collatio. uel hu*n*c sensu*m*, qui absurdissimus est, haberi velis, quasi transgressio accidens ex infirmitate, *et*

---

[1] These words, from "qui firmus in corde suo", are borrowed from I Cor. vii, 37, where they are used in quite a different connection, and refer in a somewhat obscure and frequently-discussed fashion to the question of chastity: "Nam qui statuit in corde suo firmus, non habens necessitatem, potestatem autem habens suæ voluntatis, et hoc judi-

will contemn the law with great arrogance, and boldly declare in public that he has contemned it, especially among his brethren, who are shocked at nothing since they deem that everything is permitted to every one; and such contempt methinks is now among your reverend men said to be trifling, to wit, because the matter is trifling. For otherwise what contempt you call trifling, I cannot understand. And unless you attach to this word a different meaning, than others have hitherto ascribed to it, you must needs confess that there always exists some other contempt which is more manifest and open, so that contempt has wherewith to increase, and grow; but how it can be lowered from its degree, so as to be called a trifling contempt, I cannot see. For it is greater in things trifling and easy to perform; and where error is nothing more than ignorance or weakness, contempt is so far from decreasing, that it does not even subsist. Whereas, as I said before, no one contemns, except he who, stedfast in his heart, having no necessity, but power over his own will, hath decreed in his heart, that he will not comply with such and such commandments of the princes, namely lest through obedience he should injure Gospel freedom; such a man I call a contemner.

At last after rashly pouring forth a number of words, you grant to me that the word transgression is understood of such transgression, as happens through weakness. But through this concession you manage to pass over to another piece of sophistry: for you say that it must needs be, that when human and divine laws are compared with each other, the very words which are used make it clear, that human law is that which is not divine. For the rest, you yourself confess that the contempt of the prince's majesty pertains to divine law. But you insist on keeping to the words, and request that they should be explained in a simple way, so that forsooth my words on human law should refer to some sort of human law conflicting with divine law. But on the other hand, if by human law I mean such a law as is founded upon and supported by that of God, the comparison, as you think, cannot hold good; or then you ascribe to it this sense, which is most absurd, namely that a transgression happening through weakness, and not reaching

cavit in corde suo, servare virginem suam, bene facit". It must be noted here that this passage, understood both by Bucer and Gardiner as referring to a father's authority over his daughters, was the starting-point and main subject of their long controversy on clerical celibacy.

citra contemptum imperij uel maiestatis, tamen seuerius coherceri debet quam transgressio legis diuinæ qualiscunque. Sicque iterum etc.[1] Hic ego appello animum attentum, ut animaduertat istam sophisticam. Ego professus sum me nolle committere iura diuina humanis, nedum anteferre humana. Propositio humanis legibus adiungit contemptum, diuinis transgressionem qualemcunque, aliam videlicet a contemptu. Humanas leges voco, non quia non sint diuinæ, sed quia, cum cor regis in manu Dei sit, ab homine sint ipsæ leges, dei tamen authoritate latæ, quarum contemptum contendo seuerius vindicandum ab homine presente vindicta, quam diuinarum legum qualemcunque transgressionem, quæ verba si tibi visum esset ingenue mecum agere, sonare tibi potuissent, id quod præ se ferunt omnem aliam transgressionem a contemptu. Compono enim contemptum et transgressionem, qualiscunque ea sit alia a contemptu. Quod si ita diserte proposuissem contemptum legis humanæ seuerius vindicandum, quam diuinæ, παράδοξον quidem fuisset: sed quod explicatum nihil haberet absurdi suo sensu: non magis quam quod in Euangelio dicitur, de eo qui neque Deum timebat, neque homines reuerebatur.[2] Quo in loco ostenditur multos esse, quos quum timor Dei non cohibeat, hominum tamen reuerentia contineat. non quasi hominum maior sit, id quod tamen verba præ se ferunt, quam Dei reuerentia. Sed quod ita fert humana natura, quæ præsentia magis et corporea et timet et veretur. Secundum quem loquendi modum etiam dicere possem contemptum humanarum legum quam diuinarum seuerius vindicandum, non quod Deus homine minor sit, aut humanæ leges diuinis preferantur. Sed quod expediat publicæ tranquillitati, homines qui Deum ignorant, et illius maiestatem non agnoscunt, hominum saltem potestatem formidare. Sed in causa religionis nunquam placuerunt mihi paradoxa, qualia multa hæc secta orbi proposuit, De sola fide, de

p. 264 seruo ‖ arbitrio, iustum in omni opere bono peccare, et alia

---

[1] Probably a reference to Bucer's own writing, which we cannot at present verify.     [2] In the parable of the unjust judge and the importunate widow, Luke xviii, 4: "Judex quidam erat in quadam

so far as contempt of sovereignty or majesty, should yet be curbed more severely, than any transgression of the divine law. And thus once again, etc. It is my turn now to appeal to attentive minds, that they may mark your sophistry. I have for my part declared that I refused to put on a par human and divine laws, and still more to give the first place to human law. In my proposition, the word *contempt* is referred to human laws, the words *any transgression* to divine laws, contempt being excluded in this case. I do not call human laws by that name because they are not divine, but because they have actually come from a man, though the king's heart being in the hands of God, they are however declared by the authority of God; the contempt of which laws I contend is to be avenged more severely by man's present punishment, than any transgression of the laws of God; which latter words, if you had been pleased to deal with me candidly, might have spoken to you what they obviously mean, that is, any transgression apart from contempt. For I place side by side contempt, and transgression, whatever the latter may be apart from contempt. If that I had thus elegantly propounded, that the contempt of human law should be avenged more severely, than that of divine law, this would have been indeed a paradox; but which being explained would have nothing absurd in its own sense; no more than what is said in the Gospel, of him that neither dreaded God, nor regarded man. In which place it is shown that there are many, whom as the dread of God does not restrain, yet regard for man holds them in check; not as if the regard of man were greater than that of God, which however is at first sight the meaning of the words; but because human nature will have it so, which mostly stands in fear and awe of things present and material. According to which manner of speech I might also say that the contempt of human law was more severely to be avenged than that of divine laws, not because God is smaller than man, nor because human laws are to be set before those of God; but because it is in the interests of public peace, that men who ignore God, and do not acknowledge his Majesty, should at any rate stand in awe of the power of man. But in the matter of religion, I have never liked paradoxes, many of which this your sect has proposed to the whole world, such as those of only faith, of the serf will, or that the righteous sin in all good works, and others without number, which breed

civitate, qui Deum non timebat, et hominem non reverebatur". The judge finally agrees to "avenge the woman of her enemy", not in order to please God, but for fear of her importunity.

191

infinita, quæ nihil aliud pariunt nisi contentiones, *et* verborum pugnas sine omni fructu. Ego uero simpliciter profiteor dissolutum iri omnem principum auctoritatem, ni orbi persuadeatur hæc sententia, vt seuerius vindicetur edictum principis contemptum ab istis fratribus qui sub obtentu verbi Dei omnem licentiam vindicant, quam qualiscunque transgressio diuinæ legis alia a contemptu. Nam si obtinere possent a suis principibus concionatores ut ipsi de omni peccato diuina lege interdicto legem ædant poenalem, in quo casu vix posset obtineri opinor, ut in mendacem, aut otiosa fabulantem, fratriue suo Racha dicentem[1] aliqua mulcta grauior irrogaretur, *et* fortasse in ebrium aut otiosa fabulantem assis vnius poenam statuere seuerum videretur *et* graue: hoc sane preiudicio principes tenerentur ut si quid velint ipsi precipere in Reipublicæ commodum, aut etiam relligionis exercitium *et* pietatis augmentum, ne audeant maiorem poenam suis preceptis addere quam diuinis addidissent, ut iam talitris opinor duobus aut tribus suarum legum contemptum hac religione absterriti vindicarent, ne preferant scilicet sua diuinis, *et* seuerius vindicent quæ sunt humana. Nam hoc esset obscurare auctoritatem legum diuinarum quia in sensu communi seuerior vindicta est argumentum maioris authoritatis secundum tuam doctrinam quæ verbo nititur *et* spiritu, quem præter verbum nisi si quis hauserit hanc doctrinam quæ ex Deo est probare haud poterit. Ista uero an non huc spectant, ut ridicula reddatur principum auctoritas? Et quamobrem quæso docetur populus tam diligenter principis offitium vestro modo explicatum, nisi ut discat contemnere? Ego tecum disputaui de populi officio, num ægre ferre debeat principum leges grauius *et* seuerius ‖ vindicari quam legum diuinarum qualemcunque transgressionem, *et* id contendo quod doceri maxime expediat ad presentem statum in quo nemo christianus damno vllo affici potest, nisi quod sibi accersiuerit. Quid autem vos tam anxie expetitis vitam

[1] Matth. v, 22: "Qui autem dixerit fratri suo: Raca, reus erit concilio". <sup>a</sup> In other words, to Bucer's assertion that Protestant doctrine is founded on the word and the spirit, Gardiner retorts that the spirit must be sought beyond the letter, beyond Scripture,

nothing but contentions, and battles of words without any fruit. But as for me I plainly declare that all princely authority will be destroyed, unless the whole world be convinced of the truth of this proposition, that more severe vengeance must be taken for the contempt of an edict of the prince by those fellows who, under cover of the word of God, lay claim to all licence, than for any transgression of the divine law apart from contempt. For suppose that preachers succeeded in obtaining from their princes, that they themselves should proclaim a penal law against every sin forbidden by divine law; in this case they would, I think, scarcely obtain that any fine at all heavy should be inflicted upon a liar, or a teller of idle tales, or him who says Raca to his brother; and perhaps it would seem harsh and grievous to inflict a fine of one penny upon a drunkard or a teller of idle tales. This precedent would be a restraint upon princes, so that if they themselves wanted to decree anything for the common weal, or the exercise of religion and the increase of piety, not daring to annex a heavier penalty to their own precepts than they had done to those of God, they would be held back by this feeling of awe-struck reverence, and only avenge the contempt of their own laws with two or three fillips, lest indeed they should prefer their own cause to that of God, and enforce more severely things merely human. For that would mean obscuring the authority of divine laws, since, in the common opinion of men, a heavier punishment is proof of a greater authority, according to your doctrine that is founded on the Word and the Spirit,—which latter if one does not seek beyond the word, he will not be able to test that doctrine which comes from God.[a] But do not such views tend to this, that they turn the prince's authority into a laughing-stock? And for what reason I pray you, is the people so sedulously taught the prince's duty, explained in your own way, if not that they may learn to contemn? As for me I discussed with you the duty of the people, whether they ought to feel aggrieved, that the prince's laws should be enforced more harshly and severely than any transgression of the divine law, and what I maintain in this respect is what may be taught with greatest profit for this present earthly life, in which no man who is a Christian can suffer any hurt, unless he bring it down upon himself.[b] But as for you, why do you so anxiously seek after a tranquil

presumably, if we may judge from his other controversial writings, in the tradition of the Church.    [b] No sufferings inflicted upon a man here below can endanger his hopes of future life; he can only lose his eternal reward through sin, and then he alone will be responsible for his loss.

tranquilla*m* *et* quieta*m* id curent Epicuræi quoru*m* Deus
venter,[1] optare id quidem liceat omnes bonos, sed de hoc
non conuenit esse sollicitos ut orbi eo nomine moueant
tragoedia*m*. Dic mihi quæso quî ista conueniu*nt* in
doctrinæ *con*stantia *et* *per*petuitate, sola fide iustificamur
*et* accepti reddimur Deo secundu*m* vestra*m* doctrina*m*, et
tamen de cibis *et* vxoribus est magna pars nostræ contro-
uersiæ, si hæc ad iustificatione*m* non pertinent, cur ab
elementis mundi redempti[2] de ijs contenditis, quasi sine
istis nihil posset esse foelix ho*mi*ni christiano. Posueru*nt*
in coelu*m* os suu*m* *et* lingua eoru*m* transiuit in terra,[3] ut
inquit psalmista. Quis non videt hæc in vos proprie
competere qui tame*n* ad inuidia*m* alioru*m* verbu*m* Dei *et*
spiritu*m* iactitatis, an uos hic tan*quam* hospites *et* peregrini
versamini, qui legib*us* p*re*sentib*us* obmurmuratis, *et* de
eo maxime conquerimini, *quo*d presentiu*m* reru*m* copia
libere frui non liceat, quasi christus legem Moysi ideo
abrogauerit, ut sum*m*a licentia om*niu*m rerum copia
frueremur? Legem ciborum distinguis a fine, quasi (*quod*
ridicule dixit Alesius[4]) subditi possint a principe, cur hoc
aut illud statuat, quærere et percontari, ut si quidem finis
sit politicus, ia*m* abstineat a cibis *et* pareat populus.[5] Sin
aliquid religio*n*is inesse putet princeps, ut populus hac
abstinentia doceatur non esse regnu*m* Dei escam *et* potum,[6]
*et* non om*n*ia sempe*r* expedire,[7] deniq*ue* castigandu*m* esse
corpus, ut in seruitute*m* redigatur,[8] ia*m* non pareat
om*ni*no populus, ne*que* faciat quod p*re*cipitur, quia videli*cet*
fide sola iustificantur ho*min*es, non operibus, ne*que* pot*est*

<hr />

[1] Phil. iii, 19: "Quorum finis interitus, quorum deus venter est".
[2] Possibly a reference to Gal. iv, 3: "Ita et nos, cum essemus
parvuli, sub elementis mundi eramus servientes". "The elements of
the world" is an expression borrowed from the philosophy of Plato,
τὰ στοιχεῖα τοῦ κόσμου, and in its Christian sense means the con-
stituent elements of the world without grace added to them, the world
without divine grace.    [3] Ps. lxxii (Authorized Version lxxiii), *v.* 9.
[4] The Scottish reformer Alexander Aless (1500–65), who fled from
Scotland to Germany in 1532, attached himself to the Lutheran party
and especially to Melanchton, lectured in divinity at Cambridge in
1535, returned to Germany in 1540 and took part in the conferences
at Worms and Ratisbon as one of the Lutheran party. He later
translated the Prayer Book of 1549 into Latin for Bucer's use.
[5] This was precisely the distinction made under Queen Elizabeth,

and quiet life? Let the Epicureans, whose god is their belly, be solicitous about such things. All good men, no doubt, may freely wish for them, but it is not meet that they should be so anxious about them as to cause a commotion throughout the whole world on that account. Tell me I pray you how these things agree in constancy and continuity of doctrine: we are by only faith justified and made acceptable to God, according to your doctrine, and yet a large part of our controversy bears upon food and wives. If those things do not pertain to justification, why do you who are reclaimed from the elements of the world contend about them, as if without them no happiness could find place in a Christian man? They set their mouths in heaven and their tongue walketh through the earth, as the Psalmist says. Who does not see that these words are peculiarly suited to you, who to make others hateful talk away in public of the word of God and the spirit? Do you spend your time here below as guests and pilgrims, you who grumble against the laws of this world, and mostly complain that you are not allowed to enjoy freely and in plenty the things of this life, as if Christ had abrogated Moses' law merely to the purpose, that we should with the utmost licence enjoy all things in plenty? You treat the law in regard to food in different ways, according to its purpose, as if (as Aless ridiculously said) subjects might ask from their prince, and inquire, why he decides this or that, so that if the purpose be political, the people may abstain from forbidden foods and obey; but suppose that, in the prince's opinion, the purpose be to some extent religious, so that the people may be taught by this abstinence that the kingdom of God is not meat and drink, also that all things are not always expedient, and lastly that the body must be kept under, and brought into subjection; in that case let the people altogether refuse to obey, and to do what is prescribed, and namely because men are justified by faith alone, and not by works, and because rules in regard to meat and

when the Parliament of 1563 re-enacted the provisions of the act on fasting days of 1552. It was now "ordered that Wednesdays should be observed as fish days as well as the Fridays and Saturdays, the days of Lent, and other days which were already by old custom so observed and in accordance with the Edwardine statute. The motive was the maintenance of the navy, and the provision appeared in an act which bore that object in its title... The act...entirely disclaimed any religious motive: the order is "meant politickly", and "not for any superstition to be maintained in the choice of meats" (W. H. Frere, *The English Church in the reigns of Elizabeth and James I*, p. 101). [6] Rom. xiv, 17.        [7] I Cor. vi, 12 and x, 22: "Omnia mihi licent, sed non omnia expediunt".        [8] I Cor. ix, 27: "Sed castigo corpus meum et in servitutem redigo".

modus cibi aut potus aliquid habere religionis sed super-
stitionis potius. || hæc etsi non tam aperte dicitis, tamen
eliciu*ntur* ex v*est*ris conclusionib*us*. Quod si huc tendant
consilia vestra ut Christus glorificetur, agat quis*que* partes
suas, pareat populus in silentio, imperent principes *et*
suos quisq*uam* fines videat periculo suo Deo redditurus
ratione*m*, cui stat aut cadit.[1]

Tractas leges de coelibatu *et* esu carniu*m*. Quod ad
celibatu*m* attinet, hoc tibi dico, si hæc est volu*n*tas Dei
sanctificatio n*os*tra, *et* Paulus dicit celibatu sanctificari
quu*m* corpus tu*m* a*n*ima*m*,[2] est opinor etia*m* per se gratus
celibatus Deo, atq*ue* hic te iubeo expendere Paulu*m*, quu*m*
in diuersa*m* sententia*m* cites illud, Non est bonu*m* homini
esse solu*m*,[3] quem textu*m* non a te sed ab Alesio[4] illo huc
citatu*m* arbitror, adeo ad Rhombu*m* nihil facit,[5] ut habet
barbaru*m* prouerbiu*m*. Quod si illud, ńon est bonu*m*
homini solu*m* esse, hu*n*c habeat sensu*m*, qui hic affingit*ur*,
id est, no*n* est bonu*m* homini esse sine uxore, vt valeat non
solu*m* in spetiem humanæ naturæ, sed in indiuidua
dictu*m*, male dixit Paulus, Solutus es ab vxore, noli
quærere vxorem.[6] Itane vero Paule, non quera*m* quod
Diuina sententia absolute bonu*m* est, aut potius ibi me
iubes consistere ubi Deus dixit non esse bonu*m*? Non est
bonum, inquit Deus, homini esse solu*m*. Apud te Paule
innupta sanctificatur tu*m* corpore tu*m* spiritu,[7] *et* tamen
Deus, cui*us* volu*n*tas est ho*min*is sanctificatio, dicit, non
est bonu*m* ho*min*i esse solu*m*. Sed valeat hæc distinctio[8]
ad concilianda*m* scriptura*m*, Deus de sexu masculino
loquitur, Paulus de foeminino: quæ pulchra est ratio
diuersitatis *et* hac tractatione digna. Quod si hoc vobis in
scripturis p*er*mittitis, quiduis *et* fi*n*gere *et* refi*n*gere pro
arbitrio poteritis facillime. Sed hæc irridenda sunt non
refellenda, si risu*m* admitteret rei indignitas.

---

[1] Rom. xiv, 12: "Itaque unusquisque nostrum pro se rationem
reddet Deo"; Rom. xiv, 4: "Domino suo stat, aut cadit".    [2] The
reference is obviously to I Cor. vii, possibly to *v*. 34: "Et mulier
innupta, et virgo, cogitat quæ Domini sunt, ut sit sancta corpore et
spiritu".    [3] Gen. ii, 18.    [4] See above, p. 265 of the MS.
[5] In one of his annotations to the tract *Quod ad illud axioma*, fol. 133 a

drink have nothing of religion about them, but rather something of superstition. Those things, although you do not speak them clearly, appear from your conclusions. If that your designs tend to this, that Christ be glorified, let each man perform his part, let the people obey in silence, let the princes rule, and let each man keep within his own bounds, who must give account of himself, at his own peril, to God to whom he standeth or falleth.

You handle the laws referring to celibacy and the eating of flesh. In respect to celibacy, this I say to you: if it be true that God's will be our own sanctification and if Paul says that celibacy makes holy both the body and spirit, celibacy is in my opinion agreeable to God even by itself; and here I bid you ponder Paul's words, when in support of a contrary opinion you quote this text, it is not good for man to be alone; which text I believe was not brought forward hither by you, but by that man Aless; but indeed it has nothing to do with the turbot, as the Barbarian proverb says. If that these words: it is not good for man to be alone, have the meaning which is here falsely invented, namely, it is not good for man to be without a wife, so that it have force not only in regard to human nature in general, but be a saying applicable to individual cases, Paul was wrong to say: Art thou loosed from a wife? seek not a wife. But in this case, O Paul, shall I not seek that which according to God's own pronouncement, is good absolutely, or rather do you bid me take my stand where God said was no good? It is not good, says God, for man to be alone. In your writings, O Paul, the unmarried woman is made holy both in body and in spirit, and yet God, whose will is the sanctification of man, says, it is not good for man to be alone. But in order to reconcile Scripture with itself, let us for one moment grant force to this distinction, that God speaks of the male and Paul of the female sex: here is a fine reason for their disagreement, and one well worthy of your handling of the matter. If you allow yourself this sort of thing in dealing with the Scriptures, you will be able to mould and recast anything most easily at your pleasure. But such things are to be laughed to scorn, not confuted, if however the baseness of the proceeding admitted of laughter.

---

(see Introduction, p. xviii), Fisher uses the same expression: "Quid hec ad rumbum?" Whether *rhumbus* here means "a spindle", "a rhumb", or "a turbot", we have not been able to ascertain, nor have we discovered anything in regard to the origin and meaning of the proverb. *Rhumbus* refers in some cases to a spindle used for charms or incantations.    6 I Cor. vii, 27.    7 I Cor. vii, 34.    8 Bucer's own distinction.

Illud de thure nihil olet ne*que* controuersia*m* habeat ubi finis in adiaphoro exprimitur impius,[1] Quis aut*em* sustineret Christianus demonijs sacrificare, ubi p*re*sertim locus est illæ scripturæ, Deo oportet obedire magis q*uam* homini-b*us*.[2] Neque video quorsu*m* p*er*tineat exemplu*m*, nisi etia*m* impiu*m* similiter putes, ut princeps interdicat esu*m* carniu*m* certis temporib*us*, cui*us* rei exemplu*m* tamen ab Apostolis petere liceat, de suffocato *et* sanguine.[3] Et ut illi rationem temporis habueru*nt* idq*ue* pie in sensim abroganda lege. Ita *et* princeps in indicenda abstinentia ea*m* inter cætera ratione*m* sequatur, ut popul*us* meminerit in abstinentia cibi peregrinationis suæ,[4] ut aliquib*us* mu*n*di eleme*n*tis aliquando moriatur,[5] *et* ne semp*er* ventri subseruiat,[6] *et*[7] in eo saginando laboret indies, *et* hæc cogitatio est homini conducibilis qua*m* lex de abstinentia pia ipsa in hoc *et* religiosa, etia*m* non superstitiosa,[8] ut quæ cogitatione*m* alit *et* bona fide obseruata etia*m* corpus attemperat, ne semper opprimatur diuinæ, ut ille inq*ui*t, particula auræ.[9]

Dum in eo laboras, ut discant principes in ijs imperijs,[10] no*n* sua*m* causam agere, sed Dei, tecu*m* non contenda*m*, modo ne doceatur hoc populus ut discat contemnere.

Quod ad ἐπιεικείαν pertinet, qua*m* Christus probauit in diuinis præceptis, tantu*m* illud dico, Christu*m* et exhibuisse nobis *et* docuisse diuina*m* misericordia*m*, cuius exemplo alter alterius misereri debeat conserui sui.[11] Sed publica ad Reip*ublicæ* commodu*m* in magistratu seueritas etia*m* diuinæ misericordiæ portio est, *et* thesauru*m* nobis

---

[1] These words refer to a new development of Bucer's thought in his memorandum. [2] Acts v, 29. [3] Acts xv, 20: "Sed scribere ad eos ut abstineant se a...suffocatis, et sanguine". [4] Cf. Eccles. vii, 1: "cum ignoret quid conducat sibi in vita sua, numero dierum peregrinationis suæ". Ecclesiastes was turned into Latin verse by Gardiner while a prisoner in the Tower in 1549 or 1550. [5] Col. ii, 20: "Si ergo mortui estis cum Christo ab elementis hujus mundi...". [6] Rom. xvi, 18: "Hujuscemodi enim Christo domino nostro non serviunt, sed suo ventri...". [7] *Sic* for *neque*. [8] *Sic* for the whole sentence, which cannot be easily construed. *Quam* probably refers to *cogitatio* and means "to wit how", but then the verb is missing, and *sit* should be supplied, after *abstinentia* for instance. [9] The quotation is a particularly apt one, the "ille" here mentioned being Horace, who in one of his satires describes the debasing effect produced both upon the body and the soul by over-indulgence ·in

This place in no way smells of incense;[a] and ought not to move a controversy, where in a thing indifferent the purpose is declared to be impious. Now what Christian would bear the thought of offering up a sacrifice to demons, especially in the face of this text of scripture: God ought to be obeyed rather than men. Nor do I see whither your example tends, unless you also think it equally impious, for the prince to forbid the eating of flesh at certain times,—a thing of which however an example may be supplied to us by the Apostles, who forbade things strangled and blood. And just as they acted piously when they took the times into account, and abrogated the law little by little, likewise let the prince also, when enjoining abstinence, have among other things this motive in view: that the people may in abstaining from food be reminded of the pilgrimage of this life, that they may die each day to some of the things of this world, and that they may not always be the slaves of their belly, and exert themselves in fattening it day after day; and it is profitable to man to meditate on this, to wit how pious and religious the law of abstinence is in that respect, also how far from superstition, since it feeds meditation, and if observed in good faith, is seasonable even for the body, and prevents that particle of the divine breath, as it is called, from being always smothered.

You strive to prove, that princes should learn in those commandments of theirs, not to serve their own cause, but that of God. I shall not contend with you here, provided the people be not taught this so as to learn contempt.

In regard to gentleness,[b] which Christ commended in his divine precepts, I shall just say this, that Christ both exhibited to us and taught us divine mercy; after the pattern of which each of us must have compassion on his fellow-servant. But public severity in the magistrate, for the public weal, is also a portion of divine mercy, and hoards up for us a treasure of

regard to food. He who has had too much of a feast overnight, he says, "animum quoque prægravat...Atque affigit humo divinæ particulam auræ" (*Sat.* II, ii, 78–9). Horace is here referring to the idea, borrowed from the Pythagorean and Platonic philosophies, and quite current in his time, that man's soul is a fragment of the divine soul. [10] The word *ijs* cannot easily be accounted for, unless we refer it to some point in Bucer's memorandum, which Gardiner had before his eyes at the time. [11] Matth. xviii, 33: "Nonne ergo oportuit et te misereri conservi tui". [a] It has not been possible to trace the origin of this expression, which may mean: "your way of handling the question has nothing to do with Christian virtue or honesty". [b] The word ἐπιείκεια occurs only twice in the canonical scriptures, in Acts xxiv, 4 (Latin *clementia*, English "clemency" in the Authorized Version) and II Cor. x, 1 (Latin *modestia*, English "gentleness").

accumulat benignitatis *et* mansuetudinis in eu*m* diem reponendu*m*, quo n*o*stra delicta Deus vindicabit, adeo lucro nobis fuerit ista vindicta, ut poena temporali uitetur æterna. Sed maior nos cura tangit pr*e*sentium *quam* futuroru*m*, sic· enim ‖ allicitur populus, ut de pr*e*senti disciplina aliquid remittatur. Quin poti*us* docetur populus præsentia contemnere a*n*imo christiano, *et* humanæ potestati parere *et* obedire.

p. 268

Quid sequitur[1] eo tendit quasi post lege*m* diuina*m* nulla supersit principibus materia legis condendæ quæ humana dicatur. videlic*et* quu*m* in lege diuina omnia contineantur. Et veru*m* est om*n*ia contineri implicite ut illi distinguunt, sed non explicite. Itaqu*e* q*uum* iubemur principi obedire, ibi certe om*n*ia implicite continentur, quæ iusserit postea princeps: at modu*m* obediendi ipse postea princeps explicat. Deinde generatim et*iam*, quæcu*n*qu*e* bona, sancta, *et* honesta sunt, ea diuina lege iubentur, quæ mala *et* quæ turpia etia*m* in scripturis p*r*ohibentur. Secundu*m* quæ no*n* illa modo quæ speciatim in Scripturis exprimu*n*tur, sed etia*m* ad illud exe*m*plu*m*, alia q*uæ* in legibus humanis p*r*ecipiu*n*tur, p*r*ohibenturue, prout ipso usu atque effectu bona, malaue uidebu*n*tur.[2] Quas leges de ijs ab ho*m*ine latas nisi humanas appellauerim*us*, frustra contendim*us* de legibus humanis quæ tuo iuditio nullæ sunt.

Placet quod dicis subditoru*m* non esse de principu*m* legibus iudicare. Sed hoc si veru*m* est, cur apud populu*m* inculcatur illud: Frustra me colitis ma*n*datis hominu*m*?[3] Cum obediens ex volu*n*tate Dei vere colat Deu*m*, illo vno fine proposito obedientiæ.

Illa distinctio contemptus, ut alius sit imperij, alius rei imperatæ, in vnu*m* facile redit, si eam adhibeas definitione*m* contemptoris, qua*m* ego proposui, videlicet qui rem imperata*m* alioqui licita*m*, statuit no*n* præstare. ‖ Hic *enim* du*m* rem imperata*m* non p*r*estat, et*iam* authoritate*m* spernit cui decreuit no*n* obtemp*er*are.

p. 269

---

[1] What follows in Bucer's memorandum.    [2] The construction of the whole sentence is far from easy, and we only risk a translation of it. We understand *secundum quæ* as "according to which (things)", and suppose that in the second part of the sentence the

mildness and gentleness, to be kept in store for that day, when God will punish our offences; this punishment suffered on earth will actually be a gain for us, so that a temporal penalty will spare us an eternal one. But the care of things present touches us more nearly than that of the future; and thus in fact is the people allured, to relax something of present discipline. Why is not the people rather taught to scorn the things of this world with a Christian mind, and to submit to and obey human rule?

What follows tends to this: you would have it that beyond divine law, no matter remains to princes to establish a law that may be called human, since plainly all things are contained in divine law. And all things, it is true, are contained there implicitly, as the distinction goes, but not explicitly. Thus when we are bidden obey the prince, this behest no doubt contains all things implicitly, which the prince will afterwards command; yet as to the manner of obeying, the prince himself unfolds it afterwards. Then again, whatever is good, holy and honest, is prescribed in general by divine law, whatever is bad and shameful is also forbidden in the scriptures; which includes not only those things which are specially mentioned in them, but also other things which human law, taking example from Scripture, prescribes or forbids, according as they appear good or bad in their very use and performance. Which laws made by man in regard to such matters, unless we call them human, it will be no use discussing on human laws, since in your opinion there are none such.

I like well what you say, that it is not the subjects' part to judge the laws of princes. But if that be true, why then do you beat these words into the people's heads: In vain you worship me with the commandments of men? Since a man who obeys by the will of God truly worships God, his obedience having no other purpose.

You distinguish between two sorts of contempt, one of the ordaining power, and one of the thing ordained; yet they are easily reduced to one, if you apply the definition of the contemner, which I for my part proposed, namely he who decides not to perform a thing ordained and otherwise lawful. For that man, while he refuses to perform the thing ordained, also spurns the authority to which he has decided not to submit.

two verbs of the former part are understood. ³ Matth. xv, 9. Cf. *De vera obedientia*, fol. 7 a. of the Berthelet edition, where the same text is put to an altogether different use.

Dum conaris meas rationes refellere, easdem astruis. Sed uidetur tibi principes etiam diuina mandata, si contemnantur vindicare debere. Et ostendis fecisse hoc multos: id quod tibi assentior. Sed non omnia tamen, non quod ea negligerent, sed quatenus humana conseruari societas queat, diuino iuditio vlciscenda reliquerunt.

Illud est plane sophisticum, quod quum ego fatear in humanis legibus non rem spectandam, sed crimen contemptus, in diuinis autem etiam rem quocunque modo, atque adeo etiamsi citra contemptum quis fuerit transgressus, eum locum ita tractas, quasi ego id dissimulassem. Ego uero in diuinis legibus loquor de transgressione, in humanis de solo contemptu, qui crimen complectitur inobedientiæ erga Deum. Ergo inquis non consistit collatio, cum vtraque pars collationis de diuina lege loquatur: reipsa fateor, quum humana lex diuina authoritate sanciatur. Sed nomine tamen ad originem internoscendam apte distinguuntur, et in altera iudicatur contemptus, in altera qualiscunque transgressio etiam sine contemptu. Illud ab homine seuere, hoc a Deo suo tempore. Sed tu transgressionis verbum trahis ad leges humanas, cum ego nunquam senserim tam inhumanos esse aliquos principes, hoc saltem cognomine dignos, et suæ conditionis tam immemores, ut in homines errore aut ignorantia lapsos tam grauiter animaduertere velint, si quid eos fefellerit. Neque enim impetitur principis authoritas, nisi malitia, quæ proprie contemptus est. Quod quereris principes ‖ nihil statuere in gulosos et ebrios, promptus est Scripturæ locus secundum vestram doctrinam, quod intrat per os non inquinat hominem.[1] Nam ita hodie in compitis interpretatur scripturam ex spiritu populus. Et tamen quædam sunt hominum vitia, quæ deflere magis quam temporaria vindicta castigare prestiterit, ne humana poena diuinæ vindictæ opinio minuatur, id quod etiam arbitrati videntur, qui hactenus a Christo nato in quædam peccata nihil statuerunt. Sed de hoc uiderint principes, nos legibus latis parere discamus, ne diuinam auctoritatem contemnere videamur.

[1] Matth. xv, 11.

While you try to disprove my reasons you actually confirm them. In your opinion, princes should also take vengeance, whenever God's commandments are contemned; and you show that many have done so, which I grant; but not in every case though, not because they disregarded such offences, but because they left them to be punished by God's judgment, in so far as the preservation of human society allowed them to do so.

When I declare that in speaking of human laws, what we have in view is not the matter of the offence, but the crime of contempt; while in speaking of divine laws, it is also the offence, whatever its nature, and even if the transgression stops short of contempt, it is plain sophistry to handle this place, as if I had dissembled. Now in speaking of divine laws I use the word transgression, in speaking of human laws I only mention contempt, which includes the crime of disobedience against God. Therefore you say the comparison cannot hold good, since divine law appears in both terms of it: indeed I confess the same, since human law is confirmed by divine authority. And yet both laws are fitly called by different names, so that their origin may be distinguished; and in one case it is contempt that is submitted to judgment, in the other case it is some transgression even without contempt, the former being punished by man severely, the latter by God at his own time. But you stretch the word contempt, and refer it to what we said of human laws, whereas I never heard that any princes, at least princes worthy of the name, were inhuman enough, and forgetful enough of their own degree, to chastise so grievously men lapsed through error or ignorance, if they have been led astray. Nor in fact is the prince's authority assailed, except it be by malice, which is properly contempt. As to what you bewail, that princes take no steps against gluttony and drunkenness, here is a text of scripture all ready for you, according to your principles: Not that which goeth into the mouth defileth a man; since nowadays the people expound Scripture in the cross-roads, according to the Spirit. And yet there are some of the vices of men, which were better lamented, than chastised with a temporary punishment; for else the effect of the human penalty might be to lessen men's opinion of the divine vengeance. Which all those seem to have agreed to, who from Christ's birth to the present day, refrained from making legal provision against certain sins. But princes should see to such matters; as for us, let us learn to obey such laws as have been made, lest we should seem to spurn God's authority.

Concionatoru*m* mun*us* est, *et* eorum qui Christu*m* pro-
fitentur, no*n* proferre populo eiusmodi sententias ex
scriptura, quæ non suo loco adductæ, aut no*n* satis ex-
plicatæ, populu*m* in no*n* prestanda obedientia fallant.
Cui*us*modi e*st* hæc: Subditi sunt tantu*m* alu*m*ni principum
et clientes, nec principibus aliter q*uam* propter Deu*m*
subditi. Tu*m* om*n*ia externa propter homine*m* diuinit*us*
esse condita *et* instituta.¹ Quæ no*n* om*n*ino falso dicunt*ur*
illa: Sed ita tamen ut popularia videantur, *et* ad ἀναρχίαν
spectent, qua*m* no*n* sine causa multi suspicantur esse
scopu*m* hui*us* sectæ, quæ diuinoru*m* obtentu, humana
interim om*n*ia studet confundere. Qui dicit legem Dei
absoluta*m* in se continere p*re*ceptionem om*n*iu*m* bonoru*m*,
*et* vetatione*m* maloru*m*, an no*n* tacite insinuat, frustra esse
omnes leges humanas? quas i*n*terdu*m* infami vocabulo
Traditiones vocant: nonnu*n*q*uam* uero adijciu*n*t Frustra
me colitis mandatis hominu*m*.

Et quam non apposite citatur illud: Nemo uos iudicet
in cibo *et* potu.² addatur etia*m* quod sequitur, in parte diei
p. 271 festæ: ut ideo nec cibi vlli*us* ‖ pro tempore interdictio, nec
feriaru*m*, aut festi celebratio ulla fiat, ne quis iudicet uos
in cibo. Imo uero ideo hæc legibus constituenda su*n*t,
ne quis iudicet uos in cibo: sed uestram laudent om*n*es
obedientia*m*, du*m* om*n*es in obedientia Deu*m* colentes idem
faciatis, in quo nulla queratur causa præter obedientia*m*,
etiamsi consequenter tu*m* corpori tu*m* animæ multa inde
sanctificatio succedat.

Breuiter doceatur populus diligere Deu*m*, que*m* per
fidem cognoscit, diligere proximu*m*, que*m* corporeis oculis
videt: obedire Deo, *et* obedire principibus à Deo missis:
in humana lege vindicanda non ægre ferat exeri humanu*m*
gladiu*m* a Deo datu*m* ad vindicandu*m* contemptu*m*.
Diuina*m* ultionem solam pertimescat populus, quæ cu*m*
infligitur ut seuerissima ita et iustissi*m*a est: corpus *et*

¹ These two sentences are not found in Scripture, hence we must
understand *sententias ex scriptura* as referring to maxims which agree
with the general sense of biblical precepts, but which are not drawn

## To sum up:

It is the duty of preachers, and of those who declare Christ, not to cite to the people such texts from Scripture, as not being brought forward in their proper place, or not being unfolded sufficiently, beguile the people into the refusal of obedience. Of which sort are the following words: subjects are only entrusted to the prince's fostering care and protection, and are not subject to princes in any other way than for the sake of God. Then again: all outward things have been founded and instituted in a heavenly way for the sake of man. Which assertions are not altogether false: but yet they are spoken in such a way as to seem in favour of the people, and to tend to anarchy; which latter is not without cause suspected of many, to be the aim of this your sect, which, under colour of godliness, endeavours meanwhile to confound all things human. If it be said that God's law contains in itself, without exception, the prescription of all things good, and the prohibition of all things evil, is it not tacitly hinted that all human laws are to no purpose? which laws are now and again branded with the infamous name of traditions: sometimes indeed the following words are added: In vain ye worship me with the commandments of men.

And how unsuitably the following text is cited: Let no man judge you in meat or in drink. What follows ought to be added: or in respect of an holy day; and thus no forbidding of any meat for any length of time, no celebration of holy days, or festivals, will be allowed, lest any one should judge you in meat. But on the contrary the very reason why such things are established by laws, is that no one may judge you in meat; and that all may praise your obedience, when all of you, worshipping God in obedience, join in the same actions, for which no cause must be sought besides obedience; even if in consequence of them much sanctification accrues as well to the body as to the soul.

In short let the people be taught to love God, whom they know through faith; to love their neighbour, whom they see with bodily eyes; to obey God, and obey the princes sent of God; let them not take it ill that the human sword given by God to chastise contempt, should be bared for the enforcing of human law. Let the people be greatly afraid of God's vengeance alone, which when it is inflicted, as it is most severe, so it is also most just; casting body and soul into the hell of

directly from the Bible. ² Col. ii, 16: "Nemo ergo vos judicet in cibo, aut in potu, aut in parte diei festi aut neomeniæ, aut sabbatorum".

animam mittens in gehennam ignis.[1] Itaque de presenti
fœlicitate nemo sibi impunitatem polliceatur, cum in hoc
sæculo non semper affligantur mali, id quod docet de
diuite parabola.[2] Et ut finiam, etiam illud bona fide ex-
primatur, *et* conuenire *et* expedire, ut contemptus legum
humanarum tum grauius tum seuerius uindicetur apud
homines, quam transgressio qualiscunque legum diuinarum
sine contemptu. Ne alioqui, si principes omnia ea susceperint suis legibus vindicanda, quæ diuina lege iubentur,
*et* gradibus poenarum delicta distinxerint, fore[3] omnino ut
tandem consumptis fere poenarum gradibus humanæ leges
poenæ ipsius uilitate ut predictum est reddantur con-
temptibiles *et* illusoriæ.

Hæc iudicent qui religionem<br>
bona fide curant.

p. 272   Verum libenter audio si quis alius, *et* veritatem cupio
promouere, quod ni fecissem, neque te neque Alesium ad
colloquium admisissem, quos homines noueram cuiusmodi
sitis, presertim Alesium.[4] nam de te, quem intellexi
palinodiam iam semel cecinisse,[5] bona spes erat, ut pari
facilitate veritati in cæteris cederes, si vrgearis. Itaque
tecum tanquam cum homine prudenti *et* pacis studioso
sum collocutus, ut agnosceres quod res est, ni principibus
sua edicta munire grauissimis poenis liceat, desperatam
fore bonis quietem *et* pacem. Neque expedire ut ad exemplum qualiscunque transgressionis diuinæ legis, quam
principes vindicare non solent, contemptus humanarum
legum vindicetur, sed acrius *et* seuerius. Cum dico qualiscunque transgressionis, de ijs speciebus transgressionis
loquor, quæ vacant contemptu: cuiusmodi multæ sunt, ut
tu fateris, id quod etiam meis scriptis explicaui.[6] Sed tu

---

[1] Luke xii, 5: "Timete eum qui, postquam occiderit, habet
potestatem mittere in gehennam". [2] Luke xvi, 1–22 (Parable of
the rich man). [3] *Sic* for *foret*. [4] Cf. Introduction, p. xliv.
[5] On the changes in Bucer's Eucharistic doctrine, and his gradual
return from Zwinglianism to a position intermediate between Zwinglianism and Lutheranism, cf. the illuminating study of Mr C. H. Smyth
in his book on *Cranmer and the Reformation under Edward VI*, Cambridge University Press, 1926. Gardiner no doubt thought that Bucer
had gone back farther than he really had, and profusely congratulates

fire. And therefore let no one who enjoys happiness on this earth, reckon upon impunity, since the wicked are not always cast down in this world, as we learn from the parable of the rich man. And to make an end, let this also be expressed in good faith, that it is both fit and expedient, that the contempt of human laws be punished among men both more heavily and more severely, than any transgression of God's laws apart from contempt; lest otherwise, if princes undertook to enforce with their own laws, all those things which are ordered by divine law, and distinguishing between offences, appointed various degrees of penalties, it should happen that, almost all degrees of penalties being at last used up, human laws should altogether become the object of contempt and mockery, as we said before, on account of the meanness of the penalty.

Let them weigh those things, who in good faith
trouble themselves about religion.

I am willing to listen to truth as much as any man living, and wish to promote truth; were I not thus inclined, I should have admitted neither you nor Aless to conference with me, for I knew you for the men that you are, especially Aless; for as to you, whom I understood to have already recanted before, there was good hope, that you should with the same ease give way to truth in other things, if you were plied hard. Therefore I have been conferring with you as with a discreet man, and one zealous for peace; so that you might acknowledge that which is a fact, namely that unless princes be allowed to protect their own edicts with the heaviest penalties, the good must despair of quiet and peace; and that it is not expedient that the contempt of human laws should be punished according to the same scale as any transgression of God's law, which princes are not wont to avenge, but more sharply and more severely. When I say any transgression, I mean such kinds of transgression, as are free from contempt; of which sort there are many, as you yourself confess, which I also explained in my writings to you. But you, in order that you may the more

him on his return to a more wholesome doctrine, while quoting him as a witness for truth, in his MS treatise *In Petrum Martyrem...querela* (B.M. Arundel MS 100). We find, for instance, on fol. 178 b the following words: "Ista...quum a sacramentario veneno sanatus, et resipiscens, Bucerus ipse testetur...". That Gardiner took Bucer for a Lutheran is clear from various passages (fols. 7 a, 43 b, 92 a, 109 a) and especially fol. 16 a: "Bucerus...qui est consubstantiationis acerrimus propugnator".     [6] Presumably the first memorandum sent to Bucer. Cf. Introduction, p. xlviii.

quo significanti*us* exprimas inuidia*m* propositionis, ita refers, quasi ego dixisse*m*, contemptus legu*m* humanaru*m* grauiu*s* puniri debet q*uam* diuinaru*m*: *et* ideo pro qualis-cu*nque* transgressionis, dicis, cui*us*libet transgressionis, quod sonat durius. Sed si quælibet transgressio diuinar*um* legum grauiu*s* q*uam* humanarum contemp*tus* vindicaretur apud ho*m*ines, sequeretur quod verbu*m* otiosu*m* temere ex humana infirmitate contingens grauiu*s* puniretur, q*uam* contemptus humanar*um* legum, ubi simul contemni*tur* ipse Deus, quod esset absurdu*m*. Itaq*ue* dixi contemptu*m* humanaru*m* legu*m* grauiu*s* vindicandu*m*, in quo est dolus,[1] q*uam* q*ua*lemcu*nque* transgressione*m* diuinæ legis, in-nuens illa*m* in qua no*n est* dolus, s*cilicet* infirmitas.[2] Atque hoc cu*m* toties inculcassem *et* presenti tibi, *et* absenti p*er* li*tte*ras,[3] redis tam*en* ad calu*m*niam tanq*uam* serpens qui obturauerit aures ad vocem incantantis sapienter.[4] Ad argumenta nihil respondes, tantum negas quod est luce clariu*s*, ‖ magis p*er*turbari Remp*ublicam* contemptu legu*m* humanaru*m*, q*uam* qualicu*nque* transgressio*ne* legis Diuinæ. Desidiosi *et* somniculosi ac otiosi congerrones seipsos corru*m*pu*nt* inertia, *et* legem Dei transgrediu*ntur*, Remp*ublicam* uero no*n* attingu*nt*, nedu*m* co*m*mouent tantu*m* abest ut perturbent. Vos ordine*m* omnem, vos Respubl*icas* conculcatis, du*m* principu*m*, *et* principaliu*m* edictoru*m* auctoritatem obliquis modis eleuare conamini, si[5] tu vicissim[6] veru*m* libenter audis. Magnificis verbis ornatis auctoritate*m* principu*m*, sed ita tamen, du*m* leges ad vestru*m* arbitriu*m* attemperant, *et* vestru*m* in diuinis iudicium sequantur. Romana*m* auc*torita*tem no*n* sustulistis orbi, sed vobis arrogastis, *et* transtulistis Wittembergam. Dominus doceat nos ipse sua*m* veritatem, sed Dei docibiles non erunt, q*ui* principib*us* non libenter obtempera*nt*. No*n* obtemperabu*nt* nu*n*qua*m*[7] libenter qui de modo legum tam anxie disputant, *et* eas de rebus adiaphoris in vniuersu*m* ferri tam grauate feru*nt*. Libenter quisq*ue* excuteret, si

p. 273

---

[1] In the theological use, *dolus* means "malice" and is opposed to *infirmitas*.  [2] *Sic* for *infirmitatem*. Another proof that this tract was penned in great haste.  [3] Cf. note 6, p. 207.  [4] The expression is borrowed directly from the Bible, Ps. lvii, 5–6: "Furor illis [pec-catoribus] secundum similitudinem serpentis: sicut aspidis surdæ,

expressly signify the hateful character of my proposition, recite it as if I had said, the contempt of human laws must be more heavily punished than that of divine laws; and therefore instead of any transgression you say, any transgression whatsoever, which sounds harsher. But if any transgression whatsoever of God's laws were chastised more heavily among men than the contempt of human laws, it would follow that an idle word, rashly uttered on account of human frailty, should be punished more grievously, than the contempt of human laws, in which God is also spurned at the same time, which would be absurd. Therefore I said that the contempt of human laws was to be more heavily punished, for in it is malice, than any transgression of divine law, meaning that in which there is no malice, but only weakness. And after I have been so many times impressing this upon you, both in your presence and in your absence by letters, yet you wrest the matter anew, as if you were the serpent that stoppeth her ears, which will not hearken to the voice of charmers, charming never so wisely. You answer nothing to my proofs, you merely deny that which is clearer than day, namely that the commonwealth is more disordered by the contempt of human laws, than by some transgression of divine law. Slothful, sluggish and idle fellows spoil themselves by their laziness; they infringe God's law, yet they do not touch the commonwealth, nor do they disturb it, still less do they cast it into confusion. But it is you who tread under foot all order, you who trample down the common weal, while you strive by covert ways to impair the authority of princes, and of their edicts, even if in your turn you are willing to listen to the truth. You adorn the authority of princes with magnificent words, yet only so long as they accommodate their laws to your own decisions, and follow your judgment in religious matters. You have not abolished the authority of Rome throughout the world, but you have appropriated it to yourselves, and transferred it to Wittenberg. Let God himself teach us his truth, but God's apt scholars will not be those, who do not willingly submit to princes. And those men will never willingly submit, who discuss so anxiously of the manner of making laws, and bear it so grudgingly that laws should be made for all men on things indifferent. Every man would gladly cast out, if he could,

et obturantis aures suas. Quæ non exaudiet vocem incantantium, et venefici incantantis sapienter ".    [5] If it be true that...    [6] The idea is that Bucer alternately professes error and gives ear to the truth.
[7] *Sic* for the double negation.

posset, quod odit. Sed de ijs hacten*us*, ego ad iter me paro,[1] nec vacat respondere, ut planu*m* tibi facia*m*, q*uam* me no*n* efferam meo luxu, ut tu vocas, qui ut me peruelleres, ornamenta legationis in crimen vocasti. Eq*ui*dem si gloriæ studerem, alia facerem, *et* fecissem hactenus. De *episco*pi munere redda*m* Deo ratione*m* vtina*m* talem qualem cupio. Interim du*m* in vobis uel confutandis uel refellendis vbi vbi locoru*m* verser, non videor mihi a grege abesse, qua gracia libentius inseruio principi meo, quem *et* Deu*m* timere scio, *et* Chr*ist*i gloria*m* ut qui maxime cupere illustrare. At uero sub Euangelicæ libertatis *p*retextu vitam Epicurea*m* induci pati non potest. Nemine*m* cogit ad coelibatu*m*, sed eos qui se castraru*n*t propter regnu*m* cæloru*m*,[2] non sinit cu*m* scandalo mutare consiliu*m*, *et* votu*m* contemnere. Omnibus patet matrimonij libertas, sed non castratis. Expecto, ut si minus tu, qui modestior es, *et* hoc saltem no*m*ine bene audis, alius tamen ex vestris, si quis legat, ludat in verbo ‖ Castrari, *et* declamet in stupra *et* adulteria hui*usm*o*d*i castratoru*m*, q*uam* uobis materiam Deus auferat. Quod si his malis coniugiu*m* mederetur, o*m*nino *et* o*m*nia casta redderet, optarim ego licere post vota ducere uxores, quod no*n* mea causa dico, sed alioru*m*. Sed inducta hac persuasione orbi qua*m* vos *p*rofitemini, ut vaga libertate o*m*nia liceant, et ducantur deinde vxores propter fornicatione*m*,[3] vereor ne coniugijs opus sit vni, no*n* coniugio, ut quocu*n*que se terrarum contulerit, noua*m* ducat vxorem, quia, ut mihi scripturam citasti, non est bonu*m* homini esse solu*m*.[4] Itaq*ue* ne a me detinearis, tu, si libet, propera ad tua*m*, *et* vale.

p. 274

[1] On Gardiner's departure from Ratisbon, cf. Introduction, p. **xlix**.
[2] Matth. xix, 12. The passage was frequently referred to in later controversy between Gardiner and Bucer.      [3] I Cor. vii, 2:

what he hates. But enough of these matters, I am getting ready to start on my journey, and am not at leisure to answer you, so as to make it clear to you, how little I seek to exalt myself with my pomp, as you name it; you who in order to revile me, called me to account for the outward apparel of my embassy. To be sure if I strove after glory, I should behave, and should have behaved hitherto, in a different manner. Of my charge as a bishop I shall render my account to God,—would that it were such as I wish. Meanwhile, as long as I spend time, wherever it may be, in confuting and rebutting you, meseems I am not away from my flock, for the sake of whom I am the readier to serve my prince with devotion, for I know how to fear him and God, and wish as much as man alive to shed a greater lustre on Christ's glory. But really that an Epicurean life should be brought in under pretence of Gospel freedom, is a thing which cannot be suffered. God compels no one to celibacy, but as for those which have made themselves eunuchs for the kingdom of heaven's sake, he does not allow them to change their resolve to the scandal of others, and to despise their vows. The freedom of marriage is open to all, but not to such eunuchs. I expect that, if not indeed you, who keep a measure in words, and at least on that head bear a good character, but yet some other among you, if he read this, will make sport of the word eunuch, and declaim against the un-chastity and adulteries of eunuchs of this sort; which matter of blame may God remove from you. If that matrimony were a certain cure for such evils, and made all men and all things chaste, even I should wish that in spite of vows, every man should be allowed to marry a wife; which I say not for my own sake, but that of others. But if the world is made to believe what you publicly avow, that a giddy freedom should be per-mitted to all, and wives be married to avoid fornication, I am afraid lest a man should need not one but many marriages, since according to the Scripture that you quoted to me, it is not good that man should be alone; so that wherever a man may betake himself on the earth, he take a new woman to wife. Therefore lest I should detain you, hasten back, if it so please you, to your own, and fare you well.

"Propter fornicationem autem unisquisque suam uxorem habeat...".
⁴ Gen. ii, 18.

# ANALYTICAL INDEX OF NAMES

Proper names only are included in this index, and among those only such as may be useful for the purpose of research, the names of authors quoted for reference in footnotes being generally left out. As there is exact correspondence between the English and Latin pages, the numbers of the latter are omitted. The letter "n" after the number of a page refers to a footnote, the letter "m" to a marginal note.

216

Gardiner, Stephen (*cont.*)
purposes, li–lii; his use of protestant forms of speech, xl, 82n.; made to appear a Protestant by the translator, 75n., 81n.; compared by him to a man with two wives, xxxvi; character of *De vera obedientia*, liv–lvi; Gardiner insincere in this work, lvi–lviii, but never declared afterwards for a divinely instituted papacy, lix; only refers to temporal supremacy of the Pope, lx–lxi; his theory of the king's supremacy, xiv, how justified in his own eyes, xiv–xv; claims spiritual powers for Henry VIII, lxi–lxii, 119n., but leaves a door open for some sort of papal primacy, lxiii

His tract against Bucer, xlviii–l, 173–211; his controversy with Bucer, ix, xlii–li; his interpretation of 1 Cor. vii., xlvi, 189n.; takes Bucer for a Lutheran, 206n., 207n.; explains his contention in his tract, l–li; the relation between the three tracts and his true feelings, li–lxviii; his thought in his third tract, xv; its character and sincerity, lxv; his theory of obedience in it, lxv–lxvi; compared with *De vera obedientia*, lxvi; his theory of citizenship, lxvii

Gargantua, 23n.
Genouillac, a French commissioner at Calais, 14n.
Germany, xiv, xxii, xxxv, 37, 37n.; Aless flies there, 194n.
Gnatho, a character in Terence's *Eunuch*, 149n.
Goldast, Melchior, his reprint of *De vera obedientia*, xl
Gratian, his *Decretum*, 16n.
Gregory the Great, Saint, Pope, 148n.
Gregory XII, one of the three rival Popes at the Council of Constance, 124n.
Grey, Jane, also called Queen Jane, xxxvii, xxxviii

Hagenau, 148n.
Hales, judge, xxxv
Hall, Dr Richard, Fisher's biographer, xx, xxn., 52n.

Hamburg, an edition of *De vera obedientia* issued there, xxviii, xxxiii–xxxv, xl; the protestant diet there, xxxi; a printer there in 1536, xxxii–xxxiii
Harbert, Sir William, xxxiv
Heath, Nicholas, archdeacon of Stafford, later archbishop of York: on an embassy to Strasbourg and Germany with Foxe, xxv–xxvi; present at Smalkalde, xxix, xxxi
Hedio, C., the Strasbourg reformer, xxvii
Henry V, King of England, 124n.
Henry VII, King of England, xviii
Henry VIII, King of England, xi, xii, xv, xvii, xxix–xxxii, xxxin., xli–xlii, li–liii, lvii, lxi, lxii, 14n., 15n., 26n., 32n., 33n., 42n., 45n., 52n., 53, 57, 59, 118n., 157, 169, 171; his *Assertio septem Sacramentorum*, 62n.; Gardiner enters his service, x, and pens his address to the legates, xii, xix, 2–9; reduces the Church to subjection, xiii; deprived of his kingdom by Pope Paul III, xxi; his conduct judged in the latter's brief, 11–19; undertakes a polemical offensive, xxiv; his personal prestige, xxiv–xxv; his propaganda in France, xxix; his policy at Ratisbon, xlii–xliii; in *De vera obedientia*: his marriage with Anne Boleyn stated to be legitimate, 87, 87m.; his conduct approved by Universities, 87; his liking for Paris University, 140n.–141n.; proclaimed the supreme head of the Church of England, 91, 91m., 91n., and rightly called so, 93–95, 95m., 97; his supreme headship agreed to by Parliament, 115–117, 117m.; his enforcement of the law of abstinence, 180n.; called Defender of the faith, 119n.; his legitimacy not questioned by Gardiner, lxivn.
Hereford, bishop of: *see* Foxe, Edward
Herod, Henry VIII compared to him, 7–9
Hesse, Landgrave of: *see* Philip
Heywood, B. A., his reprint of *De vera obedientia*, xli
Heywood, John, 163n.

Muller, Prof. J. A., his biography of Gardiner, ix–x, xxii

Norfolk, duke of, an English commissioner at Calais, 14n.
Northampton, the marquis of, xxxiv
Nuremberg, xliv

Œcolampadius, the Swiss reformer: Fisher and Gardiner write against him, xviin.
Orleans, University of: its opinion on Henry VIII's divorce, 34n.
Orvieto, Clement VII takes refuge there, xii; Gardiner joins him there, xii, 150n.
Osiander, the German reformer, his debate with Gardiner, xliv
Ossory, bishop of: see Bale, John
Ostia, bishop of (later Pope Paul III), 32n.

Palmer, William, his poem on Gardiner, lvi
Pantheon, the Roman, 148n.
Paris, 4n.; Paris University: its opinion on Henry VIII's marriage, 34n., 35n.; praised by Gardiner, 141, 145; why, 140n., 141n.
Parker collection at Corpus Christi College, Cambridge, xlviii–xlix
Parrhasius, the Greek painter, 140n., 141, 141n.
Paul III, Pope: see also Farnesius, cardinal, Ostia and Velletri, bishop of, liii, lvii, 15n., 25n., 29, 33, 45, 45n., 50n., 59, 61, 63, 65; makes Fisher a cardinal, xx; his two letters on Fisher's execution, xxi; his brief to Francis I, 11–19; tried to obtain Francis I's intercession in favour of Fisher, 26n., 46n.; his alleged change of opinion on the divorce matter, 32n.–34n., 33–35; his surmises about the Calais negotiations right, 57n.; gibingly compared with St Paul, xxii, 25, 158n., 159
Paul, St, the apostle, 75, 76n., 81, 89, 97, 97n., 99, 101, 107, 138n., 147, 159, 161, 174n., 176n., 178n., 185, 185n., 188n., 194n., 195n., 196n., 197, 198n., 199n., 204n., 210n., 211n.; Paul III compared with him, xxii, 45, 59, 65, 158n., 159;

Gardiner compares himself to him, lviii, 71; his views on celibacy and marriage, xlvii–xlviii
Pecock, Reginald: rejects Constantine's donation, 40n.
Peter, St, the Apostle, 81, 89, 97, 99, 101; the real nature of his primacy, lix, 135–137, 135n., 136n., 141; his position misrepresented by the bishops of Rome, 147, 147n., who ought to imitate his primacy of virtue, 147, and might claim his spiritual primacy, 155; Christ's words to him, 157, and special favours to him, 156n., 157; punished lying with death, 178n., 179
Petre, Sir William, possible translator of Si sedes illa, xxiii
Petrucci, Cardinal, his execution, 50n.
Petrus Hispanus, the logician, 140n.
Philip, Landgrave of Hesse, xxviin., xli
Philip II of Spain, King of England, xx
Phocas, a Byzantine emperor, said to have granted a grace to Pope Boniface IV, 149; but wrongly so, 148n.
Phormio, Terence's play, 58n.
Pilkington, James, xxxiiin.
Pisa, the council of, 124n.
Plato: mentions the Silenus, 22n.; his philosophy, 194n., 199n.
Plautus, 46n., 179n.
Pole, Reginald, xiii; Henry VIII tries to gain his support, xxx; receives De vera obedientia and writes De unitate, xxx–xxxi, xxxin.; Gardiner tries to get into touch with him at Ratisbon, xliii
Pope, the: see also Rome, bishop of, Clement VII, and Paul III; xiii, xv, xxxi, xxxii, xxxiv, xlii, xlvii, li, lii, lviii, lix, lxii, lxiii, lxiv, 3, 5, 129, 129n., 157n.; his position and primacy according to Gardiner, xiv, lix–lx; allows England great freedom in Anglo-Saxon times, 122n.; his position at the Council of Constance, 124n.; his powers in England in the fourteenth and fifteenth centuries, 125n.; not yet a full sovereign at Rome in the seventh century, 149n.

219

Standish, Henry: declares against privileges of the Church, lxi

Stevens, William: his reprint of *De vera obedientia*, xl

Stokesley, John, bishop of London: sent to Fisher to win him over, xx; writes a defence of the supreme headship for Pole, xxiv

Strasbourg, xxvii, xxviin., xxix, xxxiii, xxxiv, xliii, 148n.; its importance in the sixteenth century, xxv; Edward Foxe calls there, xxv–xxvi; *De vera obedientia* printed there, xxv–xxix, xl; *De unitate* published there, xxxi

Sturm, John, the Strasbourg reformer, xxviii

Sylvester, Pope: Constantine's donation to him, 41n.

Terence, 46n.; his *Eunuch*, 9n., 57n.; his *Phormio*, 58n.

Thomas Becket, archbishop of Canterbury: *see* Becket, Thomas

Thraso, a character in Terence's *Eunuch*, 9n., 149n.

Titus: St Paul's epistle to him, 89

Toulouse, University of: its opinion on Henry VIII's divorce, 34n.

Tregonwell, Sir John: a possible translator of *Si sedes illa*, xxiii

Trent, the council of, xlii

Trinity Hall: Gardiner's college at Cambridge, xvi

Tullius: *see* Cicero

Tunstal, Cuthbert, bishop of Durham: sent to Fisher to win him over, xx; opposes the king in the Northern convocation, xxiv, xxivn.: writes a defence of the supreme headship

for Pole, xxiv; deposes at Gardine'rs trial, lvii

Turner, William, xlvi, xlviin., lv

Tyndale, William: his theory of obedience, xvi, xvin.; unlike that of Gardiner, liv; as well as his attack on the Papacy, lxi

Vadianus, the, St Gall reformer, xxvin., xxviii, xxviiin.

Valla, Laurentius: rejects Constantine's donation as spurious, 40n.

Velletri, bishop of (later Paul III), 32n.

Venice, 29n., 43n.

Warwick, earl of, lvi

Wiltshire, earl of, xxxiv

Winchester, xii, xxi; bishops of: *see* Beaufort, Henry and Gardiner, Stephen

Wittenberg, 209

Wolsey, John, cardinal, 150n.; Gardiner enters his service, x; his interview with Fisher in 1527, 2n.; bullies the Pope, xi; a judge in the divorce case, xii, xviii, xix, 6n.

Wood, Michael, a printer, possibly at Rouen, xxxv

Worms, the diet of, 194n.

Wriothesley, Sir Thomas, his handwriting, xviii, xviiin., xix, xxii

York, archbishops of, deposed by Anglo-Saxon kings, 122n.; *see also* Heath, Nicholas

Zurich, xxxiii

Zwick, Johann, the Swiss reformer, xxvi, xxvin.

CAMBRIDGE: PRINTED BY
W. LEWIS, M.A.
AT THE UNIVERSITY PRESS

Demco 293-5